D0915374

DANGEROUS TALK

DANGEROUS TALK

SCANDALOUS, SEDITIOUS, AND TREASONABLE SPEECH IN PRE-MODERN ENGLAND

DAVID CRESSY

OXFORD
UNIVERSITY PRESS

OXFORD
UNIVERSITY PRESS

Great Clarendon Street, Oxford OX2 6DP

Oxford University Press is a department of the University of Oxford.
It furthers the University's objective of excellence in research, scholarship,
and education by publishing worldwide in

Oxford New York

Auckland Cape Town Dar es Salaam Hong Kong Karachi
Kuala Lumpur Madrid Melbourne Mexico City Nairobi
New Delhi Shanghai Taipei Toronto

With offices in

Argentina Austria Brazil Chile Czech Republic France Greece
Guatemala Hungary Italy Japan Poland Portugal Singapore
South Korea Switzerland Thailand Turkey Ukraine Vietnam

Oxford is a registered trade mark of Oxford University Press
in the UK and in certain other countries

Published in the United States
by Oxford University Press Inc., New York

© David Cressy 2010

The moral rights of the author have been asserted
Database right Oxford University Press (maker)

First published 2010

All rights reserved. No part of this publication may be reproduced,
stored in a retrieval system, or transmitted, in any form or by any means,
without the prior permission in writing of Oxford University Press,
or as expressly permitted by law, or under terms agreed with the appropriate
reprographics rights organization. Enquiries concerning reproduction
outside the scope of the above should be sent to the Rights Department,
Oxford University Press, at the address above

You must not circulate this book in any other binding or cover
and you must impose the same condition on any acquirer

British Library Cataloguing in Publication Data
Data available

Library of Congress Control Number: 2009928984

Typeset by SPI Publisher Services, Pondicherry, India
Printed in Great Britain
on acid-free paper by
MPG Books Group, Bodmin and King's Lynn

ISBN 978–0–19–956480–4

1 3 5 7 9 8 6 4 2

UWEC McIntyre Library
DISCARDED
Eau Claire, WI

KD
8026
C74
2010

Acknowledgements

My previous book, *England on Edge*, dealt with two tumultuous years. This study covers half a millennium. I have tried, wherever possible, to base my work on primary sources, but have also found guidance in modern scholarship. The notes and bibliography acknowledge my debt. I am especially grateful to the following scholars, who have offered insights, suggestions, and corrections: Lloyd Bowen, Whitney Dirks-Schuster, Susan Doran, Lori Anne Ferrell, Steve Gunn, Tim Harris, Cynthia Herrup, Daniel Hobbins, Clive Holmes, Ian Gentles, Paulina Kewes, Newton Key, John Morrill, Christopher Otter, Geoffrey Parker, Nicholas Rogers, Buchanan Sharp, Keith Thomas, and Alison Wall.

I am extremely grateful to the Bogliasco Foundation for a residency at the Liguria Study Center, where much of this book was written. I am grateful to All Souls College, Oxford, where the award of a visiting fellowship allowed me to bring the work to completion. I am indebted, too, to the Department of History and College of Humanities at the Ohio State University for supporting this work with a seed grant in 2006 and two quarters of sabbatical leave in 2008. Appointment as the Town and Gown lecturer in the Division of Late Medieval and Reformation Studies at the University of Arizona in February 2008 allowed me to test some of this material on a public audience. Seminar discussions at the universities of Cambridge, London, and York helped me sharpen my argument. After-dinner discussion with the fellows of All Souls of '*verba brigosa* and crimes of the tongue in early Stuart Oxford and Cambridge' extended my knowledge of law and language. Archivists and librarians in Britain and the United States have been unfailingly professional. Without their assistance this book could not have been written.

Valerie Cressy has listened to every word of this book and has made countless suggestions. I dedicate it to her.

Contents

Preface

This book examines dangerous talk among ordinary people in England from the late Middle Ages to the present. Its central focus is on the early modern era, from the sixteenth to the eighteenth centuries. It sets out to eavesdrop on lost conversations, to recover the expressions that got people into trouble, and to follow the fate of some of the offenders. It shows how casual speakers collided with the law, how their words became treason or sedition, and what sanctions or punishments followed. It is possible to do this because a record-keeping culture set down in writing some of the words that people were said to have uttered. In a world before tape recording or electronic surveillance we cannot listen to historical voices or hear the actual expressions that alarmed the authorities; but we can read Privy Council reports or judicial transcripts that claimed that such or such a person made scandalous, undutiful, or treasonable remarks. And, if that person was arrested and interrogated, or sent to trial, we may read the testimony of the accused and statements of witnesses admitting, denying, or offering excuses for the incriminating or offending words. Sources containing information of this sort are in fact abundant, though they have been little exploited by historians. The documentary evidence for the chapters that follow comes from law reports, official correspondence, parliamentary papers, assize records, and the proceedings of quarter sessions. From the end of the seventeenth century the record is augmented by newspapers. Contemporary sermons, tracts, pamphlets, and treatises round out the picture.

Most of the modern scholarship on popular politics and the state focuses on published writings. Discussions of liberty, citizenship, and censorship deal primarily with written expression. Recent historical study has exposed the surreptitious circulation of manuscripts and libels, but still it concentrates on the written word. This project, by contrast, seeks to incorporate a more elusive body of utterance, including words that were never intended to be written down. Although actual spoken language was lost to the wind, the historical record yields redactions, quotations, and representations of what was purportedly said. Even allowing for scribal interventions and lapses of memory, we find fragments of forgotten conversations, reports of words spoken in carelessness, in anger, or in drink. The evidence is often compromised, frequently opaque, and occasionally stunning. Anyone interested in the ideas and opinions of ordinary people, as well as the responses of the elite, does well to pay attention to this hidden transcript.

'Words are but wind' was a popular expression, but speech could hurt as hard as sticks and stones. The social, political, and religious history of early modern England was filled with the debris of discourse. Malicious tongues caused dispute between neighbours. Seditious words endangered the state. Scandalous and impious language disturbed the community of believers. 'It would make a man's heart to bleed', wrote the Elizabethan Calvinist William Perkins, 'to hear . . . how swearing, blaspheming, cursed speaking, railing, slandering, chiding, quarrelling, contending, jesting, mocking, flattering, lying, dissembling, vain and idle talking, overflow in all places'. 'Lamentable and fearful' were these abuses of the tongue.[1]

While considering all kinds of transgressive utterance, the emphasis here is on talk that concerned the state. Certain kinds of speech could be treasonous or seditious, though lawyers disputed the criteria for 'treason by words'. To call the king a fool or to describe the queen as a whore was certainly unwise, but was it also a crime? To declare that a particular monarch had no right to the throne, or was unfit to govern, had dangerous political implications. Such words cut to the heart of the polity, demeaning and dishonouring royal government and challenging its legitimacy. How the state responded to such verbal assaults reflects the composure or vulnerability of changing political cultures. Successive regimes, from the house of Plantagenet to the house of Hanover, coped variously with disruptive or seditious language, and found different ways of monitoring dangerous talk. At one time an offender could be hung, drawn, and quartered for treasonous expressions. At other times similar words could be dismissed with a shrug. Changing political circumstances prompted different conversations, and led to changing reactions by councillors and courts.

Nobody could know for certain who was listening or who might construe conversations as dangerous. Magistrates and officials policed an escalating register of speech offences, from defamation to slander, sedition to treason, with punishments that ranged from moderate reprimand to public execution. Enforcement depended on hearsay, reportage, and the examination of witnesses and offenders. Loyal listeners claimed to have responded:

'take heed what you say of kings', 'it is not fit for us to meddle with such matters', and 'many a man hath been laid upon an hurdle for less'. It was unclear in practice what limits applied to spoken expression, and how the regime might react.

The dominant dynamic of English history has been the relationship between the crown and people, *rex* and *grex*, the governors and the governed. We occasionally learn what kings thought of their people, but rarely can we hear what ordinary people said about their kings. This book offers a selection. Rather than claiming these voices to be representative, I recognize them as the disorderly sounds of a minority. Nonetheless, the kind of speech captured here touched a raw political nerve, prompting centuries of state retaliation. Some governors may have feared the prophetic power of cursing, as if wishing ill to the monarch could bring about that effect. Most worried that seditious talk might prove contagious, and undermine allegiance at large. The response, over time, involved a mixture of policing and propaganda, monitoring and surveillance, judicial and political intervention, and the crafting of new legislation.

Every generation remade its politics, but the courts also drew on statute, precedent, and legal memory. Edward III's treason statute of 1352 governed cases beyond the eighteenth century. Precedents established in the 1460s and the 1620s shaped outcomes a century or more later. Several of the episodes discussed in the following chapters exercised legal theorists from the age of the first Queen Elizabeth to the second.

'Freedom of speech', a topic of enduring concern, has changed its meaning over centuries. In Tudor times 'freedom of speech' was something to apologize for, an outspoken or uninhibited expression, whether sharp or blunt. By the seventeenth century the phrase was associated with politics, especially parliamentary politics, referring to the privilege of counsel and commentary in the House of Commons. The 1689 Bill of Rights guaranteed 'that the freedom of speech and debates or proceedings in parliament ought not to be impeached or questioned in any court or place out of parliament'. This became generalized to cover writing and printing as well as vocal expression, and by the eighteenth century it extended to the rights of the subject, no longer constrained as privilege but integral to 'the birthright of an Englishman'. Modern discussion of 'freedom of speech' is bound up with the politics of censorship, civic rights, and notions or charters of 'liberty'. This book traces some of the bumps along the road.

My aim, wherever possible, is to reconstruct the circumstances of speech offences and the personal dynamics and ideological frictions that may have underlain them. By examining depositions, answers, and rebuttals, as well as letters, indictments, accusations, and commentary, I hope to calibrate the weight and force of dangerous utterances. Research of this sort is slow and frustrating, with gems of information among many dead ends. But piece by piece it reveals the workings of English justice, the relationship of crown and subjects, and the political force of everyday language. It contributes, I hope, to an integration of social and political history, historical socio-linguistics, and the history of law.

Chapter 1 examines 'sins of the tongue' and restraints on political conversation. It contrasts prescriptions against 'meddling' discourse with the recognition that plebeian speech was irrepressible. Chapter 2 reviews the variety of 'abusive words' and the circumstances of their expression. It examines the language of insult between parties, and the damage done by rumour and false news. Chapter 3 deals with the medieval law of treason and its development to the mid-sixteenth century. It reviews case histories from the reign of Henry VI to the reign of Philip and Mary, with extended analysis of treasonous words in the reign of Henry VIII. Chapter 4 uses judicial records and government correspondence to capture seditious voices from the reign of Elizabeth I, including attacks on the queen's gender and sexuality. Chapter 5 follows subjects who called James I a fool. Chapter 6 presents a detailed case history from the 1620s in which Hugh Pyne, a lawyer, called Charles I 'as unwise a king as ever was'. Pyne's case produced an important judgment on the law of treason by words. Chapter 7 offers many more instances from the reign of Charles I in which subjects demeaned, derided, or even offered to kill their monarch. Chapter 8 traces similar sentiments in the revolutionary decades of the mid-seventeenth century, and shows seditious language reverberating against parliament and Protector Cromwell. Chapter 9 follows anti-monarchical speech in the reign of Charles II, when the law was tightened to punish treasonous expressions. Chapter 10 shows the difficulty of policing popular sentiments from the reign of James II to the time of Queen Anne. Chapter 11 looks at the loosening of restraints on political conversation in the eighteenth century, and renewed assaults on seditious speech in the later Hanoverian period amidst calls for reform and revolution. A final section brings the story to the present, showing how speech that once led to trial and punishment became 'the birthright of an Englishman'. The concluding chapter reviews the cultural politics of anti-authoritarian speech, community responses, excuses, and consequences, across the early modern era. Spelling and punctuation have been modernized, except in the titles of printed sources. All printed works were published in London unless otherwise noted. Dates are given 'old style', though the year is taken to begin on 1 January.

Words misreported, though by an echo, or but an echo of an echo, third or fourth hand, have oft a louder sound than the voice itself, and may sound disloyalty, though the voice had nothing undutiful or illoyal in it.

(Speaker of the House of Commons to Charles I in 1626, quoted in John Rushworth, *Historical Collections*, i (1680), 397)

I

Sins of the Tongue

Humans alone have the power of words. The 'noble gift of speech', which distinguishes man from other creatures, serves 'to multiply our delights, to mitigate and unload our sorrows, but above all to honour God and to edify one another', according to the early Stuart minister Edward Reynolds. 'The force and power of speech', he continued, 'can inflame, excite, allay, comfort, mollify, transport, and carry captive the affections of men'.[1] Our voices allow us to praise the lord, as God no doubt intended, with words both silver and golden. But they can also be forked and venomous, venting vanities, back-biting, slander, profanity, and sedition. For our tongues, as moralists observe, bring out the best and worst in humanity. 'No member of the body is subject to so many moral diseases as the tongue is . . . it is either the best or the worst member of all,' declared another seventeenth-century minister, Edward Reyner.[2]

Unruly Tongues

Post-Reformation England inherited some of the language and many of the concerns of early church fathers and medieval confessors about the 'sins of the mouth' and the 'sins of the tongue'.[3] Many a tract and sermon addressed the perils of the unguarded tongue. An Elizabethan compendium of biblical verses gathered references to 'the tongue, and evil speaking' to demonstrate 'the vanities of this world, leading the way to eternal damnation'.[4] The tongue was 'an unruly evil', a source of sin, worse than the serpent and offensive to God, claimed another Elizabethan author.[5] The tongue, repeated the Jacobean moralist William Vaughan, was one of 'the detracting instruments of Satan'.[6] Spokesmen for the established order blamed misuse of mankind's vocal gift for dissension in families, division in churches, and turmoil in the state. The tongue was the instrument of voice, voice the medium of speech, speech the utterance of meaning, and words the elements that gave language its benign or malignant power. All were double-edged instruments, both beneficial and damaging to society.

'Lamentable and fearful' were the abuses of the tongue, wrote the great Calvinist educator William Perkins. 'It would make a man's heart to bleed', he wrote, 'to hear and consider how swearing, blaspheming, cursed speaking, railing, slandering, chiding, quarrelling, contending, jesting, mocking, flattering, lying, dissembling, vain and idle talking, overflow in all places'.[7] A chorus of moral reformers complained of 'scolding, cursing, swearing, slandering, shameless and filthy-speaking', as well as scorning, scoffing, reviling, and back-biting, that imperilled not just the social order but the soul of the Christian who failed to maintain 'religious vigilancy' against these 'sins of the tongue'. The list could be extended to include grumbling, murmuring, haranguing, defaming, spreading false rumours, and speaking treason or sedition. Other Stuart authors offered 'a bridle for the tongue', 'a cure for the tongue evil', or a remedy against 'the abuse of the tongue and speech' that offended against sociability and religion.[8] Offering *Some Generall Directions for a Comfortable Walking with God*, the Northamptonshire preacher Robert Bolton, condemned 'men of intolerable conversation and very scandalous discourse' who spoke 'the language of hell'.[9] His colleague Joseph Bentham cited graphic examples in the Bible where sinners by tongue-smiting 'escaped not the sharp and smarting punishments of the Lord'.[10]

An array of aphorisms, scriptural texts, proverbs, and encapsulations of customary wisdom offered counsel on the governance of the tongue. Moral, religious, and civic advisers agreed on the necessity of controlling, bridling or disciplining that unruly member. 'Keep thy tongue from evil and thy lips from speaking guile', urged the psalmist (Psalms 34: 13). Those who lacked 'faithfulness in their mouth', whose 'throat is an open sepulchre', or who rebel or flatter 'with their tongue', faced the vengeance and judgement of God (Psalms 5: 9–10). 'Death and life are in the power of the tongue', warned the book of Proverbs, 'the wicked is snared by the transgression of his lips' (Proverbs 12: 13, 18: 21). 'The words of a wise man's mouth are gracious; but the lips of a fool will swallow up himself', advised Ecclesiastes (10: 12).

The New Testament amplified these warnings. 'The tongue is a little member, and boasteth great things. Behold how great a matter a little fire kindleth,' wrote the apostle James (James 3: 5). 'The tongue is a fire, a world of iniquity: so is the tongue among our members, that it defileth the whole body, and setteth on fire the course of nature . . . The tongue can no man tame; it is an unruly evil, full of deadly poison' (James 3: 6, 8). 'For he that will love life and see good days, let him refrain his tongue from evil', instructed Peter (I Peter 3: 10). 'Their throat is an open sepulchre; with their tongues they have used deceit; the poison of asps is under their lips: whose mouth is full of cursing and bitterness,' offered Paul (Romans 3: 13–14). There were texts here for countless tracts and sermons, providing counsel to the godly, and reproof to speakers of lewd, light, or dangerous words.

Conventional wisdom taught that the tongue was an 'unruly member', a troublesome appendage, that inevitably drew comparison to man's other bone-less member, the penis.[11] The character Ferdinand in John Webster's play *The Duchess of Malfi* (1613) observes that 'women like that part which, like the lamprey, hath ne'er a bone in't', explaining, when the Duchess protests, 'nay, I mean the tongue'.[12] The tongue is 'a little member', preached the Jacobean cleric Thomas Adams, paraphrasing the apostle James, but 'what it hath lost in the thickness, it hath got in the quickness'.[13] It was remarkable, remarked another Jacobean minister, William Vaughan, 'how this small member can work such turbulent tumults throughout all the circuits of man's little world'.[14]

A misogynist strain held that women's tongues, in particular, were dangerous instruments. 'Woman, for the most part, hath the glibbest tongue,' observed the preacher Thomas Adams.[15] A woman's tongue was 'bitterer than gall', wrote one early Stuart writer.[16] It was like 'a poison, a serpent, fire, and thunder', wrote another.[17] No venomous snake 'stings like a woman's tongue', claimed a popular ballad in 1634.[18]

It was a gentleman's part to control his tongue, to display 'temperance and moderation in his language'.[19] 'A well-tempered tongue' was a mark of good standing.[20] 'Speak not before thou thinkest what thou wouldst deliver' was conventional advice for 'decency in conversation'.[21] Many moralists agreed with the Italian Jacopo Affinati (translated by Anthony Munday in 1605) that 'it is much better to keep silence than to talk'.[22] But, sadly, even gentle tongues were at risk.

Some people believed, with the classical authority Pliny, 'that the tongue of a man hath two veins, one correspondent to the heart, the other agreeable to the brain'.[23] Even if this proved physiologically unsound, it remained rhetorically persuasive. It was widely accepted that the tongue gave voice to the inward thoughts of the heart, as if that organ, not the brain, was the source of will and action. 'What the heart thinketh, the tongue speaketh,' was a common saying.[24] 'The heart', wrote the Elizabethan Catholic

Thomas Wright, 'is the peculiar place where the passions allodge'.[25] Villainous talk proceeded from 'a corrupt and traitorous heart', claimed Lord Keeper Egerton in 1599.[26] The speech of 'ill-tongued traitors' was 'derived from their own corrupt nature', declared a well-known book on language.[27] A traitor's words, early Stuart judges agreed, revealed 'the corrupt heart of him that spake them', and betrayed the 'traitorous . . . imagination of his heart'.[28]

Early modern moralists commonly remarked that 'the tongue of man is the heart's interpreter', and that 'speech . . . is the gate of the soul'. It was observed that 'he that is rotten in his heart is commonly rotten in his talk'.[29] Proverbial wisdom declared speech to be 'the index of the mind' or 'the mirror of the soul'.[30] 'Fools carry their hearts in their mouths, wise men their mouths in their hearts,' declared Thomas Wright.[31] 'What his heart thinks his tongue speaks,' said Don Pedro of Benedick in Shakespeare's *Much Ado About Nothing*.[32] 'The tongue is so slippery, that it easily deceives a drowsy or heedless guard,' warned Richard Allestree,[33] as if the tongue was possessed of a mind of its own.

The tongue 'betrayeth the heart when the heart would betray God', warned Thomas Adams. A good tongue knew its task was to praise God, but 'if it be evil, it is a wild bedlam, full of gadding and madding mischiefs'.[34] Speech, another Jacobean author noted, was 'the key to the mind . . . to express the meaning of the heart'. The tongue, he repeated, was 'the mind's messenger', but so pervasive was human corruption that 'wickedness breaketh out'. The tongue was like the rudder that steered the ship, so that 'he who wanteth a good tongue is in as great peril as a ship in the roughest sea, that wanteth both stern and pilot'. The result could be shipwreck for the commonwealth, church, and state.[35]

In his *Rules for the Government of the Tongue* (1656) the Lincolnshire minister Edward Reyner reminded readers that God heard every word and would demand 'account thereof in the day of judgement'. Even casual words could have dangerous consequences.

The arrows of idle words, though shot out of sight . . . will hereafter drop down upon the heads of such as drew the bow. Words are but wind, is the common saying, but they are such wind as will either blow the soul to its haven of rest . . . or else sink it in the dead sea and bottomless gulf of eternal misery, if idle, profane, frothy, and unprofitable.

Though they might think that 'what is spoken is transient and passeth away', speakers of 'tongue transgressions' needed reminding that 'histories are full of remarkable judgements upon offending tongues'.[36] No matter who else was listening, every word was captured by an all-seeing, all hearing, ever-attentive God.

Nobody thought that words were harmless. Though words were but wind, they had the power of flying arrows or stinging bees. To one Stuart author they were not just wind 'but whirlwinds'.[37] To others they were instruments of destruction. 'The stroke of the tongue breaketh bones,' declared the Bible, which several times likened the tongue to a sharp sword.[38] 'The tongue breaks bones, though itself has none,' said a popular proverb. 'Her tongue is no edge tool, but yet it will cut,' repeated another.[39] 'Malicious tongues, though they have no bones, | Are sharper than swords, sturdier than stones,' rhymed the early Tudor poet John Skelton.[40] 'Talk may brew drink of damnable blame,' warned an early Elizabethan ballad, for an enemy might strike 'with knife or tongue'.[41] William Vaughan concurred: 'a wicked tongue is worse than any weapon.'[42] 'I would be loath to trust his hands, that bans me with his tongue,' wrote another Stuart moralist.[43]

'Though slanderous speeches and menaces be but words, and may be taken but only as a smoke, a breath, or blast of wind and so to vanish and be dispersed in the air like dust, yet . . . they be used as firebrands of private and open grudges, quarrels, conspiracies, and most other tragical and turbulent stratagems,' explained the Jacobean lawyer Ferdinando Pulton. 'The very root and principal cause' of the kingdom's ills, he thought, could be found in the 'menaces, threatenings, and other bitter words . . . gushing out of contentious spirits and venomous tongues'. There was no limit, he feared, to 'the sea of mischiefs, miseries, and calamities, which daily do flow from evil tongues'.[44] Majesty, magistracy, order, and piety were all imperilled by unruly tongues or corrupt conversation. So too did 'scoffing speeches, railing voices, and slanderous words' undermine 'the true church of God', according to the Elizabethan minister Anthony Anderson.[45] Seventeenth-century statesmen knew to their cost 'that grievous words do but stir up strife'.[46]

'Tattling news carriers . . . intermeddlers . . . makebates . . . and wranglers' disturbed civil quietness, wrote the Jacobean preacher George Webbe.[47] The 'poisoned arrows' of gossips, rumour mongers, and backbiters robbed people of their credit, and sowed discord in the community, complained the Restoration minister Stephen Ford.[48] To Robert Burton, author of *The Anatomy of Melancholy*, a smiting tongue could inflict sharp wounds, 'worse than any lash; a bitter jest, a slander, a calumny, pierceth deeper than any loss, danger, bodily pain or injury whatsoever'.[49] Stephen Ford agreed, that 'a reproaching and back-biting tongue is so full of deadly poison as that it will kill a man at a great distance, yea further than any other viper, adder, or any serpent can'.[50]

Innocent of 'speech act theory', early modern authors knew that words had consequences, that spoken utterance caused situation-altering effects.[51] They knew from the Bible, from literature, from legal proceedings, and from everyday discourse that speech could provoke violence, discord, unhappiness, or sedition. An oath or a slur, an insult or a curse, a joke or a lie, could all intensify divisions within communities and erode the fabric of society. These 'sins of the tongue' could damage reputations, set neighbour against neighbour, and undercut the authority of the crown. They became 'crimes of the tongue' when the state retaliated and its proceedings entered reports of spoken words into the written historical record.

The standard explanation for the sins of the tongue held that people were inherently sinful, and the sinful were naturally loquacious. 'The nature of the ungodly is to be quarrellous and contentious,' observed one Elizabethan author.[52] Because 'the heart of man by nature is a bottomless gulf of iniquity', wrote William Perkins in 1593, it was small wonder that people so often engaged in 'imprecations and cursings, either against men or other creatures'.[53]

The worst culprits, by common account, were the vulgar masses. They were 'light and seditious persons' who spread 'vain rumours and bruits, rashly discoursing upon the great and most weighty affairs touching the queen's highness' royal person and state of the realm', claimed a proclamation of 1553.[54] They were 'the idle, the ignorant, the unfortunate . . . which have no good success in their own affairs', who were most likely 'to deprave the doings of other men, and give themselves to speak evil', claimed a later sixteenth-century treatise.[55] It was 'the rude and ignorant sort of subjects . . . the wicked and wilful needy sort of inferior' people, who gave in to 'ambition, envy, malice, heart burnings, discontentment of mind, murmurings and grudgings', according to an early Jacobean treatise. Led by 'the devil, that old experienced and thoroughly practised enemy of mankind', they had 'blind, ignorant, obstinate, wilful, rebellious, malcontented hearts and busy brains . . . to murmur, grudge and mutiny against government'.[56]

Speech against Power

The most dangerous abuse of the tongue was when it whipped against magistrates and monarchs. A powerful strain of sanctions addressed the politics of language, linking the sins of blasphemy and sedition. Relentlessly deployed by preachers and propagandists, a battery of biblical verses demonized speech against the crown: 'Thou shalt not revile the gods, nor curse the ruler of thy people,' commanded Exodus (22: 28). 'Curse not the king, no not in thy thought,' enjoined Ecclesiastes (10: 20). It was a filthy sin to 'despise dominion, and speak evil of dignities', wrote the apostle Jude (1: 8). Other well-worn texts gave royal authority scriptural blessing: 'By me kings reign, and princes decree justice' (Proverbs 8: 15); 'Where the word of a king is, there is power: and who may say unto him, what doest thou?' (Ecclesiastes 8: 4); 'Fear God. Honour the king' (1 Peter 2: 17); 'The powers that be are ordained of God' (Romans 13: 1).

These rhetorical resources were available to every monarch, but they had extra purchase at times of crisis or rebellion. They were deployed in the context of the Pilgrimage of Grace against Henry VIII, the northern uprising against Queen Elizabeth, and the wars and revolutions that engulfed Charles I. The same texts helped to sanctify divine-right kingship under James I, and to remind subjects of Charles II of their dutiful subjection.

Early modern monarchs were especially sensitive to challenges to their authority, and took pains to guard against verbal affronts. Writing in 1536, the Henrician propagandist Richard Morison excoriated sowers of sedition 'that with their venomous tongue sting and poison the fame of them that are set in office'. Unguarded speech led to sedition, and sedition to rebellion, which Plato called 'the greatest sickness that can come to a commonwealth'.[57]

'Contemptuous talk' and 'unbridled speeches' led to 'factions and seditions', warned Queen Elizabeth's Lord Keeper Bacon in 1567. They 'maketh men's minds to be at variance with one another, and diversity of minds maketh seditions, seditions bring in tumults, tumults make insurrection and rebellions'. Unquiet tongues could be ruinous to the kingdom, Bacon argued, for disorderly talk became sedition, and sedition was the harbinger of treason.[58]

Drafted a few years later, in the wake of the northern rebellion, the Elizabethan *Homilie agaynst Disobedience and Wylful Rebellion* warned 'murmurers against their magistrates' that they risked a 'horrible punishment' in this world and the next. God was so 'displeased with the murmuring and evil speaking of subjects against their princes' that he had such speakers 'stricken with foul leprosy . . . burnt up with fire . . . consumed with the pestilence . . . stinged to death . . . [and] swallowed quick down into hell'. Even 'speaking once an evil word against our prince, which though any should do never so secretly, yet do the Holy Scriptures show that the very birds of the air will bewray them'.[59] They were 'monsters of men, that without regard of duty or conscience, and without fear of God or man, cease not in the abundance of their malice, to traduce her majesty . . . and to slander her counsellors and ministers, not only by railing open speeches but also by false, lying and traitorous libels'. So declared the Star Chamber judges in 1599.[60]

Merely to think disloyal thoughts was dishonourable, thought some Elizabethan theorists, but to voice them was both dangerous and damaging. 'Seditious thoughts, like an inward malady, be hurtful to the heart wherein they rest, therefore are they to be avoided; but seditious words, like a contagious disease, do infect others, therefore are they more to be abhorred,' argued Edward Nisbet in 1601. Such words, he wrote, 'pierceth the head and heart of my sovereign'.[61]

Catechists routinely taught that the fifth commandment—'honour thy father and thy mother'—applied not just to natural parents but to 'all that be in authority or worthy of reverence . . . as princes, magistrates, ministers of the church, schoolmasters, learned men, wise men, aged men, men of worship, and such like'. If anyone disobeyed or dishonoured his superiors, warned Alexander Nowell, they 'shall come to a sudden, speedy, and shameful death, or else shall lead a life more wretched and vile than any death; and finally, for their disobedience and wickedness, shall suffer everlasting punishment in hell'.[62]

William Gouge's early Stuart catechism (seven editions by 1635) demonstrated how the fifth commandment required 'reverence to all that have any excellency above us, and obedience to all that have authority over us'.[63] John Ball's catechism (eighteen impressions by 1637) likewise taught inferiors to be 'subject, reverent and thankful to their superiors, bearing with their wants, and covering them in love'.[64] John Dod's *Plaine and Familiar Exposition of the Ten Commandements* (eighteen editions by 1632) took sixty-four pages to expound the six words from the Decalogue, 'honour thy father and thy mother'. Subordinates should exhibit 'reverence, obedience, and thankfulness' to their masters and betters, and should never use rough, unseemly, or undutiful words. To do otherwise, Dod instructed, risked 'the curse of God'. 'Cruel and bitter words are heard oft times from the mouths of wicked and unnatural children', so evil speech was a mark of childishness as well as rebellion and sin.[65]

Jacobean authors developed these ideas within the divine right theory of kingship. Although James I faced no popular uprising, the Gunpowder Plot cast long shadows, and the potential for sedition was ever present. It was the duty of 'every good and true subject', Jacobean officials insisted, to report 'all lavish and licentious speeches tending to the scandal, dishonour or depraving of [his majesty's] royal person, state or government, or of the nobles and great men' of the realm.[66] 'All railing and evil speaking' against monarchs and magistrates was forbidden, declared *The Doctrine of the Bible*, because kings were 'the anointed of God, and sovereign rulers of the people . . . to speak against them is to speak against God'. The familiar words from Exodus hammered home the injunction: 'Thou shalt not revile the gods, nor curse the ruler of thy people.'[67]

Passing sentence against a sower of sedition in 1604, the Star Chamber judges warned: 'let all men hereby take heed how they complain in words against any magistrate, for they are gods.'[68] The honour of the king 'ought not to be violated so much as in thought, much less in words and action', declared Attorney General Sir Edward Coke.[69] Any 'spot or derogation' against princes and governors was *laesa maiestas* or 'a high and capital offence', declared Sir John Melton in 1609.[70] 'The Lord doth expressly forbid all unreverent thoughts and speeches' against rulers, repeated George Webbe.[71]

Reared in this tradition, Charles I demanded heightened reverent subjection. Ruling by divine right, he saw himself as 'God's instrument . . . the fountain of government . . . the light of the commonwealth . . . like the sun in the firmament'. Like his predecessors, his sacred majesty was supreme governor of the church, commander of the ship of state, head of the body politic, and the keystone of order and justice.[72] Since kingly power came from the law of God, to disobey or disparage it was a sin. With church and state so tightly fused together, there was little distinction between blasphemy and sedition. 'The most high and sacred order of kings is of divine right,' so to criticize it was 'treasonable against God as well as against the king', said the church canons of 1640.[73]

'The people must honour, obey, and support their king,' preached William Laud soon after King Charles's accession. Any dishonouring of the king and his councillors (the 'pillars' of the state) undermined the commonwealth, Laud continued, 'for to murmur and make the people believe there are I know not what crack and flaws in the "pillars", to disesteem their strength, to undervalue their bearing, is to trouble the earth and the inhabitants of it'. Scandalous and seditious talk was intolerable, in Laud's view, because 'the strength of a people is in the honour and renown of their king; his very name is their shield among the nations'.[74] Kingship was 'sacred', Laud later preached, 'and therefore cannot be violated by the hand, tongue, or heart of any man'. It was 'blasphemous iniquity' to murmur against kings, a sin to revile any monarch. Only 'distempered spirits breathe sour' upon God's blessings, and 'that man cannot deserve so much as the name of a Christian, that prays not heartily for the king'. Let no one 'whet your tongues, or sour your breast, against the Lord and against his anointed'.[75]

Other supporters of the Stuart crown sustained the attack on seditious speech. They were 'filthy dreamers (as holy Jude calls them) who despise dominion and speak evil of dignities, woe unto them', preached the royal chaplain Isaac Bargrave in 1627.[76] They were 'monsters in a kingdom, who endeavour by all means possible to enervate and weaken authority, thereby to make it contemptible', wrote Thomas Hurste in 1637. They were 'mutterers and rash discontented people' who 'offer[ed] violence with their tongues'.[77]

Writing in 1639 of 'the duty of all true subjects to their king', Henry Peacham called for reverence 'in words, deeds, as also in our very thoughts ... We ought to speak of them with all honour and respect, not to traduce them nor their actions in public or private among inferiors.'[78] But alas, railed Henry Valentine in the same year, 'these latter times have produced a generation of vipers ... who instead of rejoicing in their king rail at him ... Oh the strife of tongues! Oh the great thoughts and divisions of heart that are amongst us.'[79] Alas, 'the strife of tongues', the 'rising up with the tongue', 'the licentious looseness of seditious tongues', and the 'murmur' of the 'virulent tongue', lamented other supporters of the embattled Charles I.[80] Later chapters will expose some of the crimes of the tongue that triggered these reactions.

Restricting the Plebeian Tongue

Early modern authorities firmly believed that the common people had no business discussing the affairs of the kingdom. Their efforts to restrict the plebeian tongue and curtail its political voice reverberated across the Tudor and Stuart era. Misled by 'blindness ... division [and] discord ... the weak and vulgar minds of the people' were unfit for 'matters of weight and gravity' or 'matters of policy', according to the early Tudor theorist Thomas Starkey. The people, he pontificated, were 'rude and ignorant, having of themself small light of judgement, but ever in simplicity'.[81] Though some of Henry VIII's subjects 'daily murmured and spake their foolish fantasies', their opinion counted little, according to the chronicler Edward Hall, for 'the affairs of princes be not ordered by the common people'.[82] 'It is no part of the people's play to discuss acts made in the parliament' or to 'intermeddle with no other man's office', declared Richard Morison in 1536. State affairs were far removed from 'the lightness of the people' and their propensity to 'false ... and lewd judgement'.[83]

Elizabethan propagandists sang the same tune. It was not for 'humble men' to occupy their heads and tongues with 'great affairs and business' that passed their 'wit and understanding', declared the court preacher John Young in 1576. It 'cannot well stand with the duty of a good Christian to intermeddle over busily in other men's callings', or 'matters which are too high for them'.[84] It was wrong, wrote Thomas Wright later in Elizabeth's reign, for men to 'dispute, or rather wrangle about matters exceeding their capacity, as a cobbler of chivalry, a tailor of divinity, a farmer of physick, a merchant of martial affairs'. Men should not 'meddle with those matters which ... surpass their capacity', for that way lay 'gross errors and absurdities' and confusion.[85] 'The vulgar sort' had no business with affairs of state, declared Secretary Cecil in 1599. To yield to 'the irregular humours of such base sorts of people' was to invite recurrence of Jack Cade's and Jack Straw's rebellions.[86]

The early Stuart regime further developed this strain, excluding the king's humbler subjects from commentary on the public business of the realm. It was not for 'base mechanical fellows' or commoners 'with poorer and weaker understandings' to 'intermeddle with the fireworks of court business and state occurrences', asserted Sir John Melton. Only 'foolish idiots' essayed 'the secretest and deepest mysteries' of state that did not concern them.[87] 'Meddle not with our princely cares', instructed a manuscript poem attributed to James I, advising 'purblind people' to avert their gaze from 'state affairs'.[88]

Prince Charles's tutor Robert Dallington taught the future monarch to beware 'the inconstant multitude' and to despise 'this many-headed monster, which hath neither head for brains nor brains for government'. It became a maxim of power that, 'as sacred things should not be touched with unwashed hands, so state matters should admit no vulgar handling'.[89] The *arcana imperii*, the secret business of the realm, belonged only to those called to it by rank and breeding. For the rest, it was no concern, no matter for knowledge or discussion. 'The scum of the commons, the tags and rags of the people, base mechanicks, men of little knowledge, less honesty, and no discretion at all', had no business speaking on public matters above themselves, preached Michael Wigmore in 1633.[90] The king's affairs were not to be judged 'by goodman the cobbler, by master the mercer, by clouted shoes and russet coats', declared Francis Rogers the same year.[91] 'It is an ambitious ignorance for men to meddle in what they understand not, and first to believe popular tales raked out of the kennel, and after to vent them to the people,' wrote John Bowles, dean of Salisbury in 1629.[92] 'Study to be quiet, and do your own business,' urged Thomas Warmstry in 1641. 'Study to be quiet,' repeated the London minister Ephraim Udall, 'meddle not in things that belong not to your calling'.[93]

The chain of authority demanded deference and acquiescence, and, if ordinary people were permitted to speak at all, they were supposed to keep to the script. Political allegiance and religious conformity both required verbal discipline. The elite expected commoners to know their place and to guard their tongues, and officials were outraged when subjects overstepped their bounds. Popular discourse on political topics could produce only 'strife and contentions'.[94]

Everybody Talks

In practice, however, as political commentators well knew, people talked all the time, and sometimes spoke out of turn. Despite repeated injunctions against popular political discourse, there was no stopping the flow of commentary and opinion. There can be no society without conversation, no community without discourse, and early modern England was no exception.

People talked wherever they gathered, shared news whenever it was available, and sometimes rashly spoke their minds. The protocols of silence and deference were widely ignored. Undutiful and unauthorized talk was abundant and distressing, as the courts and councils of every age knew to their chagrin. Everyday conversations veered unpredictably onto forbidden topics, and reports occasionally reached the authorities. Given their belief that humanity was inherently corrupt, and that commoners had weak control of their tongues, officials were not surprised to hear of talk that was scandalous, dangerous, or seditious.

Instead of a cowed and silenced populace, closed off from the great affairs of the realm, we should imagine England energized by a constant hum of chatter. Instead of a dutiful and deferential hierarchy, imbued with the spirit of the fifth commandment, we should see a seething and rumbustious community, overflowing with noise and opinion. Everyday sociability thrived on comment and response, observations about the weather, enquiries about a neighbour's health, remarks about a minister's sermon, and occasional reflections on the business of the kingdom or the crown. The common greeting on everyone's lips was 'what news?' and this led easily to controversy and trouble.

A seventeeth-century print depicted 'the several places where you may hear news...at the bakehouse...at the conduit...at the ale house...at the market...at the church', as well as laundry places, bath houses, and childbeds, indeed wherever gossips might tattle and where men and women might comment on the world around them.[95] The Jacobean poet Richard West identified 'makebates and tattling gossips' among participants in this everyday exchange of information:

> You that at conduits, and such other places,
> The ale-house, bake-house, or the washing block
> Meet daily, talking with your brazen faces,
> Of peoples matters which concern you not'.[96]

John Taylor observed people in 'taverns, ordinaries, inns, bowling-greens and alleys, alehouses, tobacco-shops, highways and water passages', enjoying each other's company, sharing the latest news, and intruding on the *arcana imperii*.[97]

Alehouses, notoriously, bred 'idle and discontented speeches'.[98] Here travellers met and workers paused for refreshment. Every encounter was an occasion for conversation, and every drink an opportunity for abuse of the tongue. Much of the seditious murmuring that came to the attention of magistrates originated in alehouses and victualling establishments. It was in 'alehouses, taverns and tippling houses' that libellous songs were composed, copied, and performed, before spreading to the streets and market places.[99] There neighbours would 'sit and talk and prate' of an evening concerning the 'king or kingdom, church or state'.[100] A fiction entitled *Newes from the North* (1579) recreates such 'alehouse actions and brabbles', in which the traveller Simon Certain and the farmer Piers Plowman progress from social pleasantries to discussion of magistracy, authority, and law.[101] Joseph

Bentham wrote disapprovingly in 1638 of the 'dunghill scurrilities, quaffing compliments, ridiculous jeerings, obscene ribaldries, irreligious tongue-smitings of men better than themselves, blasphemous oaths, and such like hellish stuff', to be heard in alehouse settings.[102] One such alehouse in Nottinghamshire was known locally as 'the parliament house of John Jeppson'.[103]

The church, as much as the alehouse, was a setting for casual conversation. Outside in the porch or churchyard, and inside, even during service time, parishioners shared news, spread gossip, and expressed opinions on both local and national affairs. In some churches, such as Haddenham, Cambridgeshire, it was 'the custom there used' after the sermon for the men of the community to 'sit still in the same church to confer of the affairs of the parish'. One such Sunday conference in April 1619 led to disorderly 'words or speeches . . . for the animating or stirring up of the multitude and common people' against the fenland Commissioners of Sewers.[104] Depositions and examination files often describe contentious exchanges or altercations that took place in the church or after worship.

So too were private houses and places of business the sites of dangerous words. We learn of exchanges at market squares and shop windows, on ferry boats and in kitchens. In July 1561, 'standing in Mr Parker's house as he was tuning a pair of virginals', Robert Munds of Norwich remarked: 'it is a wonderful thing to hear men talk nowadays.' He was jawing with Edward Boston, servant to a Norwich alderman, who answered, 'if that you had heard as much as I have done it would make the ears burn off your head'. On this occasion the conversation was about the bishop of Norwich, John Parkhurst, who had been scandalously described as a 'whoremaster'. Boston recited the words attributed to a local worsted weaver, that 'nowadays there was none that preach but adulterers and fornicators'.[105] But, as we shall see, the conversation could equally have included local or national politics, or even the person of the queen.

At times of political or economic crisis the murmuring grew louder and the flow of chatter more heated. It was hard to be indifferent to war or rebellion, uncertainties about the succession, or alterations in official religion. Royal foibles sparked comment, and the fiscal demands of the state quickened public conversation. A subject's personality, passion, anger, or intake of alcohol could also affect his or her judgement. People often forgot themselves, or forgot to bridle their tongues. Although it met with their disapproval, commentators repeatedly remarked on the popular appetite for political conversation. There was a primitive public sphere as early as the fifteenth century, where commoners exercised their curiosity about the larger political world.

The late medieval commonalty, though unenfranchised, was not necessarily uninformed. Popular political commentary could be heard at alehouses like the Bell in London's Fleet Street, the Tabard at Chichester, or the Hart in Salisbury, all sites of discourse that brought patrons under scrutiny. People spoke as though they had a stake in the affairs of the kingdom, and sometimes their commentary verged on sedition.[106] The early English morality tract *Mum and the Sothsegger* observed that everyone was 'bolde to bable what hym aylid, and to fable ferther of fautz and of wrongz' regarding 'the misse-reule that in the royaulme groved' (people boldly spoke their minds about the ills of the kingdom and the misrule of those in power).[107] John Skelton rhymed about the popular taste for information, 'For men now be tratlers [sic] and tellers of tales: | What tidings at Totnam, what newes in Wales?'[108] Cardinal Wolsey worried in 1523 that parliamentary matters were no sooner spoken than they were 'immediately blown abroad in every alehouse' in Westminster.[109]

Though authorized political discourse belonged only to 'gentlemen of blood and quality . . . full of duty and understanding', and to 'the wisest and best experienced men of the state', the Elizabethan elite were aware that 'the vulgar sort' meddled in matters that did not concern them. 'Some at ordinaries and common tables, where they have scarce money to pay for their dinner, enter politic discourses of princes, kingdoms, estates, and of councils and councillors, censuring every one according to their own discontented and malicious humours . . . with many false, malicious and villainous imputations,' so fulminated Lord Keeper Egerton in 1599.[110]

Despite inhibitions on 'meddling', there were some among the queen's subjects 'making evident digressions and excursions into matters of state, debating titles and jurisdictions, quarrelling with laws and acts of parliament, examining treaties and negotiations, and every way presuming to move question of the proceedings both abroad and at home'.[111] There was 'common murmuring amongst the people, continual wresting of the word, derision of God's ministers, division between father and son', wrote Charles Gibbon in 1590.[112] If anyone wished to discuss the war with Spain, English problems in Ireland, the affairs of the Earl of Essex, or the likely succession to the throne, they were stirring dangerous waters. Yet these were the topics at the tip of many a tongue.

Similar problems troubled the early Stuarts. Despite the frown of authority, commoners persisted in discussing the state of the church, the plight of Bohemia, or the matching of the Prince of Wales. We know that commoners in a victualling house in Lombard Street, London, were 'meddling' in the high political world and discussing the affairs of the nobility, because one of them, an illiterate tailor named Harry Bond, was investigated in 1606 for saying that 'my Lord of Salisbury ... was suspected in these businesses about the court'.[113]

King James would 'well allow of convenient freedom of speech', so he said, but not 'a greater openness and liberty of discourse' or 'a more licentious passage of lavish discourse and bold censure in matters of state, than hath been heretofore or is fit to be suffered'. Matters of state (*arcana imperii*) were 'no themes or subjects fit for vulgar persons or common meetings' or for 'the boldness of audacious pens and tongues'. Repeated proclamations in 1620 and 1621 instructed 'good and dutiful subjects [to] take heed how they intermeddle by pen or speech with causes of state and secrets of empire ... above their reach and calling'.[114] But the conversation only grew louder and more reckless.

Under Charles I the popular buzz was as noisy as ever. Sermons were not just preached and appreciated but 'bruited abroad and commented upon'.[115] The affairs of the king, the queen, the duke, or the archbishop were commonly on people's lips. In country parishes, complained a Northamptonshire vicar, 'there is such a vein of refractory disposition amongst many, that though some of them speak never so vile against God, the king, and the church, and sow sedition, yet will not the rest be witnesses against them, though they both hear and see disloyalty never so plainly'.[116] Ballads, libels, pamphlets, and newsletters circulated alongside spoken observations, in both scribal and printed form. The foreign news corrantos were suppressed in 1632, 'that the people's heads might not be filled with idle discourse',[117] but the oral flow of information was unimpeded. Though historians have striven to recuperate the news culture of early modern England, through both scribal and printed sources, they have barely penetrated the ephemeral world of face-to-face conversation.[118] Later sections of this book will explore how far that is possible, and will attempt to capture some of the noise.

2

Abusive Words

Out of earshot, and far removed in time from their first hearers and reporters, we have only limited retrieval of the dark discourse of dangerous words. Most of what we know comes from depositions of witnesses and examinations by magistrates concerning private and controversial exchanges. We can never be sure of the truth of the matter, any more than early modern justices and councillors could tell if a story was fabricated or misheard, or shaped by malicious purposes. Too often the reports refer to words that were 'scandalous, seditious or treasonable' without actually citing them.

Words were but wind, and most were soon forgotten, but fragments of speech entered the historical record. This chapter examines some of the ways in which private exchanges became part of the public transcript. It uses the records of local and national courts, councils, governors, magistrates, and diarists to recover the words that early modern authorities deemed transgressive. It attempts to reconstruct the circumstances of these exchanges in order to eavesdrop on past conversations. And it offers a sample of the disorderly speech that came before the courts. The records yield echoes of antisocial language, insult, and scolding; scandal, slander, defamation, and libel; and the spreading of rumour and false news. These were products of social interactions that commonly gave voice to the sins of the tongue. The politically sensitive matter of undutiful speech, unsubjectlike utterance, seditious talk, and treasonable words against the crown is reserved for the following chapters.

Words are but Wind

Preachers and moralists often claimed that, though 'what is spoken is transient and passeth away', God was always listening to offending conversations.[1] The state too was interested in 'tongue transgressions', and had means to identify and punish offenders. A chain of reaction and reportage brought representations of offensive speech to the attention of the authorities and into the purview of historians.

First, someone had to say something that someone else thought inappropriate, dangerous, or actionable: a lie, an oath, a curse, or a grumble. But no words were recorded until a listener complained. A drinker in social company might first appeal to the landlord; another auditor might call for a constable; sometimes the words were recollected later in the course of some other dispute. Eventually the tale might reach a magistrate, who would dutifully examine the alleged speaker and witnesses. Only then would the allegation and answers be transcribed into text. Before sending the matter to the assizes, or some other legal venue, the magistrate might write to a superior for advice or to demonstrate his assiduity. Hundreds of letters reached the Privy Council with reports of 'scandalous', 'scornful', 'vile', or 'uncomely' utterances. Files of documents expose 'railing and reviling speeches' and 'unseemly and opprobrious words'. If the alleged expressions were thought traitorous or seditious, or in any way threatened authority, the Council might well press for further examinations, or take over the investigation itself.

In other circumstances involving dangerous or damaging language the victims might retaliate against personal vilification. If their reputation was attacked, their honour sullied, or their name besmirched, they might seek redress through the law. Depending on the status of the parties involved and the nature of their verbal injuries, the matter might go before the local ecclesiastical courts, King's Bench or Common Pleas, Star Chamber, High Commission, or the High Court of Chivalry. These were all record-keeping agencies, generating allegations, presentments, indictments, orders, or depositions. All offered opportunities to prosecute 'crimes of the tongue'.[2] A standard interrogatory asked, 'at what time and in what company and in whose presence were any such words spoken?'[3] Witnesses, defendants, and officials all contributed to the written record, creating partial transcripts of past conversations. Though the processes of law and the mediation of scribal recording rob these words of immediacy and inflexion, they nonetheless capture the flavour and patterns of heated and intemperate speech. Since most heated conversations were indeed lost to the wind, the recorded fragments represent a minimum of dangerous discourse.

Insult and scolding

Many a parish suffered an exceptionally noisy trouble-maker, a woman like Sara Prine in Herefordshire, 'a common scold' who inflicted 'many curses ... with great oaths and protestations' upon her long-suffering neighbours,[4] or Joan Allen of Essex, who berated the churchwarden and constables with 'most bitter railing and taunting speeches' and 'opprobrious and scandalous' words.[5] Equally common were men like Abel Wanseworth of Rayleigh, Essex, described as 'a horrible swearer, a common barrater, a sower of false and slanderous reports, and disturber of the peace and quiet of the whole town',[6] or John Wall of Hereford, who 'did scold and rail' at a female neighbour, 'calling her whore, common whore, and rotten whore', and abusing a man as 'false forsworn knave'.[7]

There was hardly a community immune from such talk. Even if they caused no other damage, abusive speakers violated the rules of civil discourse and threatened to impair the peace. Often enough their words led to blows. Local authorities made occasional attempts to curtail loud and foul language, to restrain 'railing and reviling speeches', and to guard respectable parishioners against 'unseemly and opprobrious words'. But only when they overreached or said something particularly offensive did scolding speakers become subject to judicial process, and thereby enter the records.

'Scolding' was notionally gendered, described by one scholar as 'the feminization of deviant speech'.[8] It was the unruly tongue gone wild. According to the eighteenth-century legal authority William Blackstone, 'a common scold, *communis rixatrix*, (for our law-Latin confines it to the feminine gender) is a public nuisance to her neighbourhood'.[9] Most foul speakers described as scolds were women, but men could be guilty of the like offence; the label 'scold' might not attach to them, but men could still be charged with 'scolding'.

Margaret Price of Kingston, Herefordshire, pursued a neighbour to the grave with a stream of scolding invective, 'cursing and using most uncharitable words against the corpse of one deceased'. At King's Sutton, Oxfordshire, in 1617 the scold Anne Chapman was heard 'contemptuously raging, blasphemously swearing by the lord's wounds and blood' against the incumbent minister.[10] Jane Nightingale of Norley, Cheshire, was described in 1630 as 'a woman of a turbulent and vexatious spirit ... in continual opposition with her neighbours, either causelessly vexing them or wrongfully slandering and defaming them' with 'slanderous and reproachful speeches', but the records do not refer to her as a 'scold'.[11]

In Norfolk in 1626 parishioners complained about Richard Sheepheard of Westwinch, 'an incorrigible and desperate tinker', whose 'ordinary talk' consisted of 'swearing, lying, slandering, and common barrating against others'. When the minister Robert Bale offered a mild reproof, 'the tinker broke forth into many violent speeches against him . . . vomiting out such fearful blasphemies, oaths, reproaches and threatenings . . . as it is not meet to be written'. One outburst triggered by attempts to collect rent for Shee-pheard's parish lodgings led to proceedings at the Quarter Sessions.[12] Three years later Norfolk magistrates heard of the 'many filthy, lewd, barbarous and threatening speeches' of Mr Thomas Violet, many of them directed at his unfortunate wife. Violet was a gentleman, who should have known how to control his temper and his tongue, but neighbours judged his utterance to be 'foul', 'tyrannical', and 'inhuman'.[13]

In more examples, Thomas Sommerfield of Ibstock, Leicestershire, was cited in 1634 'for brabbling and scolding in the church' and speaking with malice 'in somewhat a high manner'.[14] William Ireland of Langton-iuxta-Horncastle, Lincolnshire, was presented at an episcopal visitation in 1636 as 'a common swearer and blasphemer of God's name, for a common slanderer of his neighbours, for a filthy and lascivious talker and sower of much discord, and a common drunkard'.[15]

Described in 1641 as 'a common quarreller, a disturber of the king's peace . . . a constant jangler and wrangler both in word and action', the glover John Holt of Hereford, 'reviled and mewed' at another glover's wife, 'calling her filthy sot and a spawn of a bastard'. When the woman's husband called on the speaker 'to bridle his tongue', Holt called him 'knave' and said 'he did not care a fart or a turd for him, nor did not care for no man or no man in England'.[16] Also in 1641, parishioners at Erpingham, Sussex, described Thomas Andrews as 'a common sower of discord and debate amongst his neighbours, a very troublesome and contentious person, full of evil and foul words'.[17] Ralph Sparke of Chester the same year was similarly known as a 'quarreler amongst his neighbours . . . breeding strife, quarrels and debate . . . apt to give foul words'.[18]

People like these were incapable of tongue discipline. Their words raised the temperature of verbal scandal and invective, and also became subjects of other people's conversations. Neighbours had to decide how much to tolerate and when to resort to the courts. A particularly virulent outburst, or an exchange that created disorder, could lead to intervention by constables, clergy, or magistrates.

The records are also rich with examples of disorderly speech among people of higher social status. Gentlemen, clerics, and members of the professions were expected to watch their language, but sometimes their passion got the better of them. Like villagers and townsfolk, the educated elite occasionally succumbed to offences of the tongues. It was always shocking to hear abusive language from people whose speech was supposed to be civil and polite.

Two Cambridge academics, fellows of Pembroke Hall, fell into a shouting match in 1611, when one of them spoke unwisely, 'in a great heat and rage'. Meeting together in the college garden, Dr Theophilus Field began to berate his junior colleague Alexander Read, claiming that Read had spoken ill of him behind his back. Field called Read a 'stiff clown', to which Read replied 'that for stiffness he had honesty in him, and further said that a man had need to have a stomach in that college to carry matters out'. Field told Read 'that he had a stomach to a piece of beef to his victuals, but otherwise that he was a base fawning fellow, a back-biter and a base rascal'. When Read in turn accused Field of being 'base and contemptible', the doctor took Read 'by the beard, saying again that he was a base rascal, or words to the like effect'. Theophilus Field was a doctor of divinity, a royal chaplain, and a future bishop of Hereford, but on this occasion he could not restrain his temper. Although the words 'were spoken in private...no man else being present', they soon became public when Field repeated them to other fellows and threatened to prosecute Read before High Commission. The altercation is reported in records of the Vice Chancellor's court.[19]

Collegiate life at Oxford was also disrupted by the speaking of 'verba brigosa', or contentious, divisive and wrangling words. The 'chiding' of two fellows of St Edmund's Hall, for example, came to the attention of the Chancellor in 1631 when one called the other 'thief' and 'dishonest' for 'stealing part of other men's sermons', and was labelled 'rascal' in return.[20]

Clergymen positioned themselves as models of verbal propriety, but reports of their excesses are common. The Kentish minister John Reading appealed in 1626 against 'the liberty of an ill governed and conscienceless tongue', but apparently gave as good as he got, calling one parishioner a 'dog among men', and justifying this language by Scripture, 'for so David called railers and persecutors'.[21] Another cleric, John Hodgeson, vicar of Stradsett, Norfolk, seemed unable to practise the verbal restraint that was required of a man of the cloth. Instead, petitioners complained in 1629, he was 'a common railer and evil speaker to his neighbours and parishioners', and reviled them 'in base and uncomely terms'. He told one parish widow that she was 'a quean and the filthiest and wickedest woman that ever lived', berated another churchgoer as 'rogue, rascal and knave', and abused Francis Piggott, esquire, the most prominent landowner in town, saying 'sirra, sirra, sirra . . . thou lyest'. 'Sirra' was a demeaning word to apply to a gentleman, but it was among the mildest of Hodgeson's verbal transgressions. Parishioners complained to the Quarter Sessions about their minister's 'beastly words' when, before thirty witnesses, he charged Edmund Chapman with encouraging Thomas Parlett to 'lay his maid down in a haycock and fuck her, fuck her, fuck her, fuck her, by God . . . with such beastly gesture and motion of his body that all the people there present except himself were ashamed of his beastliness'.[22]

Other clergymen overflowed with rage and called their parishioners 'base', 'greasy', or 'saucy fellows', 'scurvy companions . . . reprobates . . . coxcombs . . . giddy headed fellows', or likened them to lowly beasts. Thomas Geary, the vicar of Bedingfield, Suffolk, railed at his parishioners as 'sowded pigs, bursten rams and speckled frogs'. Another Suffolk minister, Robert Shepherd of Hepworth, insulted his congregation as 'black mouthed hell hounds, limbs of the devil, fire brands of hell, plow joggers, bawling dogs, weaverly jacks, and church robbers, affirming that if he could term them worse he would'. Edward Layfield of All Saints, Barking, allegedly lashed out at his enemies as 'black toads, spotted toads, and venemous toads, like Jack Straw and Wat Tyler', when parishioners protested his ceremonial innovations.[23] Handbooks for ministers warned them to avoid 'foolish, ridiculous and . . . undecent' or 'unbefitting' terms,[24] but in times of stress they found it hard to contain the anger in the breast.

Even lawyers were capable of abusive language. In 1634 William Fanshaw, an auditor of the Duchy of Lancaster, spoke contemptuously of Chief Justice Thomas Richardson, 'calling him a foul blabber-lipped blockhead, fitter to be a bearward than a judge'. Richardson brought legal action against Fanshaw 'for speaking of scandalous words', and 'his too lavish speeches of his betters', but the suit redounded to the Chief Justice's discredit. The Norfolk gentleman Thomas Knyvett wrote home from Westminster that 'this business was mightily canvassed at the Common Pleas bar, to the great scorn and derision of all the hall . . . His great lordship [Richardson] is so jeered all the town over for bringing this business in question . . . The king, they say, is mightily angry at him for disgracing himself and his place so much.'[25]

Defamation and Slander

Everyday victims of defamatory language could seek redress in both the ecclesiastical and secular courts. The church courts handled defamation suits when one party spoke ill of another. The common law provided remedies for 'injuries affecting a man's reputation or good name . . . by malicious, scandalous, and slanderous words, tending to his damage and derogation'.[26] These were not criminal prosecutions by the crown or the church for violations of the law, but rather litigation between members of the community. In principle, an aggrieved party might sue for damages in a secular court, seeking money by way of compensation. An ecclesiastical court, by contrast, might vindicate a person's honour but could impose only spiritual sanction, such as excommunication or public penance, on a layman or suspend a clergyman from his ministry.[27]

Historians have made extensive use of the records of ecclesiastical courts—in episcopal, archidiaconal, and peculiar jurisdictions—to investigate charges of defamation. Surviving in bulk from the late Middle Ages to the eighteenth century, the allegations and depositions in these cases yield detailed accounts of verbal exchanges and altercations. The number of such suits expanded in the later sixteenth century, in what some people called 'the bum court' or the bawdy courts. Most concerned assaults on a person's probity, honesty, or honour, through abusive or vituperative language.[28]

A high proportion of defamation cases before the ecclesiastical courts involved sexual insults. Both men and women could suffer sexual defamation, but the most common cases involved someone—either male or female—calling a woman 'whore', 'harlot', 'jade', 'quean', or, in the Latinized records of the late fifteenth century, '*meretricem communem*'.[29] In the early Tudor diocese of Norwich, for example, Margaret Malyett of Norwich defamed Elizabeth Banyard in 1511, 'thou art an harlot'. And a few years later Emma Wilby of south Norfolk charged Katherine Googe, 'thou art a false forsworn quean'.[30] Elizabethan cases typically involved someone saying, 'you are a damned bitch, whore, a pocky whore', or calling a married woman 'whore . . . a cart is too good for thee'.[31] In 1586 the taunts of a Wiltshire woman against her neighbour—'Mistress stinks, mistress fart . . . mistress jakes, mistress tosspot and mistress drunkensoul'—brought her before the ecclesiastical court. Others defamed their enemies as 'brazen-faced quean, hacking jade, filthy bawd, and hot tailed whore'.[32]

Popular usage gave many of these words a heightened derogatory effect. 'Quean' originally meant no more than 'a young woman', but it took on the meaning of 'prostitute'. A 'jade' was originally 'a worn-out horse', but it too came to apply to a woman of easy morals. The word 'harlot' once meant a young man or knave, then a vagabond or beggar, before becoming a synonym for 'whore'. A Yorkshire court heard in 1634 that 'by the word bawd hath been and is understood such a woman who hath herself formerly been a whore and prostituted her body to the lust and use of several men, and doth keep or procure other women to offend in the like kind of incontinency'. To call a woman 'whore', 'quean', or 'bawd' was as defamatory as calling a man 'a cuckoldy witwally fool' or 'a whoremaster bankrupt rogue'.[33] But disparaging a woman's housekeeping could be as damaging as deriding her sexual honour.[34]

Gendered defamatory language fell as commonly from women's tongues as men's, with men and women abusing each other. Defending himself in one such case in Tudor Norfolk, one man acknowledged that he called a woman 'whore', but meant only that she was a 'whore of her tongue', not a 'whore of her body'.[35] In a case from Stepney, Middlesex, in 1608, George Bryan 'did call Mrs Bowers, the vicar's wife, quean and drab in contempt of the ministry', after she 'called him a knave' and spat in his face.[36]

Whereas a woman might be defamed for her sexual incontinency, as a 'harlot', 'whore', or 'quean', a man was more likely to be attacked for his character, as 'rogue', 'rascal', 'varlet', 'churl', or 'knave', often preceded by the adjective 'false'. A man's principal asset was his honesty, and once that was questioned his credit began to suffer. A 'churl' was base born, of the lowest rank or credit. So too was a 'varlet', a man or boy of menial condition. A 'rascal' belonged to the rabble, of the lowest and least trustworthy sort. The word 'knave' originally meant 'male', but came to connote someone unreliable and worthless. A 'rogue' was an idle vagabond, with the character of an unprincipled beggar. Nobody could allow such words to be used of them, even if they were true.

But insults of a sexual nature also applied to men, with 'whoremaster' and 'cuckold' among common terms of abuse. According to the late Stuart Justice Sir John Holt, 'to say whoremaster of a man is the same with whore of a woman, which is an ecclesiastical slander', that lay within the jurisdiction of the ecclesiastical courts.[37] A 'cuckold', of course, was a man who could not keep his wife from straying to other men. A 'whoremaster', by contrast, was a sexually promiscuous man or someone who kept a woman for sexual purposes.

In the early Tudor diocese of Norwich Peter Baldwin of Dunwich, Suffolk, called William Saxmundham 'a busybody', Peter Melton called him a 'knave', and Saxmundham retaliated by calling Melton a 'whoremonger'. In 1510 John Humme of Southwold called Hugh Williamson 'a false stinking cuckold'. The antique usage applied in 1521 when one man called another 'a false harlot', though later the word more commonly referred to a woman. Other cases hinged on such words as 'false knave', 'false churl', or 'false rogue or varlet'. All ended up before the bishop's consistory court.[38] The common defamatory language that rained on male Elizabethans ranged from 'whoreson', 'whoremonger', 'harlot monger', and 'cuckoldy knave', to 'villain', 'forsworn rogue', 'varlet', 'rascal', 'fool', and 'dog'. 'You are an old whoring rogue and a bastard-getting old rogue,' said one Norfolk man to another.[39] The words could not be unsaid, but the courts provided a venue where damaged honour might be mended.

Defamatory words from the alehouse or the street were only marginally less inventive than the insults of Shakespeare's characters. In *The First Part of King Henry IV* the prince calls Falstaff 'thou whoreson, obscene, grease tallow catch', and 'thou whoreson impudent embossed rascal'.[40] Petruchio in *The Taming of the Shrew* addresses Grumio, 'you whoreson malt-horse drudge'.[41] Doll Tearsheet in *The Second Part of King Henry IV* curses, 'a pox damn you, you muddy rascal . . . you scurvy companion . . . you poor, base, rascally, cheating, lack-linen mate, away you mouldy rogue', and calls Pistol 'the foul-mouth'd'st rogue in England'.[42] In *The Comedy of Errors* Antipholus berates Dromio, 'thou whoreson senseless villain', and calls Adriana 'dissembling harlot, thou art false in all'.[43] 'You whoreson dog, you slave, you cur,' shouts King Lear at the hapless Oswald. The disguised Duke of Kent calls the same unfortunate character 'knave . . . rascal . . . rogue . . . and varlet' in a powerful cascade of abuse.[44] 'Rogue, rogue, rogue,' cries Timon of Athens to the philosopher Ademantus.[45] These were dramatized versions of the speech reported in hundreds of defamation cases. Ordinary verbal exchanges may have been less artful, but they were no less damaging to those affected, and no less demanding of redress.

Certain kinds of defamatory language could be actionable in the crown courts if they implied that a crime had been committed. To say of someone, for example, 'thou art a false knave', might not be actionable at law if the words were merely insulting. But if the speaker said 'thou art a perjured knave', or 'thou art a thief, and hath stolen my beans', a case might be made because the defamation imputed a crime. Similarly, to say of someone 'thou keepest a house of bawdry' was determinable at common law, whereas simply calling that person a 'bawd' was a matter for the spiritual courts. The law gave lawyers endless opportunities to argue which words in which settings would bear an action for slander.[46] In some jurisdictions, faced with particular language, the law was unwilling to act, for example, 'for calling the plaintiff quean . . . by reason of the uncertainty of that word'. The word 'knave' by itself was not always actionable, for 'knave originally was no word of reproach, but signified a man servant, and a knave child a man child'.[47]

Towards the end of the sixteenth century the secular courts were increasingly willing to punish language that caused its victims harm, such as damage to their office, calling, or credit. A case in the Court of Common Pleas in 1577, for example, turned on the plaintiff saying, 'thou art a false deceitful knave and I will prove thee a false deceitful knave, thou art a rogue and worthy to be set on the pillory'. In another case in 1585, when Joan Coxe of Packington, Leicestershire, called Ralph Leeson 'a false knave', the Court of Common Pleas took note that, 'by reason of the speaking and pronouncement . . . the same Ralph is not only injured in his good name and fame, but also is grievously harmed in his dealings with divers honest persons'. In 1593, when Richard Ingram of York complained that Elizabeth Knowles called him 'whoremaster, whoremonger harlot', his lawyers urged 'that by reason of the utterance of these defamatory words, the status, good fame and reputation of Richard Ingram are greatly and grievously injured and lessened'. These were *'verba opprobosia injurioisa convitiosa contumeliosa ac diffamatoria'*—opprobrious, injurious, abusive, reproachful, or defamatory. The words were defamatory, not just because of what was said, but because their victim suffered damage by them. By the same token, to call someone 'villain' or 'villein' was not necessarily defamatory, 'because these are common and usual words of reproach by a master to servant, and no slander in credit'. But to use the word in a way that 'touches upon the repute of blood and liberty, of all the land and of all the goods of the plaintiff' might well be incriminating at law, so said King's Bench judges in 1595. Offensive words were 'of greater effect' if spoken of an office-holder than of someone who was not in office, argued the great Elizabethan lawyer Edward Coke.

By amplification, they were all the more scandalous, verging on treason, if spoken about the monarch.[48]

Words against Authority

Words between neighbours could be slanderous or defamatory, but they were not as dangerous to society as insults against magistrates. To speak ill of someone in authority was to violate the fifth commandment and to imperil the political establishment. Any speech against a magistrate was 'a great scandal and offence to the king', wrote Ferdinando Pulton in 1610, for it might tend 'to the breach of the peace, to the raising of quarrels, and effusion of blood'.[49] Nevertheless, as the records make clear, angry subjects in every reign hurled dangerous abuse at officers of the crown.

Abusive words were often triggered by official demands, such as an attempt to collect taxes or impose fines. If a sheriff's man came to distrain a debtor's goods, he might also receive a tongue lashing. If a justice rebuked a parishioner, he might hear rude words in return. The early modern state made myriad demands on its subjects, and sometimes lawful business provoked scandalous verbal responses. Fragments of these exchanges are preserved in the records of quarter sessions and other crown courts. Sometimes the words were 'so odious that they are not fit to be published in open court nor anywhere else', and the incriminating phrases are missing. Such was the case of the 'very railing speeches against the justices' by Thomas Holman, vintner, of Terling, Essex, when he was presented in 1608 'for a common drunkard and for keeping ill rule in his house'. 'Admonished to keep the peace and to remember that he was bound to his good behaviour', the same foul-mouthed vintner declared that he cared not, 'casting up his leg and layering his hand on his tail, making a mouth in a very contemptuous sort'.[50] A popular theatrics of insult added actions to vocabulary, through derisory gestures of the face, limbs, hands, or thumbs.

In many cases, to secure conviction, a court sought to render the actual incriminating words. In 1599, for example, when magistrates attempted to enforce orders about corn in a time of dearth, one local landowner protested, 'they are knaves, I will keep none of their bastards, my goods are mine own, they nor the queen nor the Council have to do with my goods, I do what I list with them'. The outburst cost the speaker an appearance before Star Chamber, a fine of a hundred pounds, and a bond 'for his good a-bearing'.[51]

In the 1630s a Yorkshire yeoman, James Parkin, of Mortomley, appeared before the West Riding sessions for using 'scandalous, malicious and contemptuous words' of a leading magistrate, saying, to the base example of others, 'I scorn Sir Francis Wortley's proposition with my arse, and I worship him with my arse'.[52] Another Yorkshireman, the peddler Thomas Beale of Marborough, declared in 1639 that 'he cared not a fart for Sir Francis Wortley', and Walter Hurt of Bradfield, yeoman, spoke similarly: 'I care not a fart for Sir Francis's warrants.'[53]

A Winchester attorney was 'suspended and barred of his practice' in 1632 for 'divers affronts and abuses to his majesty's justices of peace'. The lawyer John Trussell had rashly made 'unseemly... unfitting... unbeseeming speeches', to the effect that one of the magistrates was a liar.[54] When Roger Wolfe of Hereford spoke derisively 'in flouting and scornful manner' of the governors of the local hospital, the Quarter Sessions forced him to apologise in writing for his 'unseemly words'.[55] Town governments also attempted to police the discourse of participants in civic life. At Cambridge, for example, 'if any shall speak any indecent or unseemly speeches' before the Common Council, they would be fined 2s. 6d.[56] The collapse of borough assemblies into tumultuous shouting in the spring of 1642 was a sign of social dislocation.[57]

To slander or defame a clergyman was also to assault the structure of authority. Mockery of the clergy was especially disturbing, because it undercut the spiritual authority of God's ministers on earth.[58] When a Lincolnshire man reviled his vicar as a 'scurvy rascal knave', when a Buckinghamshire parishioner dismissed his minister as a 'tinkerly parson', when a Norfolk parishioner railed at his rector as 'a wide-mouthed rascal', and a Yorkshireman compared 'his minister to a pedlar and his ministerial function to pedlars' wares', the ecclesiastical authorities were outraged.[59] Other parishioners who called their ministers 'fool', 'ass', 'liar', 'varlet', 'rogue', 'knave', 'rascal', 'palterer', or 'jackanapes' were called before episcopal courts or the court of High Commission.[60] Their words disparaged and demeaned the holy ministry, violated the norms of neighbourliness, and undercut the deferential and reverential conventions on which English religious culture was based. The speakers transgressed against decency and charity, and bruised the honour of a sensitive professional caste. Faced with an outspoken papist in Lancashire in 1618, Archbishop Abbot judged it

'fit' to have him 'scoured . . . that other of his sort may learn by his example to
bridle their tongues, and not to raise slanders at their pleasure'.[61] When the
Dorset tailor Walter Bayly spoke rudely of Silas Bushell, the rector
of Bridport, in 1640, saying that he was 'a base knave, a dangerous knave, a
base rogue, a dangerous rogue, and sought the blood of honest people',
Bushell reported the matter not to his bishop but to the secular magistrates,
who ordered Bayly to appear at the next assizes.[62]

Scandalum Magnatum

An especially transgressive form of abusive speech was when someone spoke
scandalously of his social superiors. Traditional English society treasured the
distinctions of rank and status, and expected everyone to know their place.
With 'kings on their thrones' ruling subjects, 'nobles in their houses'
ordering servants, 'magistrates on seats of justice' punishing offenders, and
'private men in their families' governing households, the entire social order
was constructed as a chain of authority and deference.[63] It was natural and
proper, within this frame of reference, that a few should 'bear rule' while the
rest were better 'fitted for subjection'. The common people had 'meaner
spirits' and 'shallower judgement', explained one theorist of social hierarchy, and should be 'content in the places wherein God hath set them'.[64]
Inferiors owed 'suit, service and homage to their superiors', preached
Thomas Hurste in 1637. It was God who decreed 'that some should ride
on horse-back while others walk on foot', God who justified 'the just power
of one man over another'.[65] It was, therefore, an offence before God, and
damaging to the state, to use defamatory or slanderous language against
gentlemen or aristocrats. It was socially disruptive, and dangerous for all
concerned, when a commoner spoke ill of a lord.

The Statute of Gloucester of 1378 criminalized the speaking of slander,
'false news, and of horrible and false lies' against the nobles and great officers
of the realm. Repeated in 1388, and still applicable throughout the early
modern era, the law set forth remedies against scandalous 'debates and
discords' that exposed the kingdom to 'subversion and destruction'. It was
scandalum magnatum to speak disgracefully against men of honour, including
the 'prelates, dukes, earls, barons and other nobles and great men . . . and
also of the Chancellor, Treasurer, Clerk of the Privy Seal, Steward of the
king's house, Justices . . . and of other great officers of the realm'. The law

provided a powerful weapon for aristocrats who believed themselves scandalized by social inferiors.[66]

Scandalous words could be anything that caused offence, no matter whether true or false. Spoken against powerful individuals, against a peer, a judge, or a councillor of the crown, they constituted *scandalum magnatum*. Two Dutchmen were gaoled at Colchester in 1577 for speaking 'lewd words of the Earl of Oxford'. They were released when they said they were sorry, 'that they mistook him for the Earl of Westmorland', though this was not the most persuasive excuse.[67]

An altercation in 1578 between a Norfolk vicar and a peer of the realm resulted in another action *de scandalis magnatum*. The law reports of Sir Edward Coke reconstruct some of the offending dialogue. In the course of an argument about preaching and the Book of Common Prayer, Lord Henry Cromwell told the vicar, 'thou art a false varlet, and I like not of thee'. The cleric Edmund Denny replied rather boldly, 'it is no marvel that you like not of me, for you like of these that maintain sedition against the queen's proceedings'. This was enough to bring suit in the court of King's Bench, and the judges found for Lord Cromwell under the law of Richard II.[68]

It was *scandalum magnatum* when the Elizabethan William Barnard impugned the honour of Lord Justice Dyer by claiming that his lordship practised sorcery and was familiar with spirits. Stephen Bell committed the like offence when he spread scandal about Lord Abergavenny. Reports of these cases record the range of punishment, from fines and imprisonment to standing in the pillory, having one's ears cropped, to being made to ride backwards on a horse.[69]

If it was *scandalum magnatum* to impugn the honour of a nobleman, it was sedition to speak words that undermined the authority of the crown. Thomas Stephens alias Hawkes of Marlborough managed both in January 1580 when he uttered 'lewd, unreverent and seditious speeches against the duke of Anjou, brother to the French king'. Anjou, of course, was the queen's suitor, so her highness could not 'in honour' allow the words to go unpunished. But the punishment in this case was light, and Stephens was let go with a whipping.[70] It contrasted with the judicial savagery employed the year before against John Stubbs, whose libellous tract against the royal marriage led to the lopping of his right hand.[71] The incident suggests that writing was more dangerous than mere speaking, and print of more consequence than script, but the more lenient response in 1580 may also reflect an evolution of the political and diplomatic environment.

A dispute between Somerset gentlemen in 1624 sharpened when one of them spoke 'scornfully and scandalously' against his higher-ranked neighbour. John Boyes 'in a very peremptory . . . and mocking manner . . . spoke disgracefully' of Sir Robert Phelips, calling him 'a fool', and telling the company, 'God's blood, I am as great a man as he'. An intermediary, Henry Wescombe, asked Boyes 'to forbear such language', but observed that 'nevertheless he doth at all times continue the same or worse whenever they meet'. These were defamatory words, likely to cause a breach of the peace, which could well have led to proceedings in Star Chamber.[72] In 1634 Star Chamber resolved a dispute between Lord Morley and Sir George Tibold, in which the baron said to the knight, 'what a proud rascal is this? I am no companion for such a base fellow, such a dunghill rogue as you are . . . Go out of the house, thou base rascal, I will cut thy throat,' and then punched him on the breast. The verbal offence was aggravated by physical violence, and made worse by taking place at court, 'nigh to the chair of state in that room where their majesties were'. Though Morley confessed that 'it was done in passion', and craved the court's mercy, his outburst cost him a fine of ten thousand pounds.[73]

A few cases of outrageous speech came before the high court of parliament, especially if they encroached on the honour of its members. The records of the House of Lords occasionally permit us to eavesdrop on conversations of this sort. In May 1628 a band of soldiers drinking at the Lion tavern at Banbury, Oxfordshire, fell into argument with local civilians. One of them, Ancient Rynd (the standard-bearer), armed with a bill he had taken from a watchman, threatened other drinkers and told them 'they were base dogs'. The altercation might have been quickly forgotten, and would not have entered the historical record, had not Rynd accused the Banbury men of complaining to parliament, 'and if it had not been for the Lord Say, that puritanical base dog, you had not sped so well, but for him he cared not a fart'. Rynd went on to swear 'God damn him', threatened 'he would send them to heaven or hell before their times', and used 'other great presumptuous words' that are not recorded. By including Lord Say in his rant, the soldier had committed *scandalum magnatum*. Neighbours who had been menaced by the soldiers told their story to the mayor and justices of Banbury, who sensed its political sensitivity and forwarded a report to

Westminster. It was one thing to insult an Oxfordshire haberdasher, quite another to spread aspersions against a noble in the House of Lords.[74]

A Buckinghamshire correspondent of Archbishop Laud complained in 1636 that the Londoner Isaac Pennington (later Lord Mayor and regicide) had committed *scandalum magnatum* by blaming the archbishop for the increase of popery and arminianism. Pennington had spoken in the parish of Chalfont St Peter, a place 'where government is so slackly looked to, men of some little fortunes are persuaded they may say and do anything against government or governors, whether ecclesiastic or laic, without control'. In this case there would be no prosecution, but Pennington became subject to increased scrutiny.[75]

Another venue for prosecuting socially corrosive language was the High Court of Chivalry. Medieval in origin, the court was reformed by the Earl Marshal in the 1620s and formally reconstituted in 1634. Here an aristocrat who had been insulted by a commoner could vindicate his honour. Armigerous gentlemen also used this court against verbal affronts to their name. If one nobleman insulted another, it might lead to a challenge at arms, but no man of breeding would stoop to a duel with an inferior. They might, however, resort to the chivalry court, until its suspension at the end of 1640.[76]

In January 1640 a meeting to set Ship Money at the Red Lion inn, Fareham, Hampshire, descended into shouting and shoving as rival gentlemen hurled insults at each other. Each 'had drunk very much wine and beer' and spoke 'in a violent and angry manner'. Robert Rigges apparently berated Thomas Badd as 'a base fellow and the son of a cobbler, and no gentleman', to which Badd responded by calling Rigges a 'rogue, rascal, no gentleman and the son of a brewer'. These were 'vilifying words . . . by way of disgrace', in disparagement of the other's breeding. Each laid claim to several generations of gentility, and each man claimed to be performing the king's service, Badd as the captain of a trained band and Rigges as a Ship Money commissioner. Each brought suit in the High Court of Chivalry for scandalous words provocative of a duel. While this case was proceeding Rigges brought another bill of indictment against Badd at the Hampshire summer assizes, for speaking scandalous words against the king. The matter lay unresolved when the High Court of Chivalry was suspended in December 1640.[77]

A flood of actions for *scandalum magnatum* in the reign of Charles I led to crippling awards of damages against defendants. Anyone foolish enough to call a noble a 'paltry lord' or 'base fellow' risked an appearance before the courts. The law survived the revolution, and was exploited vindictively and for profit in the reign of Charles II. The Earl of Pembroke prevailed in 1672 against a commoner who called him 'a pitiful fellow' of ill reputation. Lord Salisbury won judgment in 1677 against another who invited his lordship to kiss his arse, saying, 'I care not a turd for him, he keeps none but a company of rogues about him'. The Earl of Shaftesbury famously brought an action of *scandalum magnatum* against a Londoner who called him a traitor. Charles II's brother the Duke of York used the same device against political enemies who blamed him for the fire of London and called him a 'papist dog'. Between 1682 and 1684 the duke launched at least ten cases of *scandalum magnatum*.[78] The rash of legal actions, with huge awards for damages, led to calls in parliament that the noble privilege be abolished. 'Commoners have had £20,000 verdicts against them; and a peer thinks himself dishonoured unless the jury gives what he demands,' complained Sir William Williams in March 1689. A peer might 'call me rogue and rascal', but if a commoner should say 'he cares for a peer no more than a dog', his lordship was likely to prevail.[79] Cases of *scandalum magnatum* became rarer in the eighteenth century, but the law that permitted them was repealed only in 1887.[80]

Disgraceful Libels

Libels, strictly, were not so much sins of the tongue as sins of the pen. Derived from the Latin *libellus* (a little book), a libel was a saying or writing, or some other form of expression, directed against someone, usually someone powerful, that offered scandal or disgrace to its intended victim. A libel against a great man could be *scandalum magnatum*, wrote William Vaughan in 1630, for 'libelling... despoils a man of his fame'.[81]

Though most libels were *in scriptis*, in the form of a handwritten epigram, statement, or verse, a libel could also be *sine scriptis*, by means of a gesture, image, or symbol. 'Speaking' could sometimes be voiceless, through a variety of insulting theatrics. Libelling could also be done 'by scandalous words, scoffs, jests, taunts, or songs', without pen ever touching paper.[82] A West Country man, Thomas Case, was fined in 1639 'for contriving a libel against John Blundell by sending him a lamb's skin with sheep's horns and cuckolds in it'.[83] Other libels were chanted aloud and spread by word of mouth. The later deployment of calves' heads (in posthumous derision of

Charles I) or turnips and cuckold horns (in mockery of George I) had similar libellous effect.[84]

Libels that were 'destructive of all government' or 'dangerous to the peace of this kingdom' might be labelled 'seditious'.[85] Any libel that offered 'dishonourable interpretations of her majesty's godly actions and purposes' was 'villainous, treasonable, and seditious', according to an Elizabethan proclamation.[86] Their effect, said Lord Chief Justice Popham, was 'to scandalize her majesty' and 'to set sedition betwixt the prince and the subjects, which is the kindling of all rebellions'.[87] Lord Keeper Egerton urged magistrates in 1599 'to search and root out such traitorous vipers' who railed or libelled against the queen or her government. 'I call them traitors', he continued, 'because the ancient laws of England account them so, for *mouere seditionem regii* is originally high treason, howsoever the statute 25 Edward III being accommodate to that time, hath dulced and qualified it.'[88] Lord Treasurer Sackville was even more outraged by the flood of 'scandalous and seditious libels' against her majesty's late proceedings in Ireland. 'These viperous and secret libellers', he declared, 'do much more in my opinion deserve death than those which commit open rebellion against the state.' Declared rebels, he argued, were easily suppressed, whereas against hidden libellers 'there is no resistance'.[89] Every libel was a 'heinous offence', declared Star Chamber judges in 1608, but libelling the monarch or the state could verge on treason.[90]

A particular problem with libels was that people were inclined to believe them; official attempts to suppress libels only added to their credibility. 'These malicious pamphlets are thought to be the flying sparks of truth, forcibly kept down and choked by those which are possessed of the state, inasmuch as they carry with them a presence and countenance of liberty of speech,' noted a late Elizabethan councillor. The only remedy seemed to be to persuade people to give libels less attention: 'answer not a fool according to his folly lest thou also become like him.' The same author declared it 'a corrupt and perverse practice of evil subjects to sow abroad libels and invectives of purpose to deface their governors', and warned that 'this pestilent infection' served 'to discourage, divide, and discredit' public officials and 'to put their country in disquiet and tumult'.[91] It did not matter in law if the substance of the libel was true, or well deserved. A libel was damaging because it was injurious, provoked disorder, or was liable to cause a breach of the peace. Even entering a libel into court in the course of prosecution risked disorder; as a Star Chamber judge noted in 1634, 'some have been punished in this court for laughing when they have heard a libel read'.[92]

Notwithstanding these strictures, the spreading of libels grew to near-epidemic proportions in Elizabethan and Jacobean England. They were found nailed to posts and crosses, on windowsills and tavern tables, or scattered in the street. Townsmen and villagers made extempore rhymed verses to spread scurrilous and insulting tales about their neighbours and betters. These libels often originated in alehouses, fuelled by alcohol and boisterous conversation, when a literate member of the company was pressed to set the words down in writing. Recent work on news culture and the origins of the 'public sphere' reveals the contribution of libels to the diversity and vitality of early modern popular opinion.[93]

Two Somerset gentlemen, Hugh Smith and John Coles, were called to account in May 1575 'for the making, rehearsing or publishing of certain slanderous rhymes made against Sir John Young, knight, a thing of very evil example and not to be winked at'.[94] In 1601 Hugh Barker, the barber of Chelmsford, Essex, asked the schoolmaster Thomas Chitham to 'pen a few verses ... upon a pretty jest I shall tell you'. Composed with 'lascivious terms and undecent speeches', the illiterate Barker's libel was 'of one Clement Pope, a glover of Chelmsford, and one Whale's wife', who had apparently committed adultery together. Barker's 'lascivious, villainous and beastly rhymes' were soon winging their way through the town, in both oral and textual form.[95]

A bawdy libel against the godly mayor of Nottingham, 'better to be sung than said, to the tune of Bonny Nell', enjoyed brief notoriety in 1616. Its offence, claimed Jacobean authorities, was 'bringing the professors of true religion and religion itself into contempt and dislike, and striking up debate and dissension in the said town'. Directed primarily at local individuals, the libel was 'seditious', claimed Attorney General Yelverton, because it undermined established authority and tended to raise tumult and sedition.[96] Another 'false and scandalous libel in metre or verse ... set to the tune of Tom of Bedlam', mocked the sexual couplings of 'the purer sort' at Rye, Sussex, in 1632.[97]

In part a response to local news, the libel itself entered the regional news stream to be remarked upon as well as repeated. Discourse engendered discourse, to be further stimulated if the victim or the authorities brought legal action.

Notorious libels in Charles I's reign targeted the Duke of Buckingham. Libellous songs against the over-mighty duke led the Star Chamber judges to recommend exemplary punishment for any who 'nourish dissention and jealousies between the king and his subjects'. Three musicians arrested at Staines, Middlesex, in 1627 for singing a libellous song were each fined five hundred pounds. But, because 'it was not expected that being poor people they could pay any part of it, and because corporal punishment was more fit for them, it was agreed they should be whipped and pilloried' at Cheapside in the centre of London, at Ware on the great north road, and at Staines on the road to the west. Noting that the offensive libel had the chorus 'the clean contrary way', Justice Richardson added the twist that the offenders should be 'carried upon horses from Westminster to Cheapside the clean contrary way, that is with their faces to the horses' tails'.[98]

In June 1628 a famous handwritten challenge appeared on a post in Coleman Street, London: 'Who rules the kingdom? The king. Who rules the king? The duke. Who rules the duke? The devil.' The libellers warned that 'if things be not shortly reformed, they will work a reformation themselves. At the sight whereof, they say his majesty was much displeased.'[99] After Buckingham's death, with the principal target for public libels departed, determined scribblers could direct their attention to the crown. 'Oh king, or rather no king...thou hast lost the hearts of thy subjects,' began a handwritten diatribe of 1629.[100] Another libel 'abusive of the state' was hung on Cheapside Cross in 1635.[101] Libels concerning the Scots were cast abroad in the king's privy lodgings and gardens in 1639.[102] More cascades of derisory libels accompanied the crisis of the 1640s, as an underground scribal culture coexisted with the radically expanded press. Moving from individuals to public causes, libels satirized the Puritans, the bishops, the parliament, and the cavaliers.[103]

The words of libels often survive in the records of the courts where they were prosecuted. Some libels were so interesting, or so scandalous, that they were shared among members of the elite. Reports of them arrived in gentle correspondence, 'to entertain you', or 'to make you a little merry withal', and some were transcribed into commonplace books.[104] The Suffolk clergyman John Rous remarked that 'light scoffing wits...can rhyme upon any the most vulgar surmises', and rhymed himself in his notebook in 1640: 'I hate these following railing rhymes | Yet keep them for precedent of the times.'[105] Fortunately for the historian, not everyone followed the advice of the Countess of Lindsey, who sent the latest libels to Lord Montague in March 1642, 'which when you have read I pray commit to the fire'.[106]

Rumour and False News

When Rumour enters, 'painted full of tongues' to begin Shakespeare's *2 Henry IV*, he calls on the audience to 'Open your ears, for which of you will stop | The vent of hearing when loud Rumour speaks? . . . Upon my tongues continual slanders ride | . . . Stuffing the ears of men with false reports.' Rumour's eager audience embraced the people of England, 'the blunt monster with uncounted heads | The still discordant wavering multitude'. The voice adopted here was of the scoundrel, but it understood the unquenchable appetite for information. The news in this case was of noble rebellion and royal battle, noised abroad though not necessarily trustworthy.[107]

The spreading of 'false rumours' or 'vain rumours and bruits' was another of the sins of the tongue. Because of its potential for sedition, the spreading of rumour was subject to law. Tales about private individuals were relatively harmless, but when rumours touched majesty or policy the state became actively concerned.

Edward I's Statute of Westminster of 1275 criminalized 'devisors of tales' who caused conflict between the king and his subjects. It became an offence to 'tell or publish any false news or tales, whereby discord or occasion of discord or slander may grow between the king and his people'. Anyone who spread such tales, or reported such rumours, was liable to be imprisoned until 'the first author of the tale' was brought into court.[108] This was powerful legislation, which later authorities could cite to show that 'slander spoken of the king is punishable under the Statute of Westminster'.[109]

The law was sharpened in the course of Henry VIII's reformation, so that certain rumours touching the king could be treason.[110] Other Tudor statutes criminalized 'seditious words and rumours' against Philip and Mary,[111] and 'false, seditious or slanderous news, rumours, sayings or tales' affecting Queen Elizabeth. Short of the capital crime of treason, offenders faced the pillory, disfigurement, and prison for their misdemeanours.[112]

The rumours that spread in the first decade of the reformation—that parish churches would be pulled down and their chalices taken, that the kingdom was about to be invaded, and that Henry VIII and his family were dead—formed part of a contested popular political culture. Similar rumours spread in every subsequent reign: that King Edward was still alive, that Elizabeth was bearing bastards, that King Charles had accepted the popish mass, that a foreign invasion threatened, or that the current ruler had died. Some people did not just spread these rumours but commented on them, voicing opinions that could be construed as seditious: that such a monarch was unfit to govern, that a foreign force would be welcomed, or that the kingdom would be better if such a ruler was dead.[113] The tongue indeed was a troublesome member, and speech a medium of peril.

3

Speaking Treason

Treason, wrote the Elizabethan legal authority William Lambarde, was foremost of those 'public felonies' that touched the crown and the commonwealth. It was, as jurists described it, the most serious offence, an attack on 'majesty itself'.[1] Treason threatened the authority, dignity, and reputation of the monarch, as well as his or her life and safety. Its practitioners subverted kingship and challenged the power of the state. Any 'denial and defacement of the just dignities and authorities of those that bear the name of majesty' was treason, that is, 'crimen lesae maiestatis, the crime of violating or abating of majesty', declared the Elizabethan lawyer Thomas Norton.[2] As a later Stuart judge told a Grand Jury, 'treason strikes at the root and life of all; it tends to destroy the very government, both king and subjects, and the lives, interest and liberties of all'.[3] 'All treasons are to be revealed, as tending to the ruin of the whole commonwealth,' advised the Calvinist theologian William Perkins.[4]

Treason and Law

The penalty for treason was death. Convicted offenders were drawn on a hurdle or sled to the place of execution, 'hanged till they be half dead, and then taken down and quartered alive'. This, says the Elizabethan commentator William Harrison, was 'the greatest and most grievous punishment used in England'. Female traitors were supposed to be burned at the stake. Aristocrats, of course, claimed the privilege of beheading, whereas felons in ordinary criminal cases were hung. Someone who refused to plead could face the agony of *peine fort et dure*, being pressed to death by weights or stones, thereby avoiding the forfeiture of their estate to the crown.[5] Though the matter was long controversial, those found guilty of treason by words faced the death penalty. But capital sentences were not always carried out. We have no figures directly relating to treason, but barely a quarter of the criminal felons sentenced to hang in the Home Circuit in mid-Elizabethan England actually went to the gallows. The fifteenth-century case of Thomas Kerver (discussed below) reminds us that the ultimate punishment was sometimes commuted.[6]

This chapter examines the law governing treasonable speech and its application in fifteenth- and sixteenth-century England. Medieval precedents carried forward into the eighteenth century, and legal scholars were always immersed in the past. Before turning to speech offences against Queen Elizabeth and her Stuart successors, we need to review some legislation and case histories from an earlier period.

The treason laws of early modern England rested on medieval foundations. Though periodically modified, strengthened, or adjusted, the framework that protected the Tudors and Stuarts was centred on the legislation of Edward III. Some lawyers discerned an older common-law tradition concerning treason, but the core of both theory and practice was derived from statute.

Addressing uncertainties in the law in the Plantagenet era, legislators in 1352 acknowledged that 'divers opinions have been before this time, in what case treason shall be said, and in what not'. Their statute in the twenty-fifth year of the reign of Edward III attempted to clarify the matter, declaring it treason,

when a man doth compass or imagine the death of our lord the king, or of our lady the queen, or of their eldest son and heir; or if a man do violate the king's wife or the king's eldest daughter unmarried, or the wife of the king's eldest son and heir; or if a man do levy war against our lord the king in his realm, or be adherent to the king's enemies in his realm, giving them aid and comfort.

It was also treason to counterfeit the king's seals or his money, or to kill his chancellor, treasurer, or justices. If other cases arose the statute reserved judgment to the king and parliament whether an offence 'ought to be judged treason or other felony'.[7]

Edward III's law created the basis for treason accusations and trials for the next several centuries. According to later interpreters, this law made treason 'any intention which pointed at the death or deposition of the king, however manifested'. But whether words by themselves could be judged treason remained open to question. The medieval statute seemed to require an overt act, like conspiracy or rebellion, but some judges held that 'the mere speaking of words might be an overt act which evidenced such an intention'.[8] The law on this point was neither stable nor resolved, and would be tested several times in courts and councils. The uncertainty that the Plantagenet statute attempted to settle remained unsettled, for in practice the boundaries between treason and misprision, *lese majesté* and seditious words, could be blurred.

Addressing '*crimen lesae maiestatis*, in our English tongue called treason', the Jacobean lawyer Ferdinando Pulton acknowledged that 'compassing and imagination is a secret thing hidden in the breast of man, and cannot be known but by open fact or deed'. Speech, however, supplied that fact or deed of treason, 'and therefore if it be uttered by words it is a sufficient signification thereof'. Others were not so sure. A quarter of a millennium after its drafting, the key Norman French phrase in the 1352 statute '*compasser ou ymaginer*' was increasingly difficult to fathom. Originally the words meant planning and plotting, involving a concrete threat to the monarch. But they could be construed to make treasonable the hatching or voicing of ideas that endangered the person or majesty of the crown.[9]

Seditious Words

Historians have long observed that 'the history of the law of sedition is in many respects obscure and needs detailed investigation'.[10] Legal scholars have sometimes questioned whether sedition is even covered in English law, and as late as the twentieth century an Attorney General could remind the British Home Secretary that 'there is no statutory definition of sedition'.[11] The courts have been more comfortable with an adjective than a noun, referring to 'seditious conspiracy', 'seditious libel', or 'seditious words' rather than raw 'sedition'. As Sir Edward Littleton observed when John Selden was charged with 'stirring up sedition' in 1629, 'we have not either in the division or explication of offences that occur in our books, an express definition, description, or declaration of it, though we meet with it sometimes mingled with other offences'.[12] Though never defined by statute, the concept emerged from common law, and has always been controversial.[13]

Though not strictly treasonous by the act of Edward III, seditious words were dangerous because they shredded the bonds of allegiance and abraded the social fabric. They brought the crown and the government into contempt and excited disaffection against the established regime. Sedition of any kind was divisive, setting subjects against each other and subjects against the crown. It was more insidious, and perhaps more pervasive, than outright treason, and had a corrosive effect on royal authority. Seditious words could be tinged with treason, or could verge on treason, or they could have treasonable import, if the courts could be so persuaded.

Though unknown to late-medieval common law or to Roman law, the legal doctrine of sedition evolved rapidly in sixteenth-century England. It was shaped as much by the Privy Council and by legal practice as by parliament. By the reign of Elizabeth I the offence encompassed all kinds of utterance and expressions that fell short of constructive treason.[14] Seditious speech could be anything divisive, contentious, or mutinous that was likely to spread discord. Like the character 'Sedition' in John Bale's play *King Johan* (written in the 1530s, revised *c.*1560), who held 'princes in scorn, hate and disdain', and fostered spiteful disobedience, seditious speakers were understood to be enemies of the state.[15]

'Contemptuous talk' and 'unbridled speeches' led to 'factions and seditions', warned Lord Keeper Bacon in 1567. They 'maketh men's minds to be at variance with one another, and diversity of minds maketh seditions, seditions bring in tumults, tumults make insurrection and rebellions'. Loose and dangerous talk could be ruinous, for sedition was the harbinger of treason.[16] *Scandalum magnatum* slipped easily into sedition because words spoken to the 'discredit or disparagement' of great men seemed likely to undermine the authority of the crown.[17] 'Sedition is a public thing . . . public and violent', said a King's Bench judge in 1578, 'for as much as it toucheth the prelates, nobles and great officers, which are the king's counsel'.[18] 'To deface a prince or governor dissolveth and subverteth the state,' declared another Elizabethan councillor in 1590, who feared that seditious words could sever 'the bands and sinews of all government next under the ordinance of God'.[19] 'If seditious talebearers (the sowers of rebellion) should not be snapped up and restrained,' warned William Lambarde, 'the hurt body [politic] would bleed to death'.[20]

Government lawyers called for sharp punishment for speakers of sedition. The crime was a high misdemeanour. Justice Roger Manwood advised in 1577 that statute law provided punishment 'by pillory and cutting of . . . ears' for 'lewd and detestable slanderous speeches towards her majesty'. And the common law, he avowed, allowed for mutilation, blinding, and even dismemberment, so that the state might punish an offender by 'burning in the face with letters, or by gagging his two jaws in painful manner, and so he cannot speak any words . . . or by burning through his tongue, or perchance cutting off his tongue, in such way as he may eat and drink and take sustenance after'.[21] The imposition of pillorying and ear-cropping was justified by reference to the statute of 12 Richard II, c. 11, although local magistrates were sometimes allowed to punish 'as they should think meet, weighing [the offender's] corrupt and cankered disposition'.[22] Seditious libellers faced fines, disfigurement, and prison.

In 1574 the government ordered the Council in the North 'to punish . . . seditious words against the queen, nobility, Privy Council, or the Council there (not being treason) by pillory, cutting off the ears, wearing papers, imprisonment, or fine, as limited by law'.[23] But at Shrewsbury that year an offender was made to sit for an hour with one leg in the stocks, with a paper on his forehead declaring, 'thus am I punished for speaking of seditious and slanderous words'. A local critic declared this too lenient, saying that the proper punishment involved three hours of restraint with both legs in the stocks.[24] (Use of the stocks to hold an offender's legs fell out of use by the early eighteenth century. The judicial use of the pillory became a rarity by the later Hanoverian era, and was abolished in 1837.)

Jacobean jurists recalled that 'in former ages speeches tending to the reproach of others were so odious that King Edgar ordained that his tongue should be cut out which did speak any infamous or slanderous words of another'.[25] Some political commentators in the reign of Charles I thought that reporters of false rumour 'are worthy to have their tongues cut out', though this was not a normal punishment in English law.[26] In early Stuart Ireland, however, a speaker of sedition could be bored through the tongue.[27] In 1639 a Scotsman in Dublin was sentenced to lose his ears, 'his tongue to be slit, his forehead to be seared with a hot iron with the letters I and S for impious slander', after speaking disrespectfully of Queen Henrietta Maria.[28]

Plantagenet Treasons

Dozens of people were punished in fifteenth-century England for words that seemed to imagine or compass the death of the monarch. Many more were investigated for 'unfitting' or derogatory remarks disparaging the crown.[29] The deposition of Richard II and the usurpation of Henry IV in

1399 precipitated a spate of treasonous remarks, along the fault lines of shifting loyalties. Some of Henry IV's subjects cursed their new king, while others spread rumours that King Richard was still alive. Several paid heavily for their words, including sixteen men executed in 1402 for voicing expectations of Richard's imminent return. Similar Ricardian rumours greeted the accession of Henry V in 1413. An inchoate news culture took shape long before the early modern era, mixing popular political prophecy, seigneurial commentary on public affairs, and shifting plebeian grievances. Out of that news culture emerged voices of treason and sedition.[30]

Another cluster of cases concerned that most incompetent and unfortunate of rulers, Henry VI (1422–61, 1470–71). In his reign too there were rumours that King Richard yet lived, and four traitors were condemned in the 1420s for saying that this 'false Richard' would shortly regain his kingdom.[31] By the time Henry reached adulthood in the 1440s there were subjects venturing to say that he was not fit to be king, and prosecutions of people who were said to have said such things. Occasionally the surviving documentation cites the actual words and reveals something of the circumstances in which they came to light. The courts took note of hostile and 'detestable' utterances, but reserved the most severe punishment for traitors who threatened the security of the realm.

A Sussex case came before King's Bench in 1441 after Thomas atte Wood, butcher of Chichester, reported his neighbour, Robert Seman, a tanner, for speaking treason. According to Wood, the two men were drinking at 'an hostelry called the Tabard' in April 1440 when Seman said 'that the king our sovereign lord was no king, nor should be, and that should be known in short time'. Both men were brought before the mayor's court at Chichester, in the presence of crown coroners, then moved up to Westminster and held in the Marshalsea prison. Robert Seman would seem to have disparaged Henry VI's title to the throne, but he was quickly released on bond and eventually discharged. His accuser Thomas atte Wood, however, spent almost a year behind bars for initiating what appeared to have been a malicious prosecution. With its origins in drunken conversation, and its furtherance through neighbourly discord, the case set the pattern for many in succeeding centuries.[32]

In a case from 1442 involving high politics rather then plebeian outspokenness, Juliana Quick used 'proud and lewd language' to excoriate the king for his punishment of Lady Eleanor Cobham, the Duchess of Gloucester, who had dabbled in sorcery, necromancy, and treason. She called

Henry VI 'that proud boy in red', and taunted him: 'Harry of Windsor, ride soberly, thy horse may stumble and break thy neck . . . Thou art a fool, and a known fool throughout the whole kingdom of England.' Perhaps she was voicing the common fame. Arraigned before King's Bench 'for her ungoodly language and foolhardiness to speak so to her liege lord the king' (though not explicitly for treason), Juliana refused to answer. Instead she suffered *peine fort et dure* (pressing to death beneath heaped irons). Her crime lay not just in her verbal mockery but in her apparent compassing of the king's death, but the circumstances remain obscure.[33]

In 1444 a Berkshire gentleman, Thomas Kerver, faced prosecution for wishing aloud that King Henry VI 'had died twenty years ago' or 'had never been born'. In saying this he evidently compassed or imagined the death of the king. Conversing with companions after the Easter service at Reading abbey, Kerver allegedly compared Henry disparagingly to the 'manful' French dauphin, and cited the biblical text '*ve regno cui puer Rex est*', repeating in English, 'woe to the land whose king is a child'. The government construed Kerver's speech as an overt traitorous act, an attempt to enlist accomplices to his 'traitorous imaginings, wishes, desires and intentions', and expended considerable effort to see him convicted. He was, the regime charged, not just an ill-spoken malcontent but a danger to the English crown. Twice tried and eventually found guilty of treason, Thomas Kerver was sentenced to be drawn, hung, and quartered, though remarkably, in this case, he was cut down from the gallows at the last minute and was pardoned to imprisonment at the king's pleasure. Early modern lawyers cited Kerver's case as an example of someone executed for treasonable words, but deep exploration of the public records (by a talented medievalist) has shown that the traitor came out alive, with a very sore neck.[34] It was a chilling precedent, though not without complications.

Thomas Kerver was not alone in describing his king as childish and unfit to rule. More than two dozen cases of this sort came before King's Bench between 1444 and 1457. A London draper said in 1446 that King Henry lacked wit and was so dominated by his ministers that 'his rule is nought'. Others remarked on the king's childish face and the setbacks suffered by the kingdom. A resident of Ely in 1449 named one of his fighting cocks Henry of England, remarked sourly on the king's defeats, and prophesied his early death. Two Southwark men in 1453 described King Henry as a sheep, and wished he had died long before. Another said that it would be better if Henry's head, not Jack Cade's, was stuck on London Bridge.[35] Hearing in

1457 that the king has been injured at the battle of St Albans, a yeoman at Westminster regretted that the injury had not been fatal.[36]

A Sussex husbandman, John Merfield, declared in 1450 that Henry VI 'was a natural fool... not a person able to rule the land'. Merfield, we learn, had sided with Jack Cade's rebels and had been included in the general pardon. But rather than accepting defeat he declared 'that he and his fellowship would arise again, and when they were up they would leave no gentleman alive but such as them list to have'. This was blood-curdling bravado, but paled besides Merfield's observations about Henry VI. Speaking in the market at Brightling, Sussex, on St Anne's day (26 July) 1450, he said 'that the king was a natural fool, and would oft-times hold a staff in his hands with a bird on the end, playing therewith as a fool, and that another king must be ordained to rule the land, saying the king was no person to rule the land'. Merfield was brought before justices at Lewes in June 1451, the case was adjourned to Chichester a month later, and thereafter the record is silent.[37]

The leading historian of late medieval and early modern treason, John Bellamy, cites these and other cases of 'treason by words' as 'novel' expansions of law associated with the Wars of the Roses. Other legal scholars have questioned whether they were congruent with common law or reasonable constructions of the 1352 statute. It seems that a verbal utterance could constitute a treasonous offence if it was associated with an actual conspiracy, or it was deemed to cause people to withdraw their love from the monarch, thereby compassing his death. There may also have been some belief that traitorous words had malefic efficacy, as if speaking depravingly of the king could actually bring about his demise.[38] Most of those charged had apparently done more than open their mouths. In practice, one should not be surprised that the law and its enforcement were adjusted to changing political circumstances.

After the battle of Towton (March 1461) the accession (or intrusion) of a talented and vigorous monarch changed the conversation but did not stop people talking. Oliver Germaine, a Wiltshire tailor, was executed that year for saying that Edward IV was responsible for the murders of Warwick and Clarence. It was treason, the judges argued, to excite the king's lieges against their rightful ruler, treason to induce subjects 'to withdraw their cordial love' from the monarch thereby compassing his death. Germaine's words, then, constituted a treasonable act. Later in King Edward's reign in 1477 Thomas Burdett was executed for saying after a royal hunt 'that he wished the buck, head, horns, and all, were in the king's belly'. But Burdett was also alleged to have engaged in necromancy, like Eleanor Cobham a generation earlier, that 'compassed the death and final destruction of the king', thereby compounding his offence.[39]

Few recorded utterances against Henry VII have survived, but the drama of his reign, which began in civil war and endured the claims of at least two pretenders, surely set men talking. The number of recorded cases, however, is low, with rarely more than one or two a year. Among them was William Haynes, a London mercer, charged in 1486 with speaking '*inhonesta* and evil-sounding words against the king and his lords', and William Styles, a Kentish labourer, who declared more menacingly in 1490: 'I would there were a pound of molten lead in the king's belly, for he did never good since he came to this land.' Haynes was released when the jury found the bill *ignoramus*, and Styles managed to escape and avoid justice.[40] A master Butlar was later heard to say that 'we need not pray for the king by name . . . for why 'tis hard to know who is rightwise king', but the speaker was not brought to trial.[41]

One of the greatest men in the land, the Lord Chamberlain Sir William Stanley, was executed in 1495 for 'words of treason' that evidenced 'the alienation of his heart from the king'. Sir Francis Bacon, who records this episode in his *History of the Reign of King Henry the Seventh*, may have been thinking as much of his own day as of the reign of the first Tudor, but his commentary is compelling. In discourse with Sir Robert Clifford, discussing the claims of the pretender Perkin Warbeck, Stanley allegedly said 'that if he were sure that that young man were King Edward's son, he would never bear arms against him'. This was tantamount to admitting that Henry VII was not the true king, a treasonous expression. Though the words were conditional, they proved lethal, and Stanley went to the block. 'That speech touched the quick,' writes Bacon, and 'no doubt pierced the king more than if Stanley had charged his lance upon him'. The consequence, he adds, 'was matter of great terror amongst all the king's servants and subjects, insomuch as no man almost thought himself secure, and men durst scarce commune or talk one with another, but there was a general diffidence everywhere'. There seems to have been a chilling of discourse, but the evidence is inadequate to determine whether this truly happened.[42] In a Star Chamber case in the 1620s Chief Justice Richardson referred to another case from 1495 in which 'one Balam made a libel against the king and for it was hanged, for it was treason', for 'alienating the subjects' affection from their sovereign is treason'. But Richardson muddled his history and may have been citing an episode from the reign of Henry VIII.[43]

Words against Henry VIII

At no time in the early modern era was it so dangerous to dispute politics as in the reign of Henry VIII. In no other reign were so many executed for allegedly speaking treason.

The king's early years yield few instances of treasonable or seditious talk, but a flood of cases followed in the 1530s. It may be that before the Reformation the king was generally popular, state surveillance less obtrusive, and the stakes not so high as they would become later. Certainly the documentation is more sparse for the early Henrician period than the era of Thomas Cromwell. Nonetheless, grumbles and grievances were still aired, and some people talked their way into trouble. A Devonshire man, John Cole, faced investigation in 1514 for saying that 'the king is but young and wots not what the matter means for his Council must order the matters, for men may have of him what they will when he is merry at tennis'. These remarks led to proceedings in King's Bench, but Cole's fate is unknown.[44] A Lincolnshire tavern drinker, Anthony Irby, made similar unguarded remarks in 1516, that Cardinal Wolsey and the Duke of Suffolk, 'which the king hath brought up of nought, do rule him in all things even as they list . . . and rule him even as a child'.[45] It comes as some surprise to hear Henry VIII demeaned in terms similar to those used against Henry VI, Edward VI, and Charles I.

A few people questioned the Tudor royal lineage, and some spoke rashly regarding the claims of the Duke of Buckingham. Robert Sherrard, the parson of Rampsham, Dorset, allegedly asserted that neither Henry VIII nor his father were 'worthy to wear the crown, for he said that the father of Henry VIII was a horse-groom and a keeper of horses . . . and he came to the crown by dint of the sword'. Sherrard voiced these words at the time of the expedition to Tournai in 1513, but they did not come to official attention until 1521 in the course of a local dispute. Though the parson denied his words, they cost him a spell in prison. His offence was scandalous speech, not treason.[46]

Ordinary ill-spoken antisocial disgruntlement occasionally reared its head, as in the case of Richard Barnard, an Essex yeoman, brought before King's Bench in 1522 for his 'opprobrious, scandalous, vilifying and rebellious-sounding words'. Barnard allegedly declared in Great Waltham church in December 1521: 'I set nought by God, by the king nor the queen, by lord nor lady, by sheriff nor sheriff's man, by bailiff nor constable, nor by no man.' This was a comprehensive rejection of the chain of authority, of the kind that might be heard in any age. We do not know whether Barnard was drunk, or furious at local officials, or perhaps the victim of malicious prosecution, but charges against him were dismissed.[47]

More pointedly, Peter Wilkinson, a Norfolk man, spoke treason in 1523 by threatening to fetch the king 'by the head and bring him down'. Witnesses reported a discussion in the vicarage at Geyton, Norfolk, in which Wilkinson complained of excessive subsidy assessments. Before long, he foresaw, 'there would be three more taxes, and every man would have to pay half what he was worth'. The only remedy, Wilkinson avowed, was for every man to follow his lead: 'he would take him by the head and pull him down.' Asked by the vicar William Pygot whom he would pull down, Wilkinson answered: 'Harry with the crown.' This may have been bluster and bravado, but it was also foolish and dangerous. The vicar bade him beware, and Agnes Whitmore (the wife of William Whitmore, the informant) declared that, had she spoken 'any such words, she were worthy to have been burnt' (the official punishment for female traitors). Report of this conversation went from Norfolk justices to councillors in London, and perhaps to the assize courts, but its final disposition is unknown.[48]

The law of treason became sharper and more dangerous when Henry VIII deployed potent new legislation to defend his break with Rome. The English Reformation, which opened access to the word of God (by promoting the vernacular Bible), was accompanied by a clampdown on popular discussion. A dozen parliamentary enactments between 1531 and 1544 redefined offences as treason. The Succession Act of 1534 (25 Hen. VIII, c. 22) made it high treason (punishable by death) to attack the king's marriage to Anne Boleyn 'by writing or imprinting, or by any exterior act or deed', and made it misprision of treason (a lesser offence, punishable by imprisonment and fines) to speak words 'to the prejudice, slander, disturbance and derogation' of their royal majesties. The Treason Act that followed later that year (26 Hen. VIII, c. 13) declared treason any act or desire, any deed or utterance, including both spoken and written words, that sought to harm the king, his wife, or his heir, or to deprive them of their title or dignities. It was now treason to call the king a 'heretic, a schismatic, a tyrant, an infidel or an usurper', as some of his subjects had been doing.[49]

Going well beyond the provisions of the 1352 act, the Henrician law made dangerous all kinds of speech that might otherwise be dismissed as ignorant, foolish, or harmless, or at worst scandalous or seditious. The new law criminalized remarks that affronted the royal honour as well as threatened the life of the king. 'Speaking is made high treason which was never heard of before,' complained Robert Fisher, the bishop of Rochester's brother, in 1535. Ordinary people could commit this offence in their casual conversations, and some of them paid for it with their lives.[50] It was scathingly remarked that 'the king will hang a man for a word speaking nowadays', and that 'a little word is treason'.[51] In 1541 the Protestant merchant Richard Hilles reported from London, 'it is now no novelty among us to see men slain, hung, quartered, or beheaded; some for trifling expressions, which were explained or interpreted as having been spoken against the king; others for the pope's supremacy; some for one thing, and some for another'.[52]

The crisis of public order provoked by Henry VIII's reformations brought hundreds of English commoners into conflict with royal authorities. As the chronicler Edward Hall recorded, 'the common people daily murmured and spoke their foolish fantasies'.[53] In response the government expended considerable energy in monitoring and punishing dissent. 'Wheresoever any such cankered malice shall either chance to break out or any to be accused thereof, his highness would have the same tried and thoroughly perused with great dexterity and as little favour as their demerits shall require'—so Thomas Cromwell instructed councillors and magistrates.[54] Local officials understood their duty to inform the Privy Council of undutiful remarks, even where the matter though 'high' was 'of small effect'.[55]

Critics and commentators came under unprecedented scrutiny in the 1530s as country justices, gentry, and informers manned a nervous network of surveillance. People who were scandalized by their monarch's matrimonial policies, who were outraged by his assault on the monasteries, or who spoke of Henry VIII as a monster became subject to official investigation. Subjects who remained loyal to the papacy or to the old religion could henceforth be construed to be traitors, especially if they voiced their opinions out loud. So too could men who disparaged government of any sort. Hundreds of cases came to Thomas Cromwell's attention, some to be monitored, others to be prosecuted with vigour. The years between 1534 and 1540 saw more than 500 investigations, over 150 trials, and more than 100 executions for treasonous words. Tudor legal historians have argued whether these numbers are excessive or modest, and whether they are marks of tyranny or of prudence. The evidence shows ordinary people to have been talking, sometimes dangerously, sometimes irresponsibly, and sometimes to ill effect, about the highest affairs of the realm.[56]

Among those held for investigation in 1535 was George Baburney, a tailor of Newport Pagnell, Buckinghamshire, who called King Henry 'a heretic, a thief and a harlot' and who hoped before midsummer to 'play football with his head'. Edmund Brocke, 'an aged wretched person' of Cowle, Worcestershire, blamed that summer's bad weather on Henry VIII, and thought it no matter if the king were 'knocked or patted on the head'. Baburney was most likely executed for his words, and for wishing 'the sword of vengeance' might light on the king and the council; Brocke, who claimed 'he was mad or drunk and wist not what he said', most likely escaped serious punishment.[57]

Another strong-voiced subject, Margery Cowpland of Henley on Thames, reportedly called King Henry 'an extortioner and knave' and Queen Anne 'a strong harlot'. When a local official, Richard Heath, warned her that he was the king's servant, she responded, 'the king's servant, the devil's turd!' Margery was in deep trouble, and her case went all the way up to the Privy Council. But it came out that her principal accuser, John Wynbok, was in dispute with her about other matters involving a covenant, a lease, and a mill, raising the possibility that this was a malicious prosecution. Margery, for her part, denied the words, but Sir William Stonor, who reported the matter to Cromwell, believed she had said them. He described her, however, as 'very aged and lacking wit' and as 'a marvellous drunken woman ... somewhat straight out of her wits, and her husband is out of his mind and hath been this twelve months and more'. Befuddlement with drink or senility was no legal excuse, but it may have persuaded the government in this case that the royal dignity was not seriously at risk.[58]

Also in 1535 Margaret Chaunseler of Bradfield St Clare, Suffolk, was examined for saying 'that the queen was a goggle-eyed whore' and 'a naughty whore', and for praying that Queen Anne, having had one child born dead, 'might never have another'. These were 'traitorous' and 'opprobrious' words, against both the Treason and Succession laws, and Margaret did not deny them. Rather, she told Sir Robert Drury, 'she was drunk when she did speak them, and that the evil spirit did cause her to speak them, and she was very penitent for her offences'.[59] Talk like this was linked to rumours about the depredation of the church and prophecies that the king's reign would come to a sudden end.[60] Other rumours had it that the king was already dead, or that the French or the Scots would soon take over the kingdom.[61]

Over the next few years the controversies of the king's matrimonial and religious policies sparked nationwide disturbance and heated discussion among subjects of all sorts. James Macock of Long Buckby, Northampton-shire, asserted in 1536 that the king had 'the foul gout or the wild gout' (that is, syphilis) and that his reign would soon be over. When news reached Essex that year that King Henry had fallen from his horse, Adam Fermour remarked, 'it should have been less loss that he had broken his neck', and offered to finish him off with arrows.[62] Among those contributing to the noise in 1536 was John Raven of Over, Cambridgeshire, who declared that 'the king was a fool, and my Lord Privy Seal another'. The constable who recorded these words warned Raven to 'deny them', for 'thou wilt sure to be hanged unless thy neighbours be good to thee'.[63] It was chilling to know you could die for saying the wrong thing, but comfort of a sort that your case still had to go before a jury and follow the process of law.

Among those prosecuted for their words in 1537, in the aftermath of the Pilgrimage of Grace, was Elizabeth Wood, wife of Robert Wood of Aylsham, Norfolk. According to local reports, Elizabeth had been resting against a tailor's shop window in Aylsham in May of that year, chatting with John Dix and William Jeckes about the men of nearby Walsingham who were on trial for an intended uprising. 'It was pity that these Walsingham men were discovered,' Elizabeth is alleged to have said, 'for we shall never have good world till we fall together by the ears, and "with clubs and clouted shone shall the deeds be done", for we had never good world since this king reigned. It is a pity that he filled any clouts more than one.' The sentiments are somewhat opaque, but they seem to have evoked a popular verse prophecy in support of peasant levelling. One of the listeners, John Dix, was troubled enough by Elizabeth's speech to ask a neighbour what to do. The neighbour, Thomas Clampe, advised him 'to take his witness with him that heard the said words, and so shortly as possible to show it unto the king's officers'. Dix duly reported the matter to the constables (John Bettes and Thomas Oakes), the constables referred it the magistrates (Sir John Heydon and Sir James Boleyn), and within two weeks the 'lewd and ungracious' Elizabeth Wood was in prison and report of her 'detestable and traitorous words' was on its way to London (Sir John Heydon to Richard Gresham, and thence to Thomas Cromwell and the Privy Council). She was convicted in King's Bench on 26 July 1537 and immediately taken to execution.[64]

The Londoner Henry Mapurley fared better, being released on a technicality after saying: 'I set not a pudding by the king's broad seal, and all his charters be not worth a rush.'[65] The Hampshire cleric Peter Bentley was held in Winchester gaol in the following year after speaking disparagingly of the king's authority: 'I set not by this seal nor by him, twysh! not this much (making a fillip with his two fingers) for I trust to see the day that all this shall be turned ups and down. A man may say what he will in his own house.' Unfortunately for Peter Bentley, and many more of the king's subjects, this assertion of domestic privilege no longer held true.[66] Loose talk was likely to be reported, and, once it had reached the authorities, an investigation would surely follow.

Reports of the dangerous speech of Robert Adeyn, a servant to Sir John Hurleston, reached the bailiffs and aldermen of Worcester in 1537. Adeyn allegedly said, 'in the presence of divers honest persons, that he would in his master's cause or quarrel fight against King Henry VIII, and if a did in the same quarrel kill the king he should not be punished otherways than he should be for killing of another man, and that is to be hanged'. These words would seem to reflect misguided seigneurial devotion rather than treason, but the bailiffs dutifully reported them to the Privy Council, who summoned the speaker to be examined. By the time the reports reached London, however, Adeyn was long gone, having fled into Gloucestershire with his master.[67]

Willing or wishing the king's death, like compassing or imagining, was clearly treasonable, and there seemed no end of such talk. As in most early modern regimes, there were subjects ready to opine that the world would never be quiet or merry while the present monarch yet lived. John Newman of Newnton, Northamptonshire, declared of Henry VIII that 'it is a pity that the king was ever crowned, for we have had more pilling and polling since he was crowned than ever we had before, and it is a pity that he hath lived so long'. A more responsible neighbour immediately warned him, 'beware what thou sayest, for thou speakest treason'.[68]

Some of the most dangerous words came from clerics who were outraged by the king's attack on their religion. William Reyrson, the parson of Kibworth, Leicestershire, went to prison in 1538 for saying that 'if the king had died seven years agone it had been no hurt'.[69] At Whitsuntide that year the Yorkshire priest Robert Keriby discussed with his parish clerk the widespread rumour that 'the king is dead'. To the clerk's comment, that 'if Cromwell were dead also, it were not a halfpenny loss', the priest responded, 'if any of the great men had had a switch at the king's neck a twelvemonth since . . . he should have had small peril for it'. William Wood, a layman who was listening to this conversation, warned them both that 'many more in the south parts hath been put to death for saying less than this'.[70] Another priest, John Colyns, predicted that Henry and Cromwell both 'will hang in hell one day for the plucking down of the abbeys'.[71]

Commoners, too, berated the king, and not only for his changes to religion. 'A vengeance on the king . . . and also of such polling harlots as you are' were the 'treasonable words' of the Nottinghamshire husbandman Nicholas Saunderson, when royal huntsmen pressed his wagon into the king's service.[72] 'A vengeance of the king', repeated the Leicestershire cook Richard Wittington, who was drawn, hung, and quartered for his treason.[73] Others predicted yet again that the king should soon be dead, and then their burden of taxation would be relieved.[74] Peter Straych of Exeter became a 'traitor' in April 1538 by saying that 'he set not a turd by the king neither by his Council'.[75] William Hamlyn of Bognor, Sussex, prayed God that 'a vengeance take the king and his Council, I would they were all hanged', after officers distrained his hog for a four-penny debt to the crown.[76] James More, a Lincolnshire labourer, was executed as a traitor in 1538 for saying that 'the king has lived overlong by three years'.[77]

Two more commoners died in 1541 for speaking treason. After shooting an arrow at a target, Lionel Haughton, a Leicestershire tailor, unwisely remarked: 'I would the king's body had been there.' John Laburne, a Lincolnshire labourer, said rather more cryptically that 'if the king came to Lincoln he would never leave, just as King Richard never left Newark'. Both were sentenced to be drawn, hung, and quartered.[78] The surgeon William Nostrum of Redruth, Cornwall, was punished similarly in 1544 for saying in exasperation, 'King Harry, King Harry, a vengeance upon King Harry'.[79]

Talk of this nature no doubt continued throughout the later years of Henry VIII's reign, though it appears less commonly in the records after the fall of Thomas Cromwell in 1540. Disaffected chatter of this sort never entirely abated, but never again would it be so dangerous to speak words that could lethally be construed as treason.

Treasonable and Seditious Speech, 1547–1558

The new Henrician treason law was repealed at the beginning of Edward VI's reign by legislators who ventured to call it 'very strait, sore, extreme and terrible' (1 Edw. VI, c. 12). Henceforth treason would be judged solely by the old law of Edward III.[80] But it still remained dangerous to speak 'by express words' against the powers, titles, or dignities of the sovereign and his government. Such talk was dangerous for the regime as well as perilous to the individual speaker. Sir John Cheke, writing in 1549, thought it 'treason to speak heinously of the king's majesty', deserving the highest punishment, but other jurists were not so sure.[81] The slippage between treason and sedition still caused confusion. Edwardian Privy Councillors were sensitive to speech against the monarch, and also to seditious words against themselves. Local officials threatened prison to commoners who spoke scandalously against gentlemen, or whose 'treasonable words' commended the 'commotion time' of 1549.[82]

In practice, as always, much depended on the councillors and judges and whether they interpreted the law to the crown's advantage. There was much blurring of distinctions, with adjectives like 'treasonable and seditious' employed in conjunction with words like 'lewd', 'slanderous', 'heinous', and 'opprobrious'. Magistrates commonly investigated accusations of speech labelled 'treasonous' or 'treasonable', only to proceed on lesser charges involving less fatal offensive words. (The word 'treasonous' meant treasonlike, whereas 'treasonable' indicated something that could be construed as treason.) Political considerations often intervened, and it might take several exchanges of correspondence between the Council and the justices, several negotiations of direction and advice, before the full weight of the offence could be measured. A felony indictment was often reduced to a misdemeanour, or the matter was dropped or referred back to local discretion.

In September 1549, for example, Sir Anthony Aucher sent William Cecil 'a bill of words spoken by George Fletcher', along with the offender's answers. 'If words may be treason,' Aucher wrote, 'none ever spoke so vilely as these "commonwealths", saying if they have no reformation before St Clement's day [23 November] they will seek another way'. But vile and dangerous though these words may have been, in a year of radical commotions, the speaker would not be treated harshly. Fletcher had not spoken directly against the king, and some in government may have sympathized with his commonwealth leanings. 'Be friendly to Fletcher, who has a wife and eight children, trusting he will henceforth be honest,' Sir Anthony Aucher counselled Cecil.[83]

In another case three years later, in September 1552, the Council asked the Chief Justice and his associates 'to consider of what importance the words contained in an information sent him enclosed, spoken by one John

Tonstall of Hetton [Yorkshire], are, and what they weigh in the law; that their opinions known, order may thereupon be given for the worthy punishment of the lewd fellow according to justice'.[84] What happened next would be affected by the standing of the speaker, the quality of the witnesses, the scandal of the words, and the circumstances of their utterance, as well as judicial and political interpretations of process and law.

In September 1552 the council took notice of 'unruly sayings . . . neither meet to be spoken, nor concealed of any hearer', allegedly spoken by the gentlewoman Elizabeth Huggons, whose family had served the late Protector. She was heard to say that 'the world doth condemn the Duke of Northumberland for my lord of Somerset's death', explaining that, by 'the world', she meant 'the voice of the people'. But this paled beside her remarks about the young King Edward. 'She said also that the king showed himself an unnatural nephew, and withal did wish that she had the jerking of him,' or could administer his majesty a lashing. Though not necessarily treasonable, these words were scandalous and seditious, and brought Mrs Huggons to the Tower for examination.[85]

The most common punishment under Edward VI for words of a seditious nature was for the offender to stand in the pillory, perhaps with an ear nailed to the post and with a paper on his head declaring the nature of the offence.[86] The authorities had discretion to decide whether one or both ears would be cropped or sheared, whether the pillorying should be repeated in more than one market place, the extent of any fine, and the length and severity of imprisonment.

A Norfolk man, William Whitered or Wissingseat, endured the pillory and the loss of an ear in February 1550, after speaking seditious words, and was then dismissed 'with a good lesson'.[87] In May 1551 one Herris, 'having spoken traitorous words against the king's majesty, denying him to be king', was referred to the next assizes.[88] The following May one Fauding, a fellow of Eton College, was detained in the Fleet prison for repeating 'certain lewd words touching the succession of the crown'.[89] Another unfortunate went to the Tower in May 1553 'for reporting of certain words touching the king's majesty's person'.[90]

The Londoner Roger Preston was set in the pillory in August 1550 and lost both his ears 'for speaking of lewd words by the Duke of Somerset'.[91] Peter Cooke suffered similarly in August 1552 for 'certain lewd and slanderous words', and was then held in prison 'till he show some tokens of repentance and amendment'.[92] Alan Hudson of Southampton lost his ears in

January 1553—one at Southampton and the other at Winchester—for speaking against the Duke of Northumberland. After two spells in the pillory with a paper on his head announcing 'a seditious reporter of lewd and slanderous words', he was allowed to go free, 'with a good lesson to beware of the like hereafter'.[93]

Against the background of dynastic problems, religious upheavals, and regional rebellions in the reign of Edward VI, these expressions of insubordination were but minor nuisances. They revealed the continuing difficulty of maintaining discipline and securing allegiance in a society destabilized by rapid change.

Mary Tudor's first legislative act was to repeal all treasons and felonies whereby men might be 'trapped and snared, yea many times for words only, without other fact or deed done or perpetrated'. Without referring to her brother's statute, which had much the same effect, she enacted that 'none act, deed or offence . . . by words, writing, cyphering, deeds or otherwise whatsoever shall be . . . adjudged to be high treason, petty treason, or misprision of treason, but only such as be declared' in the statute of 25 Edward III. The new regime thereby relied for its security, so it said, on 'the love and favour of the subject toward their sovereign ruler and governor', rather than 'the dread and fear of laws made with rigorous pains and extreme punishment'.[94] At least that is what they said before they started burning heretics.

New powers, however, were rapidly added to the Marian disciplinary arsenal. When Mary of England and her husband Philip of Spain set out to restore the authority and religion of Rome they armed themselves with 'An act against seditious words and rumours' (1 and 2 Phil. and Mary, c. 3, 1554–5). This enacted penalties for words spoken to the reproach of the king and queen that were seditious and slanderous, though not strictly treasonous. Persons found guilty of speaking such 'false, seditious and slanderous' words faced an array of judicial punishments short of a traitor's death. A first offender might lose his ears at the pillory and face a fine of one hundred pounds and three months' imprisonment. Repeat offenders risked lifetime incarceration. Authors of seditious 'writings, rhymes, ballads, letters, papers and books' were to have their right hand cut off. Those who repeated such slanders could lose an ear or pay a fine. The offence of the tongue and the pen was to be imprinted on the offender's body. The law required justices of the peace to commit without bail any person 'vehemently suspected' of saying or reporting slanderous or seditious words against the crown.[95]

If that were not enough, 'An act for the punishment of traitorous words against the queen's majesty' (1 and 2 Phil. and Mary, c. 9) made it high treason for anyone to pray 'by express words or sayings, that God should shorten [the queen's] days or take her out of the way', as some of the queen's 'heretical' subjects were allegedly doing. Another statute of 1555 threatened forfeiture and imprisonment for a first offence, and a traitor's death for a second, to any who by 'words or sayings' denied Philip and Mary's right to the English throne (1 and 2 Phil. and Mary, c. 10). Stern-minded historians have called these Marian laws 'ferocious', but also 'a weapon which no effective sixteenth-century government could avoid'.[96] They were certainly less stringent than those of Henry VIII.

In practice, however, these laws too could be dispensed with or superseded. Some offenders were dismissed without censure, while others experienced the full wrath of the regime, extending to hanging, drawing, and quartering. As always, the outcome depended on circumstance, opinion, perceived danger, and personal connections.

Several men were referred to Star Chamber in November 1553 'for their lewd reports touching that the late king should be yet alive', thereby challenging the basis of Queen Mary's rule.[97] It was a recurrent popular fantasy that the current monarch was dead, or that a predecessor was still miraculously living. John Smithfield was imprisoned in April 1554 for his 'malicious and traitorous words against the queen's highness'.[98] Thomas Burchall, one of princess Elizabeth's servants, spent two months in the Marshalsea in 1554 for 'sundry lewd and seditious words of the estate of the realm'.[99] Unfortunately the records of the Privy Council give no further particulars about these offending speeches. Nor do we know what the Middlesex labourer Thomas Sandesborough said when he 'reported certain false and seditious rumours against the queen's highness and the quiet state of this realm'. In May 1554 the Council ordered Sandesborough to stand in the pillory at Stepney with one ear nailed to the post, 'and having stood so a convenient time, to cut off his ear from his head, to the terror and example of others that would attempt the like'.[100] At Michaelmas 1557 another offender, 'one Oldnoll, yeoman of the guard', was indicted 'for horrible and slanderous words spoken of the queen...whereby scandal might grow in the kingdom between the lady the queen and...her people'. The government was determined to proceed in such cases, and, after much discussion of which law to apply, they fined and imprisoned Oldnoll under the 1275 Statute of Westminster rather than more recent legislation.[101]

The London diarist Henry Machyn records several instances between 1554 and 1558 of people 'set on the pillory . . . for speaking seditious words', some with their ears nailed to the post.[102] The martyrologist John Foxe records the case of the Sussex iron-master Richard Woodman, who was investigated for 'seditious words' before being burnt as a heretic.[103] Foxe also memorializes Alice Driver of Grundisburgh, Suffolk, whose ears were cut off in 1558 for likening Queen Mary to Jezebel, before being burned at the stake for her views against the papacy and the mass.[104]

On rare occasions the records are rich enough to capture the flavour of treasonable or seditious language and to indicate the circumstances of the offending conversation. The mayor's court records of Norwich reveal that in February 1554 a company of artisans were 'sitting by the fire talking of the rebellion that was at London and upon matter of religion'. The restoration of Catholicism and Wyatt's rebellion were evidently hot topics of conversation. John Toppelow, carpenter, said that the change in religion was 'not good', to which Thomas Hammond, worsted weaver, responded 'that whosoever speak against the queen's proceedings were very traitors'. Toppelow persisted, however, warning that, if Queen Mary married Philip, 'we should lie in swine sties in caves and the Spaniards should have our houses, and we should live like slaves and be glad to drink a pot with water'. The speaker, it emerged, had been with Wyatt's rebels and had escaped back to Norfolk. Another participant in this conversation, John Chamber, a gentleman's servant, told him 'it was a pity he came away to bear any tidings', and counselled, 'I pray God, John, turn your heart from any such seditious conversation'. Toppelow, however, had the last word, warning that 'it was not ended, and . . . all England should repent it, and it would cost a thousand men's lives'. Even allowing for the likelihood that these deponents rendered their own words in the most favourable light, while tarring others with sedition, the documentation affords a remarkable glimpse of plebeian political discourse.[105]

Other echoes of dangerous speech appear in the Middlesex sessions records. In June 1555, after Richard Smith, yeoman, of Shoreditch, spoke 'seditiously and publicly', spreading false reports 'that the queen is dead', the court ordered him to be put in the pillory in the market place, both ears to be cut off, to be fined a hundred pounds, and imprisoned for three months. The Privy Council confirmed his punishment, 'to the example of others,

according to the statute of the last parliament for spreading false rumours'.[106]
Councillors continued to press local magistrates to examine the speakers of
slanderous and seditious words, and to discover the sources of 'these
shameful rumours'.[107]

Sitting in an alehouse at Deptford, Surrey, on Maundy Thursday 1556,
William Harris, a carpenter and gunner on one of her majesty's ships,
complained that 'the queen hath given this day a great alms [the Maundy
money], and given that away that should have paid us our wages'. At this
point he should have shut his mouth, having already spoken above himself.
But Harris pressed on, opening himself to charges of sedition. He continued, with reference to the queen: 'she hath undone us and hath undone
this realm too, for she loveth another realm better than this.' The Privy
Council took note of these words, to which Harris confessed, but his
ultimate fate is unknown.[108] Other mariners found guilty of sedition were
flogged from ship to ship or hauled down under the keel.

A final glimpse comes from Kent, where in January 1558 a chain of
reports from the mayor of Canterbury, through the Lord Warden of the
Cinque Ports, to the Council in London informed Queen Mary of the
'seditious words' of Robert Cockerell and Francis Barton. Their actual
words are not recorded, but they were evidently deemed dangerous and
offensive. In this case the queen herself instructed the Warden to proceed
against Cockerell by martial law, so that his execution might be 'a terror to
others'. The recourse to martial law, in the militarized Cinque Ports, points
to the difficulties of proceeding under the law of treason. Cockerell was
hung as a felon, not hung, drawn, and quartered as a traitor. A correspondent, William Oxenden, reported Cockerell's death: 'The last word he spoke
was blaspheming, swearing, "by god's soul, now I go". So, leaping from the
ladder, he departed.' The other offender, Francis Barton, was treated more
leniently, being set in the pillory at Canterbury on market day with papers
on his head, as an example to others 'to be wary what they speak by the king
and queen or any in authority'.[109]

4

Elizabethan Voices

No monarch had taken greater care to preserve religion, peace, and plenty than her majesty, declared Lord Keeper Egerton towards the end of Queen Elizabeth's reign. The queen not only counted upon but deserved 'the entire love and affection of her good and faithful subjects'. Unfortunately, however, Gloriana's kingdom also harboured 'some wicked and traitorous persons, monsters of men, that without regard of duty or conscience, and without fear of God or man, cease not in the abundance of their malice, to traduce her majesty . . . and to slander her counsellors and ministers, not only by railing open speeches but also by false, lying and traitorous libels'.[1] These 'monsters' included men and women who were unable to govern their tongues. This chapter tells some of their stories. Rather than simply quoting remarks by way of illustration, I have tried, wherever possible, to reconstruct the circumstances of the exchange and the reactions of the authorities. By combining letters, indictments, depositions, and judicial examinations, it may be possible to retrieve parts of the lost conversations of Elizabethan England, and to recover the audible *frisson* of dangerous words.

Elizabeth Tudor, like most of her predecessors and successors, was dogged by disloyal rumours and treasonous allegations about her illegitimacy, inadequacy, or failings as a monarch. Despite the prevailing doctrine of majesty and the developing mystique of the Virgin Queen, a sub-current of seditious speech swirled through Elizabethan England. Magisterial pronouncements and customary sanctions failed to silence critics of authority. Attentive listeners heard persistent allegations that the queen was a bastard, a whore, a begetter of bastards, and that her gender, her religion, or her character rendered her unfit to rule.[2] Topics of this sort 'became a common talk in alehouses and such like places, whereupon ensued dangerous or undutiful speeches of her majesty's most gracious government', according to a report from the early 1560s.[3] Seditious rumours surfaced throughout the reign, shaded by confessional aspirations and reinforced by hopes or fears that the regime would soon change. Petty offenders, as usual, faced the pillory and the loss of an ear, and a brief spell in prison; most were made to acknowledge their fault and to secure bonds for their future good behaviour.[4] More serious transgressors risked being tried for treason, especially if they denied Elizabeth's title to the throne.

Sharp Laws

Many of the strictures and some of the legislative phrases from the reign of Queen Mary were incorporated into new Elizabethan law. A statute of Elizabeth's first parliament in 1559 gave the new queen the same protections as her sister. It became a felony by 'express words or sayings' to 'say, publish, maintain, declare or hold opinion' that she was not rightly queen. To compass the queen's death or to impugn her title was again 'deemed and adjudged high treason' (1 Eliz., c. 5). Another statute applied the Marian law against 'false, seditious or slanderous news, rumours, sayings or tales' to Queen Elizabeth, with the like punishment of pillorying, disfigurement and prison for offenders (1 Eliz., c. 6).[5]

Faced with a vulnerable female monarch, a troubled and uncertain succession, disaffections within the nobility, and a populace whose religious loyalties were unproven, anxious Elizabethan councillors sought new weapons to guard against treason. Their sense of urgency was heightened by the northern rebellion of 1569, the papal bull of excommunication in 1570, the Ridolfi plot of 1571, and the machinations of Mary Queen of Scots. Later crises, wars, and rebellions further tested the regime and the law.

Writing from York in 1570, Sir Thomas Gargrave advised Sir William Cecil:

I neither wish bloody laws nor death in matters of conscience, yet by experience I see that in Henry VIII's days sharp laws kept the evil quiet, where now they be both fierce and stout . . . Long sufferance of evil breeds hardness, whereof ensue troubles and dangers; it is time to stick earnestly to the church, and stoutly to resist the malice of the enemy.[6]

It was time to provide new legislation, modelled on the tougher treason laws of the 1530s.

The result in 1571 was 'an act whereby certain offences be made treason', declaring it treason for anyone to 'compass, imagine, invent, devise or intend' the death or destruction of the queen, or to dispute her title, 'by writing, printing, preaching, speech, express words or sayings'. As it had been under Henry VIII, now it was again under Elizabeth a treasonable offence to call the queen 'heretic, schismatic, tyrant, infidel, or an usurper' (13 Eliz. I, c. 1).[7]

The Elizabethan regime also used proclamations to respond to the threat of sedition. A proclamation of 1570, following the Northern Rebellion, required those seeking pardon to report anyone involved in 'seditious matters', including any who 'speak any slanderous words of the queen's majesty or of any of her councillors'.[8] In 1576, responding to 'certain infamous libels full of malice and falsehood... tending to sedition and dishonourable interpretations of her majesty's godly actions and purposes', the government sought to suppress these 'villainous, treasonable, and seditious attempts'. A similar proclamation in 1601 addressed 'traitorous and slanderous libels... stirring up rebellion and sedition'.[9]

New legislation in 1581 criminalized the seditious words of 'light and evil-disposed persons' and others 'evil-affected towards her highness' who disturbed 'the common tranquillity' of the realm. The new law imposed harsher sanctions against speakers of 'false, seditious and slanderous news, rumours, sayings or tales against our most natural sovereign lady the queen's majesty'. Those found guilty of speaking 'seditious words and rumours' faced a spell in the pillory and the loss of both ears, a fine of £200, plus up to six months in prison. Simply to repeat or report such words risked similar punishment. The law also criminalized any casting of the queen's nativity, calculation of her life span, or speculation about who might succeed her on the throne, threatening offenders with the 'pains of death' (23 Eliz., c. 2).[10] The medieval treason law continued to apply, buttressed by Tudor provisions.

Treasonable, seditious, and scandalous talk was strictly forbidden, but there was no way to close down popular political discourse. Ordinary people felt compelled to comment on the qualities and failings of their ruler, as well as the likely nationality, gender, and religion of their next monarch. Commoners discussed *arcana imperii* (the secrets of state) in ale-houses and markets, churchyards and private homes, and their conversations sometimes came to official attention. Elizabethan assize indictments and Privy Council files dealt repeatedly with people who spoke disparagingly or undutifully of their queen.

Indictments in Elizabethan courts sometimes distinguished between 'scandalous words', which touched the person or dignity of the monarch, and 'seditious words', which affected the security of the realm. The distinction was by no means rigid, and often collapsed in the course of judicial or administrative process. Accusations of treason might mutate into indictments for sedition, and charges of sedition could be modified to mere speaking of 'heinous' or 'opprobrious' words. It could be treason to say 'that the queen's majesty was base born and not born to the crown',[11] sedition to wish the queen's reign over or to wish her enemies to invade England,[12] but merely 'scandalous' to comment on the queen's sexuality or to say that her Council had 'no more mercy than a dog'.[13] A Kentish yeoman, William Grene of Deal, spoke 'scandalous words' when he declared in 1591 that the queen was 'a maintainer of starched ruffs and pride, which when she was dead it would be laid aside'. His mention of the queen's death turned merely scandalous speech into words of sedition.[14] How such expressions were treated in practice depended on a host of factors, including the religion, status, or gender of the speaker, whether the words accompanied other overt acts, and the public anxieties of the moment. The matter was dynamic and unstable, with councillors, judges, magistrates, and ordinary people disagreeing about the danger in particular words. Not surprisingly, in practice, the application, interpretation, and extension of the law was subject to shifting political pressures.

A society of laws, like Elizabethan England, took care to follow legal procedures, though only so far as was appropriate and convenient. Before punishing the speakers of 'lewd' or 'treasonable' words it had to be determined that such words had actually been spoken. Much of the examination of witnesses and correspondence between magistrates and Privy Councillors that ended up in the State Papers was concerned with such matters.

The law required the testimony of two reliable witnesses to prove a spoken offence. Cases of treason, misprision of treason, and sedition turned on 'the testimony, deposition and oath of two lawful and sufficient witnesses', who were to confront the accused 'face to face'.[15] A key question was whether there was any malice or 'spleen' between the parties that might interfere with 'equity and justice', or whether the alleged offender was 'wrongfully charged and molested'.[16] When Edward Bell of Chelmsford was charged with speaking sedition in May 1582, he claimed that the accuser James Hapton had a grudge against him, 'upon some falling out at football play more than a month before at the town of Writtle'.[17]

Neighbourly and financial disputes sometimes coloured other accusations. If the charge was false, the informer might be made to satisfy the accused's 'costs and credit', although the damage could not be completely undone.[18]

Short of a confession, and with only one witness, it was almost impossible to obtain a conviction. Yet the Council repeatedly insisted that 'lewd speeches' should not go unpunished. Suspects could be held in gaol while further evidence was collected, and while lawyers decided what else should be done.[19] In complex cases Privy Councillors sought advice from the Attorney General and the Lord Chief Justice, or 'her majesty's learned counsel of law'.[20] None could be sure exactly what the law was, or how it might be applied.

Cases usually began with an overheard remark that was reported to a constable or justice of the peace. They might ultimately be determined in local or national courts, like Quarter Sessions, Assizes, King's Bench, or even Star Chamber. Privy Councillors could intervene at any point in the process, to quicken or direct the justices, or to send the matter to legal limbo. When a Kentish court absolved John Parmore of using 'certain lewd speeches against her majesty' in December 1576, the Council considered punishing the jury.[21]

It was a justice's duty, according to William Lambarde, to commit 'any person being vehemently suspected of saying or reporting of any slanderous news or tales against her majesty'. Magistrates were to investigate all 'seditious words and rumours uttered against' the monarch, and Quarter Sessions were to enquire 'if any person have...spoken any false, seditious and slanderous news or sayings of the queen's majesty'. Cases of treason were supposed to be referred to the assize judges, but in practice the distinction between treason and sedition was blurred. Lay witnesses might think certain words treasonous that a lawyer knew to be unactionable. Magistrates might press for felony charges but settle for a misdemeanour.[22]

Handbooks for country lawyers instructed that, in the case of a libel concerning a 'public person, the finder ought presently to deliver the same to some magistrate, to the intent that by the examination and industry of such magistrate the author may be found out'.[23] A similar procedure applied to the hearers of seditious or treasonous words, who were supposed to report the offensive speech to a justice of the peace. The justices were supposed to apprehend and examine the alleged offender, and commit him or her to custody pending trial or other proceedings. They were to take evidence from witnesses 'and put the same in writing', and then, at their discretion, 'to send an account immediately of all the particulars to a secretary of state'.[24]

Failure to report sedition was almost as bad as speaking it oneself. A Kentish yeoman, John Rade of Benenden, was scrupulous in reporting seditious utterance in 1594, so as not to 'come in danger for not revealing it', in case 'it might come to pass according to his speech and then it were too late to redress it'.[25] In 1587, when Lewis Herbert was 'accused to have uttered lewd and undiscreet speeches punishable ... by the pillory', the Privy Council advised the Council of the Marches of Wales that he be duly punished, 'for the example of others, and restraining that liberty of speech'.[26] Dangerous 'liberty of speech' was a menace, to be curtailed by all means possible.

Elizabethan assizes typically punished seditious words by making the offender sit in the stocks or stand at the pillory, wearing a paper declaring details of the offence. The written word would thereby recall the sins of the tongue. Some offenders had the additional misfortune to have their ears nailed to the pillory, or to have one or both ears clipped. Others were whipped, fined, held in the house of correction, or remanded in gaol until they entered security for their future good behaviour.

The public execution of traitors was a relatively rare event, after the Henrician bloodbath, and few Elizabethans were convicted of treason by words. The government used its discretionary powers, choosing whether or not to proceed, what sanctions to apply, and whether to be friendly or to proceed *in terrorem*. While eager to investigate disloyal utterances, the Elizabethan authorities generally exercised leniency and discretion. Hundreds of undutiful speakers were found not guilty, or judged guilty of a lesser offence. The Privy Council often allowed local justices to punish 'as they should think meet, weighing [the offender's] corrupt and cankered disposition'.[27] Their principal concern was to maintain the boundaries of acceptable public discourse. As Lord Keeper, Nicholas Bacon advised in 1567, with regard to the circulation of libels and rumours, 'better it were for a man to be twice whipped than once hanged'.[28]

Faced with clear evidence of their seditious words, and the prospect of painful punishment, some speakers claimed to have been 'overcome' by excess drinking, as if the alcohol, not the heart or tongue, did the talking. Though dangerous expressions could not be retracted, their power was diminished because the person who spoke them was not fully in command. Friendly or collusive witnesses made supportive observations about the speaker's intoxication, as if this excused the torrent of offensive words. In 1600, for example, when Sir Edmund Baynham and his men appeared at Star Chamber for their violent conduct and seditious words, they explained that a long session at the Mermaid in Bread Street had left them 'in disorder and excess of drink', and that their behaviour stemmed only from 'drink and heat'.[29] Returned to sobriety, most Elizabethans claimed to be dutiful subjects who, this lapse apart, always accepted the queen's authority.

Another cluster of speakers was said to be brain-sick, though the insanity defence was not always effective. When Robert Knight in 1575 was 'taken as a rogue about the court speaking very lewd words not meet to be suffered', he was held in Bridewell 'until it may be examined whether he spake it of madness or malice'.[30] Robert Threel of Hastings was likewise held in the Tower in 1578 until the authorities determined whether his 'lewd speeches . . . proceeded of malice or some infirmity'.[31] Henry Houghton, an ironmonger from Chester, was gaoled in 1578 for his 'slanderous speeches against the queen's majesty', but evidence emerged that he was 'commonly troubled with a lunacy', and that his words may have been 'misconstrued by his accusers'.[32]

William Williams of Newport, Monmouthshire, was gaoled at Gloucester in 1581 'for certain undutiful speeches uttered against her majesty', but was freed when the Council determined he was 'at the time of the speeches uttered, and yet is, frantic'.[33] So too was William Calverley, who spoke 'very undutiful and disloyal speeches' in 1596. When witnesses testified 'that he was lunatic at the time of uttering' them, the Council ordered his release, 'with sufficient sureties . . . to be of good behaviour, and not to repair within ten miles of the court'.[34]

Edward Alive

One recurrent Elizabethan rumour claimed that Edward VI was still alive, so that neither of his half-sisters could be lawful monarchs. This echoed the challenge that dogged the Lancastrian Henrys that Richard II was not yet dead, and the rumour troubling Henry VII that Edward V and his brother had escaped death in the Tower. These virulent fantasies encouraged the emergence of pretenders, and fed the circulation of conspiracy theories. Their tenacity in popular discourse reflects a propensity to wishful thinking as well as anxiety about the royal succession.

In 1578, for example, the London yeoman Robert Mantell was indicted for telling people at Maldon, Essex, 'that King Edward was alive', and that he (Robert) was that king, and that if he 'would find one that was trusty he could disclose that which should rejoice them all'. The case became more complex in July 1579, when Mantell managed to escape from his confinement in Colchester Castle. Lord Darcy and Sir Thomas Lucas were sent to investigate, and eventually the gaoler of Colchester, Richard King, spent six months in the Marshalsea 'for the escape of one Mantell, naming himself King Edward'. The pretender was eventually re-captured, held at Newgate, then sentenced to a traitor's death at the 1581 Essex Lent assizes.[35]

In March 1587 an Essex blacksmith, William Francis, faced indictment at Chelmsford for perpetuating the rumour of Edward VI's longevity. When Edmund Earle asked him 'what news was at London', Francis replied knowingly 'that there was one in the Tower which sayeth he is King Edward'. When Earle observed, sensibly enough, that King Edward was dead, Francis replied, 'I dare not say so', and claimed 'he did know the man that carried King Edward in a red mantle into Germany in a ship called the Harry'. Edmund Earle, by his own account, scorned this information, pointing out that Edward was dead and buried 'where they use to bury kings'. To this Francis objected 'that there was a piece of lead buried that was hollow, but there was nothing in it, and that it was but a monument'. Attempting to terminate a potentially dangerous conversation, Earle declared that 'these are naughty words, which ought not to be spoken'. To which Francis concluded: 'I will say no more . . . . [I] will not say that he is dead or alive.' This remarkable fragment of historical discourse allows us to eavesdrop, at least at a distance and with all sorts of mediations, on a conversation among Elizabethan artisans. And it finds them conversing on topics of high significance and great risk, well above their station, some twenty-nine years into the virgin queen's reign. The assize judges found William Francis guilty of spreading false news, presumably to face the pillory and imprisonment but nothing worse.[36]

A variant rumour claimed not that Edward VI was alive but that he had been foully murdered. A Colchester yeoman, Gregory Clover, was indicted for seditious words in 1579, for claiming that Lords Warwick and Leicester were traitors who should have lost their heads 'for making away of King Edward'. The Privy Council urged that Clover be used 'with as much severity of law as may be' for 'speeches so maliciously devised . . . to stir up some tumult'. Found guilty at the Chelmsford assize, his punishment was to stand in the pillory at Colchester 'on market day with one ear nailed to the pillory'.[37]

Elizabeth's Bastards

No subject drew such lively interest, or such creative speculation, as the queen's sexuality. While some of Elizabeth's subjects complained that the queen could not rule because she was a woman, and the realm wanted a good governor, others linked her womanhood to whoredom and sin. Scurrilous comment was recurrent about the queen's claimed virginity, and her alleged dalliance with prominent courtiers. Robert Dudley, later Earl of Leicester, was only the most commonly mentioned of her majesty's putative lovers. The queen's Catholic enemies may have spread some of this gossip, but it flourished among tattlers perennially interested in dirt.

While visiting London late in 1559, Thomas Holland, rector of Little Burstead, Essex, heard the rumour that the queen was with child. He learned from a Hertfordshire minister (who might have picked up gossip from Elizabeth's household at Hatfield) that someone had been sent to the Tower for words to that effect. Holland then apparently disseminated this falsehood in Essex. By June 1560 he was under investigation for words 'by him maliciously uttered against the queen's excellent majesty'. As soon as report of Holland's words reached local justices, they took him into custody and delivered him to the Earl of Oxford, John de Vere, Lord Lieutenant of Essex, for further interrogation. Oxford, who was concerned to demonstrate his own trustworthiness to the new Elizabethan regime, sought harsh treatment for one who had so foully slandered the queen. But, Oxford wrote:

being but words, the punishment of the law extendeth but to the loss of his ears or one hundred pounds fine, so far as I can learn; and yet the heinousness of the offence might have tended very much to withdraw her majesty's subjects from their allegiance and due obedience. It standeth doubtful unto me what might thereof be construed.

Not sure whether Holland's words verged on treason, and unable to derive more information from his questioning, the earl asked the Privy Council for guidance.[38] We do not know what legal penalty Holland paid for his indiscretion, but it appears to have cost him his ecclesiastical living. Collated by the Marian bishop Bonner, he had been rector of Little Burstead only since November 1558, and he had 'resigned' by the time his successor was installed in February 1561. Local records suggest that he was a conservative cleric, who fell foul of parish evangelicals associated with Richard Lord Rich.[39]

Examined a few weeks later in August 1560 for 'words spoken and spread abroad' that touched her majesty's honour, Anne Dowe of Brentwood, Essex, was held in gaol while local magistrates considered her offence. She had spread the gossip that Robert Dudley 'had given the queen a new petticoat which cost twenty nobles', prompting the retort, 'no no, he gave her a child I warrant'. One witness reported Anne saying 'that Dudley and the queen had played legerdemain together', and that, if he had not fathered a child on the queen already, Dudley 'hath put one to making'. Another recalled her saying 'there is a Dudley which beareth more rule than ever did his father' (the executed Duke of Northumberland)—a breath-taking reflection on high politics from the mouth of a plebeian woman. A local tailor who heard Anne Dowe's words warned her 'that greater fools than he or she did talk of that matter', adding, 'take heed what you sayest, though thou be drunk now thou wilt repent these words when thou art sober'. Whether she did repent and how she was punished remains un-known, though most likely she was whipped and sent home.[40]

The rumour of royal indiscretion was impossible to suppress. A Suffolk man, Edmund Baxter, was held in Melton gaol in January 1563 for saying 'that Lord Robert [Dudley] kept her majesty and that she was a naughty woman and could not rule her realm, and that justice was not administered'. These were not only slanderous comments on the queen's chastity, but seditious remarks about the governance of the realm. Baxter's wife Joan had passed on a comment from Lady Willoughby, that while the queen was at Ipswich she looked very pale, 'like one lately come out of childbed'. It was not surprising that women should share such gynaecological observations, but it became dangerous when gossips' chatter touched matters of state. When the menfolk repeated the rumour, it became the concern of magis-trates, who dutifully informed the Privy Council about these dangerous expressions.[41]

Commentary on the queen's liaison with Dudley continued beyond his elevation to the earldom of Leicester in 1564. It was not confined to alehouse gossips, but also resounded in more reputable quarters. At the time of the Northern Rebellion in 1569, the dean of Lichfield cathedral,

Lawrence Nowell, allegedly remarked 'that this realm was plagued by the sins of the queen and of the Earl of Leicester'. There was no need to identify those particular sins. Loyal listeners judged Nowell's speech to be 'foul words', 'evil words', 'lewd and slanderous words', 'lewd and malicious words', or even 'traitorous words' against the queen's majesty. His enemies invoked them in a dispute between vicars choral and the cathedral chapter, and, although dean Nowell 'utterly denyeth the said speech', there was strong evidence of his effort to cover it up. However, he weathered the storm and remained dean until his death in 1576.[42]

The rumour about Elizabeth was still going strong a decade or two later. Stern investigation and exemplary punishment failed to halt its circulation. Although vulgar comment sheds no light at all on the queen's actual conduct, it reveals a popular propensity to imagine her majesty as a lustful woman, no better than anyone else. Thomas Playfere, an Essex labourer, was indicted for treason in 1580 for claiming that the queen had two children by the Earl of Leicester, 'and that he did see them when they were shipped at Rye in two of the best ships the queen hath'. The assize at Brentwood found him guilty not of treason but of seditious words, and sentenced him to the pillory and a brief spell in prison.[43]

In March 1581 came news from Norfolk that one Henry Hawkins was making 'certain traitorous speeches', to the effect that 'my Lord Robert [Dudley] hath had five children by the queen, and she never goeth in progress but to be delivered'. The preacher Thomas Scot, who relayed these words to the Council, described them as 'heinous' and 'villainous', and blamed their circulation on 'papists' who preyed on the credibility of the 'unruly . . . multitude'. It was, he thought, the work of England's enemies to spread traitorous and scandalous remarks about the queen.[44] Catholic propagandists certainly embraced every dark story about the so-called virgin queen, but the tale spread ecumenically among Protestant parishioners. A Surrey woman, Alice Austen, faced indictment in 1585 for saying that 'the queen is no maid, and she hath had three sons by the Earl of Leicester'.[45] Such remarks would be demeaning and defamatory to any woman, but were especially scandalous and seditious when applied to the anointed queen.

Another conversation in Surrey in 1586 moved into dangerous territory when Thomas Bellowe (or Le Ballewe), buff leather dresser, a Huguenot refugee from Picardy, claimed that in France the papists commonly said that 'the queen of England is a whore and hath two bastards'. Bellowe was drinking with other Southwark artisans, including leather dressers, a nail maker, and the keeper of a victualling house, when he made his 'vile and slanderous speeches' against Queen Elizabeth. Stirring resentments against resident aliens, he also said 'that the queen of England . . . did love strangers (Walloons and Frenchmen) better than she loved Englishmen'. Rising to this, Thomas Ashley, nail maker, upheld the honour of his queen and country by telling the Frenchman, 'hold your peace, ye villain, a pox upon thee . . . get hence'. Bellowe repeated his assertion 'six or seven times', and Ashley 'very sharply rebuked' him in exchange. Eventually the company 'caused the goodman of the house to send for a constable and to apprehend [Bellowe] and so they did'.[46]

We are fortunate in this case to have the Privy Council report and some of the related judicial records. Arrested by the Southwark constable, Bellowe was examined by magistrates and indicted at the Surrey assizes, where he was identified as a yeoman. Witnesses claimed that they had rebuked Bellowe for asserting that the queen 'is a whore, and that she hath had two children . . . but he spake the more earnestly, uttering the said speeches after that a three or four times'. Although Bellowe attributed this canard to 'the papists' in France, his enthusiastic repetition of it was an act of sedition. Found guilty, he was sentenced to stand in the pillory, to have his ears cut off, and to spend three months in prison, unless he paid a fine of a hundred marks.[47]

One of the by-blows of Elizabeth's dalliance with Dudley allegedly turned up in Spain in 1588, the year of the Armada. The English agent Edward Palmer reported to Secretary Walsingham that 'the varlet that called himself her majesty's son is in Madrid, and is allowed two crowns a day for his table, but cannot go anywhere without his keepers, and has a house for his prison'. The claimant named himself as Arthur Dudley, the Earl of Leicester's illegitimate son by a royal mother, but was most likely a ship-wrecked mariner trying his luck.[48] The Spanish were willing to sustain the story, even if they did not believe the teller.

Remarks about the virgin queen's children followed Elizabeth into old age. Some accounts were graphic and specific. Denise Derrick, a widow of Chipping Hill, Essex, reportedly remarked in April 1590 that the queen

hath had already as many children as I, and that two of them were yet alive, the one being a man child and the other a maiden child. And further, that the other[s] were burned . . . She said my lord of Leicester was father to them, and wrapped them up in the embers in the chimney which was in the chamber where they were born.

Found guilty at the Chelmsford assize of speaking 'slanderous words against her majesty', Denise was sentenced to stand in the pillory during market time with a paper on her head acknowledging her fault.[49]

Robert Gardener, an Essex husbandman, was similarly sentenced in 1590 for publicly saying 'that my lord of Leicester had four children by the queen's majesty, whereof three of them were daughters and alive, and the fourth a son that was burnt'.[50] Tattle tales about the Virgin Queen's childbearing never fully dissipated, and variants would persist for the rest of the queen's reign and beyond. The Cornish recusant John Trevelyan declared in 1628 that 'Queen Tibb (meaning Queen Elizabeth) was as arrant a whore as ever breathed, and that she was [tupped?] by Essex and Leicester and others'.[51] Well into the 1670s there was popular report that Queen Elizabeth had a daughter named Jane.[52]

Some time in 1596 one Edward Francis of Melbury Osmond, Dorset, employed the rumour of the fornicating queen in his attempt to seduce Elizabeth Bayley 'to lead an incontinent life with him'. When she refused, 'alleging the foulness of the evil before God, and the danger of the law in that behalf', Francis replied 'that the best in England [meaning the queen's majesty] had much desired the pleasure of the flesh, and had also three bastards by noblemen of the court . . . two sons and a daughter, and was herself base born'. Elizabeth Bayley's mother then joined the conversation, not to protect her daughter's honour but to ask if it was known 'who should be heir apparent to the crown?' Francis answered that 'it was', but he did not identify a particular claimant. He did, however, venture the opinion 'that this land had been happy if her majesty had been cut off twenty years since, that some noble prince might have reigned in her stead'.[53]

This was dangerous talk, not just 'familiar speech' but words approaching treason. Edward Francis was made to understand that in compassing the queen's death he had gone too far. 'A learned man told him' that for 'wishing the cutting off of her majesty twenty years past' he might hang, whereas 'the rest of the words were but a pillory matter, which he cared not for'. At first he tried to minimize his remarks, saying, 'tush, tush, they are nothing'. When Elizabeth Bayley recalled his speech, he told her, 'they were foolish words . . . and though I spake them I did not think to hear of them again'. He then set out to discredit the Bayleys as 'simple creatures' and 'base creatures of no credit', mere women. When this failed he offered 'great gifts . . . to stay his accusers from proceeding against him' and 'to deny the words they had charged him with'. The bribes apparently had some temporary effect, but in 1598 he was bound over to answer at the Dorset assizes, then summoned to appear before the Privy Council. Rather than face justice Francis fled the county, forfeiting his £500 bond. Before leaving he gave away his horse and some prized candlesticks, as though he knew he would never need them again.[54]

Outlandish tales of Elizabeth's bastard-bearing re-emerged among the English community in Germany in 1600. The Council heard that year of a traveller, Hugh Broughton, who fell in with another Englishman, William Knight, on the road from Frankfurt to Strasbourg, where Broughton made 'most monstrous and unnatural speeches of her majesty our sovereign'. Shocked by these 'untruths', Knight understood his duty as a 'true subject' to report them to London. Broughton, he wrote, 'has sown such lies about [the queen] in these parts of Germany that I could not suffer longer in silence, and have signified this, that his tongue should be shortened'. It was not just that Broughton maintained that the queen was 'an atheist and a maintainer of atheism', nor his unwise speculation about the English succession that upset William Knight. It was the lurid story of sex, murder, and deception that recalled him to his duty. According to Knight, Broughton 'said that her majesty had a daughter, which should be or was affianced unto the Prince of Condé, to succeed after her majesty's decease; also that her majesty had been, of long time past, married to Lord Chancellor Sir Christopher Hatton had not Mrs Ratcliffe hindered the same'. But this paled besides Broughton's next recitation. He told of a midwife, 'taken in a coach by sundry ways to a palace at Hampstead, and carried up into a secret chamber where a lady lay in travail'. There she was commanded to do her best and preserve the lady, whatsoever became of the child. The newborn, by this report, was a daughter, who was immediately destroyed 'in a very great fire of coals'. The midwife, her work done, was rewarded with gold, was given a drink of poisoned wine, and died six days later, 'but revealed this before her death'. The lady, the story insinuates, was 'her majesty'.[55]

All the elements of this story had been circulating in England for decades, but it was still shocking to hear such 'monstrous speeches' about the virgin queen. A barrage of black propaganda emanated from Catholic Europe, and malicious rumours about Queen Elizabeth stirred conversations on both sides of the Channel. False rumours swept Antwerp in August 1589 that Elizabeth of England was dead, and the following month at Brussels there was 'continued bruit of the queen's infirmity, said to be madness'.[56]

A Pox on the Whore

A stream of anti-authoritarian belligerence plagued every early modern monarch, and Elizabeth came in for her share of abuse. Like most of the Tudors and Stuarts, she was sometimes called a 'bastard', a 'rascal', or a 'rogue', words with cruelly demeaning connotations. In Elizabeth's case, however, the insults were strongly gendered. Some subjects disparaged her majesty because she was a ruler, but others expressed contempt because she was a woman who presumed to govern. Some of the same language that defamed market women and village wives—'whore', 'quean', 'jade'—became attached to her royal highness, the governor of England's church and head of state.

Customary home-grown invective was also fed by vituperation from abroad. The doctors at Louvain insisted that Elizabeth was 'not a righteous queen, and ought to be put out of her seat'.[57] Another 'seditious and hurtful' book circulating in Flanders described her as 'the She of Babylon'.[58] It was well known that continental Catholics and Irish rebels called her majesty 'Jezebel' and 'the worst of names'.[59] The rebel Sir Brian O'Rourke defaced a statue of Queen Elizabeth and had his men beat it with axes. Another Irishman in France, Patrick Dones or Duffe, 'often called the queen Jezebel, and said he hoped to see her dragged at a horse's tail'.[60] Even Sir John Perrot, Elizabeth's lord deputy in Ireland, railed against her majesty as 'a base bastard pisskitchen woman'.[61] (The word 'pisskitchen', not in the *Oxford English Dictionary*, suggests a slovenly housekeeper or an incontinent skivvy—grossly defamatory to the queen.) Reports of these insults enjoyed an international currency and a surreptitious domestic circulation.

Queen Elizabeth's regime was barely half a year old when the vice chancellor of Cambridge wrote to Secretary Cecil in March 1559 about 'a young man of St John's College named Clyburne' who was held under surety for speaking 'unseemly words of the queen's majesty', referring to her as 'a rascal'. This was a serious breach, for the word was deeply demeaning. The informers, George Withers and George Bond of St John's, declared, 'this is treason to slight the honour' of the queen, but vice chancellor John Pory allowed in mitigation that Clyburne's ill speaking 'was found to proceed of a cross stomach'. Cecil noted the accusation and the excuse, and took no further action.[62]

In November 1577 the mayor of Doncaster, Robert Birks, informed the Earl of Huntingdon (President of the Council in the North) about the 'open, vile and threatening speech' of a fellow Yorkshireman, Richard Keddye, who had 'repeated such words against her majesty as I am not only ashamed but afraid by word or writing to recite'. Keddye, it transpired, had already had his ears clipped for a previous indiscretion, and on this occasion, the mayor warned Huntingdon, he might not reach York alive: 'The grudge is so great in people's hearts that . . . the people would needs have torn him in pieces.' We do not learn what Keddye said, but it was evidently outrageous. Huntingdon referred the matter to Secretary Walsingham, describing it as 'a lewd action in speech which deserves a sharper punishment than Mr Gargrave [a fellow councillor in the north] thinks can be imparted by law, for hanging is too good for him'.[63]

Justice Manwood weighed into the issue, reviewing the arsenal of punishments available by common law and statute. Keddye, for his 'lewd and detestable slanderous speeches towards her majesty', had been justly punished 'by pillory and cutting of his ears according to the statute'. But having 'aggravated' his offence by speaking again against the queen, he now deserved 'a more grievous punishment'. All the resources of the law and state should be used to make him an example and secure his repentance.

The statute provided perpetual imprisonment and forfeiture of goods for a second offence. But common law also allowed mutilation, blinding, and even dismemberment for 'slanderous rumours and speeches against the nobility and council of the prince'. In light of the heinous quality of Keddye's offence, Manwood suggested, he should suffer 'burning in the face with letters . . . gagging his two jaws . . . so he cannot speak any words . . . burning through his tongue, or perchance cutting off his tongue', though it is unlikely such mutilations were implemented.[64]

Among other Englishmen who spoke disparagingly of her majesty, the Middlesex yeoman Peter Moyses of Bromley was cited in 1584 for telling a neighbour 'the queen is a rascal'.[65] John Pullyver, clerk of Writtle, Essex, was pilloried in 1580 for saying 'that some did say that we had no queen'.[66] Mark Wiersdale, another Essex minister, talked himself into trouble by saying in 1588 that Queen Elizabeth was not queen of France. The archdeacon's official who heard this remark said it tended to high treason, and Wiersdale conceded that he spoke in ignorance.[67]

Few went so far as Jeremy Vanhill, a labourer of Sandwich, Kent, who declared before witnesses on 1 April 1585: 'shite upon your queen, I would to God she were dead that I might shit on her face.' He further 'wished that the queen were as sick as Peter Aveger then was', referring to a neighbour who was gravely ill and died that night. The Rochester assizes found Vanhill guilty of speaking seditious words, and sentenced him to a felon's death by hanging (not the traitor's death with quartering), but what other crimes he had committed and whether the execution was carried out cannot be readily determined.[68] In 1592 two sailors were set in the pillory at Wapping, Middlesex, after 'scandalously and seditiously' saying 'shit upon the queen'.[69]

Casual curses of this sort kept coming, with predictable consequences. A London yeoman, John Clarke, found himself before the Middlesex sessions in June 1602 after using 'scandalous and seditious words to the queen's defamation' at Uxbridge. When the constable invoked royal authority, Clarke allegedly responded, 'why dost thou tell me of the queen? A turd for the queen.'[70] A similar encounter with a minor official the same year led another London yeoman, James Doggett, to cry 'a pox and a vengeance' on all authorities and 'a pox of all those that would follow her majesty any more'.[71]

Because she is a Woman

Gendered insults abounded, not all of them compounded by sexual derision. They were as likely to emanate from women as from men. Mary Cleere of Ingatestone, Essex, disparaged the queen's authority in 1577 by saying 'that it did not become a woman to make knights'.[72] A Surrey woman, Joan Lyster of Cobham, spinster, declared scandalously in 1586 that 'the bishop of Canterbury and the Council make a fool of the queen's majesty, and because she is but a woman she ought not to be governor of a realm'.[73]

When the minister of Aldham, Essex, John Wylton, allegedly 'spake openly in the church' in 1589 'that the queen was a whore', his parishioner, the tailor John West, claimed to be 'stupefied' by these 'horrid and diabolical words'. The report was apparently stirred up by the yeoman Thomas Wenden, who explained that 'the queen is a dancer, and Wylton sayeth all dancers are whores'. In the event the minister was exonerated, but Wenden was bound over for a year for spreading misinformation.[74] A London baker, Thomas Garner, told listeners at Rotherhithe in 1590 'that the queen's majesty was an arrant whore and his whore, and if he could come to her he would tear her in pieces, and he would drink blood; and that he would set London on fire, and it would be a brave sight unto him'. The Surrey assize judged this ferocious outburst to be 'seditious' and remanded the speaker in gaol.[75]

'Let us pray for a father, for we have a mother already', remarked John Feltwell, labourer, of Great Wenden, Essex, in the summer of 1591. When his neighbour John Thurgood asked, 'what mean you by that?' Feltwell replied, 'let us pray for a king'. Thurgood rebuked him, 'we have a gracious queen already, wherefore would you pray for a king?' To which Feltwell answered:

the queen was but a woman and ruled by noblemen, and the noblemen and gentlemen were all one, and the gentlemen and farmers would hold together one with another so that poor men could get nothing among them, and therefore we shall never have a merry world while the queen liveth, but if we had but one that would rise I would be the next, or else I would the Spaniards would come in that we may have some sport.

For this seditious outburst Feltwell was set in the pillory for two hours and remanded to the next sessions.[76]

Much higher in the social hierarchy, a nobleman and a knight were charged with speaking against the queen. In July 1601 the Council dealt with 'certain speeches used by the right honourable the Earl of Lincoln at his house in Cannon Row two or three days after the arraignment of the Earl of Essex' the previous February. Lincoln's indiscretion was to say, in the hearing of servants: 'I cannot be persuaded that the queen will be drawn to consent to the death of one with whom she has been so familiar, as with the Earl of Essex . . . . I myself have seen her kiss him twenty times, and methinks in reason that she should not then cut off his head.' The servant William Wright, who reported these words, also accused Lincoln of involvement in a confederacy on behalf of the king of Scots.[77]

Wright also reported speeches of Sir Arthur Gorges 'concerning her majesty's growing tyrannies'. But because he spoke them 'only in the hearing of the Lady Elizabeth his wife, I durst not without further proof reveal them'. As Gorges's servant, Wright continued, he 'stood in fear to deal against one so mighty who might at his lordship's pleasure bring actions of account against me of great reckoning'. Now, however, when the mighty were falling, he was willing to present his information.[78]

The charges against Lincoln and Gorges may have emerged from back-stairs gossip, but they had potentially dangerous consequences. Lincoln in particular was concerned to rebut them, in order, he said, to dispel slanders and to retain her majesty's good opinion. The accusations, he told Secretary Cecil, were 'vexatious charges . . . false and ridiculous . . . malicious surmises'. He was incensed that a traitorous ungrate (William Wright) should 'alter the sense of words spoken at my table'. The word of a nobleman outweighed that of a backbiting servant, and Lincoln's indiscretions, if that is what they were, were soon forgotten. Indeed, his lordship might even bring charges of *scandalum magnatum*.[79]

It was Never Merry World

Seditious remarks were sometimes driven by undutiful thoughts in favour of a different religion or an alternative occupant of the throne. Many were couched in the form of aggrieved nostalgia or hopeful yearning, as 'it was never merry world since (a regretted past event, such as the death of a former monarch)', or 'it would not be merry world until (a future happy occurrence, such as the succession of a prince)'. Some subjects went further than regretting the queen's accession, and forecast or wished for her imminent death.

William Appleforth, curate at Newington by Tottenham, was walking home from the Temple in London late in 1561 when someone told him of a man being examined before the Council for saying that 'her grace should not live unto Christmas', and that 'the old laws should be up again in despite of all that would say nay'. Arrived at home, 'by the fire talking . . . thinking therein no harm', Appleforth repeated this news, not reflecting that it might be dangerous or seditious. One of those listening, perhaps a servant, reported that the curate spoke 'certain words against the queen', and Appleforth was hauled to the Gatehouse for sowing sedition. Though he had not originated the offensive words and did not endorse them, they still caused him difficulty. Simply repeating seditious words, or reporting their utterance by someone else, was an offence against the law. It emerged, however, that Appleforth had made other remarks that attracted the government's attention. He struggled to explain: 'I said that an archbishop is above a queen, because I have heard it spoken of learned men in the old times . . . Where I spake of tempestuous weather, death and sickness, I did read it in the prognostication of the year last past.' As to the suggestion that he did not love the queen or her laws, Appleforth protested, 'I do pray for her daily and hourly' at all religious services. 'If this be not true,' he concluded, 'let me be hanged, drawn and quartered.' Talk of a traitor's death, however, was unnecessary, for the offence, if any, was the misdemeanour of speaking sedition. The evidence was inadequate to determine whether Appleforth posed a threat to the regime, or whether he was just another loose-tongued religious conservative.[80]

Seditious remarks by the Kentish yeoman Bartholomew Taylor on May Day 1568, that 'we shall never have a merry world so long as we have a woman governor, and as the queen lived', led to his indictment at the Maidstone assizes. Found guilty, he was sentenced to a year's imprisonment and a fine of £10.[81] A few years later Randall Duckworth, a labourer of Bradwell, Essex, was made to stand in the pillory with a paper on his head for saying that 'it was merry England when there was better government, and if the queen die there will be a change'.[82]

When Richard Jones, servant to a Shrewsbury merchant, allegedly declared in 1574 that 'there should be wars shortly in this land, and that before Michaelmas next this land should be conquered by strangers, and that the old religion should be up again', his words were reported to the Council in London. These were 'seditious words', according to the report, prejudicial to the crown, the realm, and the law, and 'tending to the ruin of them all'. Though the speaker belonged to a papist network, supporting the claims of Mary Queen of Scots, local magistrates were lax in their duty and allowed the offender to escape.[83]

It could also be seditious to report that the queen had been targeted for assassination. Richard Lockie of St Albans was examined in March 1579 for saying 'that her majesty in the fourteenth year of her reign [1572] should have been [i.e. was] shot at with a gun'. The Council construed this to be a seditious rumour, and perhaps also a compassing of the queen's death.[84] Once again, a casual conversation veered onto dangerous ground.

'This world will be in better case shortly', prophesied the Essex labourer William Medcalfe in 1586, who expected the king of Spain and the Earl of Westmorland to 'avenge the death and blood of the late Duke of Norfolk' and remove Elizabeth from the throne. Apparently a Catholic as well as a traitor, Medcalfe was given 'judgement according to the statute', presumably execution.[85] Similar words shocked listeners in other counties. 'There would never be a merry world before there were a new alteration . . . and, by god's wounds, the queen is a whore,' alleged the Kentish tailor, John Massee of Minster, in 1591. Indicted at the Kent assizes, he was pilloried and 'well whipped' for scandalously repeating these words.[86]

Also in 1591 a Middlesex yeoman, Nicholas Haslewood of Islington, allegedly 'spoke with malice and feloniously against the queen, saying he wished her death'. Haslewood, who was most likely a Catholic, also declared that 'he hoped to see his enemies burnt in Smithfield before Michaelmas'. The sessions court found him not guilty of a felony, but guilty of trespass and contempt, and sentenced him to appear in the pillory with a paper on his head explaining the nature of his offence.[87] Edward Ewer, a husbandman of Beckenham, Kent, allegedly said in 1596 'that it would never be a merry world till her majesty was dead or killed; and that her majesty was ruled by her lords at their pleasure, but we must not say so'. At the Kent assizes he was sentenced to death by hanging, but other felonies, including horse theft, compounded his offence against the state.[88]

A few of those who wished the queen dead had the means, or at least the inclination, potentially to achieve their ends. A few were desperate plotters, Catholic malcontents, men of action as well of words, who conspired to have Elizabeth killed. Among them was Sir William Stanley, a former military commander, who plotted with Catholics at Douai in 1593 to kill the queen. One of Stanley's associates, the soldier William Polewhele, revealed the details of the conspiracy. Singing for his life in February 1594 before attorney general Thomas Egerton and solicitor general Edward Coke, Polewhele accused Stanley of 'using many vile speeches', including the remark that 'if mistress Elizabeth were dead (meaning the queen) we should have good sport'. Stanley also allegedly said that 'if they can by any means procure the death of her majesty upon the sudden', then Spanish forces from the Netherlands would 'repair into England and hope to have all at their own pleasure'. One of the conspirators, Jacques di Francischi, steeled Polewhele to the task of killing the queen, warning him that, if the attempt failed, 'then all the devils in hell will not be able to prevail against England'. The achievement, said Jacques, 'would make him glorious before God, she being a wicked creature and like to be the overthrow of all christendom'. Polewhele was supposed 'either to stab her majesty or to shoot her with a pistol as she should go abroad or to a sermon'. But his courage failed him and he abandoned the enterprise and told his tale to the authorities.[89] It was a conspiracy of words, whipped up by bravado and hatred, but perhaps not unique in the late sixteenth century.

The Wrong Religion

The stressful circumstances of a contentious and unsettled reformation produced dangerous talk among religious enthusiasts. Unreconciled Catholics sometimes veered towards treason, while Protestant zealots sometimes spoke sedition. The papal bull of excommunication, the execution of Mary Queen of Scots, and the long war with Spain exacerbated religious tensions. The crown used the prerogative court of High Commission as well as the network of magistrates to quash or quarantine deviant opinions, and their effort preserves scattered remarks in the documentary record.

From the very beginning of Queen Elizabeth's reign some subjects challenged their monarch's religion. 'The queen is not worthy to bear rule or to be supreme head of the church,' asserted Peter Hall, a Kentish clergyman, who also remarked in 1559 that 'the queen's proceedings are not of God'. When Robert Nethersole, gentleman, reported these words to a neighbouring husbandman, the neighbour retorted, 'said he nothing but this? He might lawfully say these words.' But others judged Hall's words to be seditious, and secured his indictment at the Maidstone summer assizes.[90]

Thomas Bedell, esquire, of Writtle, Essex, faced indictment in 1574 for 'scandalous and seditious speeches against the queen' after demanding of a local official in the churchyard, 'what, is the queen become a papist now?' This challenged Queen Elizabeth's stated position, which, as the indictment insisted, abhorred 'all papal and papistical doctrine' and strove 'to eradicate and abolish the same within her realm'. Bedell had spoken in defence of the vicar of Writtle, Michael Mayshort, who had just delivered an anti-papist sermon. It was the issue of a writ against the vicar, in the queen's name, that triggered his outburst. He did not help his case by enlisting the support of 'others who are called puritans', including the presbyterian Thomas Cartwright, who he said made similar allegations about the queen and popery. The sessions jury at Brentwood found Bedell guilty of 'false, scandalous and seditious words . . . indecently and irreverently spoken'. As a gentleman, however, he was unlikely to lose his ears at the pillory, and with the Council's approval Bedell compounded by paying a fine of a hundred pounds and expressing his repentence in writing.[91]

Another cleric, John Williams alias Floud of Grays Thurrock, Essex, drifted into sedition in 1578 when he preached on God's anger at Balaam's covetousness and Israel's fornication with the damsels of Balak, which caused 'the chief rulers of the people...to be hanged up against the sun'. 'Even so,' said the preacher, 'if Elizabeth with the Council and other magistrates were hanged up against the sun there would not be so much wickedness done as there was'. Thomas Kightle, gentleman, reported the preacher's 'seditious words', but the county assize found him not guilty.[92]

In the following year John Flower of Northampton spent a month in gaol, awaiting further investigation by the Privy Council, for asking in conversation, 'What if we have a wicked prince? What, shall we obey her conscience? No, I will not!'[93] Resistance theory had few open advocates, and the correct answer, at least from the official viewpoint, was that subjects should endure and obey.

Roger Nowell, the Puritan vicar of Heybridge, Essex, was indicted in 1582 for speaking 'false, seditious and scandalous [words], advisedly and with malicious intent of his own imagination and contradiction of the queen...in pernicious example to other subjects'. He had apparently declared: 'If I am an enemy to the word preached, the queen is an enemy to the word preached,' saying this in church, 'in disturbance of the queen's people', some of whom reported him to the authorities.[94] A Kentish labourer, Thomas Farrington of Leysdown on Sea, was indicted at the Rochester assizes in 1599 for saying 'that the queen's majesty was antichrist, and therefore she is thrown down into hell'. Farrington confessed to these seditious words, and was sentenced to time in the pillory and the loss of his ears.[95]

The regret and nostalgia of religious conservatives led to dangerous and seditious utterances. A pamphlet of 1588 laid much of the blame for seditious discourse on 'the envious tongue of false and lying papists', whose 'false lying speeches...strike a terror in the hearts of the common people, or else to make them dislike of those that are in authority'.[96] Scraps of evidence from the courts and Privy Council show the authorities working to restrain the more reckless expressions.

'It was never merry in England since the scriptures were so commonly preached and talked among such persons as they were,' declared John Howard, petticoat-maker of Bury St Edmunds, over dinner in November 1577.[97] 'It was a merry world when the service was used in the Latin tongue, and now we are in an evil way and going to the devil and have all nations in our necks, for there is no Christian prince that hath such cruel laws as to burn men through the ears, which are now used in this realm,' protested David Brown, a husbandman of East Tilbury, Essex, in 1581. The only remedy, he suggested, was for the exiled Earl of Westmorland to come into England from Ireland with Spanish military support. 'And being demanded that if the Earl of Westmorland should come in to this realm whether he would help him and take part with him to the best of his power, he answered that he would do the best he could.' Brown's 'scandalous words' brought him before the Essex assize, which judged him guilty, though his ultimate fate is unknown.[98]

Another Roman Catholic, Henry Beare, was detained at Salisbury in 1581 for 'most lewd and slanderous speeches... affirming that mass [was] said daily in her majesty's chapel'. The Council advised Wiltshire authorities to consult someone 'skilful in the law... to consider how far the said Beare may be touched either by the late statute for slanderous speeches against her majesty, or by some other statute heretofore made for the punishing of the like', and to deal with him at the next assizes.[99]

In 1582 the authorities charged John Hamerton of Hellifield, Yorkshire, 'for certain traitorous words by him... most undutifully and wickedly spoken and uttered against the queen's majesty and her highness's proceedings'. Hamerton was a militant Catholic who said that the queen and her Protestant subjects were all heretics, and that Campion and other martyrs had been unlawfully put to death. He drew further attention to himself by claiming to have been 'Bonner's man, and helped to set fire to the faggots in Smithfield [burning heretics under Mary], and rejoice[d] to think how they fried in the flames, and what service he had done God in furthering their death'.[100] As late as 1590 a Catholic yeoman in Shropshire, William Wier, labelled priests' wives 'whores, and their children bastards', and said 'it was pity the queen did reign, to suffer them unhanged or unburnt'.[101]

In 1596 Tristam Cotterill of Lincoln's Inn reportedly 'fell into speeches against the queen, denying the supremacy... and said that in Spain the queen was commonly called the whore of Babylon'. Cotterill allegedly made these remarks while riding with Richard Vennard in Hampshire. But there were reasons to suspect that the proceedings were malicious, because by the time Vennard reported these words he was imprisoned in the Fleet for debt, blaming his troubles on 'certain recusants' connected to Cotterill, who was now his enemy.[102] Joan Gurr, a spinster of Lamberhurst, Kent, who said in 1596, 'I pray God either convert or confound her highness,' may also have been a member of England's Catholic community.[103]

An Uncertain Succession

The question of the royal succession concerned humble Elizabethans as well as privy councillors and magnates. An illicit buzz of conversation flared up whenever this topic was raised. Clandestine books from Edinburgh and Antwerp fuelled the debate on behalf of Catholics or Protestants, Spaniards or Scots,[104] but the principal discourse was local and domestic. Its ingredients included recurrent prophecy that the queen was likely to die, false reports that she was already dead, and speculation about her likely successor. Among those mentioned were Mary Queen of Scots, her son James Stuart, the Earl of Essex, Lord Beauchamp, the king of France, and the king of Spain. The statute of 1571 made it treason to dispute the queen's title, and the act of 1581 threatened death for illegally discussing the succession, but the law was incapable of imposing silence.

Mary Cleere was convicted at the Essex assize in March 1577 for saying 'that the queen's majesty was base born and not born to the crown, and that another lady [presumably Mary Queen of Scots] is the right inheritor thereunto'. She also said 'that it did not become a woman to make knights'. Her sentence was to be drawn and burnt (*trahatur et comburatur*), not drawn and hanged, as has been mistakenly recorded. Burning was the designated punishment for female traitors, though we cannot be sure that in this case it was actually carried out. Associated with Lady Petre's Ingatestone Hall, a hotbed of Catholic recusancy, Mary Cleere had espoused the position of Catholic Christendom. Her sentence, which seems to have been unique, may have been the response of a panicked government at a moment of heightened emergency. John Payne, a Douai priest, had been arrested at Ingatestone Hall in February 1577, just a month before Mary's trial.[105]

Discussing the potential aftermath of Queen Elizabeth's death, a yeoman of Southwark, John Carre, told friends in 1584 that he 'heard in a song that the Scottish king shall be our governor'. When a woman in the company questioned him, Carre responded, 'hold your peace woman, for the king of Scots shall be your governor', adding 'that this realm was spoiled for want of a good governor'. These were seditious remarks, for which Carre was judged guilty at the Surrey assize.[106] Another Surrey yeoman, Matthew

Freeland of Esher, was likewise indicted in 1600 for saying 'that the king of Scots was right heir apparent to the crown of England', although in this case he was found 'not guilty'.[107] Hugh Broughton, an Englishman in Germany, was reported for saying in 1601 'that the king of Scots is the right successor to the crown', among other scandalous remarks about her majesty.[108] The variability in sentencing and punishment points to the difficulty of policing seditious and treasonable speech.

George Binks, a tailor of Finchingfield, Essex, and a diehard papist, was indicted in 1592 for saying 'that the pope is supreme head over all Christendom, and that King Phillip is right king of England'. If the queen commanded him to do any service, he said, 'the same would go against his conscience'. As for Sir Francis Drake and his men, who had sailed against Portugal in 1589, Binks declared they 'do rob and spoil the king of Spain of his goods, which is the right king of England'. These were bold words, apparently treason, but the evidence to convict was insufficient and Chelmsford assize found him 'not guilty'.[109]

In the course of a complicated and controversial episode at midsummer 1596, a leading Essex gentleman spoke treason and his principal retainer uttered dangerous and seditious words. Sir Thomas Lucas was exercising the trained band of citizen soldiers in the windmill field outside Colchester when Sir John Smyth rode up with other gentlemen and attempted to raise the troops in rebellion. Riding up and down among the bowmen and pikemen (mostly Colchester clothiers and tradesmen), he appealed to them as 'my fellow soldiers', and declared 'that there are traitors about the court, and that the Lord Treasurer is a traitor of traitors' who intended 'to bring in the king of France'. 'About the queen there are many traitors, and the king of France shall be brought in,' he repeated. Smyth asserted 'that the common people had been of long time oppressed', and invited the men to join with him for 'redress' and 'a reformation of your troubles'. He told the troops, 'you have long been in bondage, but if you will go with me you will be free', but none of them stirred. As further inducement he introduced 'a nobleman of the blood royal, and of the house of the Lord Beauchamp, that shall be your captain', thereby raising the stakes and turning a social protest into a dynastic insurrection. (The nobleman, younger brother to Edward Seymour, would have been in the line of succession had the Grey–Seymour marriage not been invalidated.)

Several witnesses reported Smyth's words, though some claimed not to understand them. The loyal Sir Thomas Lucas collected the testimony of 'gentlemen of good account and sufficiency', other 'witnesses of good credit', and the words of 'a plain honest man, and well thought of amongst his neighbours', and sent them to the Privy Council.

Smyth was quickly arrested, but excused himself by claiming 'that he was overcome by drinking that morning of a great deal of white wine and sack'. Lucas, however, was able to ascertain that Smyth's company, 'being at the least a dozen persons', had only consumed three pints of wine and three pints of sack between them. Half a pint per person was not enough to render them senseless or reduce their culpability. Lucas also found out that Smyth had stockpiled arms, bullets, and other 'things for war' at his house at Coggeshall, and this too he reported to the Council. Rather than an impulsive folly driven by drink, a piece of midsummer madness, it appeared that Smyth and his company had planned to raise rebellion. For this they could have been executed, but Smyth was held in the Tower and eventually released on house arrest.[110]

News of Sir John Smyth's 'attempt' spread rapidly, and grew with the telling. Later that evening, villagers at Aldham, a few miles west of Colchester, sat on a bench in the midsummer twilight, recalling the exploits of the day. One of them, Thomas Wenden, described by Sir Thomas Lucas as a man 'most desperate and lewd both in word and deed', repeated Smyth's claims about the traitors at court. He also spread rumours of 'five or six thousand men slain about Greenwich, and lay upon heaps, that men might go over the shoes in blood'. When Clement Cowey of Little Tey heard this gory news, he prayed, 'God save the queen', to which Wenden responded, 'I pray God it be not too late', adding that 'by Monday morning if not this night . . . you shall hear all the bells in the country ring'. Although he did not say it outright, he seemed to be anticipating, and perhaps compassing, a change of regime.

Thomas Wenden was a retainer to Sir John Smyth and a party to his intended rebellion. (He was, perhaps, the same Thomas Wenden, yeoman and trouble-maker, who had been bound over for a year in 1589 for implying that the queen was a whore because she was a dancer.) Wenden's mouth now brought him more woe, and he was indicted at the Essex assizes in 1596 for 'certain seditious words' spoken of the queen. Sir Thomas Lucas advised the Council that Wenden 'by law ought to have lost his ears, for which he was a long time after kept in gaol, yet by means made to Sergeant Puckering, then justice of assize, had no trial but was delivered, for that Sergeant Puckering said it was too filthy a matter to be brought in open place'.[111]

The question of the succession prompted more chatter as the childless queen aged. In 1597 an Essex labourer, William Stevens, told neighbours 'that he had heard that our queen's majesty is made away and dead', and that councillors 'were gone to fetch another prince'.[112] Lancashire Catholics in 1599 heard 'bruits of her majesty's death' and speculations 'that the Earl of Essex was the worthiest to [be] king'.[113] Even in 1603, when King James of Scotland was preparing to move south, there was popular chatter on behalf of other candidates.[114]

Cheering for Spain

A surprising strain of seditious discourse spoke favourably of the king of Spain, who had shared the throne with Queen Mary and hoped to govern England again. The Essex tailor George Binks, indicted in 1592, was not alone in considering Philip II 'the right king of England'.[115] Nor were all Elizabethan Hispanophiles Catholics in search of a religious champion. Some were deeply disgruntled Protestants, fed up with queenship, or led on by bravado and drink.

The London weaver Stephen Slater declared in 1585, the year that war broke out,

that King Philip was a father to England and did better love an Englishman than the queen's majesty did, for that he would give them meat, drink and clothes. And that he thought that the queen was not queen and supreme head of England but said, I pray God she be. And being afterwards charged for saying he thought her majesty was not queen and supreme head of England, he said, he said so and so would say before the best in England, for he was pressed to serve as a soldier in Flanders by commission, and had not those things which he was promised, and that if her majesty were queen, she had villains under her.[116]

Not a papist but a man with a grudge, Slater talked himself into serious trouble. So too did John Feltwell, labourer, of Great Wenden, Essex, who in the summer of 1591 invited his neighbours to 'pray for a king'. 'We shall never have a merry world while the queen liveth', he continued, 'or else I would the Spaniards would come in that we may have some sport'.[117]

Another Essex man, Wilfred Lutey, a scrivener of Aveley, was indicted at Chelmsford in 1594 for saying 'that all those that her majesty sent over into the Low Countries were damned because the king of Spain is our anointed king . . . and that all the estates of the Low Countries were drunkards and cobblers, and all those that her majesty sent over were rebels and damned, because they fought against their lawful king'. Notwithstanding the scandal of these ostensibly treasonous words, the court found Lutey not guilty, and bailed him to the next assize. He was apparently the victim of malicious prosecution.[118] By contrast, a Southwark yeoman, William Whiting, was found guilty at the Surrey assize for saying, in 1594, 'that there were better laws and justice [and charity] in Spain than is here in England'.[119]

Other commoners faced indictment in 1596 for disloyal remarks in favour of Spain. A brickburner, John Feer, was remanded at the Hertford assizes in March 1596 for saying: 'I would that all the Spaniards of Spain were landed here in England to pull out the boors and the churls by the ears; and that twenty thousand of them were about Mr Capell's house (meaning Arthur Capell of Little Hadham, esquire) for then he . . . should be much set by.'[120] Nicholas Howlett, labourer, of Snodland, Kent, was indicted at Maidstone assizes in July 1596 for publicly saying: 'I would [the Spanish] would come. I would strike never a blow against them.' Charged with treason, he was found guilty of the lesser crime of speaking seditious words, and was sentenced to the pillory and to further remand in gaol.[121]

Another Kentish labourer, Alexander Oven, was indicted in 1596 for complaining that the Spaniards 'be long a coming; it is no matter if they were come, and I would they were come, for the people here be all nought. A plague of God light upon them all (meaning the queen's subjects).' Tried at the Kent Quarter Sessions, he was found guilty of speaking these words, but 'not of speaking them maliciously'.[122] At Hertford assizes in March 1597 a gentleman, Roger Slye, was found guilty of saying that the Spaniards 'would shortly come amongst us, whereby he hoped to see such rule in England as he should domineer over that knave Ralph Conningsby', a local adversary.[123] Like scores more Elizabethan men and women, these people spoke recklessly and unguardedly, and paid the price of enmeshment with the law.

5

Words against King James

Queen Elizabeth's laws against treason and sedition expired with her death. But though there was no fresh legislation, Jacobean lawyers made sure that their king was protected against malicious and disloyal tongues. A West Country magistrate assured the Privy Council in 1606 'that no syllable escaping the mouth of any disloyal subject, or information touching my king and sovereign coming to my knowledge, should be passed or permitted without speedy certification to your lordships'.[1]

The statute of Edward III still prevailed, and could be interpreted to cover treasonable words. To drive home the point, Lord Chancellor Egerton declared in 1605 that 'maintainers and movers of sedition . . . deserve the greatest punishment next to treason'.[2] Star Chamber judges in 1608 declared that libelling the king or the state was treason.[3] Treason could be 'in the heart, in the hand, in the mouth, in consummation', declared the prosecutors of Sir Walter Raleigh in 1618.[4]

Jacobean jurists had good cause to reflect on treason, especially after the unfolding of the Gunpowder Plot. But there was no consensus on the consequence of disloyal language. Sir Edward Coke seemed to contradict himself, over a long career, while some of Coke's fellow judges took a much harder line against treason by words.

It was treason, wrote Sir Edward Coke, 'to make the king a subject and to despoil him of his kingly office of royal government'. But could this be accomplished simply by speaking? There had been laws in England by which 'bare words or sayings should be high treason', including various Tudor statutes, but these were now repealed or expired. Treason, Coke insisted, required an overt act. 'It is commonly said', he asserted, 'that bare words may make an heretic, but not a traitor without an overt act.' In Rex versus Owen in 1616 Coke laid down that 'merely speaking scandalous words of the king was not treason', though 'words which incited to his murder were an overt act which proved the compassing of his death'. So it was clearly treason to say that 'the king, being excommunicate by the pope, may lawfully be deposed and killed by any whatsoever, which killing is not murder'.[5] To disparage his majesty otherwise was merely seditious, a high misdemeanour but no capital felony.

About the worst that anyone said of James I was that he was foreign, and that a Scot should not wear the crown of England. One or two people called the king a fool, perhaps echoing the remark attributed to Henry IV of France, that King James was 'the wisest fool in Christendom'. A few suggested that the king was unreliable in religion. One or two imagined his death. But scandalous and treasonable remarks, of the kind that dogged the Tudors, seemed to quieten down or move to a lower register. Perhaps there was general relief that the kingdom at last had a king, and a king with male heirs; that the long war with Spain was over; and that the Church of England seemed to be secure. Nobody, so far as we know, commented aloud on that aspect of King James that most fascinates modern scholars—his homosexuality. There was a surfeit of gossip about Jacobean courtiers and politicians, but surprisingly little dangerous talk about the king. Although there were executions for treason in James I's reign, and even burning for heresy, no one went to their death just for treasonable words.[6]

He is no King

Amidst the celebrations for the new king's accession a few subjects spoke rashly against the intrusion of a Scottish monarch. It would take several months before the new dynasty secured full acceptance, and more than a few Englishmen were unwilling to give their allegiance until King James was actually crowned. There was enough uncertainty and dissatisfaction in 1603 for the claims of alternative candidates to be aired. Exceptionally detailed assize records allow us to recover some of these spoken expressions.

On hearing the proclamation of the new reign on 25 March 1603, William Fletcher, a saddler of Lewes, Sussex, protested 'that we ought rather to mourn for the death of her majesty, and ought not to rejoice for that any foreign prince should reign over us . . . and that if any foreign prince did inherit the crown the nobles were perjured, and that he would never take him for his king until he was crowned'. Found guilty at the assize of speaking these seditious words, Fletcher was sentenced to be pilloried for two hours with a paper above his head describing his offence, and then to be remanded in gaol.[7]

Likewise indicted for seditious words, Thomas Brown, a Hertfordshire yeoman, was said to have declared at Royston within days of Elizabeth's death in March 1603 'that we who looked for the queen's death these twenty years will not be made fools now...and that whilst he lived a Scot should not wear the crown of England, and that although all the men of England would join with the king, yet he would be against him'. Brown also spread the rumour 'that the Earl of Hertford was ready in the West Country with thirty thousand men to withstand the king's coming into England...and that he, the said Thomas, with his policy would procure one thousand men more to join with the earl against the king'. Unable to contain himself, Brown further offered to 'drum to encourage the king's enemies against him; and that when the king should come into the country, he, the said Thomas Brown, would tell him that he was come into a place whereof he was not worthy'. Found guilty of sedition at the Hertford assize, Brown had no opportunity to offer this speech to his new monarch, but was remanded in gaol pending sentence.[8]

A Kentish weaver, John Dawley of Lewisham, spread similar reports that the new king 'would hardly be crowned because the Lord Beauchamp was up with fifty thousand men'.[9] A Kentish blacksmith, Robert Vincerst, declared on 31 March 1603 that the Spanish Infanta was coming 'with a great troop of men to be queen of England, and that the king should not live to be crowned'.[10]

Richard Hartropp, a labourer of Maidstone, Kent, complained in 1603, 'what rogues are these of the late queen's council that would not suffer her to marry while she was young that by her we might have had an heir to have been our king, whereas now we must have a strange king come out of another land with a company of spaniels following him'. Speaking in company in June 1603, Hartropp predicted that the new king was 'in danger to be killed before Michaelmas day next'. Asked how the king should be killed, Hartropp suggested, 'with an arrow or a gun out of a cellar', and predicted that 'after his death by the space of four years there shall be no king in England'. Hartropp's words had more than a whiff of treason, but the Jacobean jury found him guilty only of sedition. His sentence was to stand in the pillory for two hours and then to be remanded in gaol until he could enter security for his future good behaviour. Gaol fever evidently did the work of the executioner, for Hartropp died unreleased before the following February.[11]

In Essex too the new reign was greeted with outbursts of hostility, along with some remarkable interpretations of constitutional law. 'It was pity the king came so peaceably to this place,' declared Henry Mullynax, gentleman of Ingatestone, who wished that the English and Scots 'had gone together by the ears'. 'What if I did speak such words, I will justify what I have said,' protested Mullynax before being remanded in prison.[12] Bartholomew Ward, a tailor of Littlebury, remarked in April 1603 'that the king that was proclaimed was not king of England till he was crowned, and that it were pity that a foreign king should be king except it were his right . . . and that there was no law till our king's majesty hath enacted a parliament but God's laws, and that there were as wise men in England to have been king as the king of Scots'.[13] John Sileto, a butcher of Earl's Colne, similarly said of King James: 'he is no king; he is no king till he be crowned.' John Walden, a blacksmith of Pleshey, declared in May 1603 'that we neither had a prince nor laws'. Edmund Hall, a labourer of Aldham, asserted that 'King James is not our lawful king, nor ought not by the word of God to be received by us as our king because he is come in as a false Christ'. Henry Collyn, husbandman of Writtle, announced publicly, 'by God, I do not care a turd neither for the king nor his laws'. Each of these speakers was judged guilty of speaking sedition, and each was remanded to gaol until they could negotiate their release.[14] Their humble artisan status in no way inhibited their voicing of political opinions.

A legalistic antinomian current recurs in these outbursts, suggesting a popular constitutional literacy that confused the king's rights by accession with the legitimacy afforded by his coronation. It was as if the death of Elizabeth created an interregnum, in which the royal writ did not run. A few people ventured the notion that the new king's reign did not begin until a parliament gave it validation. Some of the conspirators promoting the cause of Lady Arbella Stuart also considered James Stuart no king until his coronation on 25 July 1603.[15]

Henry Glascocke, a husbandman of High Easter, Essex (apparently a Roman Catholic), took advantage of this liminal moment—between the death of one monarch and the coronation of the next—to declare his violent hatred of Protestant clerics. He concluded a diatribe on 31 March 1603 by saying, 'if I might have the blood of one of these priests I think it would be the means whereby I should enjoy heaven'. Cautioned by his neighbour Hugh Osborne to be careful what he said, Glascocke retorted: 'I care not what I say, there was no law now.'[16]

A similar notion prevailed in the Lincolnshire fenland, where commoners took advantage of the change of regime to resist 'the drying and laying dry of the said fens and wastes'. A riot against invasive drainage broke out at Deeping St James on 1 April 1603, less than a week after King James's accession, when William Smith, labourer, and Roger Horner, a fisherman, made 'lewd and seditious speeches' and threatened to kill some of the drainage workmen, 'openly saying that there was no danger...for until [King James] was crowned there was no law, wherefore they might do what they would, for that the parliament could clear all'. Another labourer, Thomas Wells, justified his violence against the fen enclosures 'as one greatly moved with the wrong done to our sovereign lord the king in his soil'. He even bid the workmen to depart 'in the king's name' because he had previously petitioned 'that the common in the fens might not be taken away from [him] and other poor people thereabout'. Though their cause was doomed and retribution swift, these poor commoners were ready to argue constitutional principles. One appealed to the authority of the crown, while another asserted that the kingdom's laws were currently suspended. Their theory was naive and muddled, but their voices were assertive and robust.[17]

Elsewhere in Lincolnshire a few months later, John Hacket, gentleman, 'not having the fear of God before his eyes, but out of his turbulent and disloyal heart...spread abroad and published many slanderous and scandalous speeches' against the new monarch, so the indictment against him declared. Hacket claimed that King James was a papist because a popish book was dedicated to him, and he warned a gathering of gentlemen and clergy 'that the king of France shall come with a backwing and murder them all, and that when the land were weakened he would alter our religion and bring up popery again'. Witnesses for Hacket allowed that he had spoken unwisely, being 'much terrified with the boasts of the papists', and one of them concealed these speeches, 'in regard that he did love and wish well unto the said Hacket, who at that time was his landlord'. But eventually these words reached the ears of the constable, and thence to crown prosecutors, who pressed charges against Hackett in Star Chamber.[18]

He Shall not Long be King

More seditious tongues wagged after King James was firmly established on his throne. In March 1605 Robert Ashby, cooper, of Rye, Sussex, was found guilty of saying, 'I would the king had never come into this country'.[19] The

Cornish yeoman John Penrose predicted in February 1606 that James Stuart 'shall not long be king'.[20] Henry Crompton of St Giles in the Fields appeared before magistrates in 1611 for saying, among other excesses, that the king 'would have his crown pulled about his head'. But after confessing in open court 'that he was drunk when he spake these words', Crompton was allowed to go free, only paying five shillings to the churchwardens for the poor of the parish.[21]

Several people threatened to kill the king, or wished him dead, though none of them was condemned for treason. In Wales in 1614, describing Llanidloes as 'a town of bad government', Evan David Thomas of Radnorshire said it 'ought to be burned, and if our king were here, he should be burnt too'.[22] In Somerset in 1617, in the course of a village quarrel, William Lavor of South Petherton struck a neighbour, 'saying he would kill him if he were King James'. These were dangerous words, but Lavor insisted that he was misquoted, he had actually raised his voice against James King, not King James. The matter might have ended there, had not one of the villagers charged the constable with concealing Lavor's treasonable words. The case went to the assizes in 1618 and was discharged 'ignoramus', but suits and counter suits between the parties were still active five years later.[23] Much more serious was the case of William Goodridge, who was awaiting trial in Newgate in 1619 'for using of traitorous speeches against our sovereign lord the king, saying if the king use us not well, we will cut his throat'.[24]

In September 1621 Norwich magistrates imprisoned 'two gentlemen who mishandled themselves' by speaking 'dangerous words concerning his majesty' after an evening at the Dove tavern. Staggering into Dove Lane, John and Thomas Woodhouse, the sons of Sir Henry Woodhouse, fell into a midnight brawl with the watch and made 'unfitting speeches' against the constable who tried to restrain them. When one of the officers attempted to confiscate their swords, Thomas Woodhouse protested 'that if the king should offer him such wrongs...he would kill him'. This was treasonous speech, which brought the Woodhouses before the sheriff and the mayor. After a few days in gaol the young men were released on bond while local authorities asked the Council for 'direction'. The only mitigating factor was that the Woodhouse brothers were 'overgone in drink', though this, the mayor noted, 'is not to be a privilege to them'. Friendly witnesses claimed that 'the said gentlemen at the time of speaking had with overmuch drinking bereft themselves of the true use of discretion and understanding'. They had, to be sure, no 'disloyalty or evil mind toward his majesty', but were so incapacitated at the time that they were 'likely to have fallen down the stairs' or 'to have fallen down in the gutter'. By Council instruction the matter was referred to the next Norwich sessions, where the powerful Sir Henry Woodhouse no doubt had some sway.[25]

Yet another alehouse conversation at Wormley, Hertfordshire, gave rise to 'vile words of the king' in April 1623. When the evening conversation turned to a recent incident of poaching at Theobalds Park (the king's estate), Christopher Chandler, a painter from Barnet, froze the room by saying: 'I would that his deer were hanged, and he too.' Edward Bashe, gentleman, the highest ranking of the drinkers, remonstrated: 'thou rogue, meanest thou to be hanged, or knowest thou what thou speakest?' Everyone construed Chandler to be speaking of the king, and by next day his words had reached the local justices. Under examination, the offender claimed to remember none of the conversation, but witnesses offered extenuating circumstances. His defence was not drunkenness but weakness of mind. Chandler, it was said, had served long before with the Earl of Essex, then became a painter, 'where by overstudying of himself he became distracted'. Twice a year for the past seven years he was said to be 'mad for the space of three weeks together', and he had once been committed to prison at St Albans 'lest he should have made away himself, his wife and children'. Allowing that Chandler was 'a kind of brainsick fellow and of so abject and mean condition', the Council decided he was 'not a subject worthy to be made an example in so high a nature as his offence deserves', and released him with a whipping.[26]

Though their words were vile and undutiful, none of these speakers threatened serious harm, and none paid the ultimate price. Their folly, their drunkenness, or their weakness of mind provided sufficient excuse. In another age, in the 1530s, such words might have cost them their lives, but, though these sins of the tongue demeaned his sacred majesty, they did not endanger the Jacobean regime.

Queen Elizabeth of Infamous Memory

A contentious strain of discourse under James I affected the king's honour by dishonouring his royal predecessors. Foul and scandalous remarks about Queen Elizabeth did not cease with the virgin queen's death, nor were the misdeeds of the earlier Tudors fully forgotten. Dynastic histories as well as *arcana imperii* were exposed to public comment in the most egregious *scandalum magnatum*.

A Norfolk gentleman, Henry Wayte of King's Lynn, was sentenced at the Norwich assizes in July 1605 'for sundry scandalous and opprobrious speeches' and 'unreverent and contemptuous words' against the late Queen Elizabeth, though his actual remarks are not recorded. The offender was made to stand in the pillory for an hour, to pay a fine of a hundred marks, and to be confined to Norwich castle for half a year. Eight years later Wayte's fine was still outstanding, and the king ordered the Exchequer to allocate it to a former yeoman of the guard in lieu of a pension, thereby reviving memories of the case.[27]

In addition to repeated tales of Queen Elizabeth's sexual misadventures there were also rumours that Lady Arbella Stuart, King James's cousin and a plausible claimant to his throne, had borne a bastard child. In 1618 the rumour was said to be 'voiced but not believed, hissed at by the common sort, slighted by the greater, listened to as a fable, till at last it landed at the ears' of the venomous countess of Shrewsbury, who spread it abroad. As the Star Chamber judges remarked, 'in state there is no greater error than addition to blood royal by fiction'. This was as true under James I as under his Tudor predecessors and Stuart successors. If such a child existed, 'great dishonour were it to have the royal blood concealed, but if counterfeit, no greater blemish to a state'.[28] From Henry VIII to Charles II, a king's bastards might be openly acknowledged, but there was no countenancing a by-blow from a queen.

A 'damnable libel' against the king was carried from the Midlands to the North early in 1606 and spread among tailors, drapers, and tradesmen. Some people allegedly copied it or recited it from memory. Writing to Secretary Cecil in February 1606, the incensed dean of Durham described the text as 'full of treasons' and historical errors. A Durham cleric who heard the libel read aloud declared it 'most abominable false and treasonable matter'. Purporting to be a letter from Jesus Christ, 'but indeed from the devil and his imps', the libel derided the royal supremacy, slandered Henry VIII and Queen Elizabeth, reminded readers that the new King James was 'a stranger', claimed he was ruled by 'ungodly counsel', and predicted the overthrow of the 'proud and mighty' persecutors of the Roman Catholic church. There was little the authorities could do except to be watchful and to attempt to trace the distributors of these 'seditious and scandalous' words.[29]

A dinner conversation at a gentleman's house in Huntingdonshire in July 1610 led to a complaint in Star Chamber about words 'tending to the dishonour of the late Queen Elizabeth'. A 'private, familiar and friendly conference' degenerated into a daggers-drawn brawl when the table talk turned to recent writings by the Jesuit Robert Parsons (1546–1610), and their refutation by the bishop of Lincoln, William Barlow (c.1565–1613). The diners disagreed whether these works were 'invectively written' or 'wittily and learnedly done', and began to raise their voices and reach for their weapons. They had evidently been reading William Barlow, *An answer to a Catholike English-man* (1609), which attacked Robert Parsons, *The judgment of a Catholicke English-man living in banishment for his religion* (1608). When John Brudnel accused Parsons of 'railing against his sovereign', Thomas Belley observed that the Jesuit, in conscience, 'did not hold the said Queen Elizabeth for his sovereign'. 'No more does the rest of them, meaning Jesuits and papists, that rail against our sovereign,' responded Thomas Bedell, to which Brudnel, 'in great heat and choler', told Bedell 'that he did lie'. These were fighting words, which led to challenges and bloodshed, and disgraced the household of the host Sir Robert Payne. The incident shows not only how readers could respond to text, and how text could spark debate, but also how speech could transform a situation.[30]

Later in King James's reign a Lincoln's Inn lawyer, Thomas Shepherd, made 'unreverent and undutiful speeches...touching the honour of the late Queen Elizabeth of famous memory, and of the Queen Anne Boleyn her mother'. Shepherd was confined to the Marshalsea for his offence, because King James found 'it touched the honour of his immediate predecessor, whereof his majesty of his princely wisdom hath been ever careful'.[31]

None, however, was so outspoken as the Jacobean Catholic Henry More, whose verbal assault on the king's predecessors is recorded in Star Chamber depositions. A recusant gentleman from the north of England, More had previously been questioned by the Council at York 'for drawing and persuading people to popery'. By 1623 he was an inmate of the Sheriff of Middlesex's prison in London. There his 'audacious' chamber talk with fellow inmates and his table talk at the prison keeper's house in Holborn brought 'scandal, dishonour and depravity' to both church and state. According to the Attorney General, Sir Thomas Coventry, More's words were 'lavish and licentious' as well as 'opprobrious, insolent and malicious'. Several witnesses reported that they heard him 'many times at dinner and supper' with 'occasion of speech and discourse', when More 'would always be talking of religion'. Most outrageously, More said that 'Henry VIII was a tyrant, a most vicious king, a sacrileger, and that the Protestant religion now professed within this realm did spring out of King Henry's codpiece, and that... King Henry was a very devil in hell'. He also said 'that Queen Elizabeth was a bastard, a tyrant, an usurper of the throne, a parallel with Pope Joan [who was a whore and had a bastard], and a pisskitchen, and... was in hell with her father'.[32] Each of these insults against the reforming Tudors served to scandalize their Stuart successor.

A Turd to the King

As in other ages, a background murmur of seditious speech echoed through Jacobean England, rising in intensity with changing political circumstances. Country magistrates wrote regularly to London citing 'words against the king's sacred majesty', enclosing copies of examinations, and acknowledging their 'duty to acquaint one of his majesty's honorable council with it', and 'to acquaint the king with it' himself.[33] The assize courts heard dozens of cases of this kind, and their records preserve scraps of remarks against royal authority. The Council generally pounced upon every hint of sedition, and attempted to distinguish disloyal language from ill-considered badinage. Seditious utterances were often rooted in local and petty grievances, fuelled by alcohol and fury, as well as religious and political frustrations. The words could be reckless, scatological, and undutiful, though the speakers often pleaded mitigating circumstances.

Thomas Huddeswell, labourer of Bonnington, Kent, allegedly declared to a neighbour in 1605, 'a turd for thee and the king', but the assize jury found him not guilty.[34] Another man, Daniel Taylor, appeared before the Middlesex sessions in May 1606 'for speaking certain scandalous and traitorous speeches against his majesty', though the offending words are not recorded.[35] Thomas Gibson, a sailor of Erith, Kent, spoke seditiously in 1607, claiming 'that the king's majesty was an ass, and that he, Thomas, would make a fool and an ass of him'.[36]

In Jacobean Wales in 1613, when the mayor and sergeant of Machynlleth attempted to arrest Humphrey Thomas, explaining that they were the king's officers, Thomas replied, 'turd to thee, turd to thy master, and turd to the king for appointing such officers as you to poll the town'.[37] In January 1615 one Scroggs of Cambridge was committed to prison for 'lewd

speeches . . . touching the King of Denmark [King James's father-in-law] . . .
his majesty our sovereign hath taken notice thereof'.[38] Later that year
Francis Rea of Billingsley, Shropshire, became a fugitive after making
'undutiful and strange speeches . . . against the king's most excellent majesty'.[39] James Howeton was indicted at the Middlesex sessions in 1617 for
speaking 'traitorous words against his majesty'.[40] In December that year,
'being distract and mad', the anabaptist William Ellis was confined to
Bedlam for his 'lewd and scandalous words against his majesty's sacred
person'.[41]

In May 1618 a London tailor, Passwater Sexbie of St Sepulchre's, committed 'an audacious villany' of wordless speech when he threw his hat at
the king's face when his majesty was passing through Holborn in his coach.
The Council determined that 'he was much distempered with drink at that
time, which may save him from that severe punishment which otherwise he
might deserve'. Sexbie was whipped at Bridewell and 'in the place where
the insolency was acted', and released after three months of detention.[42] The
incident reveals how close a commoner could get to King James.

Another young Londoner, the apprentice Matthew Mason, was examined in April 1619 'for divulging by letters certain false, scandalous and
seditious news concerning the sacred majesty of the king and the state of the
realm'. Mason's crime was to include in a letter to his family in Lancashire
news of a prophecy 'that there is like to be great change in England', and
reports that an apparition of 'a hand and a sword risen out of the ground' had
so frightened the king that he had taken to his bed. The letter was read aloud
in the streets of Wigan, and a copy was plastered on a chest, so the words
passed into public parlance. For his part in this scandal, Mason was whipped
and held at Bridewell by order of the Privy Council.[43]

Also in 1619, a Lincolnshire clergyman, Avery Partridge of North Scarle,
came under scrutiny 'for speaking of certain scandalous and seditious words
against his majesty'. There was no apparent religious edge to these words,
but they were dangerous nonetheless. While he walked in the fields with
George Thompson, discussing the tithing of Thompson's hay, conversation
turned to 'the cheapness of corn and the scarcity of money, and the reason
thereof'. Partridge allegedly asked, 'how can money be plentiful, seeing that
the king hath given leave for the transportation of gold out of England? . . .
We dare not say that the king is a traitor to our land, but we may say he is a
traitor to our purses and a robber unto our country.' These were dangerous
words, which farmer Thompson was quick to report. Local justices took up

the matter, and held the minister in Lincoln castle without bail until the Privy Council could make its determination. Partridge, for his part, denied the offensive words and said that he and Thompson spoke 'mere matters of husbandry'. Evidence emerged that the accusation had been 'devised and forged in malice', after an argument between Thompson's and Partridge's wives about seating in church. Claiming to be 'like sheep without a shepherd', parishioners loyal to Partridge sought their minister's reinstatement. They also testified that his accuser, George Thompson, 'hath always been a very troublesome fellow, and malicious, daily living in so many contentions, quarrels and suits with his neighbours, and so full of dissembling, crafty devices, flatteries, scoffings, backbitings, lies, railings and such kind of bad actions'. Parson Partridge, on the other hand, always prayed for the king and exhorted his people 'to all obedience and reverence unto his majesty and his laws'. Each man was guilty of sins of the tongue, but it could not be proven that anyone had spoken treason or sedition, and the matter was allowed to rest.[44]

In October 1620, 'falling in talk of the wars in Bohemia', the butcher Hugh Drayton made offensive remarks that incurred the wrath of the Jacobean regime. A former soldier aggrieved about his lack of pension, Drayton allegedly said that, 'if the king commanded him to go to the wars, God confound him body and soul if he would not go; and further said, in respect he had not his pension, that he [the king] was a villain and that the king of Spain would prove a better man'. This scandalous and unpatriotic outburst led to Drayton's imprisonment at Warwick, and then to a series of letters and petitions as his family and friends tried to get him released. Nobody denied that he had offended, but instead they used the common excuse that he was 'so far in drink' that he knew not what he said. A petition subscribed with seventy-seven names declared Drayton 'inoffensive to us his neighbours'. However, they explained, 'he hath a weak brain, by reason of many wounds given him in wars and otherwise on his head, whereby it comes to pass that a little drink doth distemper his brain, and makes him to speak and do at those times such things as he is sorry for afterwards'. Another certificate declared Drayton 'a man *non compos mentis*' who 'cannot bear his drink', who had been 'provoked by the devil' into speaking against the king. His punishment, after six weeks in prison, was to be chastised by whipping, 'in some such sort as may not be too open and public'.[45]

Dennis Mannings of Bingham, Nottinghamshire, was reported in June 1621 for 'dangerous and seditious words ... which both concern matter of state and reflect particularly upon his royal majesty'. The offensive words are not recorded, but they precipitated a flurry of administrative activity. Magistrates at Mansfield referred them to the Privy Council, who referred them back to the justices of assize, with instructions 'to take the cause and the merits of it seriously into your consideration, and thereupon to proceed according to law and justice'.[46] Later that year one Whitby was held in gaol at Chester for his 'scandalous speeches against the king.[47] Also in 1621, when Devonshire magistrates advised the Privy Council of William Sharpe of Tiverton's 'unseemly speeches delivered of his majesty... to us much odious', the Council thanked them for their diligence, but referred the case to the Devonshire assizes because they were preoccupied with 'many other matters of greater importance for his majesty's service'.[48] Amidst a worsening international situation, with English reluctance to back the Protestant cause, the Council became aware of a spate of seditious speech, including the claim that King James favoured Spain and the Scots while putting down England and the Welsh.[49] It was about this time that the French ambassador in England reported to his masters, how strange was 'the hatred in which this king is held, in free speaking, cartoons, defamatory libels—the ordinary precursors of civil war'.[50] Officials judged some of this speech to be treasonable, but no speaker is known to have suffered a traitor's death.

There is no telling what Thomas Keppins, husbandman, of Kingswood, Hampshire, said that caused him to be gaoled at Winchester in January 1622, but his speech included 'vile and treasonable words... touching the sacred person of the king'. Found guilty at the spring assize, he was reprieved from execution 'till his majesty's further pleasure be known'. Keppins was still imprisoned in March 1622, but his ultimate fate is uncertain.[51]

A Surrey man, Robert Blinckerne, was accused in March 1622 of uttering 'treasonable speeches touching his majesty'. In the course of an argument the previous August over the sequestration of some hay and corn, when the sheriff's deputy displayed his royal warrant Blinckerne 'bid the pox take [the king] with divers other railing speeches against his majesty'. He insisted he would keep his corn 'in despite of the king', and then said 'that the king was an unjust king, an usurper, and not worthy to wear his crown', and 'that he would be revenged of his majesty'. Blinkerne's principal accuser was Timothy Pinckney, a gentleman with an interest in the disputed corn, who presented his information half a year after these 'lewd and disloyal speeches' had been spoken. However, Southwark magistrates advised the Council, 'well knowing that malice may inform a truth, in a case of so dangerous a consequence we offer nothing by way of excuse to extenuate the offence of the said Blinkerne, in uttering any disloyal or undutiful speeches concerning the sacred person of his most excellent majesty'. Ordering a full examination, the Council observed that 'the words are of so high a nature as they are in no wise to be slighted nor passed over'. Blinkerne himself claimed not to remember his words, but used the common excuse that he had 'taken too much drink, whereby he was much distempered and knew not what he said'. Witnesses described him as 'drunk and mad', his outburst fuelled by alcohol and anger. This was not the most honourable excuse, but it evidently achieved his discharge, 'to be corrected with the whip' at Bridewell and then released.[52] Another offender, Thomas Russell, went to the Gatehouse in July 1623 for 'words spoken against the king's majesty', and was still in prison three months later.[53]

Finally, in August 1624, an argument between two gentlemen inmates of the Marshalsea prison grew into words of treason. According to Robert Mortlock, his cell-mate John Bailey used 'uncivil language', threatening to 'kick him about the yard', adding 'that he would kick him that wore the crown of England if he talked so to him'. Mortlock 'advised him to forbear such speech, and not to meddle with or mention the king or lords of the council', but this only triggered another outburst: 'Bailey grew hereupon more outrageous and swore God damn him, he would kick the king himself.' Mortlock, 'according to his duty, knowing such speeches were not to be concealed' (and no doubt imagining that his own penal circumstances might be improved), reported them to the prison authorities next morning, who relayed the information to the Council.[54] There was little chance of prosecution with only one witness, but the government persisted in examining these incidents of disloyalty and disaffection.

Catholic Disgraces

In the contested religious culture of early modern England it was hardly surprising that religious passions should lead to seditious language. Religious enthusiasts of all persuasions, godly Puritans as much as Catholic recusants, could readily talk themselves into trouble. Most Jacobean Catholics stayed quiet or avoided trouble for as long as possible, but a few, like the prisoner Henry More, more than made up for the general passivity.

The Cornish yeoman John Penrose, who predicted in 1606 that King James 'shall not long be king', was 'a recusant, a man of mean estate and condition, and yet an intelligencer to and from London to recusants' in the West Country, according to justice Nicholas Prideaux. As a matter of 'duty and loyalty', concerning the safety of the realm, he was someone to be watched. But magistrates also discovered an enmity between Penrose and his brother's family, who may well have accused him out of malice. When Penrose's sister-in-law told him late in 1605 'that his cattle would be driven for the king... he replied, let him drive them quickly for he shall not be long king'. When she related these words to the authorities, it was, Penrose claimed, 'to abridge him of his life, because after his death a tenement... will be profitable for her'.[55] The Privy Council, like the historian, could only guess whether Penrose was part of a Catholic threat, the victim of family jealousy, or simply someone troubled that his cattle were about to be distrained.

One of the most notorious cases concerned the lawyer Edward Floyd, whose 'disgraceful speeches... derogatory to his majesty and his royal blood' exercised both houses of parliament in 1621. Floyd, an Inner Temple lawyer of Welsh gentry origin and by report a crypto-papist, served as steward to two aristocrats, the late Lord Chancellor Ellesmere and the Earl of Suffolk. For complex reasons involving land and politics in Wales, and 'abuses offered to Sir Francis Eure', Floyd found himself a relatively privileged prisoner in the Fleet prison; it was a parliamentary investigation of the warden of the Fleet that brought his verbal indiscretions to light.[56]

Sometime around Christmas 1620 Floyd heard news of the battle of the White Mountain near Prague and the collapse of the Protestant cause in Bohemia. Conversing in the Fleet with Dr Pennington, another elite prisoner, he remarked 'he heard that Prague was taken, and that goodwife Palsgrave [Princess Elizabeth] and goodman Palsgrave [Prince Frederick] have taken their heels and were run away... What would now become of the lad, Bess must come home again to her father.' When Floyd said this, according to Pennington, 'he garnished his face with laughter and made himself merry at it'. Pennington staunchly proclaimed it the duty of every Englishman to redeem the Stuart princess, to which Floyd responded, 'go to, I see thou art a fool'. He then offered to 'drink a health to the confusion of the king of Bohemia, who had as much right to that kingdom as he

[Floyd] had to be king of Wales', to which Pennington replied (with reference to the Gunpowder Plot) that he was 'fit only to blow up parliament houses and to murder kings'. Report soon spread of this scandalous exchange, and the speakers and witnesses were called to answer before the House of Commons. For almost a month, from 28 April to 26 May 1621, parliament concerned itself with an episode of dangerous speech of the sort normally handled by the Privy Council, local magistrates, and justices of assize.

Floyd's reported comments touched a spray of raw nerves. 'I hear the honour of two incomparably noble princes called in question by a fellow as base as they are worthy,' quoth Sir Francis Kinistone. To call the king's daughter 'goodwife' and his son-in-law 'goodman', and to refer to them familiarly as 'the lad and Bess', was insulting and demeaning, reducing the blood royal to the level of commoners. To laugh at this tragedy for the house of Stuart, this disaster for international Protestantism, was to reveal a diabolical heart. The worst suspicions were confirmed when search of Floyd's quarters yielded rosary beads, an *agnus dei,* a friar's girdle, a crucifix, and varied relics, including ' a piece of our Lady's petticoat and of the cross'. This cache of Catholic devotional material was almost too good to be true, and some might wonder whether it was planted. Sir Edward Coke observed, 'he is a very pernicious fellow and hath a popish heart, though outwardly he conform'.

Though Floyd denied the alleged speeches, the Commons found the accusation convincing. His words, they agreed, were 'disgraceful . . . false, malicious and despiteful . . . contumelious and derogatory . . . lewd and dangerous'. They were clearly scandalous and undutiful, even if they could not be construed as treason. The question was what to do about them. In an extraordinary debate on May Day 1621, members of the House of Commons vied with each other to propose the most severe punishment. 'If we do not punish such in time, we may cry oh Lord it is too late,' warned Sir Robert Phelips. Others suggested ways to 'make this incomparably wicked man an example to all others'. Several proposed that he be whipped, and one, Mr Whittson, suggested the refinement of 'hot bacon dropped on him at every six lashes'. Others thought Floyd's tongue should be slit, or bored through, and that he should be branded in the face. Sir George Goring thought he deserved to be hung. 'Ill words merit blows, ergo, stripes, pillory,' said Sir John Strangeways, to which Mr Angel added, 'gag in his mouth that he may not cry to have any man pity him'. Members were at risk of making intemperate speeches themselves until Sir Edwin Sandys cooled the frenzy. 'He is a gentleman, let him not be whipped till degraded . . . let us not be so overcarried with affection as that we punish illegally and irregularly. And because his words are not slander but contempt, lay all contempt on him, pillory, papers, prison, fine.' The house concluded that Floyd should pay a fine of £1,000, stand in the pillory at Westminster for two hours, ride backwards on a horse to the Old Exchange to be pilloried again, then return to harsher incarceration in the Fleet.

In their urgency to punish Floyd the Commons had not fully considered their jurisdiction in the matter. It was unprecedented for the lower house to pass sentence of that kind. The king thanked the Commons for their 'zeal to punish such as would cast a blot of dishonour upon his blood', but Floyd, he reminded them, was *his* prisoner. John Chamberlain reported what 'most say . . . that the king thinks better to suppress such scandalous speeches than by [Floyd's] punishment to blaze them further abroad'. The Lords, meanwhile, asserted their privilege as a court of record with jurisdiction over servants of the nobility. Committees and subcommittees conferred, and the Commons yielded judgment. Sentenced more severely by the upper house on 26 May, Floyd was now 'to pay five thousand pounds, to be ungentlified (or to bear no arms), to ride with his face to the horse tail (and the tail in his hand) to the pillory in Cheapside, there to have the letter K branded in his forehead with a hot iron'. (Prince Charles, who was learning statecraft, rejected the planned S for slander, and 'would have it a K' for knave.) A few days later Floyd was to be pilloried in like manner at Westminster, then whipped to Newgate, and there to lie in the dungeon during life'. All this was carried out, Chamberlain wrote on 2 June, except the whipping, 'which was remitted in regard of his age, being about three score'.

Writing to Dudley Carleton, Chamberlain remarked that 'the sentence is by all or most thought hard and severe enough for any words how malicious soever (except blasphemy), and the censure given by the lower house was commended as more reasonable, whereupon much speech and dispute hath grown'. Joseph Mead's letters also tell Floyd's story. The news networks of Jacobean London were abuzz with commentary upon this punishment for dangerous talk. If anyone remarked on the irony of a parliament obsessed with its own privileges punishing the speech acts of others, it is not preserved in the record.[57]

In the end Floyd's fate was not so bad as it might have been. He escaped the whipping, though not the disfigurement and the ordeal in the pillory.

The fine was crippling but unpayable, and it may have been remitted. The horror of perpetual imprisonment ended after six weeks when the king exercised his prerogative of mercy, and Floyd returned to obscurity. Floyd's wife even recovered the trunks and writings that had been seized from his prison chambers, once the 'popish beads and popish books' had been removed.

Another Catholic prisoner, the priest Edmund Cannon, faced examination in March 1622 for his allegedly dangerous words the previous summer. A privileged prisoner in the Clink, Cannon enjoyed dining in the prison governor's house at Upminster. On one occasion, when conversation turned to the whipping of some London apprentices, Cannon allegedly said 'that we were all base in respect of the Spaniards, and the king of England in respect of the king of Spain was base'. This led to the prison-keeper's wife, Mrs Davison, rebuking him, 'that he durst not speak those words, if any magistrate or person in authority should examine it'. The servant Sybil Brusse, who was waiting at the table, reported this exchange to a justice. Cannon, however, denied the incriminating words, claiming that the informer had 'inveterate malice' against him, he having reproved her for being drunk. The Privy Council evidently took Cannon's part, for it was the servant, not the priest, who was whipped and held at Bridewell.[58]

Henry More, too, was in prison in London in 1623 when he made his scandalous remarks about Queen Elizabeth and Henry VIII. He also said that 'all the bishops in England are rebels to the pope', declared that King James 'did the pope great wrong', for 'the pope was supreme head over all the churches in England', and prophesied that 'a Roman bishop' should replace the present Archbishop of Canterbury, 'to decide matters spiritual and temporal'. As for English Protestants, they 'should all have fire and faggots'.[59]

Not surprisingly, More also praised the Gunpowder plotters of 1605 and wished they had been successful. It was, he said, 'a pity that he who undertook to blow up the parliament house was not hanged up presently, not so much for attempting the deed as for that he did it not'. He bragged that 'he was once indicted at York for high treason, saying that if he had been hanged for it he had been a saint in heaven'. And, when conversation turned to the crisis in Bohemia and the loss of the Palatinate, More said 'it was pity and not fit that the Lady Elizabeth and her children should come over' to England, and 'he would not have them have any maintenance nor means from our king'. Sharing Edward Floyd's opinion, More declared that

King James's daughter and grandchildren could go begging. Warned by fellow prisoners not to speak so against the king and state, More answered, 'the devil's turd in his teeth if he spared him'. This was a seditious tirade, no less actionable because the speaker was already in prison.

Henry More's defence was that, as a Catholic, he had been misrepresented by his Protestant accusers, and was prosecuted out of malice. One witness, Robert Blofield, a Suffolk attorney, had apparently made 'libels or songs in scorn of the Roman religion, to stir or provoke the defendant to anger', including 'a song of a bald-pated friar'. Another, the cleric Nicholas Lounds, took offence when More said he was no graduate. A third, the yeoman Gregory Church, hated More for calling him 'dogbolt' and for accusing him of picking another prisoner's pocket. There were 'bitter words' aplenty among these Holborn inmates, though none could pin down precisely the day, time, or circumstances of More's verbal indiscretions. Nonetheless he was found guilty, and sentenced to a spectacular (though not capital) punishment.

News of Henry More's extravagant denunciations of the English Protestant crown rapidly entered the national conversation. People were talking about his words. The young diarist Simonds D'Ewes noted on 11 February 1624 that 'in the Star Chamber one master More was deeply censured for having spoken most unworthy and scandalous words of Queen Elizabeth, saying that the Lady Anne her mother was a whore and she herself was illegitimate'.[60] The Dorset diarist William Whiteway recorded that 'a popish lawyer about London was censured at the Star Chamber for saying that King Henry VIII did piss the protestant religion out of his codpiece', and noted More's sentence, 'to have his ears cut off, his nose slit, his forehead marked with B for blasphemy, whipped about London, and fined twelve thousand pounds to the king'.[61] John Chamberlain wrote to Dudley Carleton about More's censure 'for speaking very lewdly and scandalously of Queen Elizabeth and Henry VIII', adding 'he laughed all the while' in the course of his punishment at Cheapside.[62] The Catholic news writer Thomas More (no relation) recounted Henry More's notorious expressions:

that Queen Mary of Scotland was a martyr and the true heir to this crown; that Queen Elizabeth was a bastard, and wrongfully withheld the right from Queen Mary and her issue; and lastly, that the religion now professed came out of King Henry VIII his codpiece. This last was urged most against him as disgraceful to one that was so worthy a prince, and the foundation of the religion now professed.

Despite his claim that 'he had said nor more but was extant in print in . . . statute laws and such other books as were set forth by public authority and approbation', the offender suffered disfigurement and stricter incarceration.[63]

Another overheard dinner conversation led to the imprisonment of a young Catholic gentleman. John Chamberlain told Dudley Carleton in May 1623 that 'Sir William Monson's eldest son is committed to the Gatehouse for arguing in favour of popery at the Earl of Nottingham's table'. John Monson was charged with making 'unfit and undecent speeches' touching religion and the king. Petitioning the Privy Council for release, he claimed not to remember the offensive words, but expressed sorrow that any speech of his should cause their lordships displeasure.[64] Unfortunately we do not know what he said that was so dishonourable to King James and the Protestant religion.

The words of Thomas Rogers, however, are rendered in detail. A defiant lay Catholic, Rogers was gaoled at Northampton in February 1624 for his 'divers speeches tending to the dishonour of God, of the king's majesty, the prince's highness, and the prince Palatine'. He taunted his Protestant gaolers by saying 'that he respected the English bible no more than a ballad, for it is false throughout [with] not five true words in it'. But this paled beside his remarks about the house of Stuart. Witnesses alleged that he bragged that 'most of the servants to the king and prince were papists, and that papists were most favoured by them; that the Infanta was married to the prince and with child by him; that the Palgrave was a rascally base fellow . . . a rascally beggarly slave' and 'that he hoped when the Infanta came to see fire and faggots amongst us'.[65] Here was another Catholic subject who would be deeply frustrated by the failure of the Spanish match or any stiffening of English Protestantism.

Puritan Seditions

Godly activists of the opposite persuasion, some clerics, others laymen, also spoke rashly and seditiously. Some were outspoken against the king's declaration of sports, which permitted lawful recreations on the Sabbath. Many were troubled by foreign policy, the proposed Spanish match, and the king's rapprochement with the Catholic powers. Puritan grievances ranged from complaints about the Book of Common Prayer to England's failure to support the Palatinate. Zealous outbursts on these topics lent support to the king's opinion that Puritans were inherently disloyal. One godly activist, John Williams of Brentwood, Essex, went so far as to declare King James antichrist, his kingdom Babylon. He appeared before Middlesex magistrates in 1618 for these scandalous words, but the outcome of his case is unknown.[66]

Eavesdropping servants in January 1619 reported the incriminating words of another godly Protestant, the London haberdasher Thomas Ashton, who, 'talking of the scriptures' in the hallway of a house in the Old Bailey, allegedly said 'that the king had more mind of swearing and hunting than of the church'. Ashton vowed 'that there should be neither lord bishops nor archbishops in this kingdom'. And he also said that 'Mr (William) Gouge of the Blackfriars was a better preacher than Doctor (Lancelot) Andrews, bishop of Ely, for that doctor Andrews leaned towards the pope'. Thomas Ashton, under examination, denied these words, which identified him as a seditious Puritan. The accusation, he claimed, was malicious, for Henry Awdy and Thomas Swanne, the young men who reported him, resented Ashton's discovery of their 'falsehood' and theft. They had, he said, stolen wax from their mistress and spent the proceeds on 'evil company'.[67]

Later in 1619 Gerard Prior, the vicar of Elderfield, Worcestershire, was investigated for speaking 'very lewd and ignominious words' against the king. Preaching the previous year about St Peter's day (29 June), Prior had denounced 'playing and dancing on the sabbath day' and then 'prayed to God to turn the king's heart from profaneness'. Another report had him praying 'to keep the king's heart from vanity and popery'. Some of Prior's parishioners claimed to have been 'much discontented' with their minister's speech, with 'much muttering' after the service. One of them, Michael Besley, turning to William Nutte in the churchyard, asked, 'is the king's heart so full of profaneness that Mr Prior had need to pray God to turn his heart from it, saying afterward it was a strange manner of doctrine'. Eventually these parishioners reported their concern to a magistrate, who reported the affair to the Privy Council and bound the minister to appear at the next assize or quarter sessions. The bishop of Worcester added to Gerard Prior's troubles by suspending him '*ab officio et beneficio*'.[68]

The parish of Elderfield, however, like many others, was deeply divided, and some of Prior's flock counter-petitioned on his behalf. Neighbouring ministers also rallied to their colleague's support. It became evident that Prior had presented certain parishioners for defamation, incontinency, and drunkenness, and that their accusation against him was by way of retaliation.

The minister had endured a spate of libels and threats, and his cattle had been wounded, before his enemies denounced his 'ignominious words'. Hearing all this, the Council decided to pursue the matter no further, and after some anxious weeks the vicar was reinstated. The Council then initiated action against Prior's malicious accusers.

Another Puritan minister, William Clough, vicar of Bramham, Yorkshire, talked himself into trouble in 1619 through a series of ill-advised public remarks. A few years earlier on Whit Sunday 1616 he had declared from the pulpit

for the Father, the Son and the Holy Ghost, he cared not for them all three a rye or brown bread toast; and if my lord's grace of York did stop his mouth, a better man than he should open it, knocking and clicking his fingers divers times in most undutiful and unseemly manner, to the scandal of the whole congregation.

This was doubly disgraceful, a heretical attack on the Holy Trinity and an assault on archiepiscopal authority. But it was only a prelude. In August 1619, after some of his parishioners had attended a rushbearing at a neighbouring parish, Clough launched into an impromptu and intemperate sermon against profanity that challenged King James and his declaration of sports. 'The king of heaven', he told parishioners,

doth bid you keep his sabbath and reverence his sanctuary. Now the king of England is a mortal man and he bids you break it. Choose whether of them you will follow. Now I will tell you why the king of England makes laws against God's laws in giving toleration to those May games and rushbearing, the reason is because he durst do no other for plain fear for the safety of his own body in his progress.

These were 'lewd and undutiful words touching the sacred majesty of the king', scandalous and seditious in official eyes, and Clough was called to answer for them before the Privy Council in London.[69]

In July 1620 the Council referred the case back to Yorkshire, where Clough's mouth again generated friction. This time he told Richard Gascoigne of Bramham that 'profane and irreligious persons' were responsible for his legal difficulties, and that 'it was a plot laid against him by the papists'. Describing to Thomas Whetherall 'how he escaped about his business at London', he explained, 'he had to do with none but fools', adding: 'the king is a fool, and good for nothing but to catch dotterels, and further said he could make as good a king of clouts, and that the king was unfit to govern his commonwealth.' Clough announced that he would soon be preaching at Paul's Cross in London, 'and there he would tell them all of these things, and how evil the land was governed'. Clough also declared 'that in former times priests did rule kings, but now kings did rule priests, adding further that there were priests before kings and an altar before a crown'.

Clough's words challenged the Trinity, denied the royal supremacy, scandalized his majesty, and threatened the security of the realm. No priest or subject could be allowed to say such things, and on 26 October 1620, by order of the Council in the North, Clough returned to gaol at York castle, where he languished all winter. Petitioning for release in March 1621, Clough described himself as 'preacher of God's sacred word' (a standard Puritan formulation), remarked on his 'woeful distress', and sought to clear himself of 'those ignominious and diabolical words supposed to be uttered' by him, or else 'to die the death of a traitor'. The ploy apparently worked, and Clough was freed from his 'long imprisonment' to answer again before the Privy Council and the Court of High Commission. But his 'adversaries', as he called them, had not finished. When neither the Council nor the High Commission would impose sanctions on the vicar, his principal accuser William Oglesthorpe pressed the case in Star Chamber. There Clough's 'seditious, indecent and irreverent speeches' against King James were recapitulated, along with his 'railing . . . seditious, irreverent and contemptuous speeches' against his parishioners, and every other charge that could be found to damage him.[70]

Nicholas Smithson, the Puritan vicar of Fuston, Yorkshire, also came before Star Chamber in 1621 for saying, among other outrages, that King James and Prince Charles 'were both of them against the commonwealth and set out books contrary to the laws of God'. He had not only preached against but violently disrupted a traditional rushbearing, and 'in a great rage and fury . . . did inveigh most contemptuously and irreverently' against the king's Book of Sports. Smithson's principal accuser, the husbandman Thomas Harrison, described the minister's words as seditious, contemptuous, unlawful, irreverent, unbeseeming, and wicked. Attempting to turn the tables, Smithson presented the disorderly rushbearers as 'very profane and irreligious', and himself as an orthodox conformist, protecting the church from their 'barbarism and rudeness'. Rather than denouncing the king's declaration, Smithson said he embraced it, and read it aloud to his parishioners; the rushbearers' festivity, he said, took place BEFORE morning service, 'contrary to the words and meaning of his majesty's book'. The case turned on words as much as actions, and each side did its best to discredit the other.

According to Smithson, the rushbearers, about forty young men and maids of the parish, entered the church as he was preparing for communion, climbed on the table, 'and did wilfully overthrow the communion cup . . . and standing with their feet and shoes upon the said table and cloth did then and there stick and set up . . . certain things called toppinels, which are pieces of wood adorned and decked with gold rings, silver rings, jewels, scarves, and other such things'.[71] The intrusion led to a shouting match in which all sides spoke somewhat rashly. To resort to Star Chamber was to use a heavy weapon in a local cultural contest. Who came out best is unknown.

Though his enemies described him too as a Puritan, it is hard to gauge the roots of Sir Robert Bindlose's crimes of the tongue. In August 1621, in the course of King James's progress to the north, 'in great contempt and scorn' of his majesty, Bindlose allegedly 'swore by God's heart that the king was of no religion at all'. He was also reported to have argued that 'they were fools that paid any of the benevolence for the king of Bohemia'. And when he heard that King James had bestowed some pieces of ordinance on the Spanish ambassador, he exploded, 'is the king gone mad to give them to our enemies, that we may be beaten with our own weapons?' Bindlose was no alehouse blowhard, but was a substantial property-holder and a justice of the peace for Lancashire. His local opponents delighted to report his venality, hypocrisy, and disloyalty, among other transgressions. The charges against him ranged from 'usurious dealing and notorious oppression of poor people' to bigamy, bastardy, and incestuous rape of his own grand daughter. Religious enmity may have underlain some of these allegations, for Bindlose's principal accuser, Thomas Musgrove, also asserted 'that under the habit and colour of puritanism [he] doth shroud himself and all his foul misdemeanours, and is the cause of procuring divers private conventicles and meetings of puritans and silenced preachers at his own house'.[72]

At the other end of England, a dispute in 1624 between two Cornish gentlemen, William Ericke and Ezechiel Grosse of Camborne, spilled over from the assize court to King's Bench and eventually Star Chamber. On Ericke's information, the Attorney General charged Grosse with making 'insolent and audacious speeches . . . of a most dangerous consequence'. He had allegedly said 'that the papists in England had more favour showed to them than any protestant could have'; that King James and Prince Charles 'were rank papists'; and that the king and most of the nobility had subscribed articles 'concerning the pope his supremacy over the Church of England'. This may have been commonplace anti-Catholic hysteria, sparked by the

intended Spanish match, but it was also sedition. Grosse further compromised himself by saying that King James 'had never done good to England, but
had beggared it by giving great gifts...raised by taxes from the poor
commonalty of this land'. All he could say in defence was that the charges
sprang from Ericke's malice.[73]

Grumbles and grievances led dozens of Jacobean subjects to speak themselves into trouble, but their voices were mere irritants to the Stuart regime.
James I was secure on his throne, and secure in himself, and chose not to
over-exercise himself about minor insults to his honour. The response
would be different in the reign of his son.

6

The Demeaning of Charles I:
Hugh Pyne's Dangerous Words

Few kings were so prickly about their honour, or more insistent on the dignity of kingship, than Charles I. Few monarchs had so extravagant a sense of their supremacy, yet such an unsure command of the love and respect of their subjects. One would not know, from recent accounts of his reign, that King Charles endured a barrage of popular derision, quite apart from attacks on the Duke of Buckingham, the Archbishop of Canterbury, and Queen Henrietta Maria. Long before the revolution, indeed from the very beginning of his reign, dozens of Charles I's subjects spoke of him in ways that the authorities deemed dangerous, dishonourable, scandalous, disgraceful, disloyal, uncivil, seditious, or treasonous. He was said to be foolish, childish, and not fit to be king, though few of these outbursts have been examined by historians.[1]

Two chapters here are devoted to the demeaning of Charles I. Chapter 6 explores a case from the 1620s in which the elements of speech, law, evidence, and reportage can be examined in detail. Chapter 7 reviews a wider range of seditious talk from the accession of Charles I to the outbreak of the civil war. Both reveal sub-currents of animosity that diminished the authority of the second Stuart monarch.

The Words

King Charles had not yet been crowned when the private words of Hugh Pyne, a Somerset magistrate and Lincoln's Inn lawyer, became matters of public consequence. Some time in the autumn of 1625, on the occasion of Charles I's visit to the West Country, Hugh Pyne, esquire, asked a neighbour 'whether he had seen the king at Hinton or no'. Given the answer 'yes', Pyne allegedly responded, 'then hast thou seen as unwise a king as ever was, and so governed as never king was; for he is carried as a man would carry a child with an apple. Therefore I and divers more did refuse to do our duties unto him,' adding 'that he could have had him at his house, if he would, as well as Mr Poulett' (who was providing hospitality for the king at Hinton St George). A short while later, in the course of the same royal visit, Pyne declared of King Charles, 'he is to be carried any whither', and then said aloud, 'before God, he is no more fit to be king than Hickwright', referring to 'an old simple fellow who was then Mr Pyne's shepherd'.[2]

To liken someone to 'a child with an apple' evoked the proverb that 'if you show a child an apple he will cry for it', and that a child, like a 'witless worldling . . . doth esteem an apple more than his father's inheritance'. To say such a thing about Charles I was demeaning to the Stuart monarchy and contemptuous of the fledgling king. To call him unfit was outrageous. Erasmus in *De Libero Arbitrio* had compared a child in pursuit of an apple to the freedom and weakness of the will, an observation that might invite both Calvinist and Arminian commentary.[3] Hovering behind Hugh Pyne's words lay the injunction of Ecclesiastes, 'Curse not the king, no not in thy thought', and perhaps the observation, 'Woe to thee, O land, when thy king is a child'.[4] Although Charles I was 25 at the start of his reign—as old as Queen Elizabeth and much older than Henry VIII when they took the throne—a flavour of infantilism attached to this monarch. It could not help that till the end of his life King James referred to his son as 'baby Charles'. It was not just a question of age, however, for a 'child' had limited mental capacity as well as slender years.

Hugh Pyne's mouth brought him trouble, for he had bitten off more than he could chew. His words were reckless, certainly unwise, and arguably treasonous. But retribution did not come for more than a year and a half, when Pyne's local, factional, and political enemies brought him within an inch of his life. From his arrest in the summer of 1627, to his discharge eight months later, Pyne's case refocused attention on the law of treason, and produced a landmark determination on the criteria for treason by words.

As a gentleman lawyer, and one who had served the court, Pyne was well aware of the prohibitions against speaking ill of divinely sanctioned authority. Unlike humble artisans and haunters of alehouses, with less controllable passions, men of Pyne's class were expected to govern their tongues, and, if they spoke rashly, in drunkenness or anger, their social position usually exempted them from examination. In the case of Hugh Pyne, a member of the elite though no friend of the central government, these inhibitions and privileges broke down.

It is worth paying attention to Pyne's case because it illuminates some of the problems of subjecthood and citizenship in an era of sacred monarchy. It shows how individual critical capacities sat uncomfortably with formal assumptions about how political society should work. The case reveals not only strains in the politics of the 1620s, relating to the dominance of the Duke of Buckingham and the unpopularity of the forced loan, but also the dangers of commentary about the untested Charles I.

More than is common, the documentation in Pyne's case allows us to eavesdrop on the world of private political discourse and to retrieve words and expressions that no one intended should be written down. The charges, letters, examinations, and depositions reveal how private utterance could become public testimony, and how chains of reportage reached official attention. They show too some of the legal and political manoeuvring of a regime that was ever watchful for sedition, protective of the royal honour, and sensitive about the dignity of the crown. They also illuminate the mechanisms available to establish the truth of the matter, and the legal basis for punishing dangerous speech. Pyne's case helped to clarify the distinction between felonious and treasonable utterance and speech that was simply scandalous, undutiful, or seditious.

'The case of Hugh Pyne, esquire, upon an accusation of treason for words spoken in contempt of the king,' appears in the seventeenth-century law reports and is featured in later compendia of State Trials. Pyne's case forms a footnote to legal history, being cited in Hale's *History of the Pleas of the Crown*, Blackstone's *Commentaries on the Laws of England*, and Holdsworth's *History of English Law*. He earns half a page in the 1982 *Biographical Dictionary of British Radicals in the Seventeenth Century*, but there is no entry for Hugh Pyne in the *Oxford Dictionary of National Biography*, nor does he make more than fleeting appearances in modern historical scholarship on the 1620s.[5]

Thomas G. Barnes in his study of Somerset notes Pyne's 'animosity towards the king and Buckingham', but finds him more interesting 'as a type than as an individual'. Barnes calls him 'pompous', 'waspish', and 'rambunctious', and seems unsurprised that 'Pyne's loose talk brought him within the shadow of the gallows'.[6] David Underdown in *Revel, Riot and Rebellion* notes Pyne's imprisonment 'for declaring that the king was 'stript and governed by a company of upstarts'', and treats it as a sign of the rising 'national political temperature' of the 1620s. The phrase about being 'stript' by 'upstarts' was found not in the legal records but in the contemporary diary of Walter Yonge.[7] Wilfrid Prest, discussing 'the rise of the barristers', also mentions 'the outspoken Hugh Pyne' and his public criticism of Charles I, quoting Pyne to say that King Charles was 'as unfit to rule as his shepherd, being an innocent', based again on Walter Yonge's diary.[8] Pyne also makes an appearance in Richard Cust's book on the forced loan, as 'a short-tempered and tactless lawyer' guilty of 'a spectacular display of defiance towards both the favourite and the king', who was 'eventually tried for treason'. Cust repeats some of the most outrageous words charged against Pyne, as well as the remark attributed to his son Arthur Pyne, 'that there would be a commotion in this kingdom and that we should shortly be at one another's throats'.[9] Apart from these references, and very few more, Hugh Pyne is invisible in the English historical record. This chapter attempts to tell Pyne's story, to reconstruct the circumstances of his verbal indiscretions, and to establish their significance and context.

The Man

Born c.1570 to a legal and gentry family, Hugh Pyne was one of four sons and six daughters of John and Julian (née Towse) Pyne of Curry Mallet, Somerset. He grew up within an extended kindred linking a dozen landed families in Somerset, Dorset, and Hampshire. His brothers were George, John, and Thomas Pyne, and his sisters Ann, Mary, Elizabeth, Dorothy, Margaret, and Frances. His parents were buried at Curry Mallet, where the monument Hugh Pyne provided them in his will still dominates the south aisle. A nineteenth-century pedigree of the Pyne family includes the coat of arms granted to Pyne of Curry Mallet and West Charlton, Somerset, in 1573.[10]

Pyne's father had been a member of Lincoln's Inn, and Hugh Pyne followed him there in the Armada year 1588 at the age of 18. He was called to the bar in 1596, and the following year married Mabel the daughter of Henry Staverton of Durley, Hampshire. (The marriage took place at Cumnor, Oxfordshire, and Pyne later made bequests for the poor of that parish.) In his will, dated 1 October 1624, Hugh Pyne refers to his 'most virtuous, loving, dutiful, dear, wise, and understandingly religious wife', who died in 1618. The marriage bore a son, Arthur Pyne, who was born at Micheldever,

Hampshire, and a daughter, Christabell, born at Monckton, Dorset. When he wrote his will in 1624, Hugh Pyne was living at Cathanger in the parish of Fivehead, Somerset, about 10 miles north of Hinton St George. He named his son Arthur executor, leaving him leaseholds at Cathanger, Somerset, and Luton, Dorset. Also named were his daughter Christabell, married to the courtier Edmund Windham, and several more relations, including 'my kinsman and servant Alexander Towse' (from his mother's family), to whom Pyne bequeathed 'my best satin suit'. In a codicil dated 19 November 1628, two days before he died, Pyne provided additional legacies of £1,000 each to his son-in-law Edmund Windham and his granddaughter Mabel Windham. The will was proved in the Prerogative Court of Canterbury on 28 November 1628.[11]

Pyne's legal career flourished under James I, and he rose to become counsel to Queen Anne of Denmark and a practitioner in Star Chamber. His work for the court gave him opportunities to observe Prince Charles before the young man became king. Pyne was a bencher of Lincoln's Inn by 1613, a reader by 1616, and treasurer from 1624 to 1626. In 1610 he contributed to the refurbishment of the Inn chambers and chapel, and was a supervisor of works by Inigo Jones. In 1624 he was one of several members paying to display his coat of arms in the great west window of Lincoln's Inn. He was evidently a prosperous and well-connected London lawyer, one of the leaders of his Inn and of his profession.[12]

Pyne also gained prominence as a country lawyer and county politician. He was a Justice of Peace for Dorset from 1614 to 1626, recorder for the borough of Weymouth from 1615 to 1628, JP for Somerset from 1616 to 1626, and acting *custos rotulorum* or chairman of the Somerset Quarter Sessions from 1622 to 1626.[13] His lands and leases spanned both counties, though he paid his £20 subsidy as a resident of Somerset. In 1627, at the height of his troubles, observers described him as 'a man of great estate, £2000 per annum at the least', and he was able to make substantial bequests in his will.[14]

Hugh Pyne was also able to wield some influence in Charles I's early parliaments. His son, Arthur Pyne, was a member for Weymouth and Melcombe Regis from 1624 to 1626, and his nephew John Pyne (1600–1678) was first elected for Poole, Dorset, in 1625, beginning a parliamentary career that continued to 1653.

Making his will in October 1624, about the age of 54, Hugh Pyne was at the pinnacle of a distinguished career. His testament of faith suggests a moderate Puritanism within the mainstream predestinarian Protestantism of the Jacobean Church of England. Pyne wrote in his will of his 'assurance by faith . . . at the last day to be established in all fullness of those unspeakable and unconscionable joys and blessed immortality, which are most undoubtedly prepared for all those that have desired to serve and fear and please' Jesus Christ, and he called on his children 'to live at perpetual peace and in all holy concord and unity', remembering God's mercies.[15] In correspondence with Henry Sherfield, the godly recorder of Salisbury, with whom he had legal differences in the early 1620s, Pyne observed he was 'bound as a Christian' to seek 'that perfect and Christianly reconciliation which God straightly requires'.[16] Other associates of the mid-1620s included parliamentary Puritans and aristocrats such as Sir Nathaniel Rich, Sir Francis Barrington, and the Earl of Essex.[17] Like other gentlemen and lawyers of his age, Pyne quoted as readily from the scriptures as from the classics.[18]

The Politics

Hugh Pyne's scandalous and undutiful remarks had both local and national reverberations. The festering issues of the 1620s—the inordinate power of the Duke of Buckingham, the mustering and movement of soldiers for dubious military campaigns, collisions between the prerogative of the crown and the rights of the subject, and the legality and cost of the king's forced loan—all impinged on the gentry of Dorset and Somerset. Charles had been king for less than a year before government finance and foreign policy split the political nation. Hugh Pyne took a stand on these issues, emerging as an upholder of law and a critic of the court. He was, in the government's eyes, one of those 'turbulent and ill-affected spirits' given over to 'mischievous' and 'malevolent' designs who deserved to be punished.[19]

In the factional and ideological divisions of south Somerset, the Pynes took the one side, in alliance with Sir Robert Phelips, while their rivals, the more powerful Pouletts of Hinton St George, took the other. Hugh Pyne had high standing among the local magistracy, while John Poulett, with court connections, controlled the county lieutenancy. It was taken as a mark of royal favour when the new king visited Poulett at Hinton, and this in turn looked like a snub to Pyne and Phelips. It was that rivalry at the time of the king's visit that provided the occasion and context for Hugh Pyne's remarks.

John Poulett (1586–1649) was a devoted follower of the Duke of Buckingham, a reliable apologist for government policies, and an implacable local enemy of the Pynes. His grandfather, Sir Amias Paulet, an Elizabethan Privy Councillor, had been the gaoler of Mary Queen of Scots, his father, Sir Anthony, was governor of Jersey, and the family claimed kinship to the Marquess of Winchester. John Poulett sat in three Jacobean parliaments (developing a sharp rivalry with Sir Robert Phelips), and was deputy lieutenant of Somerset by 1624, with plentiful opportunities to clash with Hugh Pyne. A pedigree made for John Poulett's younger brother Philip c.1627–35 shows the noble and illustrious descent of the Pouletts with bloodlines back to Henry III.[20] John Poulett worked hard to ingratiate himself with the court, telling Secretary Conway in September 1626 that he had 'no other ambition in the world than to live in his majesty's good opinion and memory'. He hosted the Huguenot leader Soubise, worked hard for the forced loan in Somerset, and subordinated his own interest in local forests to the financial needs of the king.[21] News writers noted the king's favour to Poulett, 'of whose nobleness all men talk'.[22]

John Poulett's rise coincided with Hugh Pyne's fall. He was created Baron Poulett of Hinton St George on 23 June 1627, about the time when Pyne was arrested. Common report had it that 'Mr Pyne's trouble . . . is wrought by my Lord Poulett, son to the marquis, and the witnesses produced against him: one to be a blacksmith, whose alehouse heretofore he had put down; another a glazier, whom for debauchedness he had bound to his good behaviour. These accuse Mr. Pyne of words spoken at his table some two years since, concerning the king.'[23] The gossipers misidentified Poulett as the son of a nobleman (William Paulet, Marquess of Winchester), but otherwise their interpretation was accurate: an outspoken godly magistrate faced retaliation from local enemies, both aristocratic and plebeian.

By the end of the year Pyne's case had become a cause célèbre, and people across the country were discussing his risky remarks about King Charles.[24] A London news writer of 23 November 1627 mentioned: 'Mr Pyne, a lawyer of Lincoln's Inn, committed for speaking some words, implying there must needs have been some defect in the chief managers of this [Isle of Rhé] enterprise. He is since bailed, but with very great bail [of £8,000]. It is doubted how he will speed, and whether his speeches, whatsoever they are, will not be tried, if they may be made capital.'[25]

The Devonshire diarist Walter Yonge noted: 'Hugh Pyne the lawyer was committed to prison, some say to the Tower, for saying the king was stript

and governed by a company of upstarts.' Yonge revisited the case a few
months later, recalling that Pyne was

accused to have said that the king was as unfit to rule as his shepherd, being an
innocent, for which he lay committed until the next parliament. His accusers, as
'twas said, the Lord Poulett, William Walrond, esquire, Sir John Stawell; and
having answered before the Council, letters were sent down to examine further
matter against him, and his adversaries, Sir John Stawell, William Walrond and
others, to examine the business.[26]

Another West Country diarist, William Whiteway of Dorchester, wrote
under December 1627, 'at this time Mr Hugh Pyne was imprisoned in the
Gatehouse at Westminster, for saying his shepherd would make as good a
king as King Charles, but it was not proved and so he was soon released'.[27]

Poulett's agents made a catalogue of Pyne's indiscretions, which they
made public in 1627. Back in 1622, they reported, when King James
declared the recent Westminster assembly to be 'only a convention and
not a parliament', Pyne warned fellow justices to take caution. 'For, quoth
he, if the king by his proclamation shall say I am no man, is he therefore to
be believed, and will you be brought to believe that I am no man, when you
yourselves knows the contrary?' Later, when the new King Charles
demanded the names of Somerset men most capable of making him a
'loan', Pyne warned one of the deputy lieutenants 'that they should be
called to answer what they had done therein the next parliament'. In 1626,
when the Privy Council ordered a countywide muster of the Somerset
trained bands, Pyne spoke against the cost of it, commenting: 'the country is
not thus to be charged upon men's pleasures and fancies.' When the deputy
lieutenants displayed warrants to use county funds for the muster, Pyne
asserted 'that it was contrary to law', warning 'that when times served they
should answer it'. Pyne spoke publicly from the bench at the Easter 1626
Quarter Sessions at Ilchester, describing certain payments to military officers
as 'extortion' and instructing the grand jury 'to make presentment of it'.
And, rather than encouraging the county's military service and discipline, as
his duty surely required, Pyne had 'animated' at least one reluctant soldier
'to make complaint and begin suits' against crown officials, one of them
John Poulett no less, with 'prejudice to his majesty's service'. Poulett's own
honour and dignity had been impugned when Pyne remarked, on the
occasion of the Huguenot commander Benjamin de Rohan, seigneur de
Soubise, lodging with Poulett in Somerset, 'that his majesty [had] committed

M. de Soubise to Mr Poulett's custody, because he knew him to be a good gaoler'.[28] Not surprisingly, Pyne was among those justices critical of the government who were removed from the Commission of the Peace in September 1626.[29]

Writing to the court on 24 September 1626 about the progress of the 'benevolence' (precursor to the forced loan), Poulett observed that Hugh Pyne and his associates did 'as much as in them lay to burden or to disorder the business'. The Buckingham network went to work to pull Pyne down, and 'Sir James Bagg was sent to the Lord Treasurer from the Duke to desire him that Hugh Pyne might be no more the deputy custos'. Pyne, Poulett informed Buckingham, was among those 'popular men' and 'ill spirits' who were 'not well affected to his majesty's service'.[30] It was at this moment, and in these circumstances, that the Poulett faction presented their accounts of Pyne's remarks regarding the character and capacities of the king. Their attack may simply have been intended to silence or discredit Pyne for his opposition to the loan, but they came close to having him hung, drawn, and quartered.

'Pyne the lawyer . . . rages, I hear, like a mad dog', wrote Poulett somewhat gloatingly to Secretary Nicholas on 27 November, 'and though the words of such men are not more to be reckoned of than the barking of dogs and hurt as little, yet when they [are] grown too impudent they are fit to be corrected, that others may by their example be made more modest, which I wish should not be otherwise than by tying up of his tongue so that he be not suffered to plead in the king's courts, which were a punishment to him who makes his living with his tongue . . . no less grievous than hanging'.[31] The lawyer's tongue built his career, but its transgressions were his undoing.

The Case

The case against Hugh Pyne developed all through 1627 and the dossier grew thicker as his enemies gathered their resources. Poulett was gathering 'proofs' and lining up witnesses 'by whom those things will be affirmed'. One report came to Poulett's notice, and thence to the Privy Council, by way of 'one Henry Harding, an attorney, who meeting with one Cheek, a servant of Mr. Poulett, told him thus much purposely that he should tell his master of it'. Other informers included Sir Edward Rodney, Mr Emmanuel Sands, Mr William Walrond, Thomas Lambert, and William Collier, gentlemen and yeomen associated with Poulett's circle. Some of these men also tried to obtain incriminating evidence from members of Pyne's household.[32]

William Walrond, the Somerset justice who had reported Pyne's remark that the muster payment warrants were illegal, added to Pyne's problems when he wrote to Poulett on 12 June 1627 with further damaging accusations. Hugh Pyne's son, Arthur, had said, apparently with his father's approval, 'that it can never be well with England until there be means made that the Duke's head may be taken from his shoulders'. Walrond had this from William Collier, who heard it from his employer Mr Windham, who was Hugh Pyne's kinsman and fellow justice. Walrond wondered whether this chain of hearsay evidence pointed to a 'plot... in practice amongst them'. It was all grist to Poulett's mill.[33]

Sponsored by Walrond and Poulett, and perhaps even prompted by them, William Collier came forth with Pyne's words comparing King Charles to a child with an apple. 'He said that the king was a simple king and a very foolish as ever was, for that he is governed as never king was, and that he was carried as a child would be carried with an apple, and therefore himself and divers of his faction did refuse to do their duties unto his majesty.' Collier also reported Pyne to say 'that the king well knows that Mr Poulett's ancestors were good gaolers, and therefore he hath committed monsieur Sabesa (Soubise) unto him a prisoner'. For good measure, and further to stir the pot, Collier did the dirt on Hugh Pyne's son, Arthur (until recently a member of parliament). Arthur Pyne allegedly said 'that it was the basest part that ever Mr Poulett did for to insinuate himself into the favour of the Duke of Buckingham, who was the county's greatest foe and like to be the undoer of this kingdom'. And Arthur Pyne had also said 'that the votes in parliament was that there would be a commotion in the kingdom, and that we should shortly cut one another's throats, by reason that the king was so governed as he was, assuring me that it would never be otherwise until the Duke's head was set further from his shoulders'. William Collier also loyally reported his own subsequent exchange with his brother Richard, asking 'whether the king were not a wise king', to which Richard gave the correct answer, 'yes, and a wise and temperate king'. George Morley, a locksmith, described being at Pyne's house during the king's visit to nearby Hinton, when Pyne asked him 'what news he heard in the country'. When Morley replied the king was at Poulett's house, Pyne answered: 'I might have had him at my house as well as Mr Poulett if I would, for he is to be carried any where.'[34]

Thus was the case laid against Hugh Pyne, esquire, counsellor at law. Disturbed by reports of Pyne's 'malicious and undutiful speeches against his majesty's royal person and dignity', the Privy Council authorized a group of Somerset justices (including William Walrond) to conduct further examinations in this 'matter so nearly and highly concerning the sacred person and honour of his majesty'. They particularly wanted to hear from one Sanders, John Frye, Joan Hawker, the daughter of Thomas Hawker, and Pyne's kitchen boy.[35]

In late June 1627, coincident with Poulett's ennoblement, Pyne's case moved to the highest political levels. Courtiers, Privy Councillors, the favourite, and the king himself all took note of the matter. The Attorney General Sir Robert Heath and Sir Nicholas Hyde, chief justice of King's Bench, examined the initial witnesses. The Earl of Manchester, Lord Privy Seal, wrote to Hyde on 26 June, mentioning the king's interest in the examinations and asking 'what your lordship conceives upon them and the matter'. The Duke of Buckingham referred Pyne's business to Secretary Nicholas on 28 June 1627, commending it to his special care.[36] King Charles had long wished that 'seditious fellows might be made an example to others', and Pyne's case provided such an opportunity. The king would remain convinced for the rest of his reign that 'malevolent persons' (like Pyne) were seeking 'to abate the powers of [his] crown'.[37]

Pyne was in for a difficult few months, as his legal income dried up and his public credit disintegrated. Removed from his county offices and held for examination, Pyne was 'first committed to his chamber in Lincoln's Inn, then to the Gatehouse', and by the end of November 1627 he was in the King's Bench prison.[38] At the least he faced censure, and, if treason could be proved, he risked a gruesome execution and forfeiture of his estates.

Baron Poulett could not resist the opportunity further to damage his adversary, while displaying his own loyalty, by supplying more reports discrediting Pyne. On 29 October 1627 he wrote to Secretary Conway commending William Walrond as 'a dutiful and affectionate servant to his majesty', who wished to report 'some confessions of words spoken in derogation of his majesty's honour and virtues (to give them no worse phrase) which he conceives stands not with his duty to conceal'. Two humbler witnesses, the yeomen William Collier and the locksmith George Morley, came up from Somerset to give evidence, receiving generous payments 'towards their charge and expense in the said attendance'. £20 was shared between these two and William's brother Richard.[39]

Walrond, a Poulett ally and a lawyer, wrote on 14 November to inform the authorities

of some things more that George Morley will confess unto me since the messenger hath been with him, which is that Mr Pyne concluded with these words [about his majesty], 'and therefore before God he is no fitter to be a king than Hickwright, which Hickwright I have heard is Mr Pyne's shepherd and a natural fool'. I pray inform my Lord Conway of this, and Morley will confirm it on oath.[40]

Responding to this on 18 November, the Council ordered further examination of Hugh Pyne. Four days later, Lord Privy Seal Manchester instructed Lord Chief Justice Hyde to continue the offender's detention. 'My Lord, whatever your opinion shall be touching the height of the offence, yet since having spoken with the king I would wish your lordship to forbear taking any bail of Mr Pyne till you have spoken with my lords, and at the least put him upon the restraint of his own chamber till you shall hear more.' The message hints at the king's continuing interest in this case, and also the Lord Chief Justice's doubts that the case could be sustained.[41]

Trusting, perhaps, in his own legal abilities and the weakness of the evidence against him, and frustrated by his continuing imprisonment, Hugh Pyne petitioned for a speedy hearing. He was, so he informed the Council, 'unredeemably prejudiced in his reputation and living by the accusation and confederacy of ill disposed and unworthy persons'. Once vindicated, he implied, he might retaliate against the parties responsible for his malicious prosecution.[42]

Pyne's counsel for Habeas Corpus were William Noy, John Bramston, John Selden, and Henry Calthorpe—a high-powered legal team if ever there was one. These were Pyne's contemporaries and colleagues from the Inns of Court who shared his opposition to Buckingham and the forced loan; Noy, in particular, was Pyne's bosom friend and travelling companion. Their pleading at Westminster on 22 November produced 'wonderful applause, even of shouting and clapping of hands, which is unusual in that place', observed a London news writer that week.[43]

Pyne's lawyers introduced a series of 'objections' questioning the witnesses against him. Had not William Collier said that 'I should have good luck if I were not put from my place before Christmas?' Had he not said 'two years since, that he was suspected by me for a spy', and did he 'not hate me' for 'being of counsel against him' in a suit for debt? Had not Collier 'reported things amiss of me' in Easter term 1626 when Pyne had refused him counsel, and had he not threatened to 'say somewhat against me because his mare was impounded by my servants?' Had he not said, 'since he came to town, that if I touch his credit he would say more than he hath already said?' And why only now did he report the alleged treasonous words, when he had many previous opportunities in the past two years to declare them?[44]

A similar roasting was prepared for George Morley, who had previously enjoyed Pyne's trust until suborned by Walrond and Poulett. Who was present 'at the speaking of the words', Pyne demanded, and who had prepared Morley's written copy of his testimony? Did he 'not solicit my servant Maune to testify against me? Whether he moved not Maune to serve Mr Walrond, and whether he did not promise him freedom from pressing, and whether he said not to him I should not stand long, and that Maune should stand by the favour of the Lord Poulett? Whether he did not tell Maune that he was to testify speeches by him heard to be spoken by me at Christmas was twelvemonth, and whether he had been in any time of that Christmas at my house or had speech with me?'[45]

Pyne did not explicitly deny the words alleged against him. Rather, his strategy was to discredit his accusers and to suggest that they had been influenced by pressure or enmity. In support of this strategy he introduced the testimony of two former servants, Hugh Maune and Richard Frankpitt.

Hugh Maune was willing to state that George Morley had come to his house one morning with a warrant, 'in the presence of my wife . . . and demanded of me whether I were not afraid of pressing' for military service. Maune answered, 'I fear it not without a special warrant', to which

Morley said that I might be afraid well enough, for its a troublesome time, but if thou wilt say what I will have thee say thou shalt never fear pressing so long as my Lord Poulett lives, and it shall be better for thee; but thou art of a stubborn nature and wilt never do thyself good, for thou dependest on thy master who hath and shall have troubles enough of his own.

On another occasion Morley threatened Maune that a pursuivant was after him for hunting deer, or 'that the pursuivant came down to serve me for words which I had spoken or could speak concerning my master, whereto I answered that I never took notice of any words that my master spake, and then he said again I was of a stubborn nature and would never do myself good'.[46]

William Collier also tried to persuade Hugh Maune to turn against Pyne. He told Maune 'that he could help me to a good master, naming Mr William Walrond whose service would be very beneficial'. Mentioning again the 'fear of pressing', a weapon notoriously threatened against opponents of the forced loan, Collier told Maune 'that I should not fear of that, for Mr Walrond would discharge me though it cost him forty pounds'.[47] Walrond and Poulett, Morley and Collier, were in close alliance and sought to turn Pyne's household against him. They threatened legal entanglement, employment difficulties, and military impressment for those not willing to cooperate.

Finally, Richard Frankpitt, gentleman, a former servant to Hugh Pyne (who was to receive a gelding or colt in Pyne's will), identified William Collier as 'a tale-bearer between Mr Pyne and Mr Walrond, which was the cause of discontent between them'. Even before the king's visit to Hinton, Pyne had suspected that Collier was 'a spy and intelligencer between my lord [Poulett] and Mr Pyne'. Collier, according to Frankpitt, was a malcontent who 'endeavoured ... to draw him ... with an ill opinion of Mr Pyne, and spake of Mr Pyne's abusing Mr Poulett in words, and said Mr Pyne must take heed he went not so far lest Mr Poulett took advantage of it'. Collier, Frankpitt explained, was a servant to Edmund Windham, Pyne's son-in-law, 'and had by that means access to Mr Pyne's house'. He abused this position by 'carrying of tales to Mr Poulett' as well as sowing dissension among Pyne's servants. Like Hugh Maune, Richard Frankpitt was invited to change sides, 'to serve Mr Poulett, promising him that he should be Mr Poulett's steward or solicitor'. The Collier brothers had used their access to the household to report words spoken by Arthur Pyne, including his threat to 'set fire on Mr Poulett's house'. So why, Frankpitt asked, echoing Pyne's own question, why until now had they 'never spake of any words that Mr Pyne should utter touching the king or Duke?' The evidence pointed not to Pyne's criminality but to 'the malice of the confederates and their practices in this business'.[48]

The Law

There seemed little doubt that Pyne had spoken most of the words reported of him. But was he guilty of treason? If treason was 'the crime of violating or abating of majesty' or 'alienating the subjects' affection from their sovereign',[49] then perhaps Pyne's words made him a traitor. The crown asked the lawyers, 'whether the words which Mr Hugh Pyne is accused to have spoken concerning the king, being legally and formally laid in an indictment of treason and proved to the jury, be good evidence to prove the offence to be treason or not?'[50] It had to be shown not only that Pyne used the words alleged, as witnesses attested, but also that their utterance constituted treason. The law on this subject was unclear. The statute of 25 Edward III made it treason to 'compass or imagine the death of our lord the king' and to adhere to the king's enemies, 'giving to them aid and comfort'. But the statute acknowledged 'divers opinions have been before this time, in what case treason shall be said', and reserved final judgment to the king and parliament whether an offence 'ought to be judged treason or other felony'.[51]

To ponder the problem, the crown commissioned a distinguished panel of judges, including Sir Nicholas Hyde, chief justice of King's Bench, Sir Thomas Richardson, chief justice of Common Pleas, Sir John Walter, chief baron of the Exchequer, and justices Sir William Jones, Sir Henry Yelverton, Sir Thomas Trevor, and George Vernon, who debated the case at Sergeant's Inn before the Attorney General, Sir Robert Heath.[52] Many of these judges had been Pyne's associates or colleagues at the Inns of Court, and their reluctance to see a fellow-lawyer condemned may have had some bearing on their decision.

The judges assigned to review the case examined legal precedents from the fifteenth century onward that showed a variety of outcomes. Traitors under Henry VI had been committed and condemned for saying 'that the king was a natural fool, and . . . not a person able to rule the land', and that it would have been better if he had never been born. Traitors under Edward IV and Richard III were hanged, drawn, and quartered for words that compassed the death of the king, their words being construed to constitute overt acts.[53]

Citing the statute of Edward III, the judges reported on 8 December 1627 that 'it is treason to imagine the death of the king. But because the imagination of the heart can be known to none but God alone, the law requires some overt act, either by deed or word, to express it.' It was up to a jury to determine the fact of the words, but the outcome of the case would depend upon the judges' directions 'upon the circumstances of the evidence'. It was the judges' consensus in Pyne's case that 'the words themselves', though 'very foul', are not treason, yet they are 'a high misdemeanour and evidence for treason'. The words themselves, they repeated, 'are not treason, yet they are good evidence to a jury to prove the intent to be treasonable'. The multiple copying of this judgment in state papers and elsewhere testifies to its landmark importance.[54]

As Attorney General Heath explained to Secretary Conway, the judges concluded that 'no words of themselves make treason; but if a person be indicted for intending and compassing the death of the king, the words spoken may be laid down in the indictment as evidence of the fact, which matter of fact is properly belonging to the jurors to try'.[55] Justice Croke's report, repeated in *State Trials*, elaborated the conclusion

that the speaking of the words before mentioned, though they were as wicked as might be, was not treason. For they resolved, that unless it were by some particular statute, no words will be treason; for there is no treason at this day but by the statute of *vicesimo quinto Edwardi tertii* for imagining the death of the king, etc; and the indictment must be framed upon one of the points in that statute; and the words spoken here can be but evidence to discover the corrupt heart of him that spake them; but of themselves they are not treason, neither can any indictment be framed upon them.[56]

Even 'to charge the king with a personal vice, as to say of him, that he is the greatest whoremonger or drunkard in the kingdom, is no treason', according to some of the judges.[57]

Pyne was off the hook. His legal problems had not disappeared, but he was not going to die as a traitor. His words, contemporaries concluded, 'cannot touch his life'. But Pyne still had to answer in person 'in the Star Chamber, *ore tenus*', and was 'still in hold' in December 1627. The case against him had collapsed, but it was not until 16 February 1628, after the end of Hilary law term, that he was fully discharged and set free.[58]

The Vindication

Within days of his release, Hugh Pyne was elected a member of parliament. On 27 February 1628 he was returned for the Dorset borough of Weymouth and Melcombe Regis, where he had long served as Recorder, filling the seat most recently occupied by his son, Arthur Pyne. His election was part of a nationwide turn against Buckingham and the court, though it may have been engineered, in part, to secure him parliamentary immunities. Weymouth had a large borough electorate (with some seventy-seven freemen), but there is no record of an electoral contest. Pyne's appearance at Westminster in March

1628, in company with other opponents of the forced loan, was a rebuff to the government and to Buckingham, and a remarkable vindication for someone recently accused of treason. Pyne's notoriety must have preceded him into a chamber where several of the members were his former friends and colleagues. He was active in debate from April to June 1628, especially in discussion of the Petition of Right (which may be interpreted as a parliamentary effort to remedy a young king's ignorance of legal history and constitutional theory).

Parliamentary diarists captured Pyne's words at Westminster, though perhaps no more accurately than his private speech from Somerset. He spoke in favour of supply and in opposition to martial law. Speaking on 4 April 1628 he said, rather gnomically, 'the king rather shows himself a man to us than a king, yet so much the more a king in being such a man'. Perhaps that was a way of dispelling the scandal of saying that the king was like a child. In a debate about parliamentary privilege on 25 April, Pyne remarked that, 'if a man in the street should say he hopes the parliament will break within this two days, the contempt is enough to send for him': this from someone who knew what it was to be sent for, to be held in custody for his words. In May he spoke several times on the Petition of Right, saying 'this declares what the law is'. In his final speech on 5 June, after Coke had called the Duke of Buckingham 'the chief and principal cause' of all our miseries, Pyne remarked: 'I think we can hardly tax the man in question without blaming a greater power.' Who that 'greater power' was remained unsaid, but it was obviously Buckingham's master, the king of England, who Pyne had earlier likened to a child with an apple.[59]

By the autumn of 1628 Pyne was ailing. The award of a commission 'to Hugh Pyne, esq. touching Kings Sedgemoor' on 12 September 1628 came too late to revive his legal practice.[60] On 16 October he paid a fine of £10 to be discharged from his reading duties at Lincoln's Inn. On 19 November, back at Cathanger, he made a codicil to his will. Hugh Pyne died at his home in Somerset on 21 November 1628, and was soon almost forgotten.[61] Buckingham by this time had been assassinated, felled by Felton's dagger, and some people wished King Charles himself dead.

7

Dangerous Words, 1625–1642

Hugh Pyne's notorious words were not the only disgraceful, undutiful, or apparently treasonous utterances to trouble the Caroline regime. Nor was Pyne alone in judging King Charles to be childlike and easily led. Dozens of Charles I's subjects scorned him with contemptuous and dishonourable remarks. A recurrent refrain depicted the king as weak or deficient, unable to assert himself against such dominant characters as the Duke of Buckingham, Queen Henrietta Maria, or Archbishop Laud. The government responded vigorously to verbal disrespect against his majesty, but few of these episodes have been noted by historians. Their traces can be found in state papers, Privy Council correspondence, and in records of county assizes.

Pyne's case would seem to have resolved the legal question of treason by words. But, despite the key judgment that 'words alone make not treason', there were 'allays and exceptions', according to Sir Matthew Hale, who was called to the Bar in 1637.[1] Caroline Privy Councillors did not necessarily concur with advanced legal opinion, and popular culture remained convinced that certain kinds of expression were 'hanging words'. Witnesses to dangerous conversations commonly reacted by protesting 'have care' or 'take heed what you say', 'thou speakest treason' or 'men have died for less matters than this', at least so they told examining magistrates. And magistrates themselves could report words they thought 'very seditious, or rather treasonable' that others would dismiss as merely 'presumptuous'.[2]

Between 1625 and 1642 the Privy Council heard repeated reports of subjects who disparaged their monarch, who impugned his character, or who even compassed his death. Despite the courtly conceit that King Charles was the best of all rulers, an undercurrent of contempt flowed through casual conversation. The king's alleged inadequacy was a recurrent motif in popular parlance, even if it was scrupulously excised from high politics. The national conversation could be crude and irreverent, with scant regard for proprieties of discourse. It certainly made up in energy what it lacked in sophistication. This chapter shows the domain of political discourse in early Stuart England to have been wider, and sometimes nastier, than historians have often imagined. It shows the cherished *arcana imperii*, notionally the preserve of statesmen, to have been constantly eroding at the edges. It shows too a rain of dangerous remarks against a monarch who was 'more jealous of his honour, or more sensible of any neglect and contempt' than any other ruler of England.[3] The material is considered here topically, and within each topic in approximate chronological order.

Light Reports

Caroline Privy Councillors avowed that they were 'not easily credulous of light reports nor apt to take impression from the vain speeches or ejaculations of some mean and contemptible persons'. Nonetheless, their 'care and providence' for the state required them to instruct local justices to hold and examine all suspected evil-speakers.[4] False news could cause panic, and commentary upon it could lead people to speak sedition. Reporters of false rumour 'are worthy to have their tongues cut out', wrote the news writer John Pory in 1625, though they were more likely to be corrected by the pillory or a whipping.[5] By the thirteenth-century Statute of Westminster, still extant, any spreader of 'false news or tales' could be imprisoned until the originator of the rumour had been discovered.[6]

A flurry of rumours spread through the fenland market town of Wisbech in the summer of 1625, to the effect that King Charles was dead, or, even more chilling, that the monarch was about to be killed. The old King James had barely been buried when rumour spoke of another royal passing. Local magistrates worked diligently to contain this misinformation and to ascertain its source. For, without a firm foundation of allegiance, deference, and order, the royal regime was in jeopardy. Within days of the rumour's first appearance at Wisbech a trio of justices relayed reports to the central authorities in London.

Wisbech was a regional commercial centre on the river Nene, 100 miles north of London. Its population in the early seventeenth century approached 1,500. News travelled slowly in this watery world beyond Cambridge, but Wisbech was by no means cut off from the affairs of the kingdom. In October 1623 the town celebrated with bonfires and bells 'in

joy for the prince's coming home from Spain', ten days after Prince Charles
had reached London. In April 1625 there was more public festivity at
Wisbech with 'beer, bread, cakes, pitch barrels, coals and faggots spent on
the bonfires . . . when King Charles was proclaimed', a week after the new
king's accession.[7] Two months later the town heard mistaken reports of
their monarch's demise.

Something of the flow of this news, and how it made its way around
Wisbech, can be recovered from the written examinations. There can be no
certainty who was telling the truth, but the reports seemed generally
plausible and coherent.[8]

The stir began around 8 June 1625 when 'a stranger came on the back side
of the town of Wisbech' and told James Thompson, labourer, 'that the king
was dead'. Thompson shared this news with his wife Ellen, who passed it to
Henry Denny, a cordwainer of Wisbech, who spread it in turn among local
shopkeepers and tradesmen. Peter Thompson, also a cordwainer, testified
that Denny came to his shop 'and told him, saying that our king was dead
and that he was made away within these three days'. Thompson then took
this news to the nearby apothecary's shop of John Stanion and shared it with
startled customers. One of them, Richard Tylney of Wisbech, gentleman,
recalled Thompson saying, 'that he could tell me news . . . of the king, and
that he should be made away with in three days'. Apothecary Stanion
testified much the same.

Robert Birback, another cordwainer, recalled that he was working in
William Eaton's shop when Denny entered, 'saying to him that he could tell
him news'. Asked 'what news?', Denny replied: 'King Charles is dead, and
I will warrant you now the world will mend, we shall be jovial boys, we
shall have old cuffing and fighting, and old men shall be regarded, for rich
men have gotten all the goods into their hands, and will be glad to give good
recompense whereby they may be aided.' This, if true, was a remarkable
speech, for Denny did not just report the death of the king but appeared to
delight in his passing. The death of the king seemed to intimate the death of
kingship and the institution of a golden age for the populace, with joviality,
benign fisticuffs, and a more equitable distribution of wealth. It suggested a
dispensation, like the space between accession and coronation, in which the
old laws did not apply.

Denny, not surprisingly, disputed this version of events. He admitted
visiting Thompson's shop, 'but being examined what speech he had with
the said Peter Thompson concerning the king's death, saith he had not any'.

Taking every precaution, the magistrates committed both Henry Denny and Peter Thompson 'close prisoners to the gaol in Wisbech' until advised by the Council in London with 'directions in this behalf'. London's response was prompt and level headed. The Privy Council thanked the Isle of Ely magistrates for their 'care in a business which soundeth to so great consequence', but noted 'it doth not yet appear upon what root those words did spring'. They decided that Thompson should be released, with sureties for his good behaviour, but Denny would remained imprisoned, 'to be proceeded with by the judges' at the next assize.[9] The ultimate determination of the case remains uncertain.

These Wisbech stirs partook of a recurrent rumour that the king was dead or dying, or was likely soon to be killed. Similar rumours had spread about previous monarchs, including Henry VIII and Elizabeth I. In this case reports imagining the death of King Charles anticipated his actual demise by more than twenty years. They were associated, perhaps, with the uncertainty that so often accompanied a change of regime, and with the liminal period before the new king was crowned.

In Essex, too, Joseph Mead informed Sir Martin Stuteville in September 1625: 'it was added in all the country over, that our king (whom God bless) was dead, the women crying and howling as if Tilbury Camp were to come again.' The prosecution of John Orris for treasonous words and William Burling for seditious speech at the Essex assize in March 1626 may be related to this scare.[10]

Another politically destabilizing rumour surfaced in the Oxfordshire town of Woodstock in the autumn of 1625, when James Hall, a tailor from Oxford, announced to the company in Thomas Godfrey's victualling house on 12 September 'that the king was gone to Scotland, and that there was a new king proclaimed there'. 'Divers people' heard this report, and some of them informed the authorities. Judging 'the same words to be very dangerous', the mayor and justices of Woodstock held Hall in custody, so they informed the Council, 'until we shall hear your lordship's pleasure therein'. It took more than a month for the Privy Council to respond to James Hall's 'lewd and pernicious words'. Their letter to the mayor of 18 October commended him for his 'care' and ordered Hall to stay in the county gaol until tried at the next assizes.[11] The rumour may have been related to comments heard in Nottinghamshire in October 1625, 'that King Charles was not the king of England but of Scotland only, because he was born there'.[12] Another 'wondrous rumour' in the autumn of 1625 was that 'his majesty was sick of the plague, and had a sore', which turned out not to be true.[13] More rumour spread from Norfolk to Yorkshire in November 1625 that the Duke of Buckingham was imprisoned 'for giving the king's majesty poison . . . but yet by God's grace he was preserved'.[14]

In January 1626 a Captain Walker heard talk 'that the king should not live to be crowned, that he is married to the Infanta of Spain', and he attempted to report these words to the royal court. A footman brought him to Secretary Conway, who apparently dismissed the report as mere wind and noise. Without specific words and witnesses, there was nothing to examine.[15] King Charles, in fact, had married Henrietta Maria of France the previous summer, and their coronation was scheduled for 2 February 1626. Not for the last time, a commoner had latched on to misinformation, and construed it in an alarming and alarmist manner.

False reports repeatedly recurred that King Charles was dead, or would die shortly. One Hopkins of the London parish of St Sepulchre told neighbours in 1628 that King Charles would not long be their king.[16] Perhaps he heard the reports spread across the Bristol Channel from Swansea to Cornwall in July 1628 that King Charles was already dead, 'slain by the cruel hands of the . . . Duke of Buckingham'. The Cornish magistrate Edward Cosoorth was so shaken by this report, fearing 'terrible distractions' in his locality, that he attempted to keep it secret until better informed by the assize judges or the Privy Council.[17] Who could tell at the time if such news was reliable?

Thomas Ematt and Nicholas Browne, two seamen responsible for spreading this 'false and dangerous rumour', were held in custody until the next assize. The Council advised the Cornish magistrates that 'his majesty, taking notice of the strange licentious liberty now taken for irreverent and undutiful speeches and false scandalous reports', required punishment of these offenders that 'may serve for a fit correction to them and a warning to others'. It was the king's pleasure, they continued, that the judges 'apply the severity of the law' in this and any 'offences of the like kind'. The central authorities particularly wanted to identify 'the author of that report' as well as its 'relators', to discover its source as well as its distribution, as the Statute of Westminster required.[18]

Nicholas Browne said that shortly before sailing from Swansea on 8 July 1628 the news was all over the market, port, and town that King Charles had been poisoned by the Duke of Buckingham. There was, he said, 'general lamentation of the whole people, who gave out that they feared that the papists would rise up in arms and kill them in their beds'. The Portreeve of Swansea had received the news, said Browne, by dispatch from the Council of Wales, and the town began to ready its defences.[19]

Now the investigation switched to South Wales, to the source of these 'wicked' and 'dangerous' reports. It appeared that the rumour spread from Carmarthenshire to Glamorgan in the wake of a hue and cry, perhaps started to divert attention from a robbery. The Welsh reports were sent up to London on 28 August 1628.[20] But by this time it mattered relatively little whether ignorant people in the south-west believed that the king had been poisoned, for the Duke of Buckingham, the alleged murderer of the monarch, had himself been killed at Portsmouth five days earlier.

That news, too, spread like wildfire, alarming or delighting people everywhere. 'Talk of the Duke of Buckingham's death doth take up all men's minds and tongues, so that nothing else is spoken of,' Sir Gilbert Gerard told Lady Barrington.[21] It joined the rumour, fanned by a Captain Tendring, 'that there is now a far more villainous, mischievous, treacherous plot intended by the priests, Jesuits and sectaries of the Romish religion, for the subversion and utter overthrow of the reformed religion, king and state, than the papist powder treason.'[22]

At Christmas 1629 the Newark tapster James Levett broadcast 'scandalous words' that he had heard from the lawyer Thomas Buller, to the effect 'that the king himself was no divine, and that most of his majesty's council were Arminians or papists'. Both men were 'reprehended . . . for meddling in matters of that nature', and bound over to the next assizes. The words were 'much published in those parts', and Lord Keeper Coventry sent reports to the Council in case they required 'any further satisfaction therein'.[23]

Another spreader of false news, James Priest, 'a very miserable poor man who . . . can neither read nor write', was held half a year in Taunton gaol in 1629 'for speaking of words concerning his majesty's person and the state'. The Somerset judges, Sir John Walter and Sir John Denham, did their duty in sending up to London a written account of the matter. The speaker, by his own account, came from Warwickshire and had served several years as a Protestant soldier in the Low Countries. Set ashore in Cornwall after the ship on which he was embarked was taken by Dunkirkers, he was travelling overland to Coventry and had a pass for that purpose. Journeying through Somerset, he 'fell into the house of one John Hooper', a minister, whom he hoped would give him some apparel, and began to brag of his knowledge of world affairs. It was Hooper, it seems, who alerted the authorities when Priest apparently said that he knew something 'touching the hurt of the king's person', adding 'that he knew more than was fit for him to acquaint him with, then being a stranger, but hereafter he might tell him more'. When the minister pressed for details, the traveller said that he heard 'that if the Duke [of Buckingham] had lived there would have been an alteration of religion . . . that the Irish men that were about Bristol were there for a purpose to have assisted some that were prepared to invade the kingdom . . . the king of Spain was in readiness with a fleet to invade', and that the names of all Catholics of note in England 'were recorded in the king of Spain's books'. In fact this illiterate adventurer knew nothing apart from common fantasy and gossip. James Priest's revelations tapped into a climate of fear, and it was not unreasonable to hold him until his story could be evaluated.[24]

More rumours circulated in the next decade, some alarmist, some incredible. Another glimpse of the process comes from examinations before Buckinghamshire magistrates in April 1633. Henry Sawyer, mole-taker, told Sir Thomas Tyringham that he fell into company with Cornelius Sympkins, a tailor, and Christopher Coorsey, a husbandman, while walking across Lathbury fields, returning from nearby Gayhurst. Coorsey apparently opened the conversation in the conventional way by asking, 'what news he did hear abroad?' Sawyer replied 'that the king was to go into Scotland the 5th of May next, and then the papists after the king's going would rise against the protestants', predicting 'that men should go over their shoe-tops in blood before Whitsuntide next'. Sympkins's immediate response to this dire prediction, so he told the authorities, was to say 'God forbid'. One of those present asked Sawyer how he came by this knowledge, to which he answered 'that they were no small birds that did say so, but rather great ones'. Brought before Sir Thomas Tyringham, Sawyer said that all he knew on the topic he learned from his father while they were catching moles, and his father had warned him 'that he should not speak of it to any body'.[25]

Henry Sawyer was one of the king's lowliest subjects (described in some reports as a 'boy'), yet he appeared to be well informed about the king's planned travels, and dangerously knowledgeable about a possible popish insurrection. (King Charles eventually left London on 11 May 1633 and arrived in Edinburgh on 14 June.) The tailor Cornelius Sympkins had asked Sawyer if he was of the same religion as Mrs Digby, who had hired him to clear moles from her grounds, and he responded, 'what is that to you?'

Though not explicit in the surviving testimony, it seems probable that Sawyer and his father, like their employer, were Roman Catholics. Lady Mary Digby of Gayhurst, Buckinghamshire, was the widow of Sir Everard Digby, who was executed in 1606 for involvement in the Gunpowder Plot. Her son Sir Kenelm Digby was a famous Catholic courtier (and sometime church papist conformist). Her presence in the neighbourhood, and her presence in the story, lent a frisson of plausibility, if not credibility, to these rumours of popish plotting.

Fearful lest the villagers had stumbled onto a dangerous conspiracy, the magistrate dutifully reported the matter to his superiors in London. Someone associated with the Digby household warned Sawyer's father that his son had been taken into custody after speaking 'that which was not fit to be spoken of, whereof note were taken'. Richard Sawyer, the father, examined a week later about his own involvement, said he heard from Robert Johnson, blacksmith, about 'the amending of the highways against his majesty's going' to Scotland, and Johnson predicted 'much hurlyburly in England . . . before his return'. When it came Robert Johnson's turn to be examined, he simply denied 'that he spake any at all about such troublesome matter, to his now remembrance'. Another crucial witness proved equally forgetful, and for a while no further light fell on these dangerous conversations.[26]

Meanwhile, rumours of impending tumults spread across several Midland counties. The prospect of blood up to the shoe-tops was an irresistible topic of discourse. A traveller from Buckinghamshire recited Henry Sawyer's words over dinner with a minister in Northamptonshire in May 1633, adding the sinister detail that Mrs Digby was stockpiling gunpowder and armour. Another carrier of the rumour identified Sawyer as being 'of the old religion', and claimed that the weaponry was sent up from London by Sir Kenelm Digby, though under examination he acknowledged only having heard that second hand.[27]

The prime perpetrators of the rumour, Richard Sawyer and Robert Johnson, were committed to London's Fleet prison and this led to a loosening of their tongues. Petitioning for release, Johnson now acknowledged his dangerous words, but said he heard them 'spoken by an ostler dwelling at the Angel inn in Stilton', who in turn was told by a Scotsman that if the king went to the Scots they would keep him, and that the English 'should not have him back again unless they won him with the sword'. Johnson had predicted that, in such an event, 'there would be much hurlyburly and many

a fatherless child', although the imagined conflict was now between England and Scotland rather than Protestants and Catholics.[28]

What do you Lack?

Hugh Pyne notoriously likened King Charles to a child with an apple, and
said he was no more fit to be king than his simple shepherd. Others
scandalously remarked on the king's inadequacy, calling him a boy or a
fool. Contemporary authorities took these comments very seriously, so it
behoves the historian to subject them to scrutiny. They stand in marked
contrast to the loyal protestations more commonly heard in mainstream
political culture. The fact that they never appeared in print has tended to
render them invisible.

A remarkable conversation among inmates of the King's Bench prison in
the spring of 1626 led to the airing of dangerous and seditious words that
directly affected his majesty. William Wraxall, William Elworthy, and
Samuel Littlewood were held in the forced intimacy of three prisoners to
a room when Wraxall, aged 55, began ranting about the crown and the
kingdom. His chamber-mates apparently took offence, but they also took
note, and reported Wraxall's words to the authorities. Lying in his bed, at
nine at night on Sunday, 5 March, they said, Wraxall declared: 'The king
had need to look to himself. His grandfather was hanged on a pear tree. His
grandmother was beheaded. His father indeed died a natural death. His
elder brother, 'twas thought he was poisoned. His sister, she is driven out of
her country. There is a curse laid upon him or the kingdom.'[29] Only missing
from this was the claim that James I too had been poisoned, most likely by
the Duke of Buckingham.

The prisoner William Elworthy, by his own report, remonstrated with
Wraxall and told him, 'he meant not well by speaking such words', adding,
'it is not fit for us to meddle with such matters'. Undeterred, Wraxall
responded, 'with a bigger voice than before, is not all this true that I have
spoken?' and turned his attention to the king. King Charles, he thought,
'had need take a course amongst them and to sit in justice himself to look to
things, having many upstarts about him . . . He is a young gentleman that
hath much to look into in the world . . . It's a disgrace to the kingdom that
they do not take a course to help the king's sister,' with more words 'very
unfitting to be spoken' to the effect that 'God doth not bless the king or

kingdom'. The recent return of the plague and reverses at war would seem to be signs of God's vengeance.

Wraxall's bedtime observations became a matter for judicial investigation the next day, when his cellmates reported them to the marshal, Sir George Reynell. Three Surrey magistrates—Sir Edmond Bowyer, Sir George Paule, and Sir Thomas Grimes—were called in to conduct examinations, and the offensive words about the king were written down. William Elworthy declared it his duty as 'a true and loyal subject' to give his information, but the other prisoners may have sensed an advantage in rendering Wraxall's words to the authorities.

When the two informers returned to their chamber, we learn, Wraxall greeted them with 'two or three great farts, and with a flearing look said, I can fart for all this, deriding at Elworthy that he did certify the justices', and warning him he 'should smart for it'. The atmosphere was highly charged, not just by Wraxall's flatulence, for he allegedly came out with 'worse words' than he had spoken the night before, such words, by Littlewood's report, 'that if he had been a man of worth he might have had his head chopped off, had it been revealed'. Unfortunately for history, though perhaps fortunately for Wraxall, these additional words are not recorded. Considering that the offender was already in prison, and there were questions about the trustworthiness of the witnesses, the investigation went no further.[30]

William Wraxall may have spoken aloud what others secretly thought about the king and kingdom. It was, however, common 'vulgar opinion' in the late 1620s that the duke had led King Charles into catastrophic military courses.[31] Dozens of people claimed, in private, that 'the king was too much ruled by the Duke'[32] or implied that his majesty was a weakling. One such speaker, the London Scot Robert Melville (or Melvin), was under guard in June 1628 for his 'foul and undutiful' aspersions, that the duke and the king had a plot against parliament, and 'with a great army of horse and foot would war against the commonwealth'. He allegedly said 'that the Duke had a stronger council than the king, of which were certain Jesuits and Scottish-men . . . that when the king had a purpose to do anything, of what consequence soever, the Duke would alter it'.[33] This built on other contemporary libels, that the king was ruled by the duke, and that the ship of state was 'not guided by the master but his mate'.[34]

When Secretary Conway heard the report he seemed half persuaded by Melville's protestations of innocence. However, he informed Buckingham, there was no alternative but to commit him, 'because that denial is nothing against two witnesses, I neither dare discharge him or advise it. But with the best judgment I have, do think that such scandalous things as these are should be silenced with contempt, or punished exemplarily.'[35]

It may be that Melville had fallen victim to a malicious prosecution. Conway's letter to Buckingham is instructive on the government's response to such matters. A single accusation might initiate an investigation, but short of a confession two witnesses were required to sustain a conviction for treasonous or seditious speech. The state could, at any time, discharge its prisoner and let the matter drop, or remand him for further examination. As always, it was a political calculation whether to bring the case to trial or smother it in silence. On this occasion, when Melville was 'brought to the King's Bench bar to be indicted upon treason, the jury would not indict him but found an *ignoramus*'.[36]

Several weeks later in July 1628, still languishing in the Gatehouse, Robert Melville petitioned the Duke of Buckingham for release. (Significantly, his appeal was to the duke, not the king.) He was, he apologised, 'drawn by the report of the common people . . . into the vulgar error of the time, and . . . was moved inadvisedly to utter some injurious speeches conditionally touching your grace's honour'. But never, he insisted, did he mean any harm. Offering as fulsome an apology as possible, and betraying a hopeful understanding of the workings of law and government, Melville asked the duke 'to intercede with his majesty for my enlargement, which I am persuaded your grace may procure from my most gracious sovereign at a motion'.[37]

In another month the Duke of Buckingham was dead, but scandalous talk about the ruler and the favourite did not cease. On hearing the news of Buckingham's assassination in August 1628, James Farrell, a servant to Lady Wotton at Canterbury, recklessly remarked 'that he thought there was ten thousand in England who had as lief the king should be dead as the Duke'. Hauled before Isaac Bargrave (Dean of Canterbury, Justice of the Peace, and a royal chaplain), Farrell protested that he meant only 'that hearing many people rejoice at the death of the Duke he thought they would not be much grieved at the death of the king himself', which was hardly better. Bargrave dutifully reported the matter to London on 3 September 1628, noting that, despite Farrell being a papist, his intentions were not necessarily 'malicious'. However, because they concerned 'so precious a point as the life of our gracious master, the light of all our eyes', the dean thought these words demanded the Council's attention.[38]

Responding on 9 September, Secretary Conway declared that a speaker of such 'scandalous and undutiful' words should be punished 'according to the strictures of the law provided against offences of that nature'. There could be no excuse, he told Bargrave, for any 'speaking rashly of the sacred person or life of the king'. Dean Bargrave, who had preached on that very subject a year earlier, did not need persuading.[39]

The Oxford-educated schoolmaster Alexander Gill, bachelor of divinity, usher, and son of the high master of St Paul's school, was another who rejoiced in the death of the Duke of Buckingham. But Gill brought serious problems on himself by also expressing contempt for the king. One evening late in August 1628 Gill and some companions were carousing in the buttery cellar at Trinity College, Oxford, when Gill drank a health to Buckingham's assassin, 'saying he was sorry Felton had deprived him of the honour of doing that brave act'. This, he confessed, 'is a common thing done both in London and other places'. Gill embellished these 'lewd' remarks by saying that, 'if there were a hell or a devil in hell, the Duke was with him'. But he might not have been in such deep trouble if he had not also spoken unadvisedly of his majesty. Disparaging King Charles for being 'led so long by the Duke', he continued: 'we have a fine wise king, he has wit enough to be a shopkeeper to ask "what do you lack?" and that is all'. William Chillingworth, a newly appointed fellow of Trinity (already a religious controversialist), reported this speech to his godfather, William Laud, and an aggressive investigation was launched. Gill's contemptuous remarks were widely circulated in the early Caroline news culture, despite attempts by the Privy Council to keep them quiet.[40] Chillingworth's subsequent turn to Catholicism made some observers suspect that his accusation had been shaped 'not . . . for love of the king but for hatred of Gill, because he is so great an antipapist'.[41]

Several sources relayed the story of Gill's words with minor variations. The Trinity tutor Thomas Atkinson, writing to Thomas Smyth at Bristol, reported Gill's 'unchristianlike railing, indeed unmanlike speeches', describing him as 'one of a strange, hare-brained, bitter disposition'. Gill's drinking companions, Atkinson suggested, had egged him on and 'vouchsafed him audience only for their mirth's sake'. At the peak of his folly the young man 'burst out at last into these speeches of the king, I am sure they are somewhat near, I think verbatim: that he was a very weak man and fitter to stand in a shop with a white apron before him than to be a king of England'.[42] Another correspondent reported Gill saying that 'the king was a weak

man, and did ill in following the Duke so long'.[43] Writing from Cambridge,
Joseph Mead had Gill saying 'that our king was fitter to stand in a Cheapside
shop with an apron before him, and say "what lack ye?" than to govern a
kingdom'. Reporting this patently seditious speech to Sir Martin Stuteville,
Mead cautiously requested, 'do pray strike out these words afore you let
anybody read the letter', a favour that Stuteville fortunately neglected to
perform.[44]

Since Gill made his remarks in an Oxford college, they might have fallen
within the purview of the university.[45] But the Privy Council entrusted the
investigation to Attorney General Heath and to Laud, who as bishop of
London had jurisdiction over St Paul's. Pursuivants plucked Gill from his
classroom early in September 1628 and took him to the Gatehouse, then to
the Tower.[46] Pyne's case the previous year had shown that words by
themselves could not be treason, but some still thought they were *lèse
majesté*. To liken the king of England to a humble shopkeeper, or to
comment on his majesty's weakness, was deeply scandalous. The use of
the huckster's phrase 'what do you lack' also echoed and parodied King
Charles's speech to parliament of 4 April 1628, that now 'he could not lack,
since he had [the people's] loves'.[47] Gill might have been excused if he had
blamed the drink and expressed remorse; but instead, under examination,
he said 'that he was not glad he had spoken the words, but he was then as
sober as now, and spoke it not without deliberation'.[48]

The case expanded when a search of Gill's papers turned up his correspondence with William Pickering MA of Trinity College, Oxford. On 10
September the Council ordered Pickering's study to be searched for any
passages between him and Alexander Gill, and any notes or papers concerning
the king, the state, the duke, or members of the Privy Council. In addition to
manuscript newsletters, 'sauced with invectives against great men', the search
produced a copy of one of the most widely circulated verse libels against the
Duke of Buckingham, apparently transcribed in Alexander Gill's hand. It
contained scandalous lines that had originally been directed at James I but
now seemed equally applicable to his son. The libel rehearsed the familiar
motif that the king was blind and needed to be helped to better vision.

> And now just God I humbly pray
> That though wilt take that slime away
> That keeps my sovereign's eyes from viewing
> The things that will be our undoing.[49]

When William Pickering was examined on 26 September 1628, he was able to confirm the gist of Gill's 'unfitting words', though none that directly touched the king. Gill, he explained, used these words in 'a mad-brained railing humour', and was far from sober when he said them. William Grinkin of Jesus College was also examined for transcribing some of Gill's verses, for which he fully apologized. Preferring not to allow the most dangerous words to be aired in open court, Laud conducted Gill's examination 'as privately as I might because the speeches are so foul', and referred the matter to the king, 'to your majesty's wisdom'. When the case came to Star Chamber two months later, we learn, 'the words concerning his majesty were not read in open court, but only those concerning the Duke and Felton'. In State Papers too the report of Gill's offensive words is partially obliterated, with the marginal notation 'read this no more'.[50]

Although the Star Chamber record of Gill's case is missing, details of his punishment are preserved in other sources. The episode was widely discussed, and letter-writers could not restrain from comment. Early in November 1628 Gill was censured to be degraded from his degree and his ministry, to lose one ear in the pillory at Oxford, the other in London, and to be fined £2,000. Observers thought that 'being a minister and a bachelor of divinity [he] will . . . for his coat's sake, escape that disgraceful punishment', at least the mutilation. And sure enough, we learn, 'upon old Mr Gill's' petition and Laud's benevolence, the fine was mitigated and his ears were left intact.[51] Referring to this case, the diarist John Rous noted this Michaelmas term a scholar 'fined and sore punished . . . for speaking words against the king'.[52] Gill spent two years under restraint before being pardoned in November 1630, and eventually succeeded his father as high master of St Paul's. His verses 'to his majesty on his birthday' in 1630 implored the royal mercy, and sought pardon for 'this much repented folly'.[53]

Other sources reveal Alexander Gill to have been a friend and correspondent of John Milton, a poet in his own right who wrote verses commending the international Protestant cause.[54] Alexander Gill had another brief moment of celebrity in 1632 when he attacked Ben Jonson's new play, *The Magnetic Lady*, the opening lines of which ask that resonant question, 'What do you lack?' Gill said the play 'stinks', but friends of the playwright retaliated by recalling the censure in Star Chamber of 'so disgraced a quill'.[55] 'Thy name it is a proverb still', recalled schoolboy verses from the 1630s, lampooning Gill's vigour with the lash, 'but now remains the vilest thing, | The alehouse barking 'gainst the king'.[56] Gill's late-night excesses were hard to live down.

Few cases are as well documented as those of Pyne and Gill, but a scatter of remarks testifies to lack of respect for King Charles. Some of this was foul-mouthed obstreperousness, which might have been directed at any monarch, but much of it was specific to the shortcomings of Charles I. Not a year went by without mutterings demeaning or attacking his sacred majesty. Many of these words had wings of their own, and were 'much spoken of' or 'often repeated', and their subsequent retelling compounded the scandal of their initial iteration.[57]

At Colchester at midsummer 1626 Robert Freeborne, 'one of Sir Henry Audley's men', engaged in a noisy argument with the watchman, 'bad a turd in his teeth', laid violent hands upon him, 'and took him by the throat'. When the watchman ordered him 'in the king's name to go with him', Freeborne answered, 'in the king of Spain's name?' To which the watchman replied, 'you shall know that you shall obey King Charles . . . there are too many such as you are'. Everyone knew that Charles and Buckingham had recently returned from Spain, and were now waging war against that kingdom. The watchman's invocation of royal authority raised the stakes, and Freeborne's rash response turned an instance of disorderly conduct into a political offence that could be construed as sedition. The incident also had a religious dimension, since Audley was head of a Catholic family, but Colchester justices decided to take it no further.[58]

Among other episodes, Anthony Spittle of Basingstoke declared to his neighbours in 1627 that he cared for the government in London, 'not so much as for his wife's turd', and no more 'than for one hair of his arse'—a fairly comprehensive denigration of public authority. Nottinghamshire labourer Thomas Haughton of Gunthorpe faced gaol in 1628 for saying 'he cared not for the king'.[59]

The Somerset gentleman Sir Robert Phelips was too cautious to speak so disloyally, but he was heard to say at the time of the general fast in 1628 that, 'there being so many plagues of the commonwealth about his majesty's person, we had never more need of such a humiliation than now'. 'The general voice is, all is nought . . . we can see no way of deliverance', wrote Joseph Mead at the height of the controversy over the Petition of Right. Opinion surfaced among the courts of Europe regarding King Charles of England's 'want of skill to govern of himself'. Intercepted Hapsburg correspondence from late

1627 referred to 'the weakness of his Council, and their want of courage in not daring to tell him the truth nor advise him for the best'.[60]

In August 1629 the Council took note of 'some disgraceful words against his majesty' spoken by one William Brookings, but seems to have taken no further action. John Williams, a man of greater worth, was held at Ilchester gaol that year 'for speaking of high and heinous words against the king's majesty'.[61] Hearing in March 1630 of 'certain fearfully ill-advised words concerning our most gracious king' spoken by 'one Hall, a tailor', the magistrate George Cotton observed that 'the first raisers of this report' were 'persons of the very lowest and basest rank and conversation'. But, finding them supported by some of 'mine honest well known neighbours', at least one of them a gentleman, he felt more confident in reporting them to Lord Keeper Coventry. Another foul speaker, John Broad, was held in Chelmsford gaol that autumn for his seditious utterance concerning 'the state of the kingdom'.[62]

Participating in 'an arbitration of debt' at the King's Head in New Fish Street, London, in July 1631, Richard Crouch gave his opinion 'that the king was indebted, and if he would pay all his debts he should be as poor a man as any then was there, and would not be worth twopence'. Warned by others present 'not to speak against his sovereign', Crouch persisted 'in the like speeches', so they reported him to the Privy Council.[63]

In August 1631, when Somerset magistrates were readjusting common rights on Alder moor in favour of the crown, a villager named Edmund Callow declared that 'the king went about to undo his kingdom'. When a neighbour 'sharply rebuked' him for these scandalous words, Callow persisted, 'so he doth'. Alarmed justices charged the offender 'with speaking of undutiful and unjust words of his majesty', and committed him to Glastonbury gaol 'till further directions might be obtained'. Sir Robert Phelips explained to the Earl of Holland that they were holding Callow as 'an example of some use to men who are too apt with liberty to traduce public actions and persons'. Callow himself was 'old, of hasty and ignorant disposition, a mere clown, and unconsiderable in every respect, more fit for contempt than indignation, yet to keep others in obedience and duty it will not . . . be amiss to have him bound to the next assizes'.[64] What happened to Callow is not known, but it is likely he was released after a pillorying or a whipping. The case allowed Phelips, whose own support for the crown had been questioned, to display his loyalty and respect while advancing his local ambitions.

A London butcher, Philip Tummey, was among those said to have uttered 'base and scandalous speeches against his majesty' in 1632.[65] George Weare of Chipping Sodbury, Gloucestershire, likewise made 'vile, impious, malicious and seditious speeches against his majesty' in 1632, which eventually came to official attention.[66] The treasonous remarks by John Stephens in 1632 are considered later.[67]

Scandalous remarks in 1633 included those of Margery Gardiner of Clerkenwell, who declared that 'the king is a bastard'.[68] A Worcestershire servant proclaimed 'that my sovereign lord King Charles was a fool'. And a London physician was charged that year with 'vain fancies' against 'sovereignty itself' for saying 'it was all one to be under the king and under the Turk'.[69]

In January 1634 the Privy Council became exercised about reports from Kent of 'wicked and malicious speeches uttered against his majesty by one Robert Wood, a vagrant rogue, which are so heinous as he justly deserveth to have severe punishment inflicted upon him'. When Wood was arrested on the Isle of Thanet and charged in the king's name, he said that the king was a knave. Earlier he had been gaoled at Canterbury for saying 'it were no matter if the king were hanged'. The mayor of Dover described Wood as 'a silly man and cracked in his brains', but he was smart enough to deny using the words alleged against him. The Council instructed the Earl of Suffolk, Lord Warden of the Cinque Ports, to 'cause the said Wood upon a market day at the full time of market to be put in the stocks by the neck, and so to continue the space of two hours, and then well and soundly whipped, and afterwards conveyed to the house of correction, there to be whipped and set to labour for his living during the time of his life'. Wood's wandering days would be over, but first he had to suffer the unusual punishment of having his neck, rather than his feet, set in the stocks, the clean contrary way.[70]

A quarrel over cattle at Somerby, Lincolnshire, in October 1634 led Maurice Bawde, a gentleman, to declare that 'he neither cared for the king nor the king's laws'. He was, perhaps, provoked to this by John Dawson, who called him 'a base, shitten, stinking gentleman' who 'could not speak one true word unless it came out of his mouth by chance'. Bawde then called Dawson 'a rogue, a base rogue, pillory rogue, hog's face, and brazen face knave', adding 'that he would have the cropping of [Dawson's] ears, and make sauce of them'. When Dawson's sister Elizabeth joined the argument, Bawde called her 'base whore and uncivil whore, and said that he would prove her a whore'. When Bawde then attempted to break open the pound and take the cattle by force, Dawson asked him if he would not obey the king's laws, triggering the outburst about caring not for the king. Bawde's violent behaviour led to a charge of riot at the Grantham assizes, to which he retaliated by suing Dawson in the High Court of Chivalry. Gentlemen, we have seen, could not always bridle their tongues, and the scandalous exchange in this case is recorded in proceedings of the Chivalry court.[71]

Others whose tongues caused them trouble in 1634 included Robert Redferne of Gloucester, who said that he could make better laws than any king or peer, and 'that the king was no better than another ordinary man';[72] Noah Rogers at Cambridge, who said 'that he hoped to die, and tread King Charles under his feet';[73] and the Kentish gentlemen Edward Boys, who spoke 'against the king and the quiet of the kingdom' in opposition to the king's Book of Sports.[74]

The conversation among villagers and travellers at Barking, Essex, moved onto dangerous ground in July 1634 when the fisherman Richard Deane alias Ottowell mentioned a recent incident in which a coachman struck a gentleman with his whip, and the gentleman retaliated by hitting the coachman with his sword. Deane got himself into trouble by saying 'that if the king had done as much to him as the coachman did to the gentleman he would have struck the king'. Attempting to get Deane to retract these words, the tavern keeper interjected, 'what, not the king if you had known him?' The local constable, Richard Walter, who was drinking with the rest, apparently arrested Deane and reported him to the magistrates, who dutifully examined the offender.

Richard Deane, in his defence, denied speaking any such words. Rather, he claimed, he had said 'that being the coachman had struck the gentleman with his whip, the gentleman, if he had been a king, could have done no less than to strike the coachman from his box'. In this completely different account the king could be imagined as doing the striking, rather than justifiably being struck. It was a lesson, perhaps, not to speak lightly of kings. In this case the authorities seemed satisfied that Deane had merely mis-spoken himself, or had been mis-heard, and let the matter drop.[75]

In July 1635 the painter James Priest declared after church at Cambridge that 'the king . . . is overruled by his servants, a company of knaves', with 'many more unfitting speeches' against Sunday sports, altars, and church organs. Examined some weeks later, Priest tried to talk himself out of trouble. He said that he could not remember the alleged words, 'and protested that he never held them in his heart'. On the Sunday in question, he recalled, he 'was much afflicted in mind' about his debts, and drank half a pint of sack at the Falcon tavern, and then another pint and a half more on coming home, which left him 'much weakened in his mind'. The alcohol, he implied, possessed a voice of its own, for which the tongue was not responsible.[76] Others investigated for 'undutiful and unsufferable speeches' or 'opprobrious and scandalous words' against King Charles in 1635 included Ralph Blackhall, a prisoner in the Fleet, Edward Loggin in Worcestershire, and Walter Gould in Dorset. Details of their offences have not survived, but their participation in popular political discourse brought them under surveillance.[77] A gentleman, Sir Nicholas Stoddard, was referred to Star Chamber in 1635 for saying 'most maliciously and in high contempt of the king... that our kingdom of England never prospered since a Scot governed'.[78] Year by year the flow of disparagement continued unstaunched.

John Lewes, a petty chapman of King's Cliff, Northamptonshire, was examined in 1636 for saying that 'the king was no better than the beggar', but he was judged to be mad.[79] In another case from 1636, Victor Johnson, 'a poor distressed stranger', was imprisoned at Plymouth for 'uttering some words to the dishonour of his majesty, but claimed he was falsely accused.[80] Anticipating the judgement of some modern historians, a Pembrokeshire man, Gerard Wright, declared in 1636 that 'King James was a wise and learned king, but King Charles wants a good head piece'. When his minister protested, 'Nay, its not so, for the king is generous and wise', Wright replied, 'Yea, in faith but it is so, and I tell you therein but the truth; for he giveth too much credit and belief to his nobility, and believeth anything they speak to him.' The minister, Edward Provard, made note of these scandalous words, and intended to relay them to the authorities. But 'living nine score miles distant from London' and temporarily mislaying his note among a trunk full of books, Provard delayed until 1639 before reporting the matter to the Council, 'who thereupon granted forth a warrant for the apprehension of the said Wright'.[81] The minister might reasonably have been worried, for just a few years earlier a man had been arrested because 'hearing of... vile, impious, malicious and seditious speeches against his majesty he did conceal them for the space of two years and did not reveal the same unto authority'.[82] The reliability of Provard's recollections were impugned, however, by testimony about 'a plot to disgrace' the alleged speaker, who was locked in dispute with the minister about fishing rights and leases.[83]

Another case in 1636 involved John Osborne of Scotswood, Northumberland, who told a gathering of gentlemen, colliers, and civic officials 'that every man was a king, and he was a king in his own house'. When Thomas Milbourne protested, 'take heed what you say of kings, for it cannot be so', Osborne pressed on, claiming 'that kings were murderers, and that King Edward the sixth did murder three wives and one of their brothers'. Another neighbour warned him, 'take heed what you say, I doubt you speak treason, and I will make report what you have said in discharge of my duty'. Osborne responded, 'what can the king do, he can but take my life', although he might also have recommended a more accurate reading of history. The conversation apparently started with Ship Money but rapidly descended into sedition. Asked by the examining magistrate, 'what occasion he had to speak discourses of any such things', Osborne answered that he recalled the matter from his study of the chronicle, but had no 'disloyal thoughts of his majesty'.[84] More 'treasonous words against his majesty' in 1636 came from John Pettit, a labourer of Saffron Walden, Essex, who, being told that King Charles was king of three kingdoms commented, 'the more is the pity'.[85]

Early in 1637, deep in drink at the Lion and the Greyhound at Lavenham, Suffolk, Thomas Skinner spoke 'dangerous and treasonable words' against the king. Quite what these words were, no one could say, for Skinner had apparently whispered them to Thomas Dandy when both men were very drunk. Dandy cried out, 'there is one in this room that speaks nothing but treason', to which Skinner responded, 'Mr Dandy had undone him, his wife and children'. Another drinker advised Dandy that 'if he were sure that the words were treasonable words he must then go charge the master of the house for the safekeeping of Mr Skinner till he did procure the constable to come'. In this case, although we do not know the actual words, we are allowed a remarkable insight into the chain of reportage that brought the matter to light. On the king's instructions the Attorney General conducted 'a full and thorough search . . . for discovery of the truth herein'.[86]

In another report to Attorney General Bankes about this time, a gentleman drinking at the Three Horseshoes in London's Fetter Lane 'said that his majesty held what he had in England by way of bastardy'.[87] Other 'desperate and treasonable speeches' in 1637 included those of Philip Stanley of Chichester, who was found to be 'distracted in his wits',[88] Ralph Whalley of Leicestershire, who said that 'the king was a dishonest man and the Lord Keeper a knave', and Lawrence Hall of Kilsby, Northamptonshire, who told his vicar 'that he owed the king nothing'.[89] Grievances against Ship Money led Thomas Chaloner to say in 1637 'that he hoped to be in the head of an army in this kingdom . . . to suppress the new levies of money now raised and to punish the inventers'. Some thought these 'desperate words would have cost him his life had he come to trial', but instead he escaped into exile.[90]

In 1638 the silkweaver Thomas Sandiford was charged 'with having uttered some dangerous speeches which, if true, ought not to go unpunished'.[91] George Pasfield, master of the *Patience*, allegedly declared that year that he cared 'a fart' for the royal warrant, and spoke 'contemptuous words against his majesty's seal manual'.[92] Alexander Jennings was held in the Fleet prison in 1638 for his 'scandalous speeches in derogation and disparagement of his majesty's government'.[93] William Walker, a Northamptonshire opponent of Ship Money, reminded neighbours in July 1638 that 'the king was under a law, as much as any subject, and that he could do nothing of himself without his subjects'. A full report of these words went to the Privy Council.[94] So too did the file on John Napier, a Scottish gentleman in London, who spoke approvingly of the Covenant and said 'that the king is deluded, seduced, and made a baby . . . *quos Jupiter perdere vult, hos dementat*'.[95]

Robert Jason, esquire, was held in prison in April 1638 'for undutiful speaking and uttering scandalous words against' the king and Privy Council. He was eventually pardoned after claiming that the offensive speeches 'were far from his tongue or thought', and that the accusation sprang from 'the plots and combinations of a brother in law and other persons of mean quality'.[96] There were also proceedings in Warwickshire in 1638 against Richard Dixon for his 'scandalous and unbefitting speeches of his majesty and his government',[97] and examinations at Cambridge for 'some factious and mutinous words uttered by one John Howell'.[98] Magistrates even investigated John Bullock, a yeoman of Fledborough, Nottinghamshire, who said rather foolishly in 1638 'that King Charles was not king of England' but rather 'of Great Britain'.[99]

The torrent of words continued in 1639, energized by the crisis in the north. John Glascock of Bedfordshire was charged in Star Chamber for 'contemptuous, scandalous and undutiful speeches' against the king, including the assertion 'that he had as good blood in him' as King Charles, that he did not love the king, and that 'he had read kings had been deposed'.[100] A Somerset man was indicted at the 1639 Lent assizes 'for speaking treason against the king', saying, 'we have a boy that governs', and allegedly wishing that the Duke of Buckingham 'had put down the king with that army (that he took into France), and set up somebody else that would have governed us better'. In the event the witnesses proved insufficient, and the offence was acknowledged to be 'less than treason'.[101]

Also in 1639, complaining about the undue influence of the Archbishop of Canterbury, the projector Francis Harris said 'that if the king were not a fool it would not be so. But when the land is governed by a fool or a child it must always groan under the burden of oppression.'[102] The words of Thomas Kerver in 1444 and Hugh Pyne in 1625 had found another echo. By this time the king was middle aged, and had ruled for fourteen years, though not everyone thought him mature.

By 1640, amidst war with Scotland and the prospect of a parliament, more people were caught up in the national conversation. The quickening crisis accelerated the flow of news and stimulated the exchange of opinion. 'Rumour and noise in the country was great, and the fear of the people far greater,' a Kentish magistrate reported in May 1640.[103] Drinking at Tamworth, Staffordshire, around that time, John Sheppard declared that he 'did not care for the king nor his laws neither'. When fellow drinkers remarked on 'the heinousness of the said words' and threatened to call a bailiff, Sheppard apparently 'wept, and said he had but a life to lose, and he could but lose it, and that his life lay in their hands'.[104] Others spoke up for the Scottish rebels who intended 'the good of this land, for they stood for a parliament here'. On 'the king's proceedings with Scotland', the London wax chandler Robert Warner declared, 'what a shame it was that our king should be so misinformed by his council', and asked, 'do you think that the king knows of this proclamation?' that had been issued in his name. The war was 'unjust', he insisted, and it was 'great pity that the king was so misled'.[105]

Respect for King Charles disintegrated further in 1641 amid more dangerous expressions of sedition. In January 1641, when the minister of Horsted Parva, Sussex, proposed prayers for the king, one parishioner queried, 'of what religion is he? I know not of what religion he is, or whether he be of any.' The churchwarden Thomas Prowle added, 'what care we for his majesty's laws and statutes?' This prompted the shocked minister to ask, 'what, do you not care for his majesty's laws and statutes?', to which Prowle answered succinctly, 'no, not we'.[106] Told by a justice in September 1641 to respect the king's authority, the alehouse-keeper Joan Allen of Pleshey, Essex, responded that 'she knew not the king, nor cared not for him . . . nor would not obey his authority'. Forced to pay a price for her 'malice and odium', she was held for a month in prison, then whipped and sent home to her husband.[107] Matthew Scott of Resdon was likewise indicted at Chester in 1641 'for giving out speeches tending to rebellion'.[108]

By spring 1642 the country was in uproar, and royal authority was palpably faltering. The Yorkshire tanner Thomas Godsey declared openly in church in March 1642: 'I care not for the king (meaning our lord King Charles) nor his laws.'[109] John Bassett of Stepney, Middlesex, said similarly at Easter 'that he did not care for the king, and that he was as good a man as the king'.[110] The Glamorganshire tailor Matthew Williams of Penmark went even further in March 1642, uttering 'certain treasonable words against the king's majesty, viz: that the king is but a private gentleman during the pleasure of the parliament'. Parliament, he insisted, 'hath power to make another king if the king will not comply and agree with the parliament'. Though voiced by a South Wales artisan with a slender grasp of constitutional theory, these 'seditious and treasonable words' were far more radical than advanced opinion at Westminster. Though local justices issued warrants for Williams to 'be brought into safe custody if he be to be found within this county', he remained at large, and could not be made to account for his words.[111]

In another alcohol-fuelled conversation on the brink of civil war, the Yorkshire squire Francis Gifford asked in June 1642 what should befall 'if the king did not keep the laws and his oath?' The reply of Knaresborough gentleman John Troutbeck was that 'he might be deposed for aught he knew', adding 'that he could live as well without a king as with a king'. His only excuse was that 'he was so overtaken by drunkenness' that he could not stay on his horse.[112]

The Archbishop and the Queen

Recurrent rumours in the 1630s commented on the king's dependence on his wife and his archbishop, both of whom allegedly pushed him towards Rome. The belief that King Charles or William Laud had abandoned Protestantism was unfounded, but it had popular adherents. Edward Parsons of Aldermaston, Berkshire, for example, declared in 1635 that Laud 'was turned papist . . . and that he was not fit for the place'.[113] Other artisans spoke 'lewd words' against the archbishop,[114] or 'scandalous and opprobrious words against my lord's grace of Canterbury',[115] calling him 'base fellow', 'an unsanctified rascal', a 'knave', a 'papist', and 'the pope of Lambeth'.[116] It was common comment in London taverns that 'my lord of Canterbury is a monk, a rogue, and a traitor to this kingdom'.[117]

After being led so long by the Duke of Buckingham, the king was now thought to be dominated by his archbishop. 'The lord of Canterbury has possessed the king with I know not what . . . He uses the king, labours with the king,' said a Mr Shepherd in 1637.[118] 'The pope of Lambeth . . . doth pluck the royal crown off his majesty's head and trample it under his feet, and did whip his majesty's arse with his own rod,' declared a drinker in Southwark in 1639. Others expressed the opinion 'that the king was overruled' by Laud and his allies, who 'would persuade the king whatever they list'.[119] Some longed for 'another Felton' to bring an end to 'the little miniken bishop'.[120] 'I must have this bishop's head . . . the head of the little man', declared the Surrey clothworker Anthony Bothway in April 1639.[121] 'It had been happier for England and Scotland if the archbishop had been made a sacrifice when he was made a bishop,' observed another drinker at Westminster earlier that year.[122]

These words were scandalous and seditious, but they could not be stopped. Laud himself prayed to 'deliver my soul from them that hate me without a cause'.[123] The archbishop's own papers include notes on the Buckinghamshire woman who said in 1634 that 'she did not care a pin nor a fart for my lord's grace of Canterbury' and wished to see him hanged, and the Surrey yeoman who declared in 1639 that 'if nobody would cut off the lord of Canterbury's head he would do it himself'.[124]

A similar line of commentary smeared Henrietta Maria. The memoirist Lucy Hutchinson remarked that 'a French queen never brought any happiness to England',[125] and this view was shared by many subjects. 'Villainous words against the queen'[126] touched on her foreignness, her popery, and her dangerous influence over King Charles.

Some blamed the queen for the collapse of the parliament in March 1629. Over dinner in Northamptonshire one servant asked another, 'what was the news?' Christian Cowper reported 'that the king was overnight well inclined to the parliament, but lying with the queen all night, the next morning his mind was changed. And she said further, that she wished the queen were ducked in the midst of the sea.' Her kinsman John Cowper added the suggestion 'with a millstone about her neck', to which Christian commented: 'you do well to put me in mind of it.' Here were household servants bantering about the high political affairs of the kingdom, remarking on the king's change of course, his intimacy with his wife, and the desirability of drowning her majesty.[127]

Under examination a month later, Christian Cowper gave the names of others who were present at the dinner, and reported that one of them said of the breaking of the parliament that 'it was thought it was long of [because of] the queen'. She acknowledged her own scandalous words about ducking Henrietta Maria, but said they were uttered 'very foolishly but without any evil intent'. Ducking was the punishment reserved for scolding women, so it was perhaps appropriate for a woman to mention it, though not to extend it to the queen. As to the further remarks about the millstone, which moved the discussion from splashing to drowning, Christian vehemently denied saying such words, although she did say that she wished the queen aboard a 'ship of the seas'. She authenticated her testimony with a mark, suggesting that she did not know how to write.[128]

Other scandalous remarks, different in content but no less offensive, were reported in November 1629. The Londoner Samuel Liston 'bravingly said' that he was 'a companion to King Charles', and then, standing up, 'laid his hands upon either side of his codpiece and said he would warm his codpiece to the queen'. The report to the Council describes this action as 'unreverent', but it was dishonourable and disgraceful, close to imagining the queen as a whore.[129] In 1630, when Henrietta Maria gave birth to Prince Charles, another Londoner named Perkins was 'like to be hanged, drawn and quartered' for calling the child a bastard.[130] The rumour would persist, to haunt later Stuarts, that the queen was unnaturally close to her counsellor Henry Jermyn, who some thought had fathered her children.[131]

The French queen was the subject of another conversation among servants in 1638 when the Londoner Rachel Thorne asked her companions 'if they knew that the queen's mother was dead'. She then used 'malicious, seditious and slanderous' words, declaring 'that the queen's mother was a whore and a cutpurse whore, and that the queen was a whore'. Another servant reported this to her mistress, who in turn sent for the constable, and Rachel was carried to Bridewell. Examined by magistrates the next day, she could not remember 'any speeches that passed in their discourse', but 'utterly denied' any words against the queen.[132] When Marie de Medici, the queen mother, came to London in November 1638, there was reported 'much dislike of her for daintiness and costliness'.[133] One minor servant at court shared his opinion 'that the queen mother was a witch'.[134]

Remarks more sympathetic to Henrietta Maria, though no less dangerous to the state, were aired in Essex around Shrovetide 1638. Thomas Porter told the authorities that, 'being in the tide boat discoursing' about the recent trial of a recusant who had championed the Gunpowder Plot, Mary Cole, a Catholic convert, declared 'that if she were as the queen she would quickly make away King Charles for dealing so hardly with that religion'. Mary Cole was a servant to the Petres of Cranham Hall, a branch of a distinguished recusant family, so her comments could be construed to be connected to Catholic plotting. Summoned before Attorney General Bankes, Mary denied the words imputed to her but claimed rather to have told Thomas Porter more innocently 'that if she were a queen and he a king she would hang him if she could'.[135]

Other witnesses offered other versions. Thomas Poulter, another servant to Mr Petre, quoted Mary to have said that 'if she were a queen she would hang the king, the keeper she meant, God save the king'. According to another witness, when Mary declared, 'if I were the queen I would have the king hanged', her son-in-law Roger Hepthrow, a labourer, interjected: 'mother take heed what you say, I have known men hanged for a less word.' To this Mary Cole answered: 'Christ save me, I meant the keeper, I pray God bless me, and sweet Jesus bless the king.'[136] The thoroughness with which these depositions were collected testifies to the importance the regime attached to uncovering such dangerous words.

The greatest danger, in godly opinion, was that Henrietta Maria threatened the Protestant religion. 'Lord, open her eyes, that she may see her saviour, whom she hath pierced with her superstition and idolatry,' preached Nathaniel Bernard at Cambridge in 1633.[137] 'I pray God convert the queen, confound and utterly destroy those that are [thy] enemies,' preached Enoch Grey at Maldon in 1638. Witnesses reported Grey's prayer, 'that God would turn the king's heart from the whore of Babel, that he would draw him out of Babylon,' because the king and queen 'lie under the plagues of the whore of Babylon'. These too were 'seditious and factious speeches', according to Chief Justice Bramston, clearly offensive to both their majesties.[138]

By 1640 report was rife in London that 'the king goes to mass with the queen'.[139] Notwithstanding King Charles's frequent assertion that he would live and die in the Protestant religion, a growing number of subjects suspected him of favouring Catholicism. In June 1640 a Mrs Thoroughgood of Clerkenwell declared to her lodger that 'the king loveth papists better than puritans'. When the lodger, Alexander West, bid her have care what she said, she replied that 'she would answer the words before the king and the Council'. She too had heard that 'the king commonly went to mass, and was turned to be a papist'.[140] Joan Worrall, a spinster of St Martin in the Fields, added the detail that 'the king's majesty had one crucifix in his chamber and did bow to it'.[141]

Villagers at Ruislip, Middlesex, digested a similar rumour in August 1640 while 'falling into discourse of the danger of the times'. Henry Wheeler, a litterman in the queen's household, told them 'that the king did go to mass in Lent last', and also spoke disparagingly of the queen mother. These were scandalous and seditious remarks, which led to Wheeler's imprisonment in the Fleet and the forfeit of his position.[142]

Others who spoke similarly included the Yorkshireman Thomas Stafford, who repeated the rumour that 'the king and queen was at mass together',[143] the Kentish glazier Edward Fairbrother, who said that 'King Charles that now is king of England is a papist',[144] and the Thameside mariner's wife Rachael Pollester, who declaimed, 'the king is a papist and a rank papist'.[145] 'We have a sinful king, we have a sinful queen,' preached 'one Mr Tutty' in London in 1641.[146] 'The king had married a Babylonish woman,' declared another London lecturer, who warned of 'the sins of wicked Manassas' and 'the scarlet whore of Babylon'.[147] We live 'now in the time of Ahab and Jezebel', declared another Puritan preacher in January 1642,[148] referring to the king of Israel and his foreign queen who led the Hebrews into idolatry and sin. Simon Zeager, a fuller from Minehead, Somerset, likewise spoke 'very seditious and traitorous words of the king's most excellent majesty' in the summer of 1642, saying that the king maintained papists against the Protestants and supported the rebels in Ireland.[149] Most of these speakers were called before courts or justices, but in the turmoil of 1641 and 1642 it was hard to secure their punishment. By this time rumours about the royal religion were overlain with tales of Irish atrocities, fears of foreign invasion, and conjectures about Catholic uprisings, threats to English liberties, and the tyrannical overreach of the parliament.

To Kill the King

To speak derisively of King Charles was a grave offence, but compassing or imagining his death could be treason. Although the Caroline regime was remarkably free from serious threats, the authorities responded vigorously to any hint of plots or designs against the monarch. Who could say for sure that no plan existed to dispatch King Charles and replace him with a more robust Protestant or a counter-reformation Catholic? Alehouse brags about wishing the king hanged were by no means as dangerous as actual assassination conspiracies, but loose talk of that nature could not go unpunished.

One of the earliest scares involved the Lancashire Catholic Sir Thomas Gerard, who had allegedly 'sworn the death of the king'. One of Gerard's female servants was overheard saying in 1625 that her brother 'is one of those that must kill the king'. By another report Sir Thomas had threatened to cut the throats of Protestant justices, and said 'that if God should call for his majesty [that is, if King Charles died], he would draw his sword to keep out the Queen of Bohemia'. A dangerous conspiracy rooted in recusant treachery was apparently revealed by the conspirators' careless chatter.[150]

Sir Thomas Gerard of the Bryn was a prominent Lancashire baronet, rich in lands, mines, and mills. His father had been involved in Elizabethan conspiracies, his uncle, the Jesuit John Gerard, had a part in the Gunpowder Plot, and his younger son Gilbert also joined the Jesuit order.[151] Though Gerard's allegiance to the Stuarts was unquestioned, his Catholicism was unshakeable, and popular Protestant opinion feared the worst. He was the principal landowner in the parish of Wigan, and a thorn in the side of local authorities. He was already subject to proceedings in the Court of High Commission when allegations of his treasonable utterances emerged.[152]

Gerard's arch enemy, Bishop John Bridgeman of Chester, lord of Wigan, and an active campaigner against Lancastrian recusants, had the baronet arrested on 23 September 1625. Two days later he sent up to London an urgent packet of information denouncing Sir Thomas, with anxious letters to Secretary Conway, Lord Treasurer Ley, and Chancellor of the Exchequer Weston. The matter concerned 'some traitorous passages against the king's person and state', according to Bridgeman, in which 'Sir Thomas Gerard of the Bryn near Wigan, baronet, had sworn the death of the king (whom God for his mercy's sake long preserve among us), and that there was a purpose of plot to be sped in Warwickshire or Worcestershire near the place where the old plot or matter was' (referring to the events of 1605). '[Gerard's] servant Robert Cowley (who is said to reveal it) lies here in prison and all the other parties are committed to several houses in Wigan.' Sir Thomas himself was lodged on bond with a kinsman until the High Sheriff of Lancashire, Edward Holland, took him into custody for transfer to

London. The Council arranged for his committal on 2 October, and Gerard was delivered to the Tower on 8 October 1625.[153]

The immediate threat seemed to be under control, but the bishop wanted 'directions' from London how to proceed. The matter was extremely sensitive, and Bridgeman's own political, financial, and ecclesiastical interests were involved. 'My good lords,' he addressed the Council, 'I conceive this business deserves very diligent enquiry, for the papists of this county have been lately more bold and busy than ever heretofore'. There had been night-time gatherings of recusants and provocations against both church and state.

The last week one Thomas Helmes of Goosnargh said openly in Preston that all protestants were damned, and that the church of Wigan, which the bishop hath lately built, should shortly be broken down with cannons. And this very instant an information was sent to me, that one widow Jaques had said these words: 'the king holds his lands wrongfully, and that he might know ere long.'

Lancashire seemed to be awash with treasonous plotting, ready to bring down the six-month-old Caroline regime.[154]

The Privy Council quite properly took this report into 'serious consideration' as a matter of 'weighty consequence' touching 'the safety of his majesty's royal person and the quiet of the state'. On 17 October they instructed the Lancashire authorities to keep their prisoners in custody and to examine them again in the hope of learning more. Sir Thomas Gerard, befitting his social standing, would be separated from other delinquents. Sir Randolph Crew, Chief Justice of King's Bench, would deal with the case in the upcoming Michaelmas term. The Council reprimanded High Sheriff Holland for allowing Gerard to be lodged with his brother-in-law Sir Richard Molineux, allegedly to keep him from being pursued for his 'many and great debts'. They reminded the Sheriff 'that a prisoner committed for any offence against his majesty, though in a far less degree than matter of treason, may not be troubled nor arrested upon any other cause or action whatsoever during his commitment'. Gerard's recusancy fines and other forfeitures left him 'in continual danger to be arrested' for debt, so perhaps he was better off as the king's prisoner.[155]

By 22 October 1625 news of the affair was widespread among court and country gossips, entering the domain of public information. Joseph Mead wrote from Cambridge to Sir Martin Stuteville in Suffolk with an intimate account of the affair. In this version, two of Sir Thomas Gerard's maidservants, washing clothes at a pit, fell a-talking together of the brave times that would be shortly for their religion: when Mr Turner, a busy justice of peace, would be turned out of office; Mr Horne, parson of Winwick, should have horns set upon his head; and the bishop of Chester, that bore himself so high, should be hoisted a peg higher to his little ease. 'And my brother Robert' (Sir Thomas's groom), saith one to the other, 'is one of those that must kill the king'. This discourse being overheard by a peddler, or some such loose fellow, who was lying sunning behind a hedge, he goes presently to an honest substantial man of the town, one Prescot, and tells him what he heard Sir Thomas Gerard's maids talking at the pit. He presently informs the parson, Mr Allen. The parson writes to the Bishop of Chester, he to the Lords of the Council. They send a mandate to the sheriff to apprehend him, which he did on Monday was sennight.[156]

In this case the Mead–Stuteville correspondence circle was accurately and promptly informed. The chain of transmission went from Sir Thomas Gerard and his groom to the maids at washing, to the eavesdropping peddler, to honest Prescot, to parson Allen, to the Bishop of Chester, to the Privy Council, to High Sheriff Holland, then to a Cambridge tutor, and so to Mead and Stuteville. Other episodes may not have had so many links, but every telling expanded opportunities for mishearing and misremembering. In this case, though willing to relay the report, Joseph Mead remained sceptical. 'The grounds are so feeble that I think it will prove no great matter,' he told Sir Martin Stuteville; 'I tell you this circumstantially because there goes stranger reports abroad, but all false'.[157]

Further examination by the authorities shed no fresh light on the matter. Responding to the Council's letters in late November, Bishop Bridgeman and the Deputy Lieutenants of Lancashire expressed frustration that the evidence of seditious words could not be proven. The recusant community had clammed silent, and testimony was unforthcoming, so that 'we cannot easily or speedily learn anything worth your lordships' notice'. Sir Thomas Gerard's involvement seemed well corroborated, but specific speech offences proved impossible to pin down.

In the more sedulous enquiry and examination of witnesses, we find them either so blanched by plea of mistaking (as that of Jaques) or so weakened by the distemper of the party accused (as that other of Helmes) or so locked up in silence ... as we can yet find nothing therein fit to be presented to your lordships' view.[158]

The original informer still held to his claim about the impending doom of Protestants, 'but none else of the witnesses do remember those words, and all of them say that the offender was far gone in drink, and had a brother died a lunatic, himself, as we conceive him, being little better'. Regarding widow Jaques, the informer who had originally acknowledged the testimony on oath 'now falls from it and saith he was mistaken'. Since a prosecution for treasonous words required two witnesses to proceed, the business with these Lancashire recusants was stalled. All that the Council could do was to instruct local authorities to keep 'an especial eye upon the conversation and intercourse' of the 'suspicious persons', and report anything 'worthy the knowledge of this Board . . . with all convenient speed'.[159]

Chief Justice Crew scrutinized the written examinations in December 1625 and concluded that 'I dare not advise any use of them in any court of justice'. One of the principal witnesses against Gerard, John Ashton, now 'lies in his grave, so as the evidence to convict is only the report of a dead man'. The words of Joan Jaques seemed 'too dark and ambiguous to ground any crime upon'. Other statements were too unstable or uncertain to present to a jury. It was true, Crew agreed, that 'Sir Thomas Gerard hath many vehement suspicions upon him, and his house is a seminary of priests and popery', but without firmer evidence a trial for treason would not stand.[160]

Sir Thomas, meanwhile, remained close prisoner in the Tower, facing forfeiture of his estates and the prospect of execution. In February 1626, five months into his imprisonment, he was reported to have become 'infirm and weak in body', and was granted the privilege of supervised access to the Tower gardens. He was still incarcerated in March, when his wife was permitted to visit him. (Lady Gerard herself was under scrutiny at this time for associating with Catholic priests at a house in Drury Lane.)[161] By July the Council was ready to release Gerard to a kind of house arrest within 5 miles of Peterborough, but Sir Thomas feared that his creditors would follow him there. He petitioned the Council that 'if he may not be freely delivered that he may be confined to the liberties of the Tower, and that his person be free from all other restraints'. One improvement in his circumstance was the king's instruction to Bishop Bridgeman, dated 26 July 1626, 'to surcease your proceedings against [Gerard] for matter of recusancy'.[162]

Gerard's ordeal finally ended when he was discharged in February 1628 (the same month as Hugh Pyne). Shortly after his release he wrote to his kinsman the Earl of Huntingdon: 'I thank God and the king I can now go whither I list, his majesty having given me his royal protection for body, lands and goods.' He was at last free to return to his 'many businesses', careful to stay out of trouble in his few remaining years.[163]

Recurrent threats required constant attention. In November 1626 Sir Benjamin Rudyerd offered portentous news to Sir Francis Nethersole:

There is a man of mean quality imprisoned and questioned, who hearing one complain of the times, said he could easily remedy all. Being asked how, he answered, by killing the Duke. The other replied, peradventure it might be as ill after. Then, said he, the king may be made away, and the queen of Bohemia with her children sent for over. The fellow doth not much deny, but says he was drunk.[164]

Rudyerd does not identify this speaker of treason, but it was most likely Thomas Brediman, who scandalized guests at a private dinner in London in October 1626. The table talked veered into politically dangerous territory when Brediman gave vent to his opinions. The gathering was in the house of John Brangston, tailor, in Drury Lane (apparently a lodging house for out-of-town visitors), and the company included Henry and Dorothy Manners of Cheswick, county Durham, and their countryman Thomas Brediman of Berwick on Tweed, a soldier, who spoke the offending words. Somebody, perhaps Henry Manners, reported the matter to the authorities, and several of the dinner guests faced examination. Being informed of these 'desperate and seditious speeches', the Privy Council on 2 November referred the matter to the Chief Justice and Attorney General for further investigation.[165]

According to Dorothy Manners, who was examined on 9 November, Brediman avowed that 'the king was too much ruled by the Duke'. When Henry Manners pressed Brediman 'to forbear speaking such things', he reportedly 'answered, I have done'. He then 'took God to witness that he spake not out of malice to the Duke or anybody, but only out of his love that he wished the state, the land, and the people well'.[166] (This was similar to the justification John Felton later gave for murdering the Duke of Buckingham, for the safety of the people and England's greater good.)

That, however, was not the end of the conversation. Henry Manners, examined along with his wife, recalled Brediman speculating aloud that the recently mustered soldiers in London might do harm to the Duke of Buckingham, and 'against the king also'. 'God forbid,' protested Mrs Brangston, and Dorothy Manners piously responded, according to her husband, 'that if such unlawful courses were taken God would not prosper them'. Everyone affected to be scandalized by the soldier's seditious outburst. Brediman, however, was in full flow, lamenting that, 'now the ancient men's counsel are refused, and justice had not lawful proceeding, and that papists increased and grew bold, unto whom it is held the Duke of Buckingham is a great patron; and he added further, that if the state stood as it doth it would not continue long'. At this point, rather than attempting to silence him, the hostess encouraged Brediman to continue, asking, 'what would become of it?' meaning the kingdom. Brediman answered, 'it may be it shall be a free state, for perhaps the Palatine and the Lady Elizabeth shall have it'. This was treasonous speech, fishing in deep waters, which could bring trouble to everyone at the table. Compassing or imagining the death of the king was a traitorous felony, and demeaning his ministers was sedition. Positing a change of dynasty was almost unthinkable. 'If these speeches were known,' observed Mrs Brangston, 'it might cost him his ears,' to which Brediman replied, somewhat opaquely, 'if it cost his ears it would cost more'. Eventually, Henry Manners recalled, 'Brediman seemed to be sorry for what he had said', and the rest of the dinner passed quietly. Manners observed that all the company were 'sober', and thought it worth remarking how little wine had lubricated their talk.[167] In this case it was the women, rather than their husbands, who responded most forcefully to Brediman's outspoken views.

The formal interrogatories administered to Thomas Brediman are preserved in State Papers, though not the defendant's answers.[168] However, with at least four witnesses against him (the Brangstons and the Manners), Brediman could not deny the charge. A London news writer picked up the story on 10 November.

The bold speakers begin to go to pound. Captain Brodeman [Brediman] was sent to the Gatehouse this last week, for speaking more than his part; and if he be not saved by twelve men, he may have liberty, perhaps, to speak his mind in his last confession. I must not repeat his words, but himself is taught better manners [a pun on the name of the informants], to put a greater difference hereafter betwixt a duke and a king.[169]

Thomas Brediman spent the winter in prison. On New Year's Day 1627, 'in all humility and penitential submission', he confessed his fault. But, 'considering the place, the accuser, the time at supper after many a cup, and I the speaker drunk', he thought he had been punished enough. Still held close in February, after 100 days' incarceration, he confessed his offence, asserted his 'loyalty and obedience', and begged again to be released. His careless words, he said, were 'my only offence in my lifetime, it being in drink or in a dream, which is as one being deprived of senses, as I was then'.[170]

It might be imagined that Brediman was then allowed to go free, to resume his military duties. But on 4 September 1627 Secretary Conway wrote to Sir John Coke about 'a poor man in the gatehouse, Thomas Brediman, who was committed by you and me. He hath been long a prisoner. I think it were very good he were released, for in punishing him we punish the king, at whose charge he lies.' In 1626 a condemned robber, compared to Robin Hood, had been sent to military service instead of execution, and a similar fate seemed likely for the veteran soldier.[171] Though never formally tried, Brediman spent almost a year in prison for his imprudent and dangerous remarks.

The suggestion that Elizabeth of Bohemia and her husband the Elector Palatine might replace King Charles on the English throne was, perhaps, not unthinkable at all. While Charles and Henrietta remained childless, the question of the succession was clouded. In 1627 the diarist John Rous wondered what might happen if 'King Charles should be stabbed, as Henry IV late in France, and then the queen regent might mar all'.[172] In June 1628 Rous noted: 'a secret whispering of some looking towards the Lady Elizabeth is fearful to be thought of, in regard of both our sovereign and also a wrong to her. Our king's proceedings have caused men's minds to be incensed, to rove and project, but as for this, it is likely to be merely the conceit of the multitude.'[173] What is remarkable here, besides treasonable conjectures about the succession, is the observation that 'the multitude' *had* 'conceits', and that popular voices invaded the most reserved *arcana imperii*.

Casual contempt for authority could easily mutate into loose talk about wishing the king dead, without much thought to its constitutional implications. So too could alehouse bluster. In May 1628 John Haberjohn, a soldier billeted in Hereford, spoke 'dangerous words against his majesty' that witnesses believed 'tend to high treason'. Report of Haberjohn's utterance quickly reached the mayor and justices, who, moved by their 'duty and loyalty to his majesty's sacred person', had the offender arrested and held in 'close prison' while awaiting further direction.[174]

The affair, like so many others, began in a drinking establishment late one night, when Haberjohn bragged 'that three of their soldiers could beat six' of the city's trained band. This prompted Richard Millard, milliner, to remonstrate, 'I pray God you be true to the king and country,' to which Haberjohn replied: 'you have spoken a bloody word.' Pressed to explain himself, Haberjohn repeatedly declared, 'I am sworn against the king,' adding, for Richard Millard's ears only, 'keep my counsel for there is treachery against the king'. It would be up to the Privy Council to determine whether they faced a plot against the monarch, or only a soldier who had too much to drink.

With greater danger, to himself as much as to the regime, a Salisbury tailor's apprentice named John Stephens said or did something around New Year 1632 that looked or sounded like treason. Brought before the city's mayor and justices, Stephens confessed 'that he had a treasonable intention to take away the life of the king's most excellent majesty'. Perhaps he said, as had others, that he wished the king dead, and was willing to undertake the task. The local magistrates took statements and examined witnesses, but, the case 'being of so high a nature and so much concerning the whole state', they sought advice from the Privy Council in London. The mayor wrote from Salisbury on 10 January 1632, and three days later the Council wrote back, ordering him to transfer all 'papers and informations' to Lord Chief Justice Richardson, and to have Stephens brought up to London 'under safe guard . . . for the discovery of the truth'. The principal witnesses, three Salisbury men and one woman, were also summoned to London.[175] There the documentary record ends, at least in State Papers and records of the Privy Council. The manuscripts do not tell us the disposition of the case, and the papers collected by Sir Thomas Richardson seem not to have survived.

A remarkable printed ballad, however, sheds light on this episode. Titled *The Godly End, and wofull lamentation of one Iohn Stevens, a youth, that was hang'd, drawne, and quartered for High-Treason*, and sung 'to the tune of Fortune my Foe', it reports the downfall of the apprentice from Wiltshire who was executed in March 1633 for treasonous speech against the king. Crude woodcut illustrations show the young man on the gallows, and his severed head and quarters spiked on Salisbury's city gates.[176]

Although we still do not learn what Stephens said that caused his doom, the ballad renders his lamentation in sensational and sentimental terms:

> Did ever any hear of one so young
> That was so bad and had so vile a tongue?
> It was the devil that wrought my overthrow,
> It was the devil that brought me to this woe.

We hear how the young man was arrested in Salisbury for his 'vile and base' offence, taken to London for examination, held for almost a year in King's

Bench prison, then returned to Wiltshire for trial at the assizes, and there
found guilty and sentenced to die. The ballad is a grim warning of the
consequences of treasonous speech. Chastised and repentant, the John
Stephens of the ballad counsels parents and children, echoing catechisms
on the fifth commandment:

> Oh do not suffer them to curse and swear.
> But train them up the God of heaven to fear,
> Teach them obedience to their sovereign king,
> And their superiors, whence doth virtue spring.
>
> Honour the king, for so the lord doth say,
> And see the magistrate you do obey.
> Unto your equals loving be and kind,
> To your inferiors bear an humble mind'.

It concludes with a loyal prayer, that seeks to erase the treason:

> Lord bless the king, and send him long to reign,
> Preserve the queen, their issue and their train,
> And God forgive me, and my prince I pray,
> Whose laws and statutes I did disobey.

While John Stephens was under investigation, one Morgan, a priest in
London, said in January 1633 that 'the king had need look about him, that
his crown and life be not brought to the stake'. Several who heard these
words reported 'divers more of worse nature'.[177] The scare prepared the
ground for the case of Arthur Crohagan, an Irish Catholic who was
executed in November 1633 after saying: 'I would kill the king of England
if I could come at him.' Crohagan's case is recorded in law reports, diaries,
and correspondence, but is more complex than at first appears. Two English
merchants, Wheeler and Elesey, testified that the Irishman spoke treason
two years earlier in Lisbon, 'in great heat of speech', vaunting his animosity
towards King Charles, 'because he is an heretic'. By one account (in
William Whiteway's diary, which misidentifies the offender as 'Patrick an
Irish Jesuit'), the traitor 'swore he would never come into England unless it
were to kill the king'. By another (in John Flower's letter to Viscount
Scudamore) the Irishman's motivation included revenge 'for the blood of
the martyrs'.[178]

Then in August 1633, when Crohagan arrived in England, 'for this
purpose', he was arrested at his lodgings in Drury Lane. Told by the arresting officer that he was now the king's prisoner, Crohagan 'most insolently

put his finger into his mouth and scornfully bit his thumb, saying, I care not thus much for your king'. This was a derisive gesture, compounding his offence with the pantomime of seditious libel *sine scriptis*. The Attorney General observed 'that in Spain the biting of the thumb is a token of scorn and disdain in the highest degree, and will bear an action of disgrace in Spain as spitting in one's face will in England'. (Compare *Romeo and Juliet*, Act 1, Scene 1, where Sampson, a retainer of the house of Capulet, offers, when Montague men appear: 'I will bite my thumb of them, which is a disgrace to them, if they bear it.')

Crohagan pleaded not guilty, but confessed under pressure 'that he was a Dominican friar and made priest in Spain. And although this, and his returning into England to seduce the liege people were treason by the statute of 23 Elizabeth, yet the king's attorney said he would not proceed against him for that cause, but upon the statute of 25 Edward III'. As the lawyer Sir George Croke commented, 'his traitorous intent and the imagination of his heart declared by these words it was . . . high treason, by the course of the common law and within the express words of the statute'. Convicted in King's Bench, Crohagan was hanged, drawn, and quartered on 27 November 1633. His last words, according to the lawyer Justinian Pagitt, were that he 'wished that he might never enter into the kingdom of heaven if he ever said those words for which he was condemned'.

Crohagan, it turns out, was actually Arthur MacGeoghegan, scion of a prominent Irish family, indeed a Dominican, who became port chaplain at Lisbon around 1630. There he fell foul of an English captain Bask or Bust, who subsequently denounced him to the London authorities. Catholic sources emphasize the captain's grudge rather than the Dominican's words, which, in their version, were misconstrued and, of course, free of malice. Efforts by Henrietta Maria and Secretary of State Windebank to save him proved fruitless, and MacGeoghegan died a gruesome traitor's death. However, contrary to custom, his quartered remains were not displayed on the gates of the city, but were retrieved by fellow Catholics for more honourable burial.[179] These cases undercut the assertion that 'there was no single case of execution for treason or crimes of state' in the 1630s—a claim that has gone from book to book, and perhaps into countless student essays.[180]

Misconstrued or misheard words led to the investigation of another possible assassination plot in the autumn of 1636. After an evening drinking in their shared lodgings at Bagshot, John Bumstead, a messenger for Sir John Thimbleby, told his chamber companion John Jonson that he had information for the Earl of Holland, 'who must speak with the queen before his business could be dispatched'. Though the inebriated messenger 'spake somewhat thick', Jonson thought he said something about 'cutting off the king's person', and reported this to the authorities.[181] Bumstead was sent to the Tower for his 'evil words and purposes to the king', and 'for saying he would cut off the king, or the king must first be cut off'. The news writer Edward Rossingham described Bumstead as 'a very poor silly fellow, but such language is not to go unpunished'. He was still in the Tower in March 1637 when Robert Reyce reported the incident to John Winthrop in New England.[182]

Other threats to the king's life emerged from casual rants against authority. John Wise, a husbandman of Rettendon, Essex, declared before witnesses in May 1636 that 'if I were a pressed soldier the king should be the first that I would aim at'. He was indicted at the assize on charges of high treason, for conspiring to depose and kill his majesty, but the case collapsed and Wise was acquitted.[183] Two years later in Gloucestershire, labourers threshing grain at Compton Abdale moved on from grumbles about Ship Money to questions of allegiance. 'The king must be served,' said Thomas Welsh, to which Thomas Mace angrily replied, 'if it be so that the king must have all, I would the king were dead'. Summoned before justices to answer for these words, Mace denied 'that ever he used any such speech at all', except to say dutifully 'that God's will must be done'. Not convinced, the justices referred the matter to the next assize.[184]

Another controversial case that raised the possibility of regicide involved Roger Moore, a Protestant adventurer home from the Low Countries, who responded to the question 'what news?' by commending the Dutch resistance against the king of Spain. Asked by neighbours at Middleton, Westmorland, in 1636 whether subjects should resist a ruler who went against their religion, he replied that 'if the king should command him to turn papist or do a thing contrary to his conscience he would rise up against the king and kill him'. The idea of regicide, or tyrannicide, was evidently not as unthinkable as some historians have warranted, and seeped into popular conversation. Another version of Moore's remarks had him saying that 'people might lawfully take arms against their prince in matters of conscience or religion', and in certain circumstances 'subjects might kill their king'.[185]

Report of these remarks spread among villagers, but the authorities took no action until Thomas Layfield, a gentleman, presented a complaint, so he said, 'out of my true subjection to his majesty'. When local magistrates examined witnesses in 1639, some two and a half years after the words had been uttered, the testimony proved contradictory. Some witnesses claimed no recollection of Moore's treasonable remarks, others that they had been misrepresented. The principal accuser, Thomas Layfield, informed Secretary Windebank that Moore was so rich and oppressive 'that almost no poor man dare speak the truth against him, for fear of an ill turn of him or his sons, who are the rudest, most drunken, desperate young men in the whole country'. Nonetheless, he urged Windebank 'to lay open this hidden treason, so nearly concerning his majesty's person'. When James Mansergh, an officer of the crown, attempted to arrest Roger Moore, his son James called the officer 'a base fellow and a base stinking shitten sheriff, and used many threatening words to him', preventing him from doing his duty. The case went to the High Court of Chivalry as well as the Privy Council.

Similarly hot-tempered, and furious at being called 'a drunken rogue', the Worcestershire gentleman John Blount swore in January 1640 that 'he would burn the town, yea if he could all England, and if the king were there present he would stab or kill him with his knife if he had it in his hand'. His adversary, Edmund Woodford, quite properly responded, 'Sir, take heed what you say,' to which Blount replied: 'I have spoken treason but I care not.' His words, he claimed later, were spoken 'more in passion than in drink', though he had consumed a vast amount of sack. Woodward conceded that Blount never 'meant the king any hurt', but local magistrates sent copies of the examinations to London in case the Privy Council wished to take the matter further.[186]

More dangerous to Charles I were the views of Thomas Stafford of Youlthorpe, Yorkshire, who 'being high flown in drink' one Sunday in January 1641 suggested that 'such a king was worthy to be hanged'. He then expressed the wish that the Scottish commander Leslie would soon be king, 'for he was a better man than any was in England'. Hauled before the northern assize, Stafford denied 'that he ever spoke any such words against the king and queen', but the evidence against him was overwhelming.[187] A Middlesex woman, Judith Castle, was also charged in January 1641 with urging her husband to go and kill the king, but confessed that 'she wished the death of her husband, and is very sorry that she spoke such words'.[188] Some of the 'rascal rabble' who mobbed the streets of the capital later that year cried out 'that the king was not fit to live, others that the prince would govern better'.[189]

Madmen and Children

Casual or drunken remarks like these did not seriously endanger King Charles, whose life, until the Civil War, was singularly unthreatened. But no compassing or imagining of the king's death could go unpunished. Even the blabberings of madmen and children would be monitored if they challenged royal authority.

In March 1634 a deeply disturbed Londoner announced himself as Henry, son of King James and Queen Anne and therefore the true king, but his claims were quietly ignored.[190] More threateningly, in September 1636 a mad man in Lincolnshire, Rochester Carr, 'broke loose into the street and said in the audience of many people, that he would go to the court... only to kill the king, and then he would marry the queen. The people knocked him down for these speeches.'[191] Early 1637 Morris Dunn, a London cobbler, startled drinkers at a house in King Street by saying: 'I came to kill the king, but that he is so fast locked up that I cannot come at him.' In this case the would-be assassin was aged almost 80 and had spent nine years in Bedlam, though he 'hath been pretty well in his wits ever since'.[192] Yet another mad man was Philip Stanley of Chichester, examined in August 1637 for 'certain desperate and treasonable speeches'. On discovering him to be 'distracted in his wits', the authorities moved him to 'the hospital and prison of Bethlehem' in London. Although Stanley posed no serious threat to his majesty, the Council commended the mayor of Chichester 'for his care and diligence herein, considering the words that were spoken were of so high a nature and importance that too much caution cannot safely be used for the preventing of danger and punishing offenders in this kind'.[193] Also apparently distracted was John Hammond alias Hendley, who claimed to have supernatural powers and said in 1639 'that he had the king's life at an hour's warning, and that if he pleased, he could put his crown upon his own head in despite of all the world'.[194]

Technically, at least, insanity was no defence in a treason case, for 'in our law *crimen laesae majestatis* is accounted so grievous an offence, to conspire against the breath of him who is the breath of our nostrils, that it is no plea for him that is *non compos mentis*, although it be for ordinary homicide', so Thomas Hurste reminded judges in 1637.[195] In practice, however, as in earlier reigns, the courts took note of a defendant's mental condition, and often preferred confinement to corporal punishment for offenders troubled in mind.

The words of children as well as madmen came under scrutiny by the ever-vigilant Caroline Privy Council. In a case from 1633, the Council sought help from Wiltshire justices 'in discovering the bottom' of alleged 'treasonable speeches' by a 6-year-old child. Based on information from the schoolmaster of Warminster, Mr Zouch,

it appeareth that one Richard Warren, the son of John Warren, a child of six years of age, standeth charged by the testimony of Drew Deadman and Francis Good-eride, children of like age, his schoolfellows, with uttering of certain desperate and treasonable speeches tending to the taking away of the life of his sacred majesty. Now forasmuch as this information containeth matter of a very tender and high nature, we have thought it meet to acquaint his majesty therewith, who thereupon declared his royal pleasure, that the said Richard Warren shall forthwith be sent up hither under the custody of Thomas Smith, one of the messengers of his majesty's chamber. And because the boy is very young and under the years of discretion, and in all likelihood inapt of his own motion to utter such desperate and devilish speeches against his majesty, but hath received the impression from some other ill-affected persons of more years, we therefore think it fit and requisite that you inform yourselves tactfully of the qualities, dispositions and professions of his parents, friends, and such others with whom he doth use to converse, and from whom he may probably be encouraged to such malicious words and thoughts. It may be more important to discover the root from which this infection hath grown than the evil itself in a child of his years.

The letter was signed by Archbishop Laud and six other Privy Councillors, and one wonders how much time they invested in this effort.[196]

In 1635 the government investigated another child offender in the same county. This time their target was 10-year-old Elizabeth Horne, servant to a village tailor, who was brought before Sir Francis Seymour and Sir Walter Smyth at Marlborough on 5 March, 'for speaking of lewd words concerning his majesty'. The morning before, being rebuked by her master, she 'wished herself hanged', and said, 'if any man would give her a hundred pounds she would kill the king'. When her master reproached her for this speech, which was heard by the whole household, 'she presently fell on her knees and wept, saying she was heartily sorry for what she had said, and prayed heartily for the king and queen, and . . . hath remained heartily penitent ever since for her offence'.

Elizabeth Horne, it seems, was a child of the parish, a bastard or an orphan, kept at the public charge. She had served William and Margaret Evans for three years, and had previously served Annis Hulett. She was, she told the magistrates, 'often frightened', and suffered pains in her legs and feet. She did not deny her outburst, but said 'she was extremely sorry', prayed God for forgiveness, and claimed 'that she had no ill intent in her heart'. But her master, William Evans of Great Bedwyn, felt obligated to report the matter to the magistrates, and they in turn took the utterance seriously, for, as they informed the council, 'we could not do less in discharge of our duties'. They held the child in the local Bridewell pending further directions from the council.

We might think the outpourings of a miserable child a trivial matter, of no public consequence. But to speak of killing the king was to speak treason. William Evans could not allow such words in his house, especially if overheard by a neighbour, without doing his public duty of informing the authorities. Anything else might associate him with his servant's sentiments. The justices responded according to their charge, by examining the parties concerned and making their report. The king himself took note of Elizabeth Horne's 'lewd words' and decided on mercy. 'Although the offence be of so high a nature, yet his majesty in his princely lenity, imputing the same rather to childish folly (she being so young) than inward malignity, doth hold it a sufficient chastisement that she be taught by a rod to have more care of her tongue hereafter.' Elizabeth was to be whipped and dismissed, leaving the authorities to reflect on the pervasiveness of incivility and sin among the common people.[197]

Two years later the 'scolding differences' of 'beggarly and angry women' at Ipswich led to investigation of the teenage Anne Dixon, who allegedly threatened the life of King Charles. Phillippa Smyth, a sailor's wife, told magistrates in 1637 that, while her husband was at sea, she and her child lodged in the house of John Dixon, caulker, paying rent of three pence a week. One Friday in September they were in company with Dixon's wife (not otherwise named), Dixon's 14-year-old daughter Anne 'who is very untoward of her tongue', among others. Dixon's wife, Phillippa recalled, 'fell to speak concerning preaching, and wished they were in New England'. Then, 'without any other body speaking any words of the king's majesty', young Anne Dixon 'spake these words: Let the king be hanged.' Phillippa reported that she instantly reproved the teenager (though that should surely have been the mother's task), saying: 'Fie, fie, let us have no more of these words, these are heinous words; upon which the said Anne said again, let the king be hanged if he would, what care I?' There the matter rested until the following Sunday morning, when Phillippa encountered Anne 'set lazing in the house', and charged her, 'you are a large girl, you set lazing there, and your mother's business to do'. The girl responded, 'be hanged if you will, and bad a turd in her teeth'. This prompted Phillippa to declare, 'you know, I can hang you, if I will', alluding to Anne's earlier remarks about the king.[198]

Examined by the authorities, young Anne related how the women had been gossiping at her mother's sickbed. Goodwife Smyth, she said, 'was telling the rest of the company of a woman who was in prison in the town for speaking of words, and [she] repeated the words that were reported to be spoken by the woman'. Anne, unimpressed, remarked, 'that is nothing'. Phillippa Smyth then 'fell on chiding' her, and Anne retaliated, 'hold your tongue and be hanged', and claimed to have said no more.

Household relations deteriorated further a day or two later when Anne Dixon discovered that Goodwife Smyth possessed a key 'that would open [her] father's cupboard where he had lain his money'. She reported this finding to her mother, who, from her sickbed, 'gave warning to the said Smyth's wife to depart out of her house'. To this Phillippa allegedly responded, 'if I depart out of the house I will make your daughter pay for it'. Leave she did, and evidently made good on her threat, telling the Ipswich justices that Anne Dixon had said, 'Let the queen be hanged.' Anne, however, 'denied that she did speak any words either of the king or the queen'.

According to Amy Hudson, the wife of a ship carpenter, who had been present when the women quarrelled, Phillippa Smyth had reproved Anne 'for being so bold in her speeches toward her, whereupon diverse words passed between the two'. Anne had said, 'Hold your tongue, you would scold by and by', adding the insult, 'be hanged'. Crucially, however, Amy Hudson denied hearing anyone 'speak any words of the king's majesty or the queen'. When Phillippa asked, 'did you overhear such a vild mauther [Suffolk dialect for 'wicked young girl'], she spake treason against the queen?' Amy responded: 'do not call me for a witness, I heard no such words spoken.' It was not even clear if the threat was to the king or his wife.

The exchange, so far as we can reconstruct it, was trivial, though in Phillippa's version at least it veered onto dangerous ground. We seem to be glimpsing a spat within a household, a gathering of gossips, in which lines of authority and deference became tangled. Phillippa Smyth, a wife and mother herself but temporarily a paying guest, seems to have taken on the task of disciplining a sluttish teenager. The girl, appealing to her own mother, and defending her father's household resources, managed to get the outsider ejected. The incident exposes some of the dynamics of domestic relations, hinging on age and gender, in a case where the men were absent. (All the females in the case made marks instead of signatures, indicating limited literacy.)

Why should the justices and bailiffs of Ipswich (William Cage, William Tyler, Robert Sparrow, and William Moysey) invest so much effort in examining this petty squabble and conveying their reports to the Privy Council? Part of the answer must be that for anyone to say 'let the king be hanged' was not petty at all but verged on treason. Such words could not be ignored, even if there was uncertainty that they had actually been spoken. The complaint 'imported matter concerning his majesty', no matter how paltry the source.[199]

But other circumstances may have drawn official interest to Anne Dixon's dangerous words. Early Stuart Ipswich was an important port and a hotbed of Puritan activity. The celebrated Samuel Ward had been town preacher there since 1605 and had himself been imprisoned briefly in 1621 for 'intermeddling with his majesty's secret affairs'.[200] Ward was under investigation again in 1634 when Matthew Wren, bishop of Norwich, cracked down heavily on Puritan irregularities, and in 1635 he was suspended from his ministry after a gruelling investigation by the Court of High Commission. Wren's episcopal visitation was the spur for William Prynne's attack on the bishops, the notorious *Newes from Ipswich* (secretly printed in 1636). The Council was always sensitive to disloyalty in East Anglia and watchful for linkages between Puritanism and sedition. Several groups of emigrants to New England set out from Ipswich, including those on the *John and Dorothy* in 1637.[201] Only two years earlier the Ipswich notary Henry Dade had declared that 'the king and his Council would be glad that the thousands that went to New England were drowned in the sea'.[202] Goodwife Dixon's apparent sympathy for the emigrants to New England may have identified her with the unruly godly, and her daughter's undutiful sentiments may have been taken as an echo of her own.

The case took a new turn in January 1638 when John Dixon of Ipswich (now described as a labourer) petitioned for his daughter's release after fourteen weeks in state custody. The accuser, Phillipa Smyth, had fled the area, leaving no reliable witness to a case that seemed driven by malice. A week later the Council ordered Anne Dixon to be set at liberty, and all proceedings against her were dropped.[203]

Undutiful Clerics

Some of the men charged with derogatory speech against Charles I were clergymen who should have known better. One of them, surprisingly, was the Arminian sacerdotalist John Cosin, whose table talk brought him legal difficulties. A rising star in the ecclesiastical firmament, Cosin had been master of religious ceremonies at the king's coronation. But at dinner with Durham prebendaries at the end of April 1628, Cosin allegedly said that 'King Charles is not supreme head of the Church of England next under Christ, nor hath he any more power of excommunication than my man that rubs my horse heels'. These were dangerous words that challenged the foundations of the post-Reformation confessional state. Though Cosin and his friends protested that no such words had been uttered, the charge brought him before Star Chamber, 'for denying the Supremacy', and dogged him for more than a decade. Correspondents could not resist retelling the story, and it passed into networks of news. One possible source of the story was Peter Smart, the Puritan-inclined Durham prebendary who was hostile to Cosin's ceremonial innovations.[204]

Cosin, for his part, protested his 'abused innocency', and asserted his devotion to 'the king's most sacred power'. The charge, he said, was an 'evil' slander, an invention spread by 'a son of Belial'. Rather, he had said no more than that the power of excommunication came from Christ to those in holy orders, and that no English monarch had taken such power upon him. As to the question of the king being head of the church, neither laws nor canons nor even the Act of Supremacy made that claim, for the king was but, under Christ, supreme governor. The 'casual discourse' that provided the setting for this conversation was among learned men, mostly clerics, who surely understood the distinction between the king's jurisdiction over the church, and ecclesiastical spiritual power that derived only from Christ. Cosin vehemently denied speaking 'any irreverent words of his majesty', or anything to 'derogate from the king's majesty's royal power', and completely distanced himself from remarks about 'horse heels'.[205]

The damage control was prompt and effective, and cleared the way for John Cosin's future preferment. But a dozen years later people were still discussing his remark that 'the king hath no more power in matters ecclesiastical than the boy that rubs his horse heels'.[206] The clash of memories in 1628 coincided with the storm over Peter Smart's denunciation of John Cosin's ceremonial excesses at Durham cathedral, Cosin's notorious espousal of quasi-Catholic devotions, and his identification with the anti-Calvinist Arminians who were under attack in parliament. To Cosin's enemies, including Joseph Mead at Cambridge, 'a great part, if not the most of the evil in our church at this present is supposed to proceed from him'.[207] Cosin was able to turn the tide from an attack on his own ceremonial practices to an attack on his enemies. Despite these controversies Cosin rose to become Master of Peterhouse (1635), Vice Chancellor of Cambridge (1639), Dean of Peterborough (1640), and, after the Restoration, Bishop of Durham.

Another prominent cleric whose table talk brought him trouble was John Williams, bishop of Lincoln and former Lord Keeper, whose fall from favour coincided with the rise of William Laud. Williams had fallen foul of Buckingham and Laud, and his enemies collected damaging reports about him. Their vindictiveness and backbiting made for a case of extraordinary complexity. Walking in an arbour at Bucdken, Huntingdonshire, in July 1627, in company with other clerics, Williams allegedly made remarks 'to the great dishonour of his sacred majesty'. Even the gardener was pressed to give evidence.[208] Later in July 1632, at a private dinner with Dr William Spicer at Westminster, Williams allegedly complained that 'the king was made against him' by his enemies, and warned that 'should there come a parliament . . . both the king and they should have cause to repent of meddling with him'. These were dangerous remarks, though perhaps not so serious as other words the informant said 'he durst not repeat'. Report of the conversation reached the royal chaplain Peter Heylyn, who felt duty bound to inform Secretary Coke that the bishop had spoken 'to the dishonour of his majesty and to the prejudice of his affairs'. Tale bearing of this kind would not stand up in court, but it kept pressure on Williams and further ingratiated Heylyn as an instrument of his patron Laud. As John Cosin and Hugh Pyne had found to their cost, private words could easily come back to haunt them.[209] In 1637 Williams was sentenced in Star Chamber for 'words spoken by him publicly of the king', including the 'strange speech . . . that he held his bishopric by as good right as the king held his crown'.[210]

Dozens more clergymen spoke rashly or disparagingly of royal authority during the 1630s. The same kind of process that allows us to eavesdrop on alehouse conversations also brings to light expressions that ministers would never have set down on paper. Despite their obligation to pray for the king, and their duty to teach obedience, these clerics clashed with state power and found themselves in trouble. Some objected to particular royal policies, like the promulgation of the Book of Sports or the war with the Scottish covenanters, while others were simply hot headed. Their stories illuminate some of the complexities of Caroline religious culture and the tensions that beset local communities.

Richard Carrier, vicar of Wirksworth and rector of Carsington, Derbyshire, was prosecuted in 1631 for 'irreligious and profane speeches to the disgrace of the state and his majesty's government', among other outrages and offences. Speaking privately and casually, he allegedly said 'that there was a double persecution in our kingdom, one against papists and another against protestants... that it was never good since there was so much preaching, and for the people, hang them, let us get what we can out of them and let them go to the devil'. He had also spoken controversially about purgatory and prayers for the dead. Such words might normally have brought the speaker before the episcopal courts or the Court of High Commission, but Carrier's many enemies made this a Star Chamber matter.[211] The case was the culmination of a series of suits and counter actions involving control of the mineral-rich Peak District.

Carrier was rich and well connected, and as Barmaster of the wapentake of Wirksworth rigorously collected his mining dues and tithes of ore and lead. One local gentleman described him as the 'arch enemy of our parish'. On one occasion Carrier's wife Jennet drew a knife against a parishioner and said, 'if I should kill one of the rogues it were but an hanging matter'.[212] The Star Chamber judges described Carrier's words as 'foul' (Chancellor of the Exchequer Cottington), 'heinous' (Chief Justice Richardson), 'scandalous' (Secretary Coke), 'ungodly' (Sir Thomas Jermyn), 'odious' (Lord Keeper Coventry), and 'malicious... and seditious' (Lord Privy Seal Montague). But fortunately for the clergyman the witnesses 'did not agree about the... scandalous words... the words were very uncertain', and many of the complainants proceeded 'out of malice'.[213]

Several of the judges expressed concern about the private and domestic occasions of Carrier's alleged ill-speaking. 'It is objected these were but table talk, and at a feast, yet they are foul things and not fit to be concealed,' observed Sir John Finch, asking 'should treason spoken at tables be concealed?' The recent judgment in Pyne's case had shown how hard it was to prove such things. 'It is hard I confess to call in question for all that is spoken at table,' agreed Justice Heath, 'and yet this should not have been a table argument.' Chief Justice Richardson blamed Carrier's host (and chief accuser), John Gell, 'for making his cups a snare, and reporting what was discoursed at his table', and complained of 'the insolency of the times [when] people will teach divines divinity, judges the law, and some will teach statesmen to govern'.[214] There was no diner's privilege, no excuse for seditious words in any setting, but no certainty either that report of these words would stand up in court.

Ultimately Star Chamber found Carrier guilty. His words alone did not condemn him, although they added weight and texture to other charges. He was fined £500, removed from the Barmote, stripped of his privileges in the lead mines, and briefly imprisoned. His wife Jennet was also imprisoned and fined £50. Carrier's ruin was compounded by the loss of his ecclesiastical living. But a decade later, when civil war broke out, Carrier would take the king's side when his old enemy Sir John Gell sided with the parliament.[215]

While Carrier's case was proceeding, two more clergymen found themselves in trouble for their words. Peter Simon, curate of Newland, Gloucestershire, ventured the levelling opinion 'that setting the king's place and quality aside, we were all equal in respect of manhood unto him'. He expressed this thought while counselling enclosure rioters in the Forest of Dean at Maytide 1631. Called before the bishop of Winchester, Simon wisely acknowledged 'that he doth with all his soul detest all anabaptistical and Jesuitical opinions and positions that oppose the authority, power, dignity, preeminency, and safety of princes; and that he doth acknowledge that there is upon kings and princes God's character which maketh their persons sacred as God's anointed'. He further assured the bishop that not a day went by 'in which he will not pray for his sacred majesty, and for the upholding of his royal dignity and preservation of his sacred person'. And, as to 'the common condition of humanity', far from espousing erroneous opinions, 'his meaning was, though kings and princes did consist of soul and body as other men, yet the endowment of God's grace and gifts of his holy spirit are greater and more abundant upon princes than inferior persons'. Suitably cowed and repentant, Simon was allowed back to his parish.[216]

Less successfully, Richard Worsley, curate of St Bartholomew the Less, London, attempted to explain the 'idle paper' he had put up 'in a public place upon a post' denouncing his vicar, Mr Hinshaw, as a crypto-papist. In this he recklessly associated King Charles with popish doctrine, confirmed by 'his going into Spain and afterward into France like a young ass for a wife'. Expecting reward rather then punishment for this libel, the writer signed his notice 'Richard Worsley, curate of St Bart. but in great hope shortly to be vicar'. Instead of preferment, however, his tactics brought trouble and investigation. A London magistrate sent the offending text to Viscount Conway, who referred it to Bishop Laud. The curate's only defence for likening his majesty to an ass was that he was 'distracted' and 'distempered'.[217]

In October 1632 a Dr Conyers of Braintree, Essex, was brought before King's Bench and committed to prison for foolish comments about monarchs. Reviewing the condition of Christendom, he is alleged to have said 'that as the Emperor is king of kings, the king of Spain king of men, and the French king king of asses, so the king of England is king of devils'. It sounds like a joke that went wrong, but words of this sort could not be tolerated. Conyers also railed at Gustavus Adolphus, and claimed that 'whosoever prayed for the king of Sweden was *ipso facto* a traitor to the crown of England, and that none but the damned crew of puritans would do so'.[218]

The London lecturer Nathaniel Bernard spoke 'treasonable words' in 1633 when he told a congregation at Cambridge that 'treason against the commonwealth' was worse than treason against the king, 'so much the worse, by how much the body is better than a member, and the whole is better than a part'. His audience at St Mary's included attentive note-takers, who reported the words to the High Commission.[219] George Preston, the long-serving vicar of Rothersthorpe, Northamptonshire, was cited in 1634 'for speaking scandalous words against the king and queen', but what he said is not recorded.[220] Likewise called before the High Commission for making 'undutiful speeches' against King Charles was Francis Doughty, minister of Sodbury, Gloucestershire, who said he was 'heartily sorry'.[221]

Another Cambridge scandal involved the Dublin-educated cleric Noah Rogers, who had recently returned from New England. Preaching at St Mary's, Cambridge, in March 1634, Rogers reportedly said

that he hoped to die, and tread King Charles under his feet, and willed [his auditors] to go to the king and tell him so. He said he was Christ's subject, and not the king's, he was free born. He said the king was not legislator, but *custos legorum*. He said the king durst not call a parliament. He said he was above the king, and would not preach unto the king unless he would obey him. If he found not justice of the king's majesty, was not the king a tyrant?

Challenged for these words, Rogers 'said he was likely to be hanged already, and was ready to suffer in any place'. Examined later by the vice-chancellor, he denied most of the speech attributed to him and sensibly 'acknowledge[d] the king to be his sovereign'. In mitigation, however, he confessed that 'he is sometimes distempered, by reason of hard study and deep meditations and melancholy, and if he have at any time overshot himself, upon his knees he beggeth pardon for it'.[222]

The republication of the king's Book of Sports drove several ministers to speak contemptuously of the crown.[223] Some wondered aloud, 'if the declaration be his majesty's', and said it seemed more the devil's.[224] One cleric who made 'sundry scandalous and ignominious speeches . . . in contempt of the king's most excellent majesty' was Henry Page, the vicar of Ledbury, Herefordshire. For preaching with 'derision and scorn' against the king's book, and for 'opprobrious and disgraceful speeches' against recreations on the Sabbath, Page was denounced to the High Commission.[225] A more subtly outspoken critic was Edward Williams of Shafton, Dorset, who told his congregation in 1634, in the words of Joshua to the Israelites: 'Choose ye whom ye will serve. But as for me and my house, we will serve the Lord.'[226]

Several clerics were charged in 1638 with seditious preaching or seditious conversation. Enoch Grey's sermon at Maldon in July was only the most outrageous. In addition to associating Queen Henrietta Maria with the whore of Babylon, he commented on the sufferings of Burton, Bastwick, and Prynne (Puritan martyrs or seditious libellers, depending on point of view). Grey warned that any 'goodman that makes profession in these times, he must look for slitting of noses, cutting of noses, and imprisonment'. However, he added, 'there is a Star Chamber in heaven' where comparable punishments would be meted out to God's enemies. He concluded his sermon by praying: 'God grant the king grace that he may be humbled, I pray God convert the queen'. A young graduate in the audience reported these 'seditious and factious speeches' to the authorities, and Chief Justice Bramston began an aggressive investigation. The state needed to know whether Grey had used 'bitter disdainful words against the bishops', had spoken 'something in derogation of the house of peers', and, above all, what else he had said 'of the king or queen in some foul unbeseeming terms'. The government intended that anyone who preached against established law and religion 'might be punished for their sauciness'. Grey, not surprisingly, became a fugitive, though he reemerged in the revolutionary ferment of 1641.[227]

Sir John Bramston also pursued the East Anglian minister Jeremiah Burroughs, whose comments in August 1638 were said to be 'full of danger'. In the course of an after-dinner stroll in the Earl of Warwick's garden, Burroughs talked first 'of the affairs of Scotland', and then went on to espouse a radical political theory akin to that of the Covenanters. Arguing with John Michaelson, the conformist minister of Chelmsford, he asked, 'what if the supreme magistrate refuse or neglect that which he ought to do and is necessary to be done, may not the people give power to some other to supply his neglect and defect?' A shocked Michaelson, of course, answered 'no . . . supreme power is in the supreme magistrate, not in the people'. But Burroughs persisted, demanding, 'whence has he this power but from the people?' Michaelson remonstrated that 'this opinion was full of danger, against clear scripture and the tenet of all sound divines, both ancient and modern . . . the powers that be are ordained by God'. Burroughs then asked, 'with a kind of indignation . . . does God say from heaven that King Charles shall be king of England or Scotland?' Yes, of course, said Michaelson, 'for the crowns or England and Scotland, like other inheritances, fall naturally and be by divine right to the next heir'. Burroughs then 'fell again upon the point of the people's power, that they did originally choose their kings and prescribe them conditions and limited their power by laws'. Not so, protested Michaelson, for kings of England and Scotland 'were never elected by the people, but had their power to govern solely and wholly from God'.

This was not an argument that either party could win, but positions hardened as they continued their walk. Michaelson described Burroughs's opinion as 'absurd' and 'dangerous', for, 'if the people should once be persuaded that all power came from them', and that they could give it 'to whom they list and take it away when they pleased, we should have as many kings as months in the year'. Burroughs gave examples of the republic of Venice and the elective monarchy of Poland, and then argued again for resistance when a king 'should exercise tyranny upon his people'. Was it not lawful, he asked, to resist such a king 'by force, and to defend ourselves and liberties by arms?' Charles I's name had already been mentioned, though the conversation was framed in hypothetical terms. At this point, Michaelson writes, 'our discourse broke off . . . because I retired myself from him', and soon after the loyal minister reported the matter to magistrates. Resistance theory had been aired before, and would become common in the 1640s, but both secular and ecclesiastical authorities found it shocking in 1638.[228]

The Scottish crisis also sparked incautious comments in some pulpits. The requirement that ministers read the proclamation against the covenanter rebels led several into sedition. In London the preacher George

Walker was arrested in November 1638 for 'divers things tending to public faction and disobedience to authority', including his remark 'that we must not too much fear great men, kings and potentates'.[229] A Norfolk minister preaching at Manchester in March 1639 'covertly insinuated to his auditors that they should pray for the good success of the Scotch rebels'.[230]

When another minister, John Kelly of Elstow, Bedfordshire, read aloud 'a manuscript of the Scottish business', which he acknowledged to be 'a dangerous paper', he was charged with 'the moving and stirring up . . . of sedition and debate'. Found guilty at the Bedford assizes in 1639, he was sentenced to a year's imprisonment, a fine of £500, and to stand twice in the pillory wearing a paper that described his crime. One of the magistrates, protective of ecclesiastical honour, proposed to Archbishop Laud that, if Kelly were pilloried, he should 'not receive that ignominy in a clergyman's habit, to the dishonour of the coat, but rather may (at least for that day) be habited as a lay man'.[231] This may have been the same Bedfordshire minister examined in 1639 for saying 'that he loves the Scots much better than the king'. He was committed to Bedford gaol to await the assizes, but 'whether for his life or for a notable misdemeanour, I know not', wrote the news writer Edward Rossingham.[232]

One more minister vehemently exercised by the Scottish crisis was John Girtam alias Haydon, who pushed his way into a pulpit at Stockport, Cheshire, during a burial service at Easter 1639, and ranted about the condition of England. Among other 'railing and unfitting speeches', he said what many perhaps felt but few dared voice:

that if Prince Henry should have been living this day, he would never have suffered such popery and idolatry as now is in England, but would have taken Rome's gate and pulled down the scarlet whore of Rome; nay, said he, if Prince Henry had been living, he would never have suffered such massacres in Germany, whereby many thousand were constrained to eat the flesh of their own arms, but would have defended the Christians from the cruelty of the Emperor; and further said, if Prince Henry had been alive at this day, there had been no rebellion in Scotland, neither durst the Scots so much as have opened their mouths against him.

Taken into custody for these words of sedition, he declared 'that he cared not for 400 constables, four score justices, nor 500 captains'. When one of the officers asked him 'if he cared for the king, yea or no', Girtam answered, 'that he cared not for all men in the world (not giving that dutiful respect as to except the king)'.[233]

As royal and ecclesiastical authority unravelled in 1641, more ministers were emboldened to speak against the crown. The Kentish minister Francis Cornewell was indicted at Maidstone in June 1641 for saying 'that if the king enjoined the Book of Common Prayer or any other testimonies or discipline that were not expressly delivered in God's words, we ought not to obey him'.[234] Enoch Grey returned to the pulpit that year to denounce 'the sins of the king'. Chief Justice Bramston planned to charge Grey with 'sedition and treason', but the king's flight from London in January 1642 brought proceedings to a halt.[235]

Catholic Crimes

A final strand of seditious speech came from the Catholic subjects of Charles I. Most Catholics, of course, held their tongues, but a few spoke boldly against their Protestant monarch. We have already heard from James Farrell who wished the king dead, Henry Sawyer who predicted a deluge of blood, and Mary Cole who talked of hanging his majesty. Catholics were always subjects of suspicion, and their words carried extra danger.

John Trevelyan, a Cornish recusant gentleman, predicted in 1628 'the utter and speedy ruin of this whole state and church', and warned his Protestant neighbours that they 'must change or choose their religion within this month or their throats would be cut'. According to testimony before magistrates at Bodmin, Trevelyan had declared that the psalm sung in church was but 'a Geneva gig', that there was 'knavery in our Bible', and that 'were it not for images we should all be atheists'. The evidence rested on a chain of hearsay, too slender to hang a suspected popish plotter. Trevelyan was a braggart and a nuisance, but the government had no real cause for alarm.[236]

The Catholic soldier John Langton, who was born in Lancashire and served in Denmark, caused consternation at an Oxford alehouse in September 1630 when he championed the Gunpowder Plot. 'It was not treason,' Langton declared, and 'Catesby, Percy and the Winters that were in the Gunpowder Treason were no traitors'. A tailor named Francis Thornton, who had been drinking with Langton, told magistrates about this remarkable discourse. Methuselah Flower, a maker of bowstrings, reported Langton to say 'that the king was a young king, and that he would serve under another king if the king would not pay him his pay'.

There was no shortage of witnesses and little disagreement about the words in question. Under examination, Langton explained that had just arrived in Oxford when 'he fell into company...and had conference with them concerning the Gunpowder Treason'. But he was so drunk at the time that he could not remember anything he said. The mayor of Oxford, however, found Langton to be 'of comely personage, well spoken', and 'very penitient', while his accusers were 'such as are usually found in alehouses in suburbs', and these factors bore in his favour.[237]

Within a week the details reached the Privy Council and came to the attention of the king. Secretary Conway wrote back to the magistrates at Oxford, thanking them for their 'care in making stay of this Langton, whose unwary tongue durst meddle with the censure of things so much above him'. The king's decision, 'of his gracious clemency', was that the soldier 'hath endured a sufficient punishment for this time of his unadvisedness', and that he should be released with a caution.[238] What is striking about this story is not just Langton's sympathy with the Gunpowder plotters, and the ease with which he got off the hook, but the evidence of tailors and bowstring-makers, tavern-keepers and travellers, casually engaged in political conversation. It illuminates once again the usually obscured exercise of citizenship, below the level of the elite, involving words that some deemed offensive.

Another alcohol-fuelled argument in Leicestershire developed into a brawl when John Belgrave declared that 'it was pity the Gunpowder Plot was not effected', and that 'they had done God good service if the Gunpowder Treason had gone forward'. The afternoon drinkers at North Kilworth in November 1633 had already tackled such topics as papist knavery and whether purgatory existed. Belgrave, if not a Catholic, was evidently a Catholic sympathizer. He also had local enemies, who may have sought to entrap him. According to Henry Cherry, husbandman, his accuser John Abbot called Belgrave 'scurvy fellow...keep you from my house...and keep not my wife company when I am gone', before announcing that he 'speaketh treason'. Reviewing the case in March 1634, Attorney General Noy found 'no proof...of words supposed by him to be spoken', and allowed the matter to rest.[239]

A potentially more serious case in 1635 concerned James Nugent, an Irish Catholic merchant based at Ostend, who allegedly spoke 'lewd and pernicious words against his majesty' while visiting Dover. He was drinking in company in the house of the widow Katherine Daniel when her son-in-law

Matthew Bennett, mariner, remarked of the fleet setting out: 'I pray God send them a prosperous voyage.' According to the hostess, Nugent then said: 'I will go with the king to hell gate and there leave him.' To which Ralph Mitchell, a merchant from Taunton, told Nugent 'his tongue was too big for his mouth'.[240]

Pending investigation by magistrates, Nugent was held in Dover gaol 'for speaking words of a high and dangerous nature against his sacred majesty'. These were not treasonous words, of the sort that got Crohagan killed, but they could be construed as seditious. Under examination Nugent denied speaking the words quoted. He did say, however, that several months before some English captains at Ostend had found fault with his religion, prompting him to ask, 'what have you to do with my religion, I am a true subject to my king, and if he go to hell I will go to the door with him'. Matthew Bennett, however, corroborated the hostess's account of Nugent's words, though he could not remember who else was present at the time. It could be that all were befuddled by alcohol, and that Nugent's Irish diction, idiom, or accent caused confusion. When the Somerset merchant Mitchell claimed not to have heard Nugent's dangerous words, the widow Daniel called him 'base rogue'.

James Nugent spent more than a month in prison while the authorities pondered his case. Petitioning for release, he again denied speaking anything against King Charles, although he acknowledged that 'the country phrase where he lives'—about going to the doors of hell—might be used by his enemies against him, and for this he apologised. His adversaries, he told the Council, were trying to ruin him 'out of malice'. Solicitor General Littleton observed in July 1635 that, if Nugent's word were 'wilful or of an ill intent, they are crimes of an high nature and deserve exemplary punishment'; but, if the defendant was to be believed, 'they merit the less correction after divers weeks imprisonment'. The Irishman offered to take the oath of allegiance, though not the oath of supremacy, for 'he knows not what that means'. Littleton was inclined to give him the benefit of the doubt, and the Council evidently concurred in this judgment.[241]

Finally, we have the case of William Pickering, a Shropshire Catholic, who faced charges in Star Chamber and High Commission in December 1635 for speeches against the king and 'scandalous speeches' against religion. 'I am a papist, and the queen a papist, and the king a papist in heart and conscience,' he boasted to Francis Huberly, yeoman. Assuring a local minister that 'all protestants were damned heretics and devils', Pickering exempted King Charles from this category, asserting 'that the king's majesty that now is is reconciled to the bishop and church of Rome'. He was also said to have declared that 'it had been a fine thing to have seen six or seven hundred heretics to have danced the morris in the air [that is, to be hanged] upon the fifth of November in their scarlet gowns'.[242]

Pickering, we learn, was prosecuted for these words, 'not in an ordinary way but by the king's own . . . direction'.[243] He and his wife Ursula were both held in prison (he in the Fleet, she in the Gatehouse), but were freed after eighteen weeks 'at the instance of the queen's majesty'. Their case continued until May 1638, when William Pickering was sentenced to stand in the pillory with a paper on his head, to be fined £10,000, to suffer a whipping, and to lose both his ears. The Lord Privy Seal recommended Pickering to be 'stigmatized with a letter L' or have his tongue bored with awl, and Archbishop Laud agreed he should have 'the highest sentence'. News of this case spread into the general stream of information, with correspondents reporting in June 1638 that 'one Pickering, a recusant, is censured in the Star Chamber to lose his ears and be bored through the tongue for saying the king was a papist in his heart and that all protestants were heretics, and making a hog sty of the churchyard'.[244] It was 'discoursing touching the censure of Mr Pickering' that summer that led the Essex servant Mary Cole to seditious speech of her own.[245]

The recurrence of cases of this nature showed that respect for the monarch could not be taken for granted. They underscore the fragility of conventional assumptions about the king commanding the people's love. They also demonstrate the impossibility of restraining ordinary subjects from meddling in matters that did not concern them. The evidence is overwhelming that commoners of all sorts, in private, domestic, or convivial settings, took a lively interest in the affairs of the crown, and were sometimes reckless in speaking their mind. By Charles I's reign such practices had been exercised for a hundred years, though never with official condonement.

Charles I's councillors encountered scores of subjects who harboured contempt for their monarch, and, because they brought certain cases to his attention, the king became aware of them too. Though much of the commentary was crude and thoughtless, and saturated in drink, it was also tinged with commonwealth theory. Some people expressed the opinion that they were as good as any monarch; some said that kings could be deposed if they failed in their duties; and some espoused a vision of elective kingship, in which there might be choice of a successor. A running motif across his reign was that King Charles was deficient—a boy, a child, not fit to govern.

At the beginning of his reign King Charles observed that it was 'more honour for a king to be invaded and almost destroyed by a foreign enemy than to be despised by his own subjects'.[246] He repeatedly invoked the politics of love, deeming 'the love of our people' amongst his 'greatest riches'.[247] William Laud told him that 'the strength of a people is in the honour and renown of their king; his very name is their shield among the nations'.[248] The Duke of Buckingham assured him that he was 'a glorious king, loved at home and . . . feared abroad'.[249] By the time his kingdom plunged into civil war, however, King Charles had endured a barrage of seditious despite. 'Poor king,' remarked one of his supporters in May 1642, 'he grows still in more contempt and slight here every day'.[250] 'There was never any king so much insulted,' observed another subject on the brink of civil war. Though addressed to recent actions by the Scottish Covenanters, the comment could serve as the epitaph for a troubled reign.

8

Revolutionary Seditions

The revolutionary crisis of 1640–2 and the Civil War that followed energized a thousand conversations. Fed by the newly freed press, and driven by extraordinary events, a politicized populus gorged on rumour and opinion. The arguments of pamphlet 'paper bullets' raged in ale-houses and churches, as the nation tore itself apart. Printed texts sparked innumerable discussions, as did the standard greeting 'what news?' Vehement exchanges brought patrons close to violence in the Angel at Norwich, the Crown at Boston, the Three Trumpets at Dover, and drinking establishments throughout the country.[1] Preachers too stirred partisan opinion in pulpits from Cornwall to Cumberland, adding to the chorus of contention and complaint. There was plenty of work for 'eaves-droppers, whisperers, or informers', as the government of the day sought to manage the 'turbulent humours of the people'.[2]

Royal authority was in tatters on the eve of the Civil War, but the emerging power of parliament commanded no greater respect. As the House of Commons swelled in ambition, it too became the target of derisory popular comment. As military leaders became public figures, they too attracted adulation or scorn. Popular royalism and popular support for parliament were both noisy and unstable, swelling and shifting as the crisis unfolded. Historical attention has focused on the major players, but a sub-current of revolutionary and counter-revolutionary ferment exposed dissensions among the multitude at large.

Our Dread Sovereign

In the face of Scottish insurrection, Puritan disturbances, and popular expressions of contempt, leaders of the established church reasserted the scriptural basis of divine right kingship. The new ecclesiastical Canons of

1640 insisted on the authority of 'our dread sovereign lord, the king's most excellent majesty', and defined all resistance to his power as 'treasonable against God as well as against the king'. Ministers in every parish were required four times a year to 'exhort their people to obey, honour and serve their king', though only the most diligent complied.[3]

The Laudian John Swan in Cambridgeshire spoke in 1640 of kings as '*patres patriae*, fathers of their country', without whom there could be no safety or quiet. Kings were 'God's anointed ones, and may not...be touched with any virulent tongue nor invectives of a bitter pen'.[4] The future bishop Henry King preached at St Paul's that 'the king is the state's pilot, and his law the compass'. Without royal authority we are 'sheep without a shepherd, and water without a bank, and a body without an head'.[5] 'Were it not for the binding force of sovereignty,' preached Richard Gardyner in London, 'our meetings would be mutinies, our pulpits cockpits...the honourable would be levelled with the base, the prudent with the child, all would be amassed and huddled up in an unjust parity, and the land overrun with inflexible generations'.[6] The king, preached Robert Mossom in 1642, is 'the defender of our faith... the preserver of our peace...the protector of our laws...cursed is he that despiseth him'.[7] The king was the 'keeper' of the people's 'civil blessings', declared another sermon of 1642. 'We should not safely meet and converse together, had we not a gracious king over us to repress our mutual violences.'[8] Urging obedience, an Essex vicar, Edward Jeffrey, allegedly preached in August 1642 that 'the king hath not only power to command all your persons, but also power to take away your goods at his pleasure'.[9] Never before had the English heard such sustained exposition of constitutional theory.

Crude and casual contempt for royal authority prompted a restatement of traditional protocols of loyalty. Conservative clerics reminded subjects of their duty, while opponents of royal policy were readying to fight their king. Royalist sermons of the early 1640s reiterated familiar phrases in support of 'the powers that be' and gave a new gloss to the injunction 'touch not mine anointed'. Laudian clerics had previously cited this verse on behalf of the priesthood, but now they applied it directly to King Charles, along with the biblical injunction to 'give Caesar his due'.[10] Conservative magistrates tried to maintain conventional discipline by prosecuting people who spoke sedition, even if they had difficulty bringing offenders to court.

Parliamentary authorities also upheld the dignity of the monarch whose policies they opposed, maintaining the fiction that 'the king can do no wrong'. With reference to King Charles, a parliamentary gentlewoman assured her royalist kinsman in 1643 that 'they esteem his person sacred, and pray heartily for his life, and desire and seek his honour and preservation'.[11] The royalist Richard Towgood conceded as much: though 'they charge his majesty's evil counsellors, they seldom ascend so high as to touch the throne'. Unfortunately, however, these principles had less purchase when the country turned from arguing to fighting. Not all on the parliamentary side were so scrupulous as their leaders, and some turned to 'the vilifying and dishonouring of sacred majesty' and 'bitter discourse against sovereign authority'.[12]

Preaching at Bristol in January 1643, Towgood warned that 'to speak bitterly and reproachfully of supreme authority, it is a very unfit, unwarrantable and unlawful thing'. Citing Job 34: 18, he asked rhetorically, 'is it fit to say to a king, thou art wicked, and to princes, ye are ungodly?' No, he answered, 'it is not fit to tax an earthly king'. He quoted Exodus 22: 28, 'Thou shalt not revile the gods, nor curse the ruler of thy people,' and Ecclesiastes 10: 20, 'Curse not the king, no not in thy thought.' And he concluded with the rallying scriptures of 1 Peter 2: 17, 'Fear God, honour the king,' and Matthew 22: 21, 'Render unto Caesar the things that are Caesar's.' It was unlawful, Towgood insisted, 'for any of the subjects to speak evil of their king, no, though he be unjust, and do but weakly govern his kingdom'.[13] 'The king can do no wrong,' another embattled royalist reminded the nation in 1647, 'the king is God's lieutenant, and is not able to do an unjust thing... The justices and ministers are to be questioned and punished if the laws be violated, and no reflection to be made on the king.'[14]

Curse the King

King Charles, however, could not please even his supporters. Thomas Elliot, who was vehement against parliament, despaired in May 1642: 'a plague upon it, his majesty will not stand to anything he saith, for if he would we should have made an end of the business long since.'[15] Even Henrietta Maria berated him in her letters from abroad.[16]

'Poor king,' wrote Thomas Knyvett from London in May 1642, 'he grows still in more contempt and slight here every day... And no wonder, when the reverence and worship of the king of kings comes to be construed superstitious and idolatrous.'[17] Referring to the biblical figure who threw stones at King David, the Herefordshire cleric Henry Rogers called on God to 'confound all those Shimeites that curse the king and esteem no more of him than of a dead dog'.[18] The majesty of monarchy was severely tarnished, as if the anti-authoritarian talk of previous decades was but a prelude. Local magistrates continued to police political discourse for as long as they could, and assizes and Quarter Sessions still sought to punish offenders. Parliament too attempted to preserve the honour of the crown as well as respect for established authority. Middlesex magistrates, in the parliamentarian heartland, sought to maintain order, propriety, and deference to traditional authority. But other courts ceased to function, or limped along with fewer judges and reduced competence. Their records, to the extent they survive, allow glimpses of popular partisan allegiance.

Many people, if pressed, would say on the eve of the Civil War that they were both 'for the king and the parliament'. Others declared with equal vehemence that 'they cared neither for king nor parliament', or 'would neither obey king nor parliament'.[19] These were common positions in the summer of 1642 that became less tenable in the months that followed. Arguing against a neighbour at Grantham, Lincolnshire, in June 1642, the apothecary William Clarke protested: 'thou hast a rotten, stinking heart within thee, for if thou wilt be for the king thou must be for the papists.' Renouncing his allegiance to King Charles, Clarke suggested that the Prince of Wales or the Duke of York should be crowned in the king's absence from London.[20]

At Leicester in July 1642 the summer assizes fined George Knight £300 for 'certain treasonous words' and 'slanderous words spoken against the king', and indicted others on similar grounds.[21] In October 1642 the Chester Sessions indicted Samuel Troughton 'for speaking words against the king's majesty tending to treason'.[22] Matthew Haman, a sawyer at Dover, reportedly said of King Charles in October, 'he is as nothing, if he were a king he would not murder his subjects'.[23] Seeing two sheep's heads on a pole in London in 1643, Alice Jackson of St Andrew Holborn said that she 'wished the king's and Prince Rupert's heads were there instead'. 'The king was an evil and an unlawful king, and better to be without a king than to have him king,' she declared.[24]

A different sensibility drove Edmund Rayner, a religious visionary of Lambeth, Surrey, who told his female followers early in 1643 'that he was as much the Lord's anointed as the king was'. When report of this reached parliament, he was held for judgment at the Surrey assizes.[25] Thomas Aldberry, a London gunsmith (whose profession did well from the war), told listeners in July 1643 that 'there is no king, and that he would acknowledge no king'. In his mind, at least, monarchy was already abolished, long before the revolutionary parliament struck it down.[26] Republican political theory was filtering down to these less tutored levels, blending with altered appreciations of an embattled crown.

Drinking at the Bell alehouse at Fincham, Norfolk, in November 1644, the glover Thomas Theodrick declared, 'the king is no king, he is a bastard, and was crowned with a leaden crown'. Francis Hubbert, yeoman, told him 'that those words were bloody words, wishing him to take heed what he spake'. Within days the exchange was reported to magistrates. Even if these Norfolk villagers were 'Roundhead rogues', as the knacker Miles Cushion called them, there could be no countenancing such seditious talk against his majesty.[27] In February 1645 the House of Lords committed one Churchman to Newgate pending trial 'for speaking treasonable words against the king'.[28] Another Londoner, Ansell Poulten, faced indictment in 1646 for saying 'that the king was run away from his parliament, and that he was no king'.[29]

'What was the king?' asked John Bamforth in a public house at Barnsley, Yorkshire, in November 1645. 'The king was just so and so,' answered Thomas Beeves, making a derisory gesture. Beeves also offered to wager £10 that 'the king's ears was scoffed off within a month', and gave his opinion that the queen 'was gone over to Holland to play the whore', and that 'all the king's issue were bastards'. 'Roundheaded rogues', cried one side of the room, and 'cavalier rogues' the other, though it did not stop them drinking together.[30] 'The queen is a whore, and she left a bastard at Newark-upon-Trent,' announced another drinker, who was fined 100 marks for his comment.[31] Anne Smith of St Giles in the Fields was likewise fined 100 marks in 1648 for her remark that 'the king's children are bastards, and that the queen was delivered of a child at Oxford when the king had not been with her a twelvemonth before'.[32]

For some Londoners it was not enough to fight the king on the battlefield, nor to belittle his authority. They wanted him dead, and expressed a willingness to assist in the task. Henry Sutton, for example, was indicted for treason in January 1643 for saying he would kill the king.[33] 'His majesty is a stuttering fool,' declared Joan Sherrard of St Dunstan in the West in 1644. 'Is there never a Felton yet living? If I were a man, as I am a woman, I would help to pull him to pieces.'[34] Another vocally empowered London woman, Mary Giles, the wife of a lawyer, announced in 1645: 'I will kill the king of England.' She was called before the Middlesex sessions for 'conspiring and designing to compass the said king's death', but it is unlikely that she paid dearly for her comments.[35]

A Pox on the Parliament

Parliament, its supporters claimed, comprised 'a select company of grave, wise, judicious and pious men',[36] who represented the interests of the nation. Its enemies, by contrast, saw Pym and his fellows as 'rogues and devils'. A competing tradition of popular commentary piled opprobrium on leaders at Westminster, especially when they began to exercise power. Being scornful of parliament, however, did not necessarily make one a royalist, any more than mocking the king made one a republican. It was possible to savour anti-parliamentary libels or verses about John Pym without taking a constitutional position.[37] It might be *scandalum magnatum* to dishonour a parliament man, and sedition to deride the institution, but the chaos of the time allowed little room for these issues to be tested. Parliamentarians themselves considered some speech against them to be 'traitorous', though such comments belonged more to rhetoric than to law.

Quarter Sessions records from 1642 contain scores of citations of ill-tempered speakers saying such 'wicked and devilish words' as 'pox confound the parliament' or 'the devil take the parliament'. The House of Commons too collected reports of 'words tending to treason and sedition'.[38] If such speakers could be apprehended, they were usually bound over to appear or held until the next sessions, though a surprising number were reported to be still 'at large'. Often the matter went no further, once the authorities had expressed their disapprobation. If a case went to trial, a jury might well find the defendant 'not guilty'. Scandalous and seditious speech rarely resulted in severe punishment at this time, though moderate doses of fining, pillorying, and short-term imprisonment were frequently recommended.[39]

The table talk at a Kentish vicarage became matter for public discussion when one of those present, the curate Mr Minis, reported the conversation to the House of Commons. At dinner, said Minis, Dr Peake and his father-in-law made 'base and scandalous speeches' and 'wicked and traitorous speeches' against parliament, the City, and the godly. 'A company of five hundred good soldiers out of Ireland would quickly vanquish them all and put them to flight,' said Peake of the London-trained bands, adding 'that it were a good deed to take the Lord Mayor, the Sheriffs, and some of the Aldermen, with others of good rank and quality, and hang them up at their own doors, the rest would soon be brought to subjection'. The conversation would seem to date from early 1642, after the king's flight from London. A version of Minis's report went into print, with hopes that 'the parliament will take these invective aspersions of such railing Rabshakehs into their grave and judicious considerations'.[40]

In May 1642 the House of Commons learned of Thomas Elliot's brag 'that he would kill any man whom his majesty should command or bid him, without questioning the cause'. As for the parliament, said Elliot, 'hang them dogs . . . they have no more religion than a company of dogs'.[41] In June 1642 they heard of Ellis Coleman's 'scandalous words' in a London shop, reviling the parliament as 'malignant'. Though parliament talked of making King Charles the most glorious king, he said, they 'only meant to fetch the king by force and put him into the Tower a prisoner and make him only a titular king not having any power of his own'. Bidding 'a turd on Pym's teeth', Coleman swore 'he would go ten miles to see him hanged'.[42]

The papermaker Henry Wheatley declared that summer that 'they were all a company of fools that would not hold with the king'.[43] A Mr Riches, drinking at the Angel in Norwich in July, brandished his knife, so he said, 'to cut all heresy into two, and to cut all the puritans' and roundheads' members off'. Others spoke of hanging or beheading the parliamentary leaders, or otherwise compassing their deaths.[44] An Essex clergyman, Edward Jeffrey of Southminster, declared in August 1642: 'a pox on the parliament, by God, we will first cut the parliament's throats.'[45]

Norwich magistrates in August 1642 stayed judgment on 'very foul and scandalous words' of 'delinquents' until they had 'acquainted the House therewith'. 'A health to our gracious king, and confusion bring to factious Pym,' offered John Coldham, calling anyone who would not join this health 'rebels'. The alehouse conversation, as reported, revealed pockets of hostility to parliament and sympathy for the embattled monarch. William Symonds told John Andrews 'that the parliament went about to take away his majesty's sons, and did condemn the parliament for doing acts against the king'. John Balls told William Youngs that he could not be 'for the king and the parliament . . . for they were severed . . . saying that the parliament was against the king, for if he should go to the parliament they would take away his prerogatives, and commit him to prison, and take off his head'. The discussion became abusive when one drinker called another 'prickears, roundhead rascal and knave, and said he was a better man'.[46]

In a similar conversation the same month at Sherston, Wiltshire, Abraham Haynes, a traveller from London, said he thought 'this parliament should be overthrown . . . then he would warrant there should never be a parliament again while England was England'.[47] A company of 'fiddlers and rogues' at Chester sang 'scandalous songs' at a dinner for the Grand Jury men in which they 'jeered' and 'scoffed further at the parliament, saying reformation would be perfected when the devil is blind'.[48] The same month a traveller from Leicestershire told a Hertfordshire innkeeper, 'he did not care a pin for the parliament, and a plague take the parliament, God bless the king, and the devil take the parliament'.[49] Similar expressions could be heard all over England as the nation descended into civil war.

The wars of the Stuart kingdoms, like all wars, put pressure on morale, allegiance, and opinion. Loyalists and royalists pledged themselves 'for the king', and spoke 'scandalous words' against the parliament. Some of the harshest antiparliamentary remarks come from within the parliamentary heartland. A conversation in the kitchen at the King's Head in Ipswich in November 1642, for example, produced 'opprobrious speeches in a scoffing way against the parliament'. A visitor from Cambridge, Edward Dawtry of King's College, told the company that 'they that fight against the king and his army fight against God', and 'there hath been a king when there was no parliament, but never a parliament without a king'. Out of their 'tender respect and due regard' for the honour of parliament, the bailiffs of Ipswich sent reports of this conversation to Westminster.[50]

In 1643 John Draycott, a Clerkenwell yeoman, called the government 'a parliament of rogues, for they have plundered all honest men and have not left above three or four honest men in the city'. A sympathetic Middlesex jury found him not guilty.[51] Sarah Dennis of St Giles in the Fields, described by the court as 'a mischievous and evil woman', fared worse and faced a fine and imprisonment in December 1643 for saying 'the parliament men are roundheaded rogues', and singling out Lord Say, 'a pox take him'.[52] In Norfolk that year, 'falling out with one of her neighbours' and 'railing with other women', Rachel Mercy of Fakenham declared 'that she cared not, for there is no king, no laws, nor no justice'. When her neighbour Elizabeth

Percival questioned her, she explained that 'there was no king... because the king was not where he should be'.[53]

Two years later in 1645 Margaret Gardner of suburban Middlesex was fined 6s. 8d. for saying 'that the parliament are roundheaded rogues and puritans'.[54] Speakers of similar seditions came before the Quarter Sessions in Essex for abusively naming 'roundhead knaves', 'roundhead rogues', or 'parliament rogues'.[55]

John Voysey, a Devonshire merchant visiting London in 1647, declared 'that some of the parliament men had the pox and were whoremasters, and some of them were rogues and rebels'. These were 'scandalous and disgraceful words', according to Middlesex magistrates, but Voysey disowned them, saying he was 'in his drink'.[56] More jeering references to 'roundhead rogues', 'parliament dogs', and 'parliament whores' can be found in the papers of the parliamentary Indemnity Commissioners of the 1640s and 1650s.[57]

Treason without a King

The revolutionary justice of January 1649 transformed England's legal and constitutional environment. Having executed the king and abolished kingship, the Rump republic sought to protect itself through new legislation. In 1649 it became treason to say 'by writing, publishing, or openly declaring' that the new commonwealth was 'tyrannical, usurped or unlawful', or to attempt its overthrow 'by any open deed'.[58] Whether mere speech could constitute such a deed was unclear. New laws in 1654 and 1656 made it treason to 'compass or imagine the death of the Lord Protector', or 'by writing, printing, openly declaring, preaching, teaching or otherwise' to assail his authority. It was treason to declare the regime 'tyrannical, usurped or unlawful', treason to plot or raise force against the state or to promote the claims of the exiled Stuarts.[59] In effect, the laws that had protected Tudor and Stuart monarchs from treasonous subjects were adapted to the revolutionary regime. As a lawyer instructed an Exeter Grand jury in 1655, 'by the word king' in the statute of 25 Edward III 'must be meant the chief officer, and the bearing of that office... let the name be whatsoever'.[60]

The new laws were primarily directed against royalist conspirators, but they also provided sanctions against activist dissidents, both cavalier and parliamentarian. They did not specifically re-enact treason by words, but they established a framework in which seditious, undutiful, or dangerous speech could be investigated and punished. The act of July 1650 'for settling of the militia' specifically charged commissioners to search out and examine conspiracies against the state 'by words or actions, spoken, printed, preached, written or published', and to secure and disarm 'all papists and other ill-affected persons' who 'shall declare themselves in their words or actions against this present parliament, or against the present government established'.[61] In practice, as earlier, an offender might be threatened with a charge of treason, only to suffer the penalties of a lesser crime like sedition.

From the Regicide in 1649 to the Restoration in 1660, England's revolutionary governments faced low-grade resistance that often took the form of nostalgia for King Charles or expressions of support for his son. Assize records of the 1650s are thick with indictments of commoners cursing the commonwealth and the protectorate. The spectre of royalist insurrection haunted each of the short-lived interregnum regimes. Stuart royalists had no love for Oliver Cromwell and sometimes said so, but disaffected parliamentarians and thwarted radicals could also be heard to excoriate the Lord General who became Lord Protector. So too could those English men and women who grumbled against authority of any kind, however constituted. Dissident speech in this period followed the pulse of public affairs, but seems not to have been severely punished.

The execution of King Charles in January 1649 elicited a groan from the crowd, but any spoken words that accompanied it have been lost. It did not take long, however, for the authorities to react to 'seditious words and speeches' from the pulpits and streets.[62] In September 1649 a Yorkshire minister, Marmaduke Richardson, was summoned to the assizes 'for praying publicly before his sermon in the parish church of Pocklington for Charles II, king of Scotland and heir apparent to this realm'.[63] William Mason of Newless, Yorkshire, a prophet though not a very good one, assured neighbours in January 1650 that 'there should be a king in England... and that very shortly'.[64]

Thomas Welsh of North Dalton, Yorkshire, drinking with soldiers of Colonel Bright's regiment, caused trouble in February 1650 by declaring 'that there is a king, and that England could never be governed aright without a king'. He then drank the king's health, saying that 'Prince Charles was crowned king of Scotland and would shortly be amongst us'. Called before the assizes, Welsh made the usual excuse of drunkenness, said he remembered nothing, and was fined £40.[65] Christopher Wright declared in a common inn at Whitby in August 1651 'that he was for King Charles, and that he would fight heartily for him so long as he did live, though he were hanged at the door cheek for it'.[66] William Bewick of Beverley, currier, declared in October 1651, 'I will drink a health to Prince Charles, King of Scots, and to his good success into England, and to the confusion of all his enemies,' then drank a silver beaker full of ale and demanded fellow drinkers to pledge likewise. Instead, they turned him in to local magistrates.[67]

Charles II had been defeated at Worcester on 3 September, and his cause was in ruins. This did not stop other royalists from pledging the exiled monarch, like John Peacock of East Ayton , who hoped that 'the sun will once again shine', or the bailiff of Rydale who drank 'to three of the best Englishmen which are out of the nation', meaning the Stuart princes.[68] John Harvey, a Suffolk gentleman, was seen 'drinking the king's health and cursing and drinking to the confusion of parliament' in April 1652, and when challenged by the magistrate told him 'he was no justice of peace, for that there was no power to make him one'.[69] The dyer Simon Warrener of Knaresborough, Yorkshire, 'made and penned a song . . . that he wished all gallant soldiers to display their banners and set King Charles in his right again', for which he was examined before the northern assize in May 1653.[70] Hundreds more drank to the 'confusion' of the parliament or protector, and 'healths' to the exiled Stuart, suggesting there could be no lawful state without a lawful king.[71] In April 1658 the Yorkshire cleric John Hitchinough was investigated for saying 'that King Charles's blood would be revenged, and that shortly'.[72]

The Devil Confound Cromwell

Without a Stuart monarch to demean, other disaffected Englishmen turned their spleen towards the governors of the commonwealth. Paul Williams and his wife, who kept an alehouse at Hammersmith, Middlesex, were indicted in December 1649 for calling the parliamentary grandees Lord Fairfax, General Cromwell, and Colonel Pride 'sons of whores', and hoping soon 'to see their downfall'. They were each fined 500 marks, a sum well beyond their capacity. They were also alleged to have called the Council of State 'rogues and murderers of the late king', and wished they would soon be 'cut off or hanged', but on this charge the jury found them 'not guilty'.[73]

In April 1650 a London tailor, John Norris of St Botolph without
Aldgate, declared 'that the late king was illegally put to death, but he
hoped that his persecutors would hereafter suffer for it'. He said too of
parliament 'that the power which they have is maintained only by the
sword, and that they do seek to infringe the liberty of the subject, which
they did formerly promise to maintain'.[74] This was plebeian political thinking, fuelled by indignation and nourished by pamphlets and conversations.
Local judicial records allow us to hear more.

Early in 1650 the schoolmaster of Beeleby, Yorkshire, William Leng,
told billeted soldiers 'that he cared not a turd for them, and that Cromwell
was the son of a whore, that the commons of England were fools, and that
he scorned their government'.[75] Turned in by a Yorkshire parchment-
maker, William Lazenby of Haxby said in January 1651 'that he hoped
within a twelvemonth to see General Cromwell's head off, and all the
heads of all the parliament men in England that now is'.[76] Anne Watson,
the wife of a Middlesex labourer, said in April 1651 that 'they that sit at the
parliament are all the sons of whores, and that she could find in her heart to
blow them up with gunpowder'. A few years earlier disaffected voices had
called for another Felton; now they were invoking the spirit of Guy
Fawkes. Despite the specificity of her words, the jury found Anne Watson
'not guilty'.[77]

James Williams of Carlton, Yorkshire, said in September 1651 that Cromwell's supporters 'would all be hanged, and called traitors and rogues'.[78] The
yeoman William Archer of Etton said in February 1652 that 'the parliament
were traitors and bloodsuckers, and that they had taken off the king's head
and intended to take off his son's, but the Lord had blessed him out of their
hand'.[79] In November 1653 an intelligencer warned Cromwell of more
'harangues of sedition', and 'so many scandalous and scurrilous aspersions
from the pulpit upon the parliament, army, Council of State, and all now in
power'.[80]

After Cromwell's seizure of power a network of agents and supporters
sought to stifle opposition and to keep the government informed. One of
the Protector's friends at Bristol assured Secretary of State Thurloe in
February 1655 that 'his highness may be confident, here are many godly
people that do so love, honour, and pray for him . . . that if they saw the least
tendency by words, gesture, or actions towards any villainy, his highness
should quickly hear of us'.[81] Always vulnerable, the Protectorate regime
relied heavily on intelligence and information.

When a former parliament man, John Williams, denounced the Protector in a sermon in Radnorshire in February 1654, an account soon reached Westminster. 'Railing much against the present times and government', and associating the protectorate with 'slavery and popery', Williams asked his congregation: 'what do you want now, a king? You have one, and that as great a tyrant as the former.'[82] Another hostile preacher in March 1654 used 'all the contemptible words that can be spoken' against Protector Cromwell.[83] In August 1654 one Yorkshireman warned that Cromwell 'will sell us all, as the Scots sold the king'. Another denounced the Lord Protector as 'an idol' and 'a devil', and his regime as 'corrupt' and 'tyrannical'.[84]

Rumours of plots abounded, and those who talked them up, like the button-maker Jasper Mottershed, spoke 'many dangerous words of most evil consequence against the government and public peace'. Mottershed was arrested in June 1654 after reckless talk in the Star inn at Maldon, Essex, about an imminent royalist uprising.[85] Also in 1654 the widow Ellen Wande of Selby hoped to see Cromwell 'come to an evil end, then clapping her hands together in a rage and passion, said, let the rogue look to himself, for there are rods in piss for him'.[86] Others described the Protector as 'a traitor' and his followers as 'rogues and thieves'. 'Cromwell is the son of a whore,' said one Yorkshireman; 'the devil confound Cromwell,' said another.[87] 'The Lord Protector was a traitor,' said the Westmorland cleric Charles Kiplin, who hoped that Cromwell 'and all that took his part would come to a shameful end'.[88] In the metropolis too there were both men and women who called the Lord Protector a 'rogue' or a 'rascal', and 'hoped to see him hanged'.[89]

Comprehensively damning his highness, one Christopher Emerson said before witnesses in September 1655

that the Lord Protector was a rogue and a rascal and blood-sucker, and that he should have his throat cut and his head cleft ere long; and that he was a cowardly rogue, and wore two pistols in his pocket, and was afraid of every dog that barked; and that he should have his throat cut by Michaelmas day, and named weapons to that purpose.[90]

Samuel Baxter, the preacher at Dibden, Hampshire, also 'cast base unworthy aspersions on his highness the Lord Protector' in 1655, calling him 'a countenancer and maintainer of all the sects and errors that were in the kingdom'. Baxter also sang 'ranting, filthy and unsavoury songs', so his enemies charged, including one 'that it would never be well until the king had his own again'.[91]

The Westmorland countryman Richard Browne of Cleaburne was so incensed against the Protector's regime in June 1655 that he 'wished that he had them all in a hot burning oven, he did swear again, God confound him if he would not set up the stone and burn them all to death'. Cromwell was 'a murderer', he said, who 'deserved to be either hanged or headed'. The regime dealt with Browne relatively lightly, fining him £10, then reducing it to £5, but holding him in prison till the money was paid.[92] A Kentish man, Thomas Bennett, said in 1656 'that the land is governed now by none but rogues, knaves and thieves, for want of a king, and that the justices of peace are fools'. Not stopping there, he called Oliver Cromwell 'a fool', named his dog after the Lord Protector, and threatened to kill him if he came near him.[93]

At Maidstone assizes in March 1656 Isaac Atkinson of Wichling, Kent, clerk, was indicted for saying: 'The Lord Protector is a rogue, a robber, and a thief . . . Within a year and half he will have a bullet in his arse, or else I will give the ears from my head.'[94] A Middlesex labourer, Morris Seiston of Stepney, drank to the confusion of Cromwell in June 1656, saying 'he the said Morris was more fit to be a Protector than his highness'.[95] Anne White, wife of William White of Stepney, was indicted at the Middlesex sessions in May 1657 for saying 'that she cared not for the Lord Protector, and would that Cromwell and all his soldiers were hanged'.[96] Her neighbour Jane Neviston said in 1658 'that the Lord Protector was a base rascal-like fellow, and that she hoped to see him hanged'.[97] Even more gruesome was the declaration of Christopher Flower of North Couton, Yorkshire, in 1658, who 'hoped to see the day to wash his hands in my Lord Protector's blood, and that shortly too'.[98] After the Protector's death in September 1658, John Simpson of Clerkenwell said that Oliver Cromwell was a rogue and that he died of the pox. Gabriel Benfield of Mile End said that Cromwell's soul was in hell.[99]

Few of these offenders faced more severe punishment than the pillory and a brief spell in prison. Some remained 'at large' and could not be brought to justice; juries found others 'not guilty'. Several were simply bound over to keep the peace. As the English revolution unravelled, the collapsing regime issued proclamations 'against all disturbers of the present government and against agitators',[100] but were no more successful than their predecessors in silencing dangerous talk.

9

Charles II: The Veriest Rogue That Ever Reigned

The Restoration of Charles II was a joyful affair for most of the king's subjects, but an unhappy turn for supporters of the commonwealth regime. Behind the accolades for the restored royal government were the mutterings of malcontents who found it hard to close the door on two decades of revolution. Although multitudes greeted their king with acclamation, a disgruntled minority continued to speak ill of the monarch. Cromwellian diehards and supporters of 'the good old cause' had no fair words for any Charles Stuart, and some would deny allegiance to any hereditary king. Several unreconstructed republicans were indicted for speaking approvingly of regicide, some going so far as to say that 'all kings' heads should be cut off'.[1] These were extreme opinions, rarely voiced, but the authorities could not afford to ignore them.

Some of this anti-monarchical language was associated with plots to reverse the Restoration, but much of it was just alehouse chatter. Dreams of a republican England became mixed with the ordinary anti-authoritarian belligerence of drunk or disgruntled commoners. The authorities remained vigilant, for nobody could tell whether loose talk betrayed a treasonable project, or how deep a conspiracy might run. The restored Stuart regime could not allow dangerous talk to go unchecked, and making an example of seditious speakers was part of the process of restoration.

Hundreds of English men and women came before authorities in Charles II's reign 'for speaking irreverent and unmannerly and uncomely words concerning the king's majesty', or for uttering words that were 'desperate and dangerous', 'scandalous and treasonable', 'treasonable and seditious', or 'words tending to treason'.[2] Most of those cited were men, and the majority were of plebeian social condition. Of 232 recorded cases of

seditious or treasonable language before the Middlesex Sessions between
1660 and 1688, 182 (78 per cent) involved men and 50 (22 per cent)
women.[3] Among 216 individuals similarly indicted at county assizes, 17
were gentlemen (8 per cent), 12 clerics (6 per cent), 68 yeomen (31 per
cent), 60 labourers (28 per cent), and the rest (27 per cent) various kinds of
artisans and tradesmen or their wives.[4] Their words posed challenges to the
restored Stuart monarchy, though they reflected only a minority opinion.

Restoration Stirs

Both Houses of Parliament concerned themselves with 'treasonable words'
in the crucial transitional month of May 1660. Francis Newport told his
uncle Sir Richard Leveson on 22 May 1660 that 'divers have been committed for treasonable words against the king'.[5] Informers reported 'very
treasonable and dangerous words' amongst soldiers and sailors, including
threats to Charles II's life. Often enough the reports were exaggerated,
malicious, or unfounded. Hearing that a Mr Trevill had said 'that he would
kill the king with his own hands', the Commons referred the matter to a
committee to discover 'the truth of the business' and to see 'what else may
conduce thereunto'.[6] The Lords took up the case of Justice Baynes, a
brewer in Southwark, who under examination denied and 'abhorred' the
'treasonable words against his majesty' attributed to him. Particularly troubling were the words of a Captain Henbury, that, 'if we must have a king, he
did not doubt but to flatter him . . . yet he hoped and did not doubt to see
the king hanged before his own gate at Whitehall within six months after he
came thither'.[7]

A dangerous strain of opinion involved nostalgia for the Commonwealth
and fantasies about alternative successions. Told that 'we shall have a king',
the Yorkshireman Richard Abbott avowed, 'if I had but one bat in my belly
I would give it to keep the king out, for Cromwell ruled better than ever the
king will'.[8] The Londoner William Hammond said likewise 'that Oliver
was as good a man as King Charles was', for which words he was cited to the
Middlesex sessions.[9] William Cox of Wapping said 'that my Lord Lambert
deserved the crown and to be a king better than Charles II'.[10] The Yorkshireman Francis Ryder spoke similarly that Lambert would have been a
better successor to Cromwell, who 'governed better than ever the king will
do'.[11] Discussion of this sort went on for decades, arguing whether Charles I

was justly executed, whether Cromwell was a better man than the king, or which of the two was the greater traitor.[12]

Speaking for other defeated republicans, the Middlesex shoemaker Edward Jones said in May 1660 that the king reigned 'on sufferance, for a little time, and it would be theirs again before it be long'.[13] 'There is a crown provided, but the king will never wear it,' and 'your king ere long will have nothing left to set his crown upon', declared the former Roundhead officer John Hodgson. Hodgson's case reveals some of the reversals of fortune and settling of scores that accompanied the Stuart restoration. Hodgson's enemies secured his arrest and imprisonment in Bradford gaol, and the magistrate at his trial was one he himself had formerly reprimanded. He was eventually freed, after five months in prison, and took the oath of allegiance.[14]

The Declaration of Breda of April 1660 had barely been promulgated when Thomas Willis, a minister at Twickenham, Middlesex, preached against 'a malignant plot to bring in Charles Stuart' and thanked God 'for delivering us from that bloody family'.[15] Others ventured the opinion that the incoming king would not live to be crowned, or that Charles I's fate would soon overtake his son. Several prophesied a short reign and a bloody one for the newly restored monarch.

On hearing the news of Charles II's accession, Margaret Dixon of Newcastle upon Tyne flew into a rage of invective:

What! Can they find no other man to bring in than a Scotsman? What! Is there not some Englishman more fit to make a king than a Scot? There is none that loves him but drunk whores and whoremongers. I hope he will never come into England, for that he will set on fire the three kingdoms as his father before him has done. God's curse light on him. I hope to see his bones hanged at a horse tail, and the dogs run through his puddins.[16]

Even before his own sexual appetites had become widely known, the incoming monarch was described as 'a rogue' and 'the son of whore'.[17]

John Botts, the minister of Darfield, Yorkshire, warned parishioners in May 1660 that Charles II 'would bring in superstition and popery'. His sermon reached its peroration: 'Let us fear the king of heaven and worship him, and be not so desirous of an earthly king, which will tend to the embroiling of us again in blood.' Report of these words brought Botts before the northern assizes, where he was allowed to plead the king's pardon and go free.[18] 'We should have nothing but popery,' feared the Yorkshireman William Poole.[19]

Edward Medburne, a glazier of Wapping, Middlesex, avowed in May 1660 'that if he met the king he would run his knife into him to kill him, and that he did not care though he were hanged for it himself'. If General Monck (the maker of the Restoration) and King Charles were hanged together, Medburne fantasized, 'he did not care if he were the hangman himself, and would spend that day five shillings for joy'.[20] Anthony Chapman, a London labourer, similarly said 'that he hoped to meet the king at the gallows'.[21]

William Fenn of St Martin in the Fields went further when he said 'that he hoped to wash his hands in the king's blood' and offered to thrust 'an old rusty sword . . . up to the hilt in his heart'. An old rusty sword was, perhaps, the sign of a Cromwellian veteran. Fenn boldly repeated his threat 'that if the king were in the room, he would run a sword that was there up to his heart'.[22]

William Sparkes of Stepney greeted the Restoration with 'irreverent and unmannerly and uncomely words' to the effect that Charles II was 'a poor and beggarly king' and that his days would not be long. The thanksgiving day for the Restoration, Sparkes predicted, 'would be the best day that ever the king should have', as if he should not live to enjoy many more.[23] Margaret Osmond likewise prophesied in June 1660 that Charles II 'shall not reign one year'.[24]

Thomas Lunn of Bootham, labourer, appeared at the Yorkshire assizes for saying in June 1660 that 'the king shall never be crowned, and if he is crowned he shall never live long. His father's head was taken off with an axe, but a bill [an agricultural hand tool] shall serve to take off his.' These were treasonous words, though what price Lunn paid for them is uncertain. Difficulties with witnesses and juries impaired the chance of conviction, and punishment could not be guaranteed.[25] Similarly cited for 'speaking and uttering desperate and treasonable words' in Middlesex, Joseph Exton avowed: 'I will be hanged if ever King Charles be crowned.'[26] Nicholas Wright, a wheelwright of Hornchurch, Essex, appeared before magistrates 'for speaking seditious words against our sovereign, by saying "if there were a king", when his majesty was proclaimed'.[27] 'A pox on all the kings,' said Mary Greene of St Paul's Covent Garden soon after the Restoration, adding that 'she did not care a turd for never a king in England for she never did lie with any'.[28]

Though most of those cited for seditious speech were commoners, outside the traditionally constituted 'political nation' they also included a few incautious aristocrats. Viscount Purbeck, a somewhat protean figure with both Catholic and Protestant leanings, both royalist and parliamentarian credentials, and claims to at least four surnames (Villiers, Danvers, Howard, and Wright), was called before parliament in June 1660 for his 'treasonable words and blasphemous speeches'. He had said over dinner with Lord Monmouth 'that it was a very commendable and just action to put the last king to death, and that if an executioner had been wanting, he would have been the person'.[29] It is not clear exactly when Purbeck said these words, if indeed he did so, but similar sentiments were aired in alehouses both before and after the Restoration.

The execution of the regicides prompted the Canterbury shoemaker Simon Oldfield to say in December 1660 that 'King Charles I had a fair and legal trial, and [the Regicides] which were lately executed for the same were executed and suffered wrongly'. Leaving no doubt about his commonwealth loyalties, Oldfield also declared that 'the king is no more head of the church than I am, and I was always against kingly government'.[30]

Rumour and gossip further discredited the restored Stuart monarchy. All sorts of defamatory stories were recited, including the claim that Charles I had helped to poison his father, and that Henrietta Maria's children were sired by the courtier Henry Jermyn.[31] A Whitechapel woman, Jane Blunstone, comprehensively denigrated the royal family, saying that 'the queen is the great whore of Babylon, and the king is the son of a whore, and the Duke of York is a rogue, and such like words'.[32] A Yorkshireman gave out that 'the king is a bastard and the son of a whore'.[33] John Tyler of St Martin in the Fields repeated the claim that 'King Charles was a bastard'.[34] Commentary of this sort had a long life, reappearing in the 1670s in the claim that Charles II was begot by one Barry, a cobbler, on 'the French witch' Henrietta Maria,[35] and that both 'the king and Duke of York were bastards'.[36] Others spoke derisively of the royal family's origins, saying 'one of them formerly run away into another land and got to be steward to some great man there, and so changed their name to be Stewart'.[37] Several subjects made the somewhat puzzling claim that Charles II was 'but a chimney sweeper'.[38]

Some of these comments reveal an almost visceral hatred for the house of Stuart. When the king's younger brother died in September 1660, 'a miscreant villain in Kent, getting into a pulpit, affronted God with thanks for the death of the Duke of Gloucester, adding blasphemous desires for the same upon the rest of the royal stock', so one gentleman informed another.[39]

A similar sentiment was heard at Guernsey in July 1663, when Thomas le Marchant responded to the question 'what news?': 'Good news,' he replied, 'the Princess Royal is dead, and I wish it were the last of the family.'[40]

Malicious and Advised Speaking

New legislation of 1661 was designed to protect the king and his government against 'all treasonable and seditious practices and attempts' and to prevent a relapse into 'the miseries and calamities' of recent years. Invoking the 'right good and profitable law' of Queen Elizabeth (13 Eliz. I c. 1, 1571), and reiterating principles dating back to Edward III, the Restoration statute made treason any attempt to 'compass, imagine, invent, devise, or intend' the death or deposition of the monarch. 'Such compassings', it explained, included hostile expressions or utterances 'by any printing, writing, preaching, or malicious and advised speaking'. Words by themselves could once again secure a traitor's death. Simply to 'affirm the king to be an heretic or a papist, or that he endeavours to introduce popery', was also a crime, short of treason, as was any writing or speaking 'to incite or stir up the people to dislike of the person of his majesty or the established government'. It became illegal to declare that parliament had a legislative power independent of the king. Those found guilty faced exclusion from office and such 'punishments as by the common laws or statutes of the realm may be inflicted', including the penalties of praemunire.[41] (Praemunire, from the Latin for forewarning, was a complex medieval law, best expressed in 16 Richard II c. 5 in 1392, which punished contempt against the crown, such as introducing a foreign or papal power into England. It had been deployed as an effective weapon in Henry VIII's reformation. The penalties for praemunire included forfeiture of property, imprisonment at pleasure, and disqualification from public office, but not execution.)

The treason statute of Charles II 'altered the former law greatly', so Lord Chief Justice Francis Pemberton explained when he used it against the Whig Earl of Shaftesbury in 1681. The ancient treason law still operated, but this 'more copious statute ... has enlarged that of Edward III in a great many particulars', to include designs 'but uttered and spoken'. 'Formerly,' Pemberton told the Grand Jury, 'words alone would not make treason; but since this act, gentlemen, words, if they import any malicious design against the king's life and government, any traitorous intention in the party, such words are treason now within this act.'[42]

One of the first to suffer under this statute was the Fifth Monarchist preacher John James, who had been overheard at a conventicle in White-chapel declaring 'that the king was a bloody tyrant, a blood-sucker, and blood-thirsty man' and 'that the death and destruction of the king drew very near'. Tried for high treason in November 1661 in King's Bench, James protested that 'there was no law of God to take away a man's life for words'. The Attorney General, however, insisted that James spoke treason, 'for which he ought to die'. The jury found him guilty after fifteen minutes' deliberation, and he was condemned to be hanged, drawn, and quartered. At his execution, however, 'the sheriff and hangman were so civil to him . . . as to suffer him to hang till he was dead before he was cut down'.[43]

More fortunate was one Alicock, charged in Hilary term 1662 to have said that 'the king is a bastard, his mother is a whore, he is gone to convey the whore out of the kingdom (the king being then gone to leave his mother at Portsmouth in order for her transportation to France) but may come short home, if I meet him I will kill him'. These were dangerously incriminating words, but the witnesses in this case included 'women of ill fame' and people with grudges against the defendant. The jury found Alicock not guilty.[44]

Even in cases where the words were undisputed, it was not always clear whether they were treasonable. Lawyers, juries, and the public at large had different understandings of the peril of the law, which tended to change with the climate of danger. To say, as did Michael Mallet in 1678, that the king was a 'rogue' could lead to both legal and political wrangling. Mallet was a member of parliament, but had spoken privately in Berkshire. Secretary of State Coventry advised the Attorney General: 'I am not lawyer enough to tell how far this is a crime, but am sure it is a great one. The Lord Chancellor thinks he should be taken into custody for treasonable words, and that there is no privilege of parliament in the case.' Despite protests from the Commons, Mallet was held in the Tower while the Council conducted examinations, and was released four months later only on grounds of ill health. It did not help that the Popish Plot was raging at this time, and parties on all sides were especially nervous.[45] The difficulty of determining the legal weight of disloyal language is suggested by reference to 'words tending to treason', words 'which we conceive import high treason or are too near it', and 'dangerous and seditious words, bordering upon if not altogether treasonous'.[46]

The readiness of juries to find political offenders 'not guilty', despite strong evidence of their seditious words, may have inclined some officials not to pursue prosecutions. Magistrates were generally more likely to treat seditious speech as a symptom of disorder than a serious threat to the state. But their tolerance for words of 'envenomed malice' varied with the politics of the moment as much as with the particularities of language. As a government lawyer advised the Duke of Beaufort in 1682, certain words spoken at Leominster 'require nimble prosecution to justice; for as long as the traitorous, saucy, and malicious tongues of the subjects are at liberty to scandalize his majesty, his royal highness and government, we cannot expect a well-grounded peace'.[47]

Punishments for crimes of the tongue included the pillory, fines, and varying periods of imprisonment. Guilty offenders would stand in the pillory in a public place for an hour at a time, often with a paper on their head describing their crime. Their necks and hands would be restrained, but there was no talk now of nailing or removing ears. Fines could range from a few shillings to several hundred pounds, but the larger sums were probably remitted for people without resources. Defendants stayed in gaol while their cases were examined, and often remained in gaol until their fine had been paid or sureties obtained. Custodial sentences were normally short, up to six months, though occasionally an offender was held at the king's pleasure. Seditious speakers against Charles II were not normally treated to a whipping, but the labourer Matthew Webb, who said in 1683 that the king 'will die as his father did', was sentenced 'to be flogged on his naked back until it shall be bloody', the flogging to continue across London from Smithfield, through St John's Street to Swan Alley, through Old Street, then Whitecross Street, 'to the door of his own house there', as well as to pay £3 6s. 8d.[48]

People continued to talk wherever they gathered, at market, at church, in the alehouse, and in the street. News and opinion spread like fractals, from the court to the city, to the suburbs, and beyond. A new venue for conversation emerged with the Restoration, the remarkable phenomenon of the coffee house. Not just in London, where their numbers grew by the dozen, but also in provincial England, coffee houses provided their customers with reading matter and commentary as well as refreshment. By 1666 the Earl of Clarendon was concerned that coffee houses were centres of sedition. They allowed, he said, 'the foulest imputations [to be] laid upon the government, and the people generally believed that those houses had a charter of privilege to speak what they would, without being in danger to be called into question'.[49]

To counter this threat, Clarendon proposed insinuating government spies into coffee houses to record dangerous conversations, perhaps along the lines of the 'mouches' employed by the police of Paris. Information gathered over the next few years, including reports of conversations in coffee houses, suggests that, at least informally, parts of Clarendon's proposal went into effect. Several members of Charles II's government proposed suppressing the coffee houses to quieten their discourse. They were targets of royal proclamations in 1672 and 1674 against the utterance of false news and 'licentious talking of matters of state'. Again in 1675 the coffee houses were condemned as places where 'idle and disaffected persons' spread 'false reports to the defamation of the govern-ment and disturbance of the peace of the realm'. A few coffee-house keepers were arrested for promulgating 'seditious discourses', but the sheer popularity of the coffee habit, and its contribution to the revenue and the economy, forced the authorities to back down. Another magistrate complained in 1683 that coffee houses were 'places where false and seditious news are uttered and spread abroad to delude and poison the people', but they continued to thrive as hubs of commentary on public affairs.[50]

Historians have become enamoured with later Stuart coffee houses, seeing them as crucial to the burgeoning 'public sphere'. The effect of the coffee bean upon demeanour and conversation has been compared favourably to the effects of alcohol.[51] But coffee houses were by no means the sole nexus of critical or dangerous talk. Nor was coffee the sole stimulant on sale at such venues. Alehouses, inns, taverns, and victualling rooms continued to attract political conversation, alongside places of business and other areas of congress. Reports of 'dangerous words' in Charles II's reign were more likely to come from such drinking establishments as the Bell in Bell Yard, the Devil in Fleet Street, the Sun in Holborn, the Swan at Sittingbourne, or the White Lion at Cambridge than coffee houses in London or the provinces. And coffee-house clients charged with speaking seditious or dangerous words were as likely to have been drinking punch or other intoxicating beverages as coffee.

A Pox on the King

Charles II was crowned on St George's Day, April 1661, and reigned another twenty-four years. Although some subjects grew to like him, and most acknowledged his majesty as a divinely anointed monarch, seditious talk continued to trouble the authorities. As Charles's character became better known, public commentary grew all the more scandalous. Out-spoken commoners frequently asserted that the king was a 'knave' or a 'rogue', that he was a 'son of a whore' and a 'keeper of whores', and, after the arrival of Catherine of Braganza in 1662, that the queen herself was a whore.[52]

In February 1661 Henry Welburne of Brandesburton, labourer, said: 'the king is a rogue, and if he does not depart the land presently he shall die the sorest death that ever king died.'[53] 'The devil take [the] king,' said Robert Thornell of St Paul's Covent Garden in August 1662.[54]

William Pierce was held at Newgate in October 1663 for 'treasonable and traitorous words' to the effect that 'the king is a rogue'. Tried on the lesser charge of uttering scandalous words against the king ('*pro propalando verba scandalosa contra regem*'), he was fined five marks, made to stand in the pillory for an hour at Westminster, Charing Cross, and New market, and then to stay in prison until his fine was paid and sureties found for his good behaviour.[55] That same autumn the Yorkshire labourer William Moul-thrope was indicted at Pontefract for asking 'is the king better than another man?'[56] The yeoman James Parker, a former Cromwellian soldier, appeared at the northern assizes in November 1663 for saying, 'as for the king, I am not beholding to him, I care not a fart for him', but the jury set him free.[57]

Cases of this sort are abundant, though the records rarely allow us to reconstruct conversations. The indictments do not necessarily reproduce the actual words spoken, though they capture the essence of the offence. They display a limited vocabulary of abuse in service to a wide range of indignation.

Peter Sourceau and Everard Blake were indicted in Middlesex in May 1664 for 'scandalous, seditious and treasonable words', saying that 'the king of England is not fitting nor capable to govern his kingdoms'.[58] The labourer Anthony Derrew of Whitechapel called the king 'a vagabond and a rogue and a knave', as well as a keeper of whores.[59] 'God damn his majesty,' cursed John Mayling of Newcastle after the second Dutch war, 'what was he more than another man, that so many men had suffered death for him?'[60] The king, said the yeoman Henry Northit, was 'a traitor to this land and nation'.[61] 'The king is the son of a whore and the veriest rogue that ever reigned, and has no more right to the crown than I have,' declared a former Cromwellian soldier in 1670.[62]

Several people in Essex heard the blacksmith Henry Newington say that 'the king had none but sons of whores and bastards belonging to him, and that he should not reign two years longer, and after him should never any king reign more in England'. Though witnesses described Newington 'as deboshed a rude and base knave as any in England . . . not fitting to live in civil society', this did not so much mitigate as sharpen his offence, which the Privy Council examined early in 1671.[63] Elizabeth Phillips had to answer at the Middlesex sessions that year for saying that 'the king keeps a company of rogues about him'.[64]

An Admiralty investigation of treasonable talk in 1673 led to more detailed information. At the Three Tuns tavern in July that year, 'discourse being had about state affairs', a Mr Hosier spoke 'treasonable words . . . that the king had betrayed his people'. One of those present, the naval officer Captain Perriman, protested that they ought not to talk of such topics, and 'noted down the words in his book'. It was Perriman's report a week later that led to Hosier being examined by the Admiralty board. When Hosier said he remembered nothing and may have been drunk, the board advised him 'to prepare a better answer to justify himself, or else we fear it will go hard with him when the Lords shall be acquainted with it. Indeed,' they noted, 'the poor man is very much afflicted at this unhappy business'. The offender's remorse, and the possibility that the case against him was driven by malice, may have led to the matter being dropped.[65]

In another conversation in 1674, Alexander Malley of St Margaret's, Westminster, derided King Charles as 'a ridiculous prince for making peace with the Dutch', and prophesied that 'the king of France will be king of England before two years come to an end, and all protestants will be made slaves as in Turkey, or be banished'.[66]

Not a year went by without somebody being cited for saying that the king was a 'rogue and knave',[67] or 'a fool',[68] or bidding the king 'to the devil'.[69] 'The king of England is no more than another man . . . and I myself am as good a man as he,' declared the yeoman Samuel Morris of Whitechapel in 1676.[70] Offering to 'drink damnation to the king and the duke', the Westminster apothecary Edward Warren said in 1677 that 'if [King] Charles were here he would fling the beer in his face'.[71] 'His majesty is a pitiful fellow and a rascally rogue,' said the labourer Thomas Sothin of Chatham, which words cost him a fine of £200 at the 1679 Kent assizes.[72] George Speke in Somerset gave his opinion in 1681 'that the king was no more fit to govern than his ass'.[73] 'God damn the king' was a frequently repeated curse.[74]

Charles II's sex life attracted lively commentary, often intermingled with discussion of the succession. John Weeden of St Giles in the Fields remarked in August 1674 that 'our king keepeth nothing but whores and he is a scourge to the nation'.[75] Henry Langley of St Martin in the Fields was charged with uttering 'opprobrious and seditious words' and bringing the king 'into hatred and contempt'. He allegedly said, 'I would the king had been burnt before he came into the land,' referring to burning with the pox rather than consumption by fire.[76] A London libel in May 1675 set down what many were saying: 'the king has given up his life, his understanding, and his conscience into the disposal of whores and ladies of pleasure, who do with him what they will.'[77]

A libel found in December 1675 on the king's statue in Lombard Street declared 'that his majesty was in a worse condition than his father, having disobliged all his friends, and that he was going to live in France with Madame Curwell, Duchess of Portsmouth' (Louise de Kérouaille). Other copies of the libel were cast in the gallery and fixed on a door at court, provoking lively conversation. A Mr Sisted, drinking at the Palsgrave's Head in Temple Bar, embellished the news to say 'that his majesty had sold Tangiers, and Madame Curwell was to have the money, and that his majesty was about selling all the foreign plantations to the French king'. A fellow drinker, James Allardice of the Strand, told Sisted that 'he deserved to be hanged for speaking such seditious and treasonable words', but Sisted insisted that it was all true. Examined a few days later by Secretary of State Williamson, he admitted repeating gossip that the king had secretly and bigamously married 'the French lady', adding that Dr Bourne's wife had told him that Madame Queroualle had told the queen 'that she was as much the king's wife as the queen, only that she was not married by a bishop'.[78]

Royal dalliances provided an excuse to Sir Matthew Pearson of Sileby, Leicestershire, who protested in May 1678 'that he kept but one whore and had but one bastard, but that the king kept twenty and had twenty bastards'. When report of these words reached local magistrates, one said it 'was of that nature that he durst not meddle with it'. The accuser, Elizabeth Church (perhaps the target of Pearson's attentions), then related the matter to Secretary of State Williamson.[79]

In 1681 the Yorkshireman William Beever remarked that 'the king is sick of the pox with using so many whores ... and there hangs a great judgement over the nation's head for his wickedness'.[80] Speaking at the Crown in Ilminster that year, the Somerset gentleman George Speke shared his view 'that the nation was governed by a company of whores', and suggested, with a nod to Henry VIII, 'let the king cut off the queen's head, and then he may marry again and have children'.[81] This was similar to the view of Gabriel Shadd, a prisoner in Wood Street Counter, who suggested in 1683 that King Charles 'ought to be divorced from the queen that there might be an heir to the crown'.[82]

Hang the Knave

Many of the most outspoken opponents of Charles II not only scorned or denounced him but wished him dead. Some predicted his early demise, while others offered to hasten him to the grave. While few of the king's subjects had the opportunity to do him harm, a surprising number acknowledged the aspiration. The unfortunately named republican shoemaker Edward King of Westerham, Kent, spoke treason in July 1662 when he declared: 'If I could have my opportunity, I would be the death of the king.' There were 30,000 of his sort, he declared, who were prepared 'at an hour's warning' for 'the biggest fight that ever was known in England'.[83]

By 1663 some people were predicting 'that there would be wars shortly again in England', or that soon 'many will arise in England and Scotland as will cut the throats of all those that were for the king'.[84] 'Before the twelvemonth's end we shall see King Charles's head in a poke, as his father's was,' predicted the knife-maker George Parkin of Attercliffe, Yorkshire, in October 1663.[85] 'I know a hundred people that would fight against the king, and I would be the first,' declared the husbandman John Bromley from Kent.[86] Rumours of plots encouraged republicans to imagine a change of regime.[87]

Talk of republican risings mingled with casual anti-monarchical bluster. 'If thou and the king were both hanged, it would be better for the common weal,' Edward Cuthbert told a neighbour at Newcastle in December 1663.[88] The former Cromwellian soldier Henry Ashton of North Shields declared in 1664 that killing cavaliers was 'as pleasant to him as killing of bucks and does', and 'he would do the like to the king if he had him'.[89] 'Hang the king, he is a knave and a whoremasterly knave,' declared Anthony Peele of Ullock, Cumberland, in September 1665.[90]

Some subjects blamed the king for the nation's ills and the increased burden of taxation. King Charles 'did take the same ways that his father did to be ill beloved', said Henry Philip in Middlesex in 1664, adding that 'the chimney money [Hearth Tax] would prove a worse burden then formerly the Ship Money was'.[91] 'The king is the only causer of the plague and pestilence,' claimed the Yorkshireman William Thomson in 1665, adding, 'if this king had been hanged when the other was beheaded we should have none of these taxes, but I think we must all rise'. Despite strong evidence of these treasonable words, the assize jury found him not guilty.[92] The clothier William Duncke of Hawkhurst, Kent, also thought the king should be 'served as his father was served', and then he might stop oppressing Quakers.[93]

Casual talk of killing the king stained countless conversations. Warned in 1667 that 'the king's watch would take her' in her drunken condition, Jane Singleton of Middlesex answered 'that she wished the king hanged on the highest tree in England'.[94] The Warwickshire mercer George Sadler was indicted in 1669 for drawing his sword against the constable and saying 'that if it had been the king himself he would have done as much to him'.[95] 'The king might be hanged, and I will hang the king and you too for a groat,' the Kentish yeoman John Cullenbeam told a tax-collector in 1671.[96]

A chain of reportage brought the words of James Dalley, 'a dissolute unlicensed alehouse keeper' of Horsell, Surrey, to the attention of the king's Council in May 1672. George Massey told Thomas Blundell, who reported the matter to the justice John Windebank, who referred it to his colleague Henry Hildeyard of East Horsley, who then wrote to Sir John Williamson, the Clerk of the Council, enclosing reports of his examinations. Dalley allegedly said 'that the king was the beginning of the wars with the Dutch . . . and wished that the king might be set in the forefront of the battle and be killed first, and then there would be an end of the wars'. Under examination, Dalley 'denied it totally, but with such perturbation and agony as amounted to a very probable presumption of his consciousness', so Henry Hildeyard told the Council; 'but as he would confess nothing, and was accused but by a single testimony, and that not precise in the time, I dared not commit him, the statute requiring two witnesses'. Dalley remained free on bond while the Council pressed Massey to remember who else had been present on the night in question.[97]

The carpenter Henry Heywood of Northbury, Cheshire, was reported to have said in January 1673 that 'he wished the king's head were off and in his hand, and his body where it is', but in this case too there was only one witness so the prosecution came to nought.[98] Anthony Croft said at York in May 1679 that 'the parliament . . . will do away with this king as they did with the last, and then we shall be men'.[99] Other subjects reportedly said that they wished the king dead, that the king would soon be dead, or that they would willingly assist in his killing.[100]

Conversation of this sort was endemic, and seemed to last as long as monarchy. 'We should never be happy in England till the king were made a John the Baptist and we had his head in a charger,' declared Ferdinando Gorges of Leominster in 1682.[101] 'I wish the king were dead, to see who would fight for the English crown,' said the Middlesex yeoman's wife Elizabeth Bryan in January 1685, as Charles II indeed lay dying.[102] The spectacle she wished for, as a political observer, was soon dramatically to unfold.

Popery and Plots

If people were suspicious of the king's religion, they were unforgiving about that of his brother. Most people accepted Charles II as Defender of the Faith and Supreme Governor of the Church of England. But he was married to a Catholic, surrounded by papists, and took popish mistresses to his bed. Although the king's own attachment to Rome remained secret, the rumour persisted that King Charles had turned papist. A dangerous strain of discourse developed, comparable to one that bedevilled Charles I, on the mystery of the king's religion.

So long as Charles II remained childless, at least through Queen Catherine of Braganza, his brother James, duke of York, was heir to the throne. After 1670 it became public knowledge that the duke had been reconciled to Rome, and some thoughts turned to altering the succession. At stake were not just the faith and devotion of the royal family but the religious orientation and discipline of the nation.

Suspicions about Charles II's religion circulated even before he was crowned. John Watson, a mariner of Stepney, Middlesex, was found guilty at Maidstone assizes in March 1661 for saying that 'the king prays and goes to mass twice a day'. For this, and for calling the king's followers 'a blood-sucking crew', he was sentenced to be pilloried and to be gaoled at his majesty's pleasure.[103] Subjects in Yorkshire also claimed that the king was for popery 'and went to mass with the queen', a canard that had previously attached to Charles I.[104] 'The king hath brought popery into this land,' declared a Surrey basket-maker in 1663.[105] The Essex blacksmith Henry Newington declared in 1670 that Charles II was a papist and a rogue, and that the money given to the king was to maintain whores and knaves.[106] King Charles was guilty both of tyranny and of aiding the popish faction, according to a libel discussed in London in 1675.[107]

Though Charles II bore the title Defender of the Faith, observed John Martin, the rector of St Andrew's, Guernsey, in 1677, it was the Catholic faith 'of his concubines'. The king, he continued, 'savoured strongly of their papistry, and he feared he would soon act accordingly like his brother the Duke of York'. Augmenting these remarks, Martin recalled that, when the king was in exile in France, 'his majesty went every day from the mass to the brothel, and from the brothel to the mass'. Reports of these scandalous words reached Secretary Williamson in September 1677, and the king himself took note of the information, initiating prosecution of the outspoken Mr Martin.[108] It was also in 1677 that the yeoman Thomas Walker of St Martin in the Fields declared that 'he hoped to see the Prince of Orange king of England, and that the king (meaning our most serene lord Charles II) should live no longer'. Walker said furthermore that 'if he were one of the States of Holland, he would fight to the last drop of his blood against all kings'.[109]

By this time belief in the king's embrace of popery was overwhelmed by suspicion of his openly Catholic brother. The duke's proximity to the throne fuelled rumours that he was actually a bastard, whereas the illegitimate Duke of Monmouth sprang from a lawful union. The king, York, and Monmouth featured in hundreds of conversations, in which people prayed for, or feared, particular outcomes. Drinking the Duke of York's health could be hazardous, but a glass raised to Monmouth or the king could also provoke a scuffle or a torrent of regrettable words.[110]

Late in December 1675 the company at the Swan at Sittingbourne, Kent, heard the 'abominable' false news 'that the king and the Duke of York had a falling out, and that the duke had stabbed or wounded the king so that he was either dead or dying, and that the duke was fled into France, and that the whole city of London was up in arms'. The bearers of this misinformation, two men from Sandwich, 'said it was very true, since they had it from a kinsman of the king's secretary'. Since these tale-tellers had disappeared by the time the authorities came to investigate, they arrested the landlord of the Swan, in whose house the words had been spoken. Eventually, in January 1676, the Sandwich men were tracked down at Thanet and taken to Dover Castle. They were identified as Stephen Wooten and Thomas Venterman, 'very honest ignorant fellows', who had served as seamen in the Dutch wars.

They 'immediately confessed they had spoken the words' and claimed that their story came from two women they had met in Southwark. At this point investigation of the rumour ceased, but on that very day, 7 January 1676, the Council drafted a new proclamation against seditious libels.[111]

Revelations of a Jesuit conspiracy to kill the king and restore Catholicism dominated the news in the autumn of 1678. By October the rumour ran from Yarmouth to Ostend that King Charles was already recently dead.[112] As told by Titus Oates and Israel Tongue, the plot ran close to the king's brother and implicated dozens of Catholics at court. Before confidence in the conspiracy crumpled, with the perjury of its principal witness, some eighty alleged traitors were arrested and fifteen put to death. The state trials of 1678 to 1681 attracted widespread attention, and details were circulated nationally by the popular press. Equally compelling were the parliamentary 'exclusion' crisis and its accompanying popular politics, through which the Whigs tried to alter the royal succession. England succumbed to a period of anxiety, in which the meanings of words and gestures were easily misconstrued. Printed pamphlets and unlicensed news-sheets augment the archival record, allowing detailed reconstruction of some episodes.

One early victim of the frenzy, in which casually seditious comments could be taken as high treason, was the London goldsmith William Stayley. Stayley, a Roman Catholic, was unfortunate to be overheard conversing in French with a foreigner in a London victualling house, the Black Lion in King Street. Their exchange took place in the presence of other diners, over 'a quart of ale and a slice of roast beef'. One of the eavesdroppers knew enough French to translate Stayley's remarks, that King Charles 'was the greatest heretic in the world, that he was a great rogue', and that 'I will with this hand kill him'. Stayley allegedly emphasized his remarks by clapping his hand on his heart and stamping his foot 'in great fury'. Though he strenuously denied the charge and said he was misheard, Stayley fell foul of the 1661 statute that made 'desperate words to be treason'. He was tried in November 1678 'for speaking dangerous and treasonable words against his most sacred majesty the king'. Despite his protestations of loyalty to the crown, Stayley knew himself to be 'a dying man by the statute'. Though he spoke no worse than several dozen others, the politics of the time were against him. The jury found him guilty, and within days he was taken to Tyburn to be hanged, drawn, and quartered. Rough transcripts of Stayley's case appeared quickly in print with such titles as *Treason Justly Punished*.[113]

In 1681 the government used the same Restoration treason law against the populist Whig nobleman Anthony Ashley Cooper, Earl of Shaftesbury. Shaftesbury had been foremost in efforts to exclude the Catholic Duke of York from the royal succession, and had helped to inflame fears of popish plotting. He was arrested in July 1681 and held in the Tower on charges of high treason. Witness after witness declared that Shaftesbury 'spake very irreverently and slightingly of the king'. He had declared with a loud voice that

the king was a man of no faith, and that there was no trust in him, and that our said lord the king deserved to be deposed as well as Richard II . . . that he [Shaftesbury] would never desist until he had brought this kingdom of England into a commonwealth without a king . . . and that our said lord the king and all his family should be rooted out.

Asked about the king's religion, Shaftesbury allegedly answered that King Charles 'hath no more religion than a horse'. He had also said that the king was 'not fit to rule, being false, unjust, and cruel to his people', that he was weak and inconstant, 'of no firm and settled resolution', and 'that the king would never be quiet till he came to his father's end'. Some witnesses even claimed that Shaftesbury spoke of other noblemen, such as the Duke of Buckingham, having as good a hereditary claim to the throne as any Stuart. Citing both the treason act of Edward III and the legislation of 1661, the indictment claimed that Shaftesbury's words 'compassed, imagined, and intended the death and final destruction' of the king, and revealed the earl's 'wicked treasons, traitorous compasses, imaginations and purposes'.[114]

Shaftesbury, by this account, was a loose-lipped lord, a magnet for malcontents, who recklessly spoke treason in his private dining room and at public gatherings. But most of the witnesses against him were of questionable integrity, men of shifting allegiance who 'made shipwreck of their consciences', so claimed the defence. In any case, the worst of Shaftesbury's remarks were no more remarkable than many in popular parlance. According to the diarist Roger Morrice, the Lord Chief Justice acknowledged 'that there was nothing but words against the Earl of Shaftesbury, and that he could not make words an overt act, and therefore the charge would not reach his life'. Without delay the Whig jury returned the bill *ignoramus*, to much 'hollowing and whooping' in the court and bonfires in the streets. Shaftesbury went free, but hastily produced accounts of his trial reported the proceedings, including the words in question, to an avid politicized public.[115]

The last years of Charles II's reign saw no abatement in the flow of malicious discourse.

High political and principled opposition fused with the chatter of the alehouse and the street. Many humbler voices than Shaftesbury's were raised against the king and his brother, their cry, 'No York, no York! A Monmouth, a Monmouth!' catching the gist of numerous conversations.[116]

'If the Duke of York was here, I would run my sword into the heart's blood of him up to the hilt,' declared the Middlesex labourer William Orpoole in February 1681.[117] 'I wonder the parliament doth not chop off his head,' mused the tailor James Groves in April that year.[118] Blamed for the fire of London, the Duke of York 'now was come again to cut our throats', claimed a commoner in 1682.[119] The Kentish labourer William Burman named the Duke as 'a great wizard' and feared 'that he is preparing for a field of blood with his witchcraft, and . . . will lay the nation in blood and popish slavery'.[120] 'If the Duke of York should succeed his brother, he would be a worse popish tyrant than ever Queen Mary was,' declared Robert Humes of Stepney, Middlesex.[121] Other alehouse patriots assailed the future James II as 'the son of a whore and worse than a murderer',[122] and 'a papist dog' who 'should be hanged at his own door'.[123]

Rumour spread that the king would soon be poisoned or otherwise murdered.[124] It was common talk in 1682 'that the king would not live another six months'.[125] Some predicted that the king's head 'would be cut off as his father's was', but 'the Duke of York shall not successively reign, nor any of the royal family'.[126] The Council learned in 1682 of bravado remarks in Southwark about 'old Oliverian boys who know how to ride',[127] and prospective rebels in Devon who 'hoped to draw a sword' against the court as their forefathers had done.[128]

Some of this noise expressed frustration at the political collapse of the exclusion movement. But elements of plebeian conversations invoked commonwealth political theory. Railing against the king in October 1682, the nonconformist Peter Bell declared: 'we trust him with our lives and fortunes like fools as we are. He governs as well by a trust from us as by inheritance, and if you had ever read the coronation oath you would find it so.' These 'scandalous' words and others brought Bell to Newgate, where he languished for several months. When his excuse that he had spoken 'in a great passion, improved by excess of brandy' failed to dislodge the charges against him, he offered to tell secrets to the Duke of York if that would get him out of gaol.[129]

Also exposed to commonwealth principles, the company at the Bell in
Thetford, Norfolk, heard William Cropley of Kilveston say in May 1683
'that the king is an elective king, and that the people, who have the power
to set up, have power to pull down'. It did not take long for report of these
remarks to reach the Privy Council in London.[130]

The Council also heard of one Aaron Smith who called King Charles 'a
damned dog to deprive his subjects of the rights of Magna Carta'. Smith
went on to damn the king 'and his co-rogue the Duke of York, they are
both worse than the devil . . . he that destroyed them and their whole family,
root and branch, did God service'.[131] Raising the stakes, a Captain Baker
swore in London in July 1683: 'God damn me, I will pistol the Duke of
York, if ever I meet him I will send a brace of bullets into his head, because
he is a villain and a traitor against his brother.' In mitigation Baker said that
he had been told that 'it was not treason to kill a duke'.[132]

Against these seditions, upholders of traditional royal authority repeated
many of the classic arguments for divine-right kingship. William Clifford
reminded listeners at Wakefield in October 1681 that 'a king is the greatest
of all earthly blessings'. He used his pulpit to excoriate those 'incendiaries'
who 'magnify the power of the people to break open the cabinet of state',
with their 'diabolical dialogue of speaking evil of dignities'.[133] John Burrell
preached on a similar theme in January 1683, insisting it was no business of
subjects to make judgements of princes, 'as though the foot must judge the
head'.[134] Preaching at Salisbury in June 1683 the prebendary Paul Lathom
built on Proverbs 8. 15—'By me king's reign'—to explain that kings 'are
great ministers of the divine providence' and instruments of God's purpose
on earth. To speak ill of them, to speak evil of dignities, was offensive and
dangerous, especially for 'men that move in lower spheres'.[135] Such pieties
had little influence on the likes of the Kentish yeoman George Brewer, who
declared in 1684, 'damn your government, I care not a fart for it'.[136] The
institution of monarchy would continue, but English kingship was forever
desacralized.

10

The Last of the Stuarts

The reign of James II saw a Catholic king in a Protestant nation, experiments in religious toleration, rebellion, high treason, foreign invasion, and a Whig revolution that put the king's daughter and nephew on the throne. The age of William and Mary saw expensive wars with France, a Dutch-dominated court, high taxation, suppression of Ireland, and a continuous Jacobite threat. Queen Anne's reign was shaped by partisan politics, religious division, more war and taxation, and a succession crisis solved by dynastic jiggery-pokery. The thirty years from the Duke of Monmouth's rebellion in 1685 to the Jacobite uprising of 1715 gave English men and women no shortage of topics to talk about. An energetic press gave further stimulus to the national conversation, in an age of growing prosperity. More people than ever were literate, by some estimate 45 per cent of men and 25 per cent of women.[1] By the end of the seventeenth century England's population exceeded five million, double its size at the start of the Tudor era, and its impact on the world was greater than ever.

God Bless the Right James

Even before the Duke of York became King James II in February 1685 there were Englishmen predicting a sticky end for him. Merrymakers aboard the *Pearl* of Whitehaven drank healths to the Duke of Monmouth in April 1684 and predicted that 'parliament will lop off (the Duke of York's) head'.[2] Drinkers in London likewise proposed healths to the Duke of Monmouth and confusion to his royal uncle.[3]

Given the long subversive tradition of traducing the reigning monarch, and the particular opprobrium attached to the Catholic duke, it was not surprising that some English men and women spoke disrespectfully of their new King James. The treason law of 1661, which penalized treasonous words, expired with the death of Charles II. But the medieval treason law still applied, and seditious speakers still faced the pillory, fines or prison. Some country districts still put unruly speakers in the stocks.[4] Most of the magistrates could distinguish undutiful speech from treasonous acts, and did not shrink from sending real traitors to execution.

Amidst conventional expressions of joy, celebrations for the accession of James II were marred by dissident voices that claimed, among other things, that the new king was responsible for the burning of London, that he had poisoned his late brother, and that he was, in any case, illegitimate. Young women in Hampshire were heard discussing an apparition of King Charles that confronted King James 'and said to him, "Dost thou think to be king that has murdered me?" and then went up into his chamber and lay down upon his bed,' so frightening the queen that she miscarried and died.[5] A Worcestershire bargeman, John Stewart (no relation to the royal family), indicted at midsummer 1685 for upholding Monmouth, also declared that Charles II had been poisoned.[6]

Deborah Hawkins, the wife of a London yeoman, appeared before the Middlesex sessions in March 1685 for 'audaciously and seditiously' telling another woman that King James 'is no king but an elective king, and if there were wars as I believe there will be, I will put on the breeches myself to fight for the Duke of Monmouth'. Before James II should be crowned, she asserted, 'this head of mine shall go off, and before that day comes there will be a great deal of bloodshed'. Her words were clearly seditious, but the court did not regard them as particularly dangerous. Treating her as an ignorant and disorderly woman, rather than a self-announced Amazon traitor, the court found her guilty but fined her the derisory amount of 13s. 4d. She had to stand in the pillory for an hour with a paper on her head declaring her offence.[7]

Deborah Hawkins was by no means alone in claiming that England now had an elective monarchy. A paper found on the road from Barking to London in March 1685, turned in to Essex magistrates, claimed that James, though declared king by the Council, was

not by the consent of the nation ensembled in parliament, and therefore no ways binding upon the people to look upon him as [England's lawful king]. His virtues no man knows. His vices are very public and unnumerable . . . burning of London and Southwark, murdering of Justice Godfrey and great Essex, and poisoning his brother to come to the crown, and these are his practices to bring England down.[8]

The claims were familiar, the stuff of popular parlance and paranoid partisan gossip.

More threatening, perhaps, were the words of John Hathaway, a yeoman of Stepney, Middlesex, who told all comers in March 1685, 'I would fight for the Duke of Monmouth', and that 'rather than the king should not be killed, I would do it'. Found guilty of sedition, but not treason, he was fined £6 13s. 4d., and whipped at a cart's tail from East Smithfield to Ratcliffe Cross, then committed to Newgate until he had paid his fine.[9]

A subversive minority drank healths to the Duke of Monmouth and urged Monmouth's claim to the throne. Some prophesied that King James would not live till his coronation (in April 1685), that there would be a bloody battle for the crown, and that Monmouth 'shall sway, and shall sway'.[10] 'I hope the Duke of Monmouth will get the better of the king. And if he doth, I will hang twenty of you,' declared Martha Tickner, the wife of a Kentish labourer.[11] Very few people were prepared to match these words with actions.

Monmouth's revolt that summer seemed to fulfil expectations of civil war. Its failure secured the second Jacobean regime. But, despite the collapse of the rebellion, and the traitor's grisly execution in July 1685, some of Monmouth's supporters refused to believe that their hero was dead.[12] Others clung to Monmouth's name, even though he was no longer a leader. James Audley was indicted in London, for example, for saying 'that Monmouth was an honester man than the king, and had more right to the throne than he hath . . . that Monmouth had more honesty in his little finger than the king had in his whole body'.[13] Similar seditious nostalgics looked back from Charles II to Oliver Cromwell, and from James I to Queen Elizabeth.

'Here's a health to the right king of England, the right king of England is alive,' cried George Wright, carrier, from the top of the market cross at Bolton, Lancashire, in 1686. Other witnesses heard Wright saying, 'I hate all papists' and 'God bless the right James, the right king of England', referring to Charles II's illegitimate son.[14] Peter Hutchinson, a Yorkshire blacksmith, offered a health to the Duke of Monmouth in April 1687 (almost two years after the rebel's execution), saying that the duke was 'alive as certainly as he was himself', and refused to have 'any of these popish dogs to be our king'.[15] 'God damn the king, for the Duke of Monmouth is alive in Holland,' declared a Westminster woman, Margaret Hambleton, also in 1687.[16]

Stephen Duffield of Ripon, Yorkshire, spread a particularly inventive rumour in January 1687 when he told a Sunday morning drinking assembly that 'the queen told the king that she could not conceive unless she drank Charles [i.e. James] Monmouth's blood . . . that unless she might drink his heart's blood it would do her no good'.[17] This may have been a joke as much as a flying report, but it quickly came to the attention of the magistrate Sir Jonathan Jennings. Duffield's remark touched the most sensitive of state issues, the highest *arcana imperii*, opening to inspection and ridicule the most intimate dealings of the king and queen and the most pressing issue of the succession. It was grotesque to imply that the queen was a ghoul, and that Monmouth's blood might give her a child. The story may have evoked the drinking of healths, as well as propitiatory eucharistic blood, but its burden was that Monmouth was alive, in crown custody, and that his life was in imminent danger. History tells that Queen Mary of Modena would indeed soon become pregnant, presumably through more orthodox efforts, giving birth to the ill-starred James Francis Edward Stuart in June 1688.

Traditional rules of deference and decorum still governed English society, but scandalous, scurrilous, and seditious words reverberated throughout James II's short reign. The young Lord Altham, second son to the Earl of Angelsea, was arrested in October 1685 'for words spoken' while drinking in a tavern, 'as if he seemed more inclinable to drink the king's damnation than his health'. According to the chronicler Roger Morrice, 'the court said that men should be responsible indeed for words they spoke in drink, but much more for actions', and fined him a hundred marks.[18]

'The queen is the pope's bastard,' declared William Pratt, yeoman of Westminster, explaining in July 1685 that 'it is no treason to speak against the queen because she never was crowned with the crown of England'. There was at least a fraction of truth in this assertion, since Queen Mary of Modena wore a newly commissioned crown in the April ceremony, but Pratt was not charged with speaking treason. His scandalous words earned him the paltry fine of 3*s*. 4*d*. (not much more than the cost of a dinner and a round of drinks), and to be whipped from Temple Bar to Charing Cross.[19]

It was by no means unusual to hear speakers declare that King James II was a 'papist and a rogue'. Paul Roach, a yeoman of Clerkenwell, Middlesex, was fined £13 6*s*. 8*d*. for such words in January 1687.[20] 'God damn the king for a papist dog,' said the Chelsea fisherman Thomas Bennett in October 1687.[21] Another Londoner, John Seyton, was found guilty of 'speaking seditious words' for calling James II 'a cheat'.[22]

Compassing the king's death, though still illegal, was not so perilous as in previous years. When Cornelius Alder, yeoman, of St Martin in the Fields

observed of the king and queen in October 1687, 'oh, what a fine opportunity the City hath to shoot them as they go by any corner', his wife Mary
chimed in, 'oh, that I were a man', implying that she might just take that
action. Report of this dangerous exchange brought the couple before the
Middlesex sessions, but a jury found them both not guilty.[23]

In November 1686 a cleric, Samuel Johnson, was degraded from his
ministry, fined 500 marks, made to stand three days in the pillory, and then
whipped 'from Newgate to Tyburn' for inciting the king's subjects to
rebellion against him. But Johnson was punished for his pen, not his tongue.
He was sentenced at King's Bench for 'writing and publishing two false,
scandalous and seditious libels, tending to sedition and rebellion'. The
printed broadsheet describing his punishment reached a wider audience
and probably stimulated more discussion than his original manuscript libels.[24]

A Dutch Dog and a Usurper

We have no conversational transcript of the crisis that unseated King James
and brought William and Mary to power. The words of the revolution are
lost to the wind. The constitutional and high political history of these
months is exceptionally well documented, but we have little access to its
popular discursive accompaniments. Licensing of the press broke down in
November 1688 and was not reimposed until the following February.
'Everything, till now concealed, flies abroad in public print, and is cried
about the streets,' the diarist John Evelyn observed, but he gave no examples
of those expressions. Widely distributed newsheets reflected and stimulated
public debate. The licensing act expired in May 1695, and journalists were
free to print the news.[25]

It comes as no surprise to find the kind of opprobrium poured on the
Stuart monarchs redirected against their revolutionary successors. Partisan
voices mixed with the usual stream of rowdy denigration. Reports reached
London in 1689 from various parts of England of men and women cited
'for uttering scandalous and seditious words against the government', for
'affronting and opposing the king', and for other utterances of 'dangerous
words'.[26] In July 1689 the Londoner Thomas Page was charged with high
treason for saying, 'God damn him, he would murder King William and
Queen Mary...Why did they come into England to take away their
father's possessions?'[27] Northern drinkers caused trouble with competitive

health-drinking, to King William or King James, and toasts of 'confusion' to the other.[28]

Dozens more were convicted at the Middlesex sessions for spreading false news or for speaking scandalous and seditious words against the new king, queen, and government. Most were made to stand an hour in the pillory at the busiest time of day at Charing Cross, Covent Garden, St James Street, St John Street, Bow Street, the Strand, or New Palace Yard. Offenders were also fined sums ranging from 5 marks to £100, and remanded to Newgate until their fine was paid. Finally, on discharge, they had to pay fees of between 4s. and 18s.[29]

The Council was unwilling to act on mere hearsay, however, and was careful to secure corroboration of alleged seditious words. Though not necessarily more tolerant than the previous government, it took care to screen out false and malicious accusations and to give the accused the benefit of the law.[30] Having ousted an arbitrary regime, it did not want to appear tyrannical itself. On the other hand, William III's government was prepared to investigate all threats to the crown, and referred speakers of 'scandalous and seditious words' to the assizes.[31] When the mayor of Exeter released a suspect charged with speaking scandalous and seditious words in December 1689, the Council reprimanded him. The Earl of Shrewsbury chastised officials who slighted his majesty's service, in the case of a crime 'which seems to tread upon the heels of treason'.[32] Prudence argued for vigilance, with arbitrariness kept at bay.

Written material worried the late-Stuart regime much more than casual conversation. Seditious papers, libels, books, or pamphlets vexed the authorities much more than seditious words. The government of William and Mary sought out unlicensed, false, and scandalous books and papers, and set out to apprehend their authors.[33] In 1691 it went after 'seditious newsmongers and incendiaries' who distributed false reports and inveighed against the government in coffee houses.[34] As a *de facto* government making extraordinary financial demands, it was ever alert to seditious publications, watchful for correspondence with the king's enemies, and attentive to dangers from the Jacobites and from France. When licensing of the press ended in 1695, newspapers occasionally reported trials 'for speaking seditious words against the king', but rarely reproduced the offensive language.[35]

A scatter of cases captures the flavour of dangerous popular speech in the 1690s. The army lieutenant James Weames was charged in September 1690 with 'speaking scandalous and seditious words', to the effect that 'the land would never be blessed' until the French had restored King James to his throne. As for King William, Weames called him 'a villain'. Character witnesses, however, affirmed the officer's good affection to the present government, and the Old Bailey jury found him 'not guilty'.[36] In 1691 the Jacobite Giles Griffiths tried to suborn one of the soldiers of 'their now majesties', saying: 'you are all lobstring faggoting dogs, rogues, rebels and traitors to your lawful king, I wish the king's ships were all on fire.' For this he was sentenced to an hour in the pillory, and then set free after paying his fees.[37]

A London woman, Ann Knot, was acquitted in 1692 after allegedly saying: 'God damn King William, I would clip off his ears for a groat if I could come at him.' She was no real threat to the crown, and the jury found the evidence insufficient.[38] A soldier who rode through the streets in 1695 shouting out that 'the king is dead' was bailed after a short stay in Newgate.[39] A mariner found guilty in 1696 of speaking treasonable and seditious words was sentenced to be carried in a boat from ship to ship with a halter about his neck, to receive 100 lashes, and then to be put ashore. Unfortunately, we do not know what he said.[40] Hanna Bromfield of Upton Warren, Worcestershire, however, declared in 1696 that 'King William is a son of a whore, and if ever King James comes in I'll be one that shall help to put down Justice Chettle's house or set it on fire, but I'll have it down'. Aflame with both local and national grievances, she had to answer for her words at the Worcestershire Quarter Sessions.[41]

Writing later in William III's reign, Justice Sir John Holt made the distinction that courts had been making in practice for several generations: 'Loose words, spoken without relation to any act or project are not treason; but words of persuasion to kill the king are overt acts of high treason.'[42] The precedent of Pyne's case cast long shadows.

Government legal advisers raised doubts whether prosecutions for seditious language would hold up in court. In the divided political culture of Williamite England it was hard to gauge a jury's sympathies and difficult to amass the weight of evidence necessary to secure a conviction. When in 1701 a Mr Bliss allegedly spoke ill of King William, the Attorney General Sir Edward Northey doubted whether there was proof enough to have him punished.

If the woman that makes it be to be believed, he is guilty of a very great misdemeanour, for which he may be proceeded against by indictment or information, as his majesty shall direct; but in regard there is but one witness, and that a woman, and one who, as appears, had declared herself to be against Mr Bliss . . . it may be a question whether she will have so much credit with a jury as on her single testimony to convict Mr Bliss.

It would not be good, the king's attorney cautioned, for the prosecution to be 'baffled by an acquittal'. Nonetheless, after due consideration, the government decided to proceed to indictment. Unfortunately for the historian, the specific words that triggered this action are not preserved in the record.[43]

A greater legal uncertainty attached to the words of one Colonel Cage, who crossed over to Calais on a packet boat from Dover in August 1701. Safely ashore in France, Cage drank a bottle of wine with the master of the ship and 'discoursed about the state of England'. The seaman Samuel Lucas affirmed that he was 'very happy in so good a king as King William', but Cage disagreed and 'spoke slighting words of King William and his government, and said there would be an alteration of the government in a little time, and after spoke in favour of King James and the pretended Prince of Wales'. When Cage refused to join Lucas in a health to King William, 'they had some hot words', and Lucas took his story to the Council in London.[44]

Colonel Cage, evidently, was a Jacobite, but had he also committed an offence? According to Attorney General Northey,

the charge is so general that no indictment or information can be founded on it, viz., that he spoke very slighting words of his majesty and his government, not mentioning any, and that he spoke in favour of the late King James and the pretended Prince of Wales, not mentioning the words. As to the words, that he said there would be an alteration of the government in a little time, I doubt they are so general that they are not criminal, without that he had further explained what alteration he meant. Besides, the words being spoken beyond sea, no information or indictment can be brought for the same; for by the law, the words must be said to be spoken in some county of England, and proved to have been there spoken; the law being defective in this case.[45]

This last may technically have been correct, but it had not prevented previous regimes, from Queen Elizabeth to Charles I, from monitoring and punishing seditious words spoken by subjects overseas.

A final case, which began in the last year of King William's reign, was tried at the Surrey assizes under his successor, Queen Anne. An account of the case was soon published, details entered the law reports, and a transcript survives in the National Archives.[46] These sources make possible a partial reconstruction of a conversation that took place in the Duke's Head victualling house in Long Lane, Southwark, on 30 January 1702, the anniversary of the execution of Charles I. James Taylor, 'a poor tanner', was discoursing with John Albery, a man of somewhat more reputable status. Taylor, the court observed, was 'a noted republican or dissenter, and a frequenter of the Calves Head Club'. Their conversation turned on the calendar, with its controversial days of embedded political significance:

TAYLOR. It is a brave holy day.
ALBERY. It is no holy day, but a solemn fast day.
TAYLOR. For what?
ALBERY. For the sins of the nation, for the heinous and barbarous murder of King Charles the first.
TAYLOR. You are one of those blockheads who believe that King Charles the first died a martyr.
ALBERY. I am one of them that you call blockheads, if you count those who love King Charles to be so.
TAYLOR. ('with a great deal of impudence'). King Charles the first was rightly served in having his head cut off, and it was also pity that his two sons, Charles and James, had not been served so at the same time.
ALBERY. This is very rude and barbarous language towards crowned heads.
TAYLOR. I never knew any good that any of the Stewarts did in their lives.
ALBERY. I never knew any mischief or hurt any of them had done.
TAYLOR. Yes, King Charles the first murdered the protestants in Ireland . . . King Charles the second minded nothing but whores; and as for King James, he was a papist.
ALBERY. Though he was so, two very good branches proceeded from him— Queen Mary and Princess Anne (which then was, but now is our most gracious queen).

Upon which Taylor spoke very factious, seditious and scandalous words against her present majesty.

Having failed to restrain Taylor's animosity towards the royal family, Albery took his information to a gentleman at court, who relayed it to the Earl of Nottingham. Eventually the case reached the Kingston assizes in March 1704, where Taylor was tried for 'seditious words' and 'speaking treasonable words of the dead'. This was a questionable legal concept, but the crown argued that the words were of 'ill consequence' and 'bad example' that could also 'affect the living'. They tended 'not only to the destruction of the very root and branch of the royal family, but even monarchy itself'. Potent historical memories and allegiances were in play, with dangerous implications for the current regime. Citing Pyne's case from 1628, the court found Taylor guilty of a misdemeanour, noting that 'this misdemeanour has a

tendency to treason, and shows a treasonable intent in the speaker'. He was
fined 40 marks and made to stand twice in the pillory, but was otherwise
unmolested.

That Brandy-Nose Bitch, the Queen

The accession of Queen Anne in March 1702 elicited the usual mixture of
polite acclaim and crude denigration. Jacobite loyalism dogged Queen
Anne's regime, along with the radicalism of the good old cause and conventional plebeian obstreperousness. Nicholas Wolstenholme, esquire, of
Enfield, Middlesex, declared to drinkers at the Bell at Edmonton that 'if the
queen were King James's daughter, I am sorry she is crowned'. John Pott, a
London grocer, had opened conversation by remarking: 'we have now a
lawful and rightful queen of our country, King James's daughter, and I like
her the better and thank God for her.' Wolstenholme responded 'that he did
not know whether she was King James's daughter or not, but if she was, he
liked her the worse'.[47] These were sensitive and dangerous remarks. To
stress too hard that the new queen was 'lawful and rightful' was, perhaps, to
imply that the late King William had been neither. To disparage Queen
Anne for being King James's daughter could be construed as opposition to
the royal house of Stuart. The Secretary of State, Sir Charles Hedges, duly
noted the information against Wolstenholme, but the accused seemed to
suffer no harm. In September 1702 he became Deputy Lieutenant for
Middlesex.[48]

Much more scandalous were the words of Thomas Wadley, a Londoner
who was walking with George Dunn of Shoe Lane in March 1703 when
conversation turned to recent legislation concerning prisoners. According
to Dunn, Wadley moved to say: 'God damn the judges and their warrants
and the parliament for making such an act, and that brandy-nose bitch, the
queen, for signing it; but I suppose she will not stay to sign any more, for
I believe she will run away after her father into France before another
parliament comes.' These were inflammatory and seditious words, but
with only one witness the offence was hard to prove. Dunn could add
only that he also heard Wadley's brother William speak words to the same
effect.[49] Though it was common parlance, though defamatory, for one
subject to tell another, 'you are a brandy-nosed whore, you stink of brandy',
it was outrageous to apply such language to the queen.[50]

Also arrested for 'seditious words' in 1703 was the dissenting preacher Campion of Wapping, who prayed aloud for God to bring 'satisfaction . . . to a languishing and complaining people who were ready to perish'. When it came time to pray for the queen, Campion prayed aloud: 'God send her counsel from heaven, for I am afraid she has none upon earth that will advise her any good.' The informer, Thomas Crocket of Symond's Inn, who brought this remark to the attention of the authorities, characterized it as 'the very trumpet of sedition and rebellion, and tending to nothing less than the sowing [of] discord in one of the most happy governments in the world'.[51] More 'words highly reflecting on her majesty' were charged against Thomas Tudway, Professor of Music and organist of St Mary's, Cambridge, who was removed from his post and deprived of his degrees, though afterwards restored on recantation.[52]

In the face of the Jacobite threat and the danger from France, the government passed an act in 1705 'for the better security of her majesty's person and government'. This made it high treason to maintain by writing or printing that Queen Anne was not the lawful and rightful monarch of the realm. Written text posed the greatest danger, but talk too could be seditious. Anyone 'maliciously and directly by preaching, teaching or ad-vised speaking' challenging the queen's title could 'incur the danger and penalty of praemunire' (forfeiture, imprisonment, and exclusion from pub-lic office). Conviction still required two credible witnesses, and the words had to be reported within three days and prosecuted within three months of being spoken. In 1707, after the union with Scotland, these provisions were extended to the entire United Kingdom.[53]

Relatively few speakers suffered from these new statutes. The Londoner John Baldwin faced charges in October 1706 after telling drinkers at the Griffin and Parrot in Drury Lane 'that he would swear that the Prince of Wales was King James's son'.[54] Another Londoner, John Denton, was fined a mere sixpence and whipped from the Bell alehouse to the Post and Chain in Cripplegate in 1708 for speaking seditious words and for profanely cursing her majesty. Several more were put in the pillory or remanded to Newgate for seditious and treasonable words against the queen, but docu-mented cases are few and slender.[55]

Without more information the government could do little about the unnamed customer in a barber's shop in Holborn in May 1710, who predicted 'that the pretender was coming over, and that Dr Sacheverell would be made archbishop'. When asked 'what was to be done with the queen when the pretender came over, he replied that she must be put aside'. The barber would not identify his client by name, but allowed he 'had spoke treasonable words'.[56]

Report reached the Council in January 1711 of 'highly criminal' talk among military officers. A witness, Richard Tilden, heard a Captain Gill say 'that kings were sent for a curse to the people'. His companion, Purser Campbell, concurred, saying he would fight for her majesty only 'so long as [she] governed to please the people and according to the constitution, but if [she] did otherwise, he swore he would then turn his sword and fight as heartily against as ever he had for her majesty'. To this Gill concurred, 'so will I'.[57] This was 'commonwealth' talk, subversive if not treasonous, but hard to prove with only one witness. It was the mere echo of a conversation, not the grounds for a case at law.

More dangerous talk stirred the air in a victualling house at Portsmouth in June 1711, when John Franklyn allegedly declared that 'the Prince of Wales is right heir to the crown of England, and the queen has no title to it'. Furthermore, he offered to part with all his money, 'to furnish them with arms to assist the Prince of Wales'. Franklyn was evidently a Jacobite, and he was almost certainly drunk when he spoke. But he may also have been the victim of a malicious accusation by an informant who owed him money. Other reports identified Franklyn as a dissenter, 'a quiet man, and not likely to have spoken such words'. He was allowed bail, to answer at the next assizes.[58]

In January 1712 Charles Collins of St Mary le Bow, Middlesex, was charged with 'speaking false, seditious and dangerous words' the previous December. Prompted by a passage in the newspaper *The Postman* about an intended royal visit, Collins declared of Queen Anne: 'she's not worthy to carry Prince Eugene's shoes after him, damn her ... she's but a mechanick, the daughter of a collier, her father was a rogue, and I am better born than she.' Found guilty, he was sentenced to a fine and the pillory.[59]

Another report of Jacobite vaunting came in February 1713, when the labourer John Shore recalled a conversation among workers at a printing house in Cripplegate. One of those present, Freeman Collins, allegedly said: 'we shall never have any good times till the Pretender come, and that he hoped to see the mass houses fuller than the churches.' The informant allowed, however, that Collins spoke 'in a jocular way'.[60] Justinian Chamnies, esquire, was tried at Maidstone in July 1713 'for speaking abominable and atheistical words with respect to God and religion and seditious words of the queen', but like many other speech offenders was found 'not guilty' on all charges.[61]

Even if convicted of political crimes of the tongue, English men and women of the early eighteenth century were unlikely to suffer gravely. The ancient punishment of nailing and clipping ears had fallen into disuse, and the stocks, a standard punitive tool since the Middle Ages, were rarely employed. Nor was whipping regularly imposed on these speakers of sedition. Even the pillory, which would stand for another hundred years, was no longer an essential instrument in sentencing. Crippling fines and extended imprisonment for speech against the crown also seem to have fallen into disuse. In most instances a token punishment was enough. The state no longer felt imperilled by dangerous words, so long as those words were not distributed through writing. By the early years of the eighteenth century the English had freedom to speak as they pleased, provided they steered clear of blasphemy and slander.

11

Dangerous Speech from Hanoverian to Modern England

Undutiful and offensive language still resounded in eighteenth-century England, within the dominant political culture of politeness and loyalism. A subdued seditious grumbling could be heard in a hundred streets and alehouses, rising to vociferous contention in moments of crisis. The noise came from all sectors, including the rougher end of the so-called public sphere. Although the English came to pride themselves as a polite and respectable people, there were many among them given to uncouth and seditious utterance.[1]

The subjects of the Hanoverian monarchs could be as outspoken as their Tudor and Stuart predecessors, as prone as ever to offences of the tongue. Larrikin irreverence, malicious jesting, conversational bravado, and alcohol-tinged obstreperousness slipped easily towards sedition, with sometimes alarming consequences. Some among the commonalty regarded the taunting of authority as the birthright of any Englishman, while Whigs in particular regarded 'freedom of speech' as the bastion of English liberty. There could be 'no such thing as public liberty, without freedom of speech, which is the right of every man', wrote 'Cato' in *The London Journal* in 1722. 'Without freedom of speech there can be no such thing as liberty,' repeated 'Cato Redivivus' in 1766.[2] By 'freedom of speech' they meant freedom of writing, but the phrase invoked both an entitlement and a slogan. It echoed the 1689 Bill of Rights, which protected 'freedom of speech' in parliament, now generalized to the nation at large.

For the most part, eighteenth- and nineteenth-century governments tolerated or dismissed abusive remarks, or inflicted no more than token punishment on speakers of scandal and sedition. From time to time, however, regimes felt threatened, and used old law against new offenders.

Jacobite scares in the early Hanoverian period, radical enthusiasms in the age of the French Revolution, and plebeian outbursts after the Napoleonic wars produced the greatest concentration of cases. This chapter follows the history of dangerous and seditious speech beyond the Stuart era, to review the voices of the disaffected and the varying responses of the state.

Mainstream legal opinion in Hanoverian England was disinclined to construe disloyal or seditious speech as treason. The statute of 1352 still applied, making it treason to compass or imagine the king's death, but most jurists denied that words alone could be treasonable. 'The great question is, whether words only spoken can amount to an overt act of compassing the king's death,' wrote the legal scholar William Hawkins, but the question was already answered in the negative. In his influential *Treatise of the Pleas of the Crown* (1716–21) Hawkins sided with the judges in Pyne's case of 1628. (He also rebuked Sir Edward Coke, who in his third *Institutes* took one view, but 'was clearly of another opinion when he was Chief Justice'.) Neither 'deliberate words' (such as, if I meet the king I will kill him) or 'conditional words' (such as, if the king arrests me I will stab him) could be treasonable, wrote Hawkins, unless they were associated with an overt act such as conspiracy or insurrection. Nor was it treason to question the king's title to the throne, unless it could be shown that 'the speaker had a design against the king's person'. Such words might be scandalous, wicked, or unwary, and subject to law as misdemeanours, but by themselves they would not imperil a person's life.[3]

Hawkins did not discuss 'sedition', which remained poorly defined in English law, but his cautious understanding of 'treason' did not leave the state defenceless. 'Words spoken . . . in contempt and disgrace of the king' remained 'highly criminal' and 'highly punishable' under the Hanoverian monarchs. Subjects who spoke contemptuously of the king, 'as by cursing him, or giving out that he wants wisdom, valour or steadiness', or whose words served to 'lessen [the king] in the esteem of his subjects and weaken his government, or raise jealousies between him and his people', still faced judicial punishment. For these misdemeanours they were 'punishable with fine and imprisonment, and sometimes with the pillory, by the discretion of the judges, upon consideration of all the circumstances of the case'.[4]

Equally cautious was Sir Michael Foster, whose *Discourses upon a few Branches of the Crown Law* appeared in 1762. Foster too reviewed 'the diversity of opinions' on the subject of treasonable words and concluded yet again that 'loose words not relative to any act or design are not overt acts of treason'. Such words were, at worst 'an high misprision' or high misdemeanour, for 'words are transient and fleeting as the wind, the poison they scatter is at the worst confined to a narrow circle of a few hearers. They are frequently the effect of a sudden transport, easily misunderstood, and often misreported.' Far from encouraging the state to police its subjects' speeches, Foster warned of 'the extreme danger of multiplying treasons upon slight occasions'.[5]

William Blackstone, solicitor general to George III, in his *Commentaries on the Laws of England* (1765–9), also separated 'mere words' from 'the highest civil crime' of treason. Though 'formerly matter of doubt', it was now

> clearly to be agreed, that by the statute of Edward III, words spoken amount only to a high misdemeanour, and no treason. For they may be spoken in heat, without any intention, or be mistaken, perverted, or mis-remembered by the hearers . . . As therefore there can be nothing more equivocal and ambiguous than words, it would indeed be unreasonable to make them amount to high treason.

The judgment in Pyne's case clearly shaped these ideas.[6] If people spoke ill of their monarchs, the law might subject them to lesser sanctions, or ignore them altogether. An unknowable number of seditious speakers never came to the attention of magistrates, but were dealt with informally by disapproving neighbours.

German George

In 1714 the preferment of George of Hanover, a German princeling, over the claims of the exiled James Stuart and other Catholic contenders imposed novel strains on English political culture. The Whig faction became dominant, the Tories were in disarray, and popular politics became divided and contentious. Jacobite disturbances broke out in many parts of England, often triggered by royal or Stuart anniversaries and stimulated by partisan health-drinking. Attachments and animosities were signalled through the deployment of emblems: white roses (for the Pretender), turnips (to mock German George), and horns (for the royal cuckold). Cries in the streets included 'away with the Whigs' and 'No King George but a Stuart', to be answered by 'King George forever, no warming-pan bastard'. Similar sentiments appeared on libels, handbills, and inscriptions chalked on walls.

Dozens of subjects were cited or indicted for their scandalous or seditious utterances. One Middlesex man was indicted for offering 'to lay fifty guineas

that the king did not reign twelve months'. Another greeted the Hanoverian accession by remarking 'King George, King Turd'. A yeoman from
Kent declared that his majesty was 'not the lord's appointed king' but was
'brought in by a parcel of bogtrotters'. A Cornish man offered to 'send the
cuckold [back] to Hanover'. The disturbances seemed to have reflected
some genuine enthusiasm for the Pretender along with insolent taunting of
the party now in power. High-level Jacobite rebels and conspirators faced
execution for real treason, but most of those caught 'drinking the pretender's health', 'cursing the [Hanoverian] king', or 'speaking seditious and
scandalous words' against his majesty faced the lesser penalties of a misdemeanour. If convicted, they were bound over for their future good behaviour, made to stand in the pillory, or charged a small fine. A few served six
months in prison. The Staffordshire feltmaker Thomas Birkes, who opined
'that King James will be our king yet', was whipped and fined one pound.
The Tyneside labourer John Sheerer, who upheld the Pretender's claims,
was fined one shilling and sent to prison. The Lancashire shoemaker Jeffrey
Battersby, who said that 'King George has no more right to the crown than
you or I', and hoped for 'flourishing times' under King James, was acquitted.[7] William Wide was pilloried and imprisoned in 1715 for saying 'God
damn King George, he has no right to the throne'. John Bournois was
found guilty of calling King George a usurper and upholding James III as the
'right and lawful king of England', but his sentence was respited. The
Londoner John Humfreys was fined 20 marks and sentenced to six months
in prison for a similar offence.[8]

The judicial response to popular seditious speech was generally measured
and restrained. As many as 80 per cent of those cited for seditious words in
early Hanoverian London were never brought to trial, and 40 per cent of
those prosecuted were acquitted. Overall conviction rates for seditious
speech in early Georgian England were little more than 25 per cent.[9] The
age of incarceration or mutilation for speaking seditious words seemed
to be over.

Juries were notoriously unreliable, and opinion on the street could be
fickle. Robert Harrison of St Botolph's Aldgate was found guilty in 1718 of
shouting out, late at night, 'King James III for ever, who dare oppose him,
God damn all his foes'. For these seditious words he was sentenced to stand
in the pillory, to pay 20 marks, and to suffer six months' imprisonment.
When Harrison appeared in public, a London mob 'did generally seem to
countenance the prisoner, giving him small money and huzzaing him', so

that officers feared he might be rescued. Angry spectators 'damned the court and the jury who condemned the said Harrison'.[10]

Other offenders suffered heavier though less public punishment. Robert Constable, one of the Proctors of the Arches Court of Canterbury, was fined £200 and imprisoned for six months in 1718 for his 'treasonable and seditious words against his majesty', though the actual words are not recorded.[11] More details survive concerning Margaret Hicks, a Middlesex woman, who cursed the king in 1719. When a neighbour told her that 'she had no business to meddle with King George', she replied: 'God damn King George and you too.' Warned that 'she might be hanged for it', Margaret Hicks answered that 'she had rather be hanged for that than anything else; if she could have his heart's blood she'd stick him' with her knife, and that 'the first time King George came by the door she would stick him'. Found guilty at the Old Bailey sessions, she was fined 40s. and sentenced to six months' imprisonment.[12] Also tried in 1719 for saying 'Huzza for the Pretender, as he had but one life to lose, he would lose it for the Pretender', Peter Thorell was acquitted on the grounds of it being a malicious prosecution.[13] Verbally compassing the king's death was no longer a hanging offence, though popular culture preserved memories of capital punishments for treasonous speech.

Quarter sessions and assizes still dealt occasionally with speakers of 'treasonable and seditious words against the king and government', but the political and judicial establishment seemed to share the view of 'Aristarchus' in *The Weekly Journal* in 1721 that the spoken word was a relatively minor threat. Unlike 'seditious writings, which are undertaken coolly and deliberately... words are often spoken passionately, inconsiderately, wine and opposition making men often drop expressions contrary to their real sentiments'.[14]

Jack Pudding King

Scandalous remarks about the Hanoverian royal family and expressions of support for the Stuart Pretender flared up from time to time in the reign of George II (1727–60). But the few cases that came to light were not especially shocking. The evidence points to pockets of disaffection rather than a regime in trouble. Seditious words had not disappeared from the political landscape, nor from the common vocabulary, but they did not reflect deep ideological divisions. The courts generally treated them as mild misdemeanours, affronts to good order, or regrettable lapses of taste, and often decided not to prosecute at all.

The early years of George II saw few recorded incidents. In perhaps the most serious, John Spencer was convicted in London in February 1728 'for uttering opprobrious and seditious words against his majesty', for which he had to stand one hour in the pillory and suffer twelve months in gaol.[15]

Dining at a London victualling house in May 1729, the lawyer William Lambe remarked of Frederick, Prince of Wales, 'God damn him, he's a fool, and looks like a fool'. Several fellow diners 'took particular note of this discourse', and one thought it his duty to report it to the Council, which took the matter no further.[16] The remarks may have been scandalous, but they were not worth troubling the law. They may even have echoed court opinion, since Prince Frederick had few friends in the royal family.

The Jacobite menace was potentially more serious, but for the moment it appeared to be a spent force. The government took note of Jacobite expressions when they were reported, but was not always able to retaliate. The authorities took no action, for example, against the unknown celebrant at Gainsborough races in August 1730 who 'threw up his cap and cried out, long live King James'.[17] In another incident from Lincolnshire that month, drinkers at the Royal Oak at Gainsborough heard Captain George Gumley say 'that Walpole was a tool to that damned son of a whore, King George'. A fellow drinker 'told him to not say so', but Gumley was unstoppable. He declared 'that King George was not the lawful king, that [neither] he nor anyone else could believe that King George was the right king of England, [and] that if he had it in his power to raise fifty thousand men, he would soon be as good a king of England as he was'. This time there was no shortage of witnesses, and Gumley was cited for his words at the Lincoln assize.[18] Another loud-mouthed Jacobite was indicted at Shrewsbury in 1738 for *seditosa et malitosa verba*—hateful and seditious words. James Dawes told loyal supporters of George II, 'Damn you and your king. My king [James] shall be king when you and your king are gone to the devil.'[19]

Drink rather than disloyalty seems to have been at the root of Thomas Dixon's 'seditious words' at an inn near Carlisle in February 1744. Dixon, an attorney's clerk, was much in liquor when he fell into an argument with a recruiting sergeant. When the sergeant cursed the Spaniards (with whom England was at war), Dixon called him 'a cowardly fellow' and offered 'a health to the Spaniards'. Uproar ensued, and Dixon found himself cited in King's Bench. Petitioning for clemency, he claimed not to remember the offensive words, blamed them on alcohol, and declared them 'contrary to his inclinations'. Neighbours attested that he was neither disloyal nor disaffected, and he was allowed to go free. The case served as a warning that walls had ears, that jesting or drunken speech could bring trouble. But it also demonstrated a reluctance to criminalize words that might just as well have been ignored.[20]

Jacobite sentiment emerged again at an alehouse at Winterbourne, Gloucestershire, in April 1744, when John Crowe (or Crane) declared: 'I wish the Pretender and all his army of men was in Frencham common, I would be the first man that should help him.' Report of these words was relayed up the chain of authority, from the village constable to the Duke of Newcastle in London. They were remarkably similar to Elizabethan brags in favour of Spanish forces, and early nineteenth-century assertions of support for Napoleon. Though they could be construed as treason, such words were more probably expressions of anger and frustration, and the authorities treated them with appropriate contempt. 'For speaking seditious words against his majesty', the offender was fined a mere shilling and stood in the pillory an hour.[21]

In 1745, the year of Jacobite rebellion, metropolitan magistrates recorded a spate of seditious commentary. Daniel Smith, an Irish labourer of the parish of St Giles in the Fields, was held in Newgate and then sent to trial for shouting 'God bless King James, King James forever, King James forever'.[22] Gabriell Service, a labourer of St Clement Danes, was likewise apprehended in 1745 for saying 'Damn King George'. Witnesses heard Service ranting at the sign of the Crooked Billet in Witch Street, and one of them recalled his remarks from a few months earlier, 'Damn King George, Damn you Jack Pudding King', and his threat 'that if he had the shaving of King George he would cut his throat'. He was also alleged to have declared that 'the king is a rascal, a rogue, and a jack pudding, and ought to be shit on'.[23] A 'jack pudding' was a jester or buffoon, but use of this term against the king did not necessarily make the speaker a Jacobite.

Comparable remarks could be heard after the Jacobite threat had passed, as in 1747 when the mariner John Clapison of Hull was indicted for saying 'damn the king and the Duke of Cumberland'.[24] Ann Dinmore of Surrey spoke similar words that year against the king and his nephew.[25] Two Oxford students, who had already been punished 'in an academical way' for speaking treasonable words, were sentenced in King's Bench in 1749 to be fined and imprisoned, 'and to go round immediately to all the courts in Westminster Hall, with a paper on their foreheads denoting their crime'.[26]

In one more case from George II's era, Charles Farrel was indicted in June 1756 for seditious words against the king. A Catholic and a Jacobite, and also seriously drunk, Farrel disturbed the company in a public house at Houndsditch by declaring King George 'a thief', damning the royal family, and saying 'he'd shoot his present majesty on the throne, and that he'd destroy them all'. Found guilty of words that a previous century might have deemed treason, Farrel was merely lodged in Newgate until he found sureties for his good behaviour.[27]

The Birthright of an Englishman

The accession of George III in 1760 attracted no significant outbreaks of disaffection. The king was young and English born, with hopeful prospects. There is little evidence of either popular or principled hostility to the crown in the first thirty years of his reign. Magistrates of the 1760s could find nothing more startling to report than the words of a Middlesex man who said that the king was 'a villain, a rogue, and never kept his word in anything', and another who called King George 'a whelp and a bastard'. According to legal analysts, it was 'arrogant and undutiful behaviour' to curse the king, or to give out 'that he wants wisdom, valour, or steadiness'. It was seditious to drink 'to the pious memory of a traitor', or 'in common and unadvised discourse' to deny the king's right to the crown. The law treated such statements as criminal contempts against the king's person, which served to 'lessen him in the esteem of his subjects . . . or raise jealousies between him and his people'. Prosecutors and judges would exercise their discretion, and juries would generally take an accommodating line.[28]

The publication of seditious writing always concerned the authorities, but, as for the spoken word, so long as it was not slanderous, people could say what they pleased. If commoners spoke ill of government, that was among the crosses that authority had to bear. Unlike *ancien regime* France, where people died for *mauvais discours* against the king,[29] nobody in Hanoverian England went to the scaffold for speaking treason, nor did anyone convicted of seditious speech lose their ears. The middle decades of the eighteenth century give the impression of a secure and confident regime, facing a less polarized and less threatening popular politics. The records of central government, the press, the courts, and legal opinion, all indicate a relaxed and tolerant view of speech offences, and a general unwillingness to press such cases at law.

Everything changed in the 1790s. The revolution in France sent shock waves across Europe, reawakening the fear of sedition in Britain. The Hanoverian ruling class braced itself for assault, and sought to protect itself through policing and law. Rumours of plots against the government and scares of saboteurs and assassins created an atmosphere of panic. By 1792, year three of the revolution, the fear of invasion from France fuelled fears of domestic insurrection. Tom Paine's *Rights of Man* sold 200,000 copies that year, and a goodly number were burnt. The Home Office received warning in November 1792 that soon 'there would be no king and it would be worse than in France'. By early December the government was 'prepared for the worst'.[30] By February 1793 England and France were at war.

In the panic of 1792 rights and practices that had seemed long settled faced new challenges, amidst fears for the safety of the country and the regime. There would be heightened surveillance of extra-parliamentary politics, increased monitoring of potentially seditious meetings, and closer scrutiny of the press. Publicans and keepers of licensed premises felt pressure to report what people said. Radical associations such as the London Corresponding Society and the Sheffield Constitutional Society were denounced as fronts for the *sans culottes*. Industrial agitators, Irish nationalists, radical preachers, and enthusiasts for the revolution in France were imagined as parts of a many-headed monster. Government lawyers took a harder line on sedition, likening it to treason that threatened authority, the constitution, and the king.[31]

An anxious proclamation of May 1792 proscribed all 'wicked and seditious writings . . . printed, published, and industriously dispersed' that might lead to tumults and disorders. Authors and printers could be prosecuted for their dangerous inflammatory words. The immediate target was written text rather than verbal utterance, but political orators also found themselves in trouble as the Pitt administration took steps against sedition. Mindful of England's constitutional tradition, the government took pains to assert that its new punitive measures were designed to protect the 'rights and liberties, both religious and civil', of the king's 'faithful and loving subjects'. The crackdown on sedition was 'for the preservation of the peace and happiness' of the kingdom.[32]

There began a decade of harassment of authors and publishers, which extended to speakers of dangerous words. The government launched aggressive legal action against radical and revolutionary voices, not only targeting the products of the press. Speech that had seemed innocuous enough in the early part of George III's reign was construed as dangerous and criminal in the era of revolution. The danger, so the government said, lay not only in particular forms of words, but in the context and circumstance of their expression. Lord Kenyon claimed in court in 1793 that 'the propriety of prosecuting for words of this sort depends a great deal upon the time and season at which those words were uttered'.[33] To damn the government and call the king 'a fool' was impropriety 'at any time, but especially at the present moment', declared another crown counsel that year.[34] To denigrate the monarchy when Louis XVI and Marie Antoinette had just been guillotined, or to uphold the French when revolutionary forces were poised to cross the Channel, would not only cause uproar in an alehouse or coffee shop but was now likely to enmesh the speaker in the complexities of the courts.

George III's government considered suspending habeas corpus in November 1792, and the legal protection was formally removed between May 1794 and July 1795 and again from April 1798 to March 1801. Critical expression became riskier, and its consequences more severe. A series of highly publicized trials in 1793—of John Frost in May, William Winterbotham in July, and Thomas Briellat in December—brought seditious speech to wider public attention. Printed accounts of these trials broadcast the words in question and exposed the arguments of both sides. These were prosecutions for words spoken, not written, and they showed that the law was a double-edged weapon. The defendants suffered heavy custodial sentences, but their words were widely publicized and they took on the character of political martyrs.[35] They were singled out as orators and activists, not casual speakers who overstepped their bounds.

John Frost, a radical lawyer and a member of the London Corresponding Society, returned from Paris in November 1792 and joined friends for dinner at the tavern above Percy's coffee house in Marylebone. As he was leaving, someone downstairs asked him his opinion about affairs in France, and Frost replied: 'I am for equality. I see no reason why any man should not be upon a footing with another, it is every man's birthright.' Pressed to comment further, he said there should be 'no kings ... no kings in this country', adding 'that the constitution of this realm was a bad one in having a king'. These words provoked an angry hissing among coffee-house patrons. Some threatened to kick him out, and someone else reported Frost's words to the authorities.

In May 1793 John Frost was put on trial for

maliciously, turbulently and seditiously intending the peace and common tranquillity of our lord the king and of his kingdom, to disquiet, molest and disturb, and bring our most serene sovereign lord George III . . . into great hatred and contempt . . . and to alienate and withdraw the affection, fidelity and allegiance of his said majesty's subjects from his said majesty.

Frost's seditious words, said the prosecutor, were 'an exceeding high misdemeanour', verging on treason. They displayed 'a seditious intention' that 'might be forerunner of seditious acts'.

Thomas Erskine, for the defence, made an impassioned speech denouncing the criminalization of casual conversation. What Englishman, he asked, would consent 'to have his loosest and lightest words recorded and set in array against him in a court of justice? . . . If malignant spies were properly posted, scarcely a dinner would end without a duel and an indictment.' But the words in question were well attested by witnesses, and the jury found Frost guilty. He was sentenced to be struck off the roll of attorneys, to be pilloried at Charing Cross for an hour, and then to spend six months in Newgate. It is said that he escaped the pillory when an angry crowd destroyed the platform, and the shameful sentence was remitted. Frost was eventually pardoned in 1813, but his professional life was ruined.[36]

More severely punished was William Winterbotham, a nonconformist preacher at Plymouth, who was tried for seditious words in July 1793. Informants testified that Winterbotham had declared in two sermons in November 1792 that he approved of the revolution in France, saying that it 'opened the eyes of the people of England'. He called on his auditors to 'stand forth in defence of your rights', adding that 'we have as much right to stand up as they did in France'. Finally, he opined that, if King George did not observe the laws, 'he has no more right to the throne than the Stuarts had'. Found guilty of sedition by a special jury at the Exeter sessions, Winterbotham was fined £200 and sentenced to four years in prison.[37]

Thomas Briellat, a Middlesex pump-maker, was tried in December 1793 for speaking similar seditious words at a cheesemonger's shop in Hackney and at a victualling house in Shoreditch. He was alleged to have said, among other dangerous utterances, that 'there never will be any good times until all kings are abolished from the face of the earth', that 'the king had lived a lazy life for a long time' and 'ought to work for his living', that 'a reformation cannot be effected without a revolution', and that he wished 'the French would land one hundred thousand men in England to fight against the government party'. These were especially inflammatory words at a time when England and France were at war, and when many Londoners feared insurrection. Briellat's defence counsel, like John Frost's, attempted to appeal to the jury. 'Gentlemen,' he warned them, 'there is not a word spoken by any of you in a butcher's shop, or any other, but it may be carried to the office of these gentlemen . . . If you think the honest character of an Englishman is still to be preserved, if you think that a freedom of speech and a freedom of communication is still to go forward between Englishmen, remember that words, if even sworn to, are a sort of thing very indeterminate, easily misconceived, and misrepresented.' The jury, however, found Briellat guilty, but recommended mercy. He was fined £100 and sentenced to a year in prison, but excused the humiliation of the pillory.[38]

The trials of Frost, Winterbotham, and Briellat stimulated legal argument and general discussion. Some hardliners sought to press charges of treason, while more liberal voices warned of the danger of 'tyranny and oppression'. Jurists reviewed the law of treason to see whether mere words could be culpable, and generally concurred that they could not.[39] Close analysis of King's Bench rolls (the work of Philip Harling) finds only fitful and sporadic enforcement of the seditious libel laws in late Hanoverian England, but no shortage of intimidation. Crown prosecutors were involved in over 200 such cases between 1790 and 1832, especially around 1793, 1808–11, and 1817–21. Many cases, however, did not proceed to indictment, and conviction rates were erratic. Some juries were reluctant to convict, and as many as two-thirds of those prosecuted escaped punishment. Most of these cases concerned radical literature or 'licentious' publications, rather than words spoken aloud.[40]

Thomas Brimble, however, was sentenced to the pillory and six months in gaol at the Somerset assizes in 1793 'for speaking seditious words of the king and constitution'.[41] William Roberts in Devon and Benjamin Ward in Nottinghamshire were found guilty on similar charges.[42] John Nuttall, a cotton spinner of Bolton, was tried at the Lancashire assizes in August 1793 for proclaiming Thomas Paine 'a better man than the king', and toasting the company in the King's Head, 'here's damnation to the king and constitution'.[43] Benjamin Booth earned twelve months in Lancaster Castle gaol for damning the king and saying, 'I would guillotine him if I could'.[44]

Another case in December 1793 concerned William Hudson (or Hodgson), who denounced the king as 'George Guelph, a German hog butcher, a dealer in human flesh by the carcass'. He spoke these words in the London coffee house, after drinking three large glasses of punch, and caused further disruption by responding to a health to 'the king' by pledging 'the French republic, and may it triumph over all the governments in Europe'. The coffee-shop keeper called for an officer to arrest the offender, and Hudson was tried at the Old Bailey. His protest that there was 'no law . . . to order him into custody for mere words' was overridden, and he was sentenced to two years in Newgate and fined £200, his imprisonment to continue until the fine was paid.[45]

A headline in the newspaper *The World* in April 1794 read 'More Prosecution for Words!!!' The rector of Shenfield, Essex, had been arrested after 'a conversation on a political subject at an inn at Brentwood'.[46] Stephen Cavern in London was sent for trial for saying that 'kings . . . are of no use in this country . . . we are governed under a tyrannical government'.[47] For his 'seditious expression against the king and government', John Sayer of Southampton earned six months in gaol.[48] George Wilkinson of Bath also earned four months in prison for crying 'success to the French', and describing the king and his ministers as villains.[49]

But the initial panic was subsiding, and juries became less ready to convict. When John Porter of Somerset was prosecuted in 1794, 'for wickedly and maliciously damning the king', the assize jury found him 'not guilty'.[50] Another Somerset man, Evan Nepean, was likewise acquitted of 'uttering seditious words' in 1794 when the case against him collapsed.[51] Juries at Leicester and at Coventry found defendants 'not guilty' after the courts refused to accept their original verdicts of 'guilty of speaking the words in the indictment, but not with a malicious [or seditious] intent'.[52] A tailor in a London pot house jested in September 1794, 'that Treason was only Reason with a T at the beginning of it'.[53]

Seditious words were still dangerous, as much to the speaker as to the late Hanoverian regime. Casual speech in drinking establishments could lead to investigation by magistrates, and public oratory from a platform was sure to be monitored by authorities. Edward Swift, a labourer of Clewer, Berkshire (also described as a slopseller of New Windsor), was sentenced to a year in prison in 1794, 'for uttering treasonable and seditious words against his majesty'. Witnesses swore that he expostulated, 'Damn the king and queen, they ought to be put to death the same as the king and queen of France were . . . Damn and bugger the king and all that belong to him . . . Damnation blast the king, I would as soon shoot the king as a mad dog.' This was a comprehensive explosion of disloyal invective, for which Swift was promptly convicted and sentenced.[54]

After Henry Yorke alias Redhead, aged 22, made an inflammatory speech at Sheffield in April 1794, local conservatives secured his indictment for high treason. Yorke had denounced tyranny and urged reform, commended the revolutions in France and America, and proclaimed his ambition 'to cause revolutions all over the world'. He described the governments of Europe, including that of George III, as 'frightful abortions of haste and usurpation'. He was also involved in pamphleteering and petitioning against slavery. The Council in London took up the case in March 1795 and advised that Yorke 'should be proceeded against for misdemeanour only', not treason. They rightly judged that a trial for speaking seditious words was more likely to result in a conviction. Eventually in July 1795 he was sentenced to two years in prison and fined £100, his supporters calling him 'a martyr to the cause of liberty'. The prosecution side of Yorke's King's Bench file bulks out to over a hundred papers.[55]

By this time Hanoverian political culture was severely agitated, with growing unrest in England, discontent in Ireland, and scandals engulfing the royal family. Demonstrators shouted 'No war. Down with George', and some called out 'no king'.[56] Courtiers might well be forgiven for fearing revolution. In October 1795 when George III took his coach to parliament he was jostled and hissed, and someone threw a stone through his window. Hearing of this, the Surrey publican Lewis Bowyer remarked: 'damn him, serve him right if they had stoned him to death . . . I wish his head was on Temple Bar.' It took the assize jury five minutes to find Bowyer guilty, despite his excuse of intoxication.[57]

In another case that autumn, Samuel Wyatt, a young gentleman from Hampshire, was drinking at the Play House in Portsmouth when 'God Save the King was called for and played'. An army officer, Lieutenant Clark, rebuked Wyatt for not taking off his hat, to which Wyatt responded: 'Damn all royalty and satellites of kings.' Later, in his defence, Wyatt claimed that 'he did not know the meaning of the word satellite' (which referred to attendant military officers). When the watch arrived to arrest him, Wyatt declared 'that he had a right to say what he pleased in a free country, if this is a free country'. A report was sent to the Treasury Solicitor in London, and Wyatt was bound to appear at the next sessions.[58]

The Treasonable and Seditious Practices Act of 1795 (36 Geo. III, c. 7, designed to expire with the death of George III) declared it high treason, punishable by death, to 'compass, imagine, invent, devise, or intend' the death of the monarch, to deprive him or his heirs of their 'style, honour, or kingly name', to levy war against his majesty, or to stir foreigners to invade the realm. Such treason could be expressed through 'printing or writing' or 'by any overt act or deed'. Authors, printers, and publishers were exposed to the terror of this law, but ordinary alehouse utterances were not covered. A further clause, however, explicitly penalized the spoken word. It would now be a 'high misdemeanour' (though not treason) for anyone 'maliciously and advisedly, by writing, printing, preaching, or other speaking [to] express, publish, utter or declare any words or sentences to excite or stir up the people to hatred or contempt of the person of his majesty, his heirs or successors, or the government and constitution of this realm'. Anyone convicted of a second offence risked banishment or transportation for seven years.[59] The Seditious Meetings and Assemblies Act, passed in the same session, required a magistrate's permission for any public meeting of more than fifty persons, and allowed the authorities to declare any meeting 'seditious'.[60]

The legislation of 1795 empowered the government to scrutinize discourse, but its bark was worse than its bite. It launched no Hanoverian reign of terror, and spawned no more than a scatter of prosecutions. Radical activists became more careful, or withdrew from public view, while ordinary people grumbled with impunity.[61] Notwithstanding the new legislation, the ultra-radical subculture of the late eighteenth century gave voice to 'a melange of ribald blasphemy, millenarianism and political treason' in alehouses and coffee houses, debating clubs and 'free-and-easies', where government spies rarely penetrated.[62] The crown itself allowed 'the right of free, of temperate, of sober, and of ample discussion . . . upon every political subject', though not seditious language that advocated the abolition of monarchy.[63] English political culture had weathered a storm, though revolutionary echoes still reverberated in the legendary toast 'may the last king be strangled in the bowels of the last priest'.[64] Dissidents may have continued to say such things, but they were rarely taken to court. And if they were tried, the government could not count on convictions.

Among the few recorded cases from the next few years, William Davies of Surrey was prosecuted at Guildford in 1798 for 'uttering scandalous and seditious words in the Swan and Castle alehouse'.[65] Peter Sequest of Somerset was found guilty that year of wishing 'success to the French, and God bless them', but was fined only a shilling and sentenced to a month in gaol.[66]

In April 1800 a Welshman, John Griffith, praised Napoleon Bonaparte and declared aloud, 'Damn King George the third, he is no king—I could make a better out of a block of oilwood, it being first painted and gilt, and then sent to parliament for their acceptance'. Despite claiming lunacy, and the fact that he spoke in Welsh, the offender was sentenced to two months in prison.[67] Later in 1800, after George III had survived a pistol attempt at Drury Lane Theatre, the Londoner Robert Chapman was remanded for saying, 'I wish I had a pistol, and I would shoot the king . . . If I had him here I would rip his bloody guts out, and lay them on the floor . . . damn his eyes.'[68]

Political talk in the Golden Lion in Cripplegate became heated later in 1800 when Jesse Hilliar, drunk on gin, said: 'Damn the king and the parliament.' The Old Bailey judge gave the jury a choice: 'if you think that this was a drunken conversation, they not knowing what they said, you will acquit the defendant; but if you think this man was of wicked disposition, and wishing to overturn the government, to be sure you will find him guilty.' The jury decided quickly, 'not guilty'.[69]

A Westminster magistrate likewise invited a jury to decide if Daniel Turner's words in 1806 were spoken with seditious intent, 'or whether they were not rather the result of a silly and obstinate spirit of opposition, in one of those ridiculous disputes about politics, that so frequently occur between such men in their ale-house meetings'. Turner, an ex-soldier, had wished success to Bonaparte, 'the universal friend of mankind', nearly precipitating a riot in the Lemon Tree public house in Haymarket. The jury instantly acquitted the prisoner.[70] In a similar case from Norfolk, one E. Stubbing said in a public house at Wymondham that 'he wished Bonaparte would come, he would be the first man to join him', and 'that Bonaparte was a better man to his country than King George is to this'. Again, to the charge of uttering seditious words, the jury promptly returned 'not guilty'.[71]

By the time of George III's golden jubilee in 1809, the king was mad, blind, and incapacitated. Savage cartoon caricatures mocked both the monarch and the regent. Nonetheless, it was generally conceded that his majesty reigned over 'a people happy, great and free', where popular loyalism drowned out noises of dissent.[72]

The Age of Peterloo

A House of Commons review in 1821 of 'the individuals prosecuted for political libel and seditious conduct in England and Scotland since 1807' noted very few cases involving mere words. Most of the political prosecutions from this period concerned the writing or printing of seditious libels, not vocal utterance, and those found guilty suffered heavier custodial sentences and stiffer fines than mere seditious speakers.[73] A few scares arose against the background of Luddite disturbances and the continuing Napoleonic war, but the danger of seditious words appeared again to have receded.

In 1813 the Yorkshire mill worker James Chapman faced prosecution for seditiously venting his 'Jacobinical and revolutionary principles', saying: 'Damn the king, he is superannuated and has been these six and twenty years. We are governed by a set of damned whores, rogues and thieves. The Prince of Wales is a damned rogue, and the Princess of Wales a damned whore.' But after very little deliberation the jury 'returned a verdict of Not Guilty, to the universal satisfaction of a crowded court'.[74] The view was widely held that an Englishman was privileged to fill his belly with beer and to say whatever came into his head. Despite the efforts of prosecutors, juries inclined to agree that a man in liquor was not fully responsible for the sins of his tongue.[75]

New fears and tensions gripped England after the end of the Napoleonic wars. Amidst economic hardship and agitation for reform, the last years of the Regency and the first years of the reign of George IV brought a new round of prosecutions for seditious speech. Some of this was alehouse bravado, of the kind that was long familiar, but the courts also targeted political orators who brought radical appeals to the public. Even more dangerous was the subversive and seditious press. As in the 1790s, an anxious government equipped itself with new legislation.

The Treason Act of 1817 (57 Geo. III, c. 6) made perpetual the provisions of the 1795 law (36 Geo. III, c. 7), penalizing all 'compassings, imaginations, inventions, devices, or intentions' tending to the king's death, expressed, uttered, or declared 'by publishing any printing or writing, or by any overt act or deed'. The principal danger resided in writing, however, and the statute did not address spoken words.[76] Habeas corpus was again suspended, and ninety-six people were detained in 1817 on suspicion of treason.[77] 'An act for the more effectual prevention and punishment of blasphemy and seditious libels' in 1819 further criminalized the composing, printing, or publishing of any libel 'tending to bring into hatred or contempt the person of his majesty, his heirs or successors, or the Regent, or the government and constitution of the United Kingdom', but it did not specifically mention crimes of the tongue.[78]

Descriptions, denunciations, and exculpations abound, but we have no voices of Peterloo, the 'massacre' of August 1819, when a festive gathering of reformers at St Peter's Fields, Manchester, was violently dispersed by the Manchester Yeomanry and the Fifteenth Hussars. At least eleven people from the crowd of 60,000 were sabred or trampled to death.[79] The orator Henry Hunt, who had planned to address the assembly, was initially charged with treason and eventually tried for conspiracy and sedition. At the York assizes in 1820 he was sentenced to two and half years in prison.[80]

Robert Wedderburn, an artisan preacher in Soho, said in October after the Manchester events 'that the revolution had already begun in blood there, and that it must now also end in blood here'. He called the Prince Regent a tyrant who had lost the confidence of his people, and claimed that, given enough wine and whores, 'the poor fool was very well satisfied, and so he don't care a damn about the people's sufferings'. Already under surveillance for his agitation against slavery, Wedderburn was convicted of blasphemous libel and sentenced to two years in prison.[81]

The Manchester events also inspired James Taylor, a Staffordshire labourer, to propose the toast 'success to Hunt' at the George and Dragon in Waterfall in November 1819. Two travelling soldiers refused to join the health, not even for 'the best bottle of wine in the house', and drank instead to the king. Taylor responded intemperately, 'Damn King George, Damn the Regent. I wish that [Henry] Hunt had fifty thousand men as good as myself . . . [to] clear the country of them', and further wished for 'the cutting off the head of the Prince Regent'. This led to Taylor's appearance at the Staffordshire assizes in March 1820 on charges of sedition, where, despite the weight of evidence, he was acquitted.[82]

In another case from Staffordshire, the labourer Edward Price was drinking at the King's Head in Wolverhampton in November 1819 when he launched into a rant against the monarchy:

I wish I had the Prince Regent and the crown here, I would trample them under my feet into dust . . . I wish . . . the Prince Regent . . . into the bottom pit of hell . . . Damn the king and all the [royal] family . . . I should wish to take them out of their coffins when they are dead and burn them to ashes.

When the landlord refused Price any more ale, he moved on to the Seven Stars, where the constable of Wrottelsey arrested him. Bound over to appear at the next quarter sessions, Edward Price was indicted for attempting 'to raise and excite discontent, disaffection and sedition in the minds of the liege subjects of our lord the present king, and to traduce, vilify and bring into hatred' the Prince Regent. Despite testimony to his good character, and observations that he became 'riotous when drunk', the court found him guilty and sentenced him to twelve months in prison.[83] More fortunate was the Yorkshireman William Brown, charged in July 1820 for saying 'the king is a bad one . . . I wish I had a bullet in the king's liver. If I had a chance I would put a bullet in.' Sufficient witnesses corroborated these words, but the Grand Jury threw out the case.[84]

Modern Crimes

By the end of the Hanoverian era, in the reigns of George IV and William IV, the monarchy fell into further disrespect. Scandal followed the royal family, and the crown was held in contempt. But with parliament ascendant and the press emboldened, it hardly mattered what ordinary people said. The accession of Queen Victoria in 1837 introduced more cordial relations between the queen and her subjects, though not without occasional scares. In November 1837 a madman calling himself 'John II, king of England', and claiming to be the son of George IV and Queen Caroline, uttered 'seditious words and threats' against the new monarch, challenging her: 'you usurper, I will have you off the throne before this day week.' Examined in the Court of Queen's Bench, Captain John Goode showed 'violent symptoms of mental derangement', and was declared insane. At one point he asked, 'why am I not tried for high treason', when charged only with 'seditious words'.[85]

A decade later a panicked reaction to Chartism led to the Crown and Government Security Act of 1848, which made it a felony, punishable by transportation or imprisonment, to engage in 'open and avowed speaking' of a treasonable nature, or to advocate treason by writing or speech against the queen.[86] Immediately dubbed 'the new gagging bill', the law became the target of seditious ballads that warned of its likely effects:

> Mind what you say by night and day,
> And don't speak out of reason,
> For everything God bless the queen,
> Is reckoned up high treason.[87]

The act was rarely used, and came to be regarded as antique and ineffective.

High Victorian opinion upheld 'freedom of speech' as a distinctly British characteristic, a hard-won right that underpinned the nation's greatness. The ability of citizens to speak and write as they pleased was taken as a sign of political maturity that distinguished modern Britain from the more repressive regimes of continental Europe and from England's less liberal past. Spokesmen for the establishment (the self-styled 'guardians of society') liked to recall these principles at times when provocative oratory or inflammatory publications tested them to the limit. England's freedom of expression excited the 'astonished admiration' of the people of Europe, wrote *The Times* in 1846, 'her liberty... stands firm and immovable, rooted in the affections of the people'.[88] Similarly editorializing in 1879, the London paper *The Graphic* remarked that

in continental countries... any language or writing which is calculated to bring the ruling power into discredit or contempt is very speedily and sharply repressed. In these islands, on the contrary, there is an almost superstitious reverence for freedom of speech, and seditious words, unless accompanied by seditious deeds, are usually permitted to be uttered with impunity.[89]

On both occasions, these writers suggested, Irish extremists had crossed the line and may have forfeited the protections of the law.

Judges too spoke warmly of English liberties when they reprimanded alleged speakers of sedition. Free speech was protected, proclaimed the Recorder at the Central Criminal Court in April 1886, 'providing always the utterances were *bona fide*, and that they involved only honest criticism for the amendment of our social and political relations, and were not made in a tone and in language which seemed to encourage acts of violence'. Words became 'seditious', he said, when the speaker 'went beyond fair discussion in considering questions affecting the constitution' and 'intended to stir up hatred and contempt for the power of the country'. Such was the case of socialist agitators at Trafalgar Square, who had denounced the House of Commons as capitalist parasites, and recommended hanging the enemies of the poor on lamp posts. The jury, however, was not convinced and found the defendants 'not guilty'.[90]

It became a precept of Victorian law, passed on to the present, that speech was free though actions had consequences. Words spoken on a political platform or in a public house were not in themselves perilous, but could become so if they caused trouble, incited crime, or led to a breach of the peace. The distinction was not always clear, and audiences, arresting officers, courts, and juries could harbour different opinions. Victorian governments, like their modern successors, were more inclined to use laws against unlawful assembly than laws against sedition to control speech they thought dangerous. But any fear that private conversations would reach the ears of the authorities was long considered absurd. The tone was set by the versatile and wide-ranging Metropolitan Police Act of 1839 that made it an offence for anyone 'in any thoroughfare or public place' within the metropolitan district to 'use any threatening, abusive, and insulting words or behaviour with intent to provoke a breach of the peace'. This was a law that could be used against political orators as well as drunks, and it remained in force until 1986.[91]

Following the end of the First World War in 1918, government officials again became concerned by threats of seditious disturbance. The culprits, or suspects, included mutinous servicemen, militant workers, unemployed labourers, communist agitators, Irish nationalists, anarchists, and suffragettes. Private conversation remained beyond the reach of the law, but seditious public oratory again became subject to investigation. Police informers infiltrated meetings to make transcripts, and members of parliament demanded action against dangerous expressions. Targets in 1919 included the Bolshevik pattern-maker, David Ramsey, imprisoned for five months for words 'calculated to cause sedition and disaffection among the civilian population, and to prejudice discipline among the king's forces';[92] agitators in the Welsh collieries whose speeches threatened 'to inflame passions and...to foster violence and revolution';[93] and speakers at Hyde Park Corner who advocated the overthrow of monarchy and capitalism. One such orator, the anarchist bus conductor Sydney Hanson, cried 'to hell with the Union Jack, the Union Jack is a flag of tyranny', and was fined 40s. under the Metropolitan Police Act for 'insulting words or behaviour' liable to cause a breach of the peace.[94]

Lloyd George's government kept its nerve and restrained the more zealous constabularies. Regional police forces were instructed not to initiate prosecutions on their own, but to report to Whitehall any speech that was 'of such a character that the question of prosecuting the speaker requires serious consideration'.[95] When reports came in from Manchester of a socialist speech at the Free Trade Hall in November 1919, the Home Office considered whether to press charges of sedition. One official urged prosecution if 'there is a distinct prospect of a trial for seditious libel resulting in a conviction'. Another pondered 'whether more harm would be done by prosecuting or by giving such speeches impunity'. A third warned that conviction could not be assured, and that even a successful prosecution would 'give a large advertisement to the circulation of dangerous views'. The official wisdom was to keep a watching brief, but to hold the powers of government in reserve. It was remarkably similar to considerations by the Elizabethan Privy Council, and to the policy that generally prevails today.[96] Public authorities had to decide how much to tolerate and when to intervene, but political judgement always offset the complexities of the law.

After the General Strike of 1926 the Attorney General and Director of Public Prosecutions prepared secret advice for the Home Secretary how to deal with revolutionary and seditious threats. In all cases, they wrote, 'the question, "what is the law?" is very closely allied to the question, "how should the law be applied?" ' The difficulty arose, they said, 'from the British theory that very full liberty should be allowed for the propagation of "opinions" as distinct from seditious "incitements" '. Whether this 'British theory' was to be treasured or regretted was a matter of opinion. It remained

exceedingly difficult to extend the law so as to strike at the propagation of subversive opinions without interfering unduly with new ideas which may seem subversive to one generation and be generally accepted by the next. English law allows the tares to grow with the wheat so long as there is no immediate danger to the safety of the state.

A further problem, of practicality rather than principle, was that the common-law offences of seditious conspiracy and seditious libel were 'triable only on indictment' and needed to be decided by a jury. As before, in so many similar circumstances, the government weighed questions of security and law enforcement against outcomes that could be unpredictable and counter-productive.[97]

By the later twentieth century the very concept of seditious speech seemed archaic. The Law Commission of England and Wales concluded in 1977 that there was no need for an offence of 'sedition' affecting political conduct, since existing public-order laws would suffice.[98] The European Convention on Human Rights, which the United Kingdom was quick to ratify, proclaims 'the right of freedom of expression' and the right 'to receive and impart information and ideas without interference by public authority'. This was enshrined in the Human Rights Act of 1998, but hedged to allow room for 'the interests of national security, territorial integrity or public safety, for the prevention of disorder or crime, for the protection of health or morals, [and] for the protection of the rights of others'.[99] Though not extensively tested in the courts, there is room here for argument on all sides.

New global threats have refocused attention on speech that sparks hatred or encourages terrorism. The modern world appears menaced by different crimes of the tongue. Britain's Public Order Act of 1986 makes it an offence for anyone to use 'threatening, abusive or insulting words or behaviour' with the intent to stir up racial hatred.[100] The Crime and Disorder Act of 1998 and the Racial or Religious Hatred Act of 2006 further criminalize offences involving 'threatening words'.[101] The 2006 Terrorism Act penalizes the 'glorification' of terrorism, prompting critics to caution that 'rants should be rejected with argument, not with police and prisons'.[102]

Modern legislation guards against disruptive or antisocial speech to protect the community's values and institutions, but it does not privilege particular persons or officeholders. Britain's royal family enjoys no special protection from verbal assault, though it is unlikely to countenance prosecution of its enemies. The modern monarchy is a fixture of celebrity culture, an anomaly in a democratic society, and critics attack not its power but its privileges. The House of Windsor lays claim to a millennium of English kingship, and inherits too the tradition of demeaning the monarch. But there is no crime now of compassing or imagining, no penalty for *lèse majesté*. It may be rude and crude to call the queen 'a harridan', her heir 'an expensively educated dicksplash', or her husband a Nazi, but one can say such things with impunity.[103] Unlike earlier declarations—that Henry VIII was a tyrant, Elizabeth I a whore, James I an ass, and Charles I a baby—these may be sins of the tongue, but nobody counts them as crimes.

12

Dangerous Talk in Dangerous Times

From the fifteenth century to the eighteenth, and no doubt most other times, the people and governors of England engaged in spirited public conversation. Multivocal, multilayered, and with many modulations, this conversation ranged over sensitive topics of subjecthood and citizenship, authority and obedience, deference and power. As we have seen, the common tongue was not always respectful or polite. Some utterances were hostile and abusive, demeaning to public authority, hostile to the crown. Others reinforced the established regime. People spoke unguardedly, recklessly or without reflection, and sometimes said things that could be judged scandalous, seditious, or even treasonable. The preceding chapters have introduced fragments of conversations that got people into trouble. This final chapter revisits material from across the period and ventures some general conclusions. It reviews examples of dangerous talk, the responses of auditors, and the excuses of those accused. It reconsiders the peril of law and the patterns of punishment for alleged offenders. And it questions the threat posed by crimes of the tongue to the security of early modern regimes.

Vocal Subjects

Despite conventional inhibitions, early modern people displayed an appetite for public information, and a propensity to discuss the affairs of the crown. All sorts of people spoke of things that official political culture prescribed off limits. Some of this chatter was disorderly, and veered towards dangerous territory by directly commenting on the qualities and character of the monarch. A tension resonated between the protection of *arcana imperii* and the energies of popular discourse. Different regimes responded to this problem through a combination of politics, administration, and law. They also depended on information from informants, and encouraged loyal subjects to report the speech transgressions of their neighbours. The state response changed over time, even as the background chatter remained incessant, because of alterations in political culture and in law. Over time, especially in the eighteenth century, the law became more lenient and the government more secure. Punishment for seditious speech became less savage, though times of political panic could see a stepped-up pressure. Every early modern regime had grounds for concern about the dutiful allegiance of its subjects, but most recognized that subversive threats and seditious challenges were more likely to stem from the culture of print than from the everyday activity of talking.

Preachers and magistrates, moralists and monarchs, nonetheless expressed horror and distaste at the torrent of unseemly discourse. Their own language deployed a host of pejorative adjectives to condemn the words that they disapproved. A powerful rhetoric of disapprobation countered and contained the most disruptive popular expressions. Henry VIII's kingship was said to be exposed to 'lewd, ungracious, detestable and traitorous' speeches, and to 'opprobrious, scandalous, vilifying and rebellious-sounding' words. His successors Edward and Mary faced 'horrible and slanderous' verbal assaults, and expressions that were 'malicious and traitorous' or 'lewd and seditious'. The Elizabethan regime coped similarly with 'lewd, detestable, slanderous' speech, and 'false, scandalous and seditious' words.[1] Councillors and justices chose these adjectives not just to express loathing, but also to echo the language of statutes and proclamations, and to highlight the offender's exposure at law.

Their reactions were perhaps appropriate in the light of subjects who called Henry VIII a 'tyrant', a 'whoremaster', a 'knave', 'a heretic, a thief and a harlot', cursed 'a vengeance on the king', and offered to 'play football with his head'. How else should one describe the language that labelled Queen Elizabeth a 'whore', a 'quean', a 'jade', a 'bastard', a 'rascal', and a 'rogue'? It was surely scandalous for a Surrey woman to say in 1585 that 'the queen is no maid, and she hath three sons by the Earl of Leicester'. It verged on treason to say, as one Catholic said in 1593, that 'if mistress Elizabeth were dead we should have good sport'. From the viewpoint of the Tudor regime, such words were indeed detestable, arguably seditious, and deserving of punishment.

James I's councillors likewise defended their king against 'insolent and audacious speeches...of a most dangerous consequence' and 'disgraceful speeches...derogatory to his majesty and his royal blood'. Undutiful speech was still 'opprobrious', though few said worse of England's first Stuart than that he was 'an ass' or 'a fool'. More menacingly, a Middlesex man prophesied in 1611 that King James 'would have his crown pulled about his head', while others offered to burn, stab, or cut the king's throat.[2] Though many of these disorderly voices might be counted as forms of resistance, among the weapons of the weak, they also suggest an intimacy with monarchy, as if his majesty was there to be mocked or rebuked. Much of the seditious speech concerning early modern rulers expressed hope that the king would govern better, not that kingship should be removed.

Charles I, we have seen, attracted a battery of derogatory commentary, from Hugh Pyne's remark in 1625 that King Charles was like 'a child with an apple', to Joan Sherrard's observation two decades later that 'his majesty is a stuttering fool'. A Kentish man in 1634 called Charles I a 'knave' and said 'it were no matter if the king were hanged'. 'Is there never a Felton yet living?' asked a London woman in 1644, invoking the memory of Buckingham's assassin and wishing his sacred majesty dead. Not surprisingly, Caroline magistrates railed against words they deemed to be 'high and heinous', 'factious and mutinous', 'wicked and malicious', 'undutiful and unjust'. Their rhetoric of vituperation waxed strong against speech they termed 'opprobrious and scandalous', 'desperate and seditious', 'vile', 'impious', 'unsufferable', 'lewd', 'very dangerous', and 'fearfully ill-advised'.[3]

The mid-century revolution saw no abatement of derogatory speech against shifting centres of power. Oliver Cromwell, like the king he replaced, was labelled 'a traitor', 'a rogue', and 'a rascal', by people who 'hoped to see him hanged', while his supporters dubbed such speech 'dangerous', 'scandalous', 'treasonous', and 'seditious'. Though political circumstances changed, the terms of the discourse proved remarkably durable.[4]

Charles II's less loyal subjects called their king a 'bastard', a 'traitor', a 'base knave', a 'bloody tyrant', and a 'rascally rogue'. Evil speakers used all sorts of 'unmannerly and uncomely words concerning the king's majesty', calling him 'a damned dog' and 'the veriest rogue that ever reigned'. Several wished his majesty stabbed, hung, burned, or beheaded, and more than one offered to 'kill the king with his own hands'. Restoration authorities characterized such language as 'desperate and dangerous', 'scandalous and treasonable', or 'treasonable and seditious', though the words were no worse than in previous reigns.[5]

The barrage of hostility continued, with later Stuart subjects calling James II 'a cheat', 'a rogue', and 'a papist dog', William III 'a damned Dutch usurper', and Queen Anne a 'brandy-nose bitch'. Their Hanoverian successors fared just as ill, with George I called a 'usurper', a 'turd', and a 'cuckold', George II derided as a 'jack pudding', and George III damned as a 'villain', a 'rogue', and a 'liar'. One man in 1795 wanted King George stoned and his head set on Temple Bar. Another in 1800 offered to 'rip his bloody guts out, and lay them on the floor'. Most contemporaries agreed that these were 'scandalous, malicious, and dangerous' expressions, but they could not be quieted. Words of this sort still stirred the authorities to action, but they were less likely now to result in convictions or grievous punishment. Eighteenth-century liberals claimed that 'the birthright of an Englishman' included freedom to speak one's mind, no matter how coarse or undutiful the utterance, and this view has largely prevailed to the present.[6] A desacralized monarchy had less at stake and could tolerate more than a regime of sacred kingship and divine right royal supremacy.

Sometimes the offensive expressions were too terrible to set forth in writing. Witnesses were reluctant to repeat them, and officials sought to prevent their circulation. The Yorkshireman Richard Keddye used 'open, vile and threatening speech' against Queen Elizabeth in 1577, but what he said is lost because the informant was 'not only ashamed but afraid by word or writing to recite' it.[7] In 1596 the trial of Thomas Wenden for seditious speech against the queen was set aside because, a government lawyer argued, 'it was too filthy a matter to be brought in open place'.[8] James I himself judged it better in 1621 'to suppress such scandalous speeches than by punishment to blaze them further abroad'.[9] The London schoolmaster Alexander Gill was tried in Star Chamber in 1628, but 'because the speeches are so foul' his most incriminating words were not read in court, and the official record is partially obliterated.[10] The dangerous remarks of bishop Williams in 1632 were allegedly such that the informant 'durst not repeat'.[11] But, despite this reticence, a wide array of opprobrious language resounds within the surviving records.

Tudor and Stuart statesmen thought seditious speech endangered society and the state. They frowned on words 'of a high nature', and expressed alarm at talk 'of high consequence'. Scandalous speech dishonoured the crown, and turbulent tongues imperilled the regime. Treasonous speech, they said, undermined the framework of order and security. Elizabethan councillors argued that loose talk 'maketh men's minds to be at variance with one another', and could sever 'the bands and sinews of all government next under the ordinance of God'. Disrespect spawned sedition, they feared, with treason not far behind, risking 'the ruin' of the crown, the realm, and the law.[12]

Early Stuart administrators shared this anxiety. There was no excuse for 'lewd and undutiful speeches', remarked Secretary Conway in 1628, no 'liberty of speaking rashly of the sacred person or life of the king'. It was the Devil's work, he said, to stir up 'undutifulness and disobedience'.[13] William Laud agreed that the 'sin of murmuring against the king' was intolerable, and that none should 'whet [their] tongues, or sour [their] breasts' against the Lord's anointed.[14]

Like its royal predecessors, the Cromwellian regime of the 1650s sought to guard itself against 'dangerous words of most evil consequence against the government and public peace'.[15] The view persisted, and was frequently reiterated, that verbal expressions had political consequence, and, if uncorrected, could undermine the state. Charles II's councillors in the 1670s claimed that undutiful words tended to 'the defamation of the government and disturbance of the peace of the realm'.[16] In 1682 they urged that such words 'require nimble prosecution to justice; for as long as the traitorous, saucy, and malicious tongues of the subjects are at liberty to scandalize his majesty, his royal highness and government, we cannot expect a well-grounded peace'.[17]

The constitution, though battered, withstood these verbal assaults. Later governments came to accept that alehouse chatter had little serious impact on the constitutional fabric, and coffee-house banter left structures of power intact. Seditious talk was treated more as an irritant to be endured than a crime to be punished. The Glorious Revolution energized political arguments and put 'freedom of speech' onto the national conversational agenda. Hanoverian authorities became broadly tolerant of verbal political abuse, though they still applied sanctions to words that would 'lessen [the king] in the esteem of his subjects and weaken his government, or raise jealousies between him and his people'.[18] As in many regimes past and present, a tension remained between national security concerns and the subject's 'freedom of expression'. Despite the scares of the French Revolution, few henceforth feared that words alone could jeopardize the fundamental stability of the kingdom. On the threshold of the modern era we hear much

less about talk that imperilled the polity, and rather more about the impropriety of language that could cause a breach of the peace. Political conversation was as boisterous and irreverent as ever, but it was essentially
decriminalized and removed from state surveillance.

Anxious Authorities

Despite the anxieties of councillors and moralists, the utterance of 'dangerous speech' generally proved more dangerous to the speaker than to the
community to which he or she belonged. The hierarchical, monarchical
society of pre-modern England disapproved of disorderly expression, but
scandalous or undutiful talk, though reprehensible, did not seriously endanger the state. The fear that seditious words would erode the bonds of
authority proved largely unfounded. Though malicious and uncivil chatter
was endemic, some of it touching the crown, successive regimes survived
largely unscathed. Once the words had been exposed to official scrutiny,
they were more likely to redound to the discomfort of the person who had
said them. Justices of the peace grilled suspects and witnesses, and magistrates pursued offenders at law. Those found guilty of sedition experienced
humiliation, incarceration, mutilation, financial distress, or public ruin.
Their punishment could include the noose, the knife, the whip, the pillory,
the stocks, imprisonment, and fines. In extreme cases, if the law so provided,
a speaker whose words were judged treasonous faced gory execution.

Whether they thought it deeply dangerous or merely undutiful, governors and magistrates long felt themselves obliged to root out seditious talk.
Local authorities under Henry VIII were tasked to search out and punish
'any such cankered malice'.[19] Elizabethan justices knew their duty to report
'any person being vehemently suspected of saying or reporting of any
slanderous news or tales against her majesty'.[20] Offensive words, the Jacobean Privy Council insisted, 'are in no way to be slighted nor passed over'.[21]
'No syllable escaping the mouth of any disloyal subject, or information
touching my king and sovereign coming to my knowledge, should be
passed or permitted without speedy certification to your lordships', a
magistrate assured his masters in 1606.[22]

Charles I's regime likewise took 'care and providence' to pursue suspected speakers of scandal and sedition, especially any whose utterances 'so
nearly and highly concern the sacred person and honour of his majesty'.[23]

Caroline magistrates became especially diligent in investigating all 'speeches against the king's honour'. As the mayor and aldermen of Barnstable explained in 1626, with reference to an offensive speaker in Devon, they 'could do no less than to lay hold of him and have him in safe custody' until the Privy Council advised 'what should become of him'.[24] Commending Sussex authorities in 1637 for reporting 'certain desperate and treasonable speeches', the Council advised that 'too much caution cannot safely be used for the preventing of danger and punishing offenders in this kind'.[25] Conscientious officers would initiate the processes of the law whenever report arose of reckless or malicious talk. It was this solicitude that generated the letters, reports, case files, and legal records on which much of the present analysis is founded. Prosecutors of treasonous words in the later Stuart and Hanoverian eras likewise spoke of their duty to uphold and defend the established order.

Uncertain Laws

Changes and continuities in the censuring of seditious speech also reflected alterations in the law. The law governing speech that touched the crown was unstable, and its application mutable and uncertain. Despite the enduring gravity of the legislation of Edward III, and its augmentation by treason statutes under Henry VIII, Elizabeth I, and Charles II, the power of the courts to punish people for words remained contestable. The law, as always, was subject to interpretation, and the savagery or lenience of its embrace varied with political circumstances. Words that in one era could take an offender to the gallows might lead only to the pillory a few decades later, or even be disregarded. The law of Edward III famously made it treason to 'compass or imagine' the death of the monarch. But whether such compassing could be done by words, and what those words should signify, was long unfathomable. Late medieval judges argued it was treason to induce subjects 'to withdraw their cordial love from the monarch, thereby compassing his death', and this could be accomplished by language.[26] Similar notions prevailed under the Tudors. In practice there was slippage between words identified as scandalous, seditious, or treasonable, with varying legal consequences.

Henry VIII's Treason Act of 1534 specifically penalized the spoken word, making it treason to call the king a 'heretic, schismatic, tyrant, infidel or usurper', or otherwise harm his title or dignities.[27] The Elizabethan regime sought similar protection. By the statute of 1571 it again became treason, 'by writing, printing, preaching, speech, express words or sayings', to call her majesty a 'heretic, schismatic, tyrant, infidel, or an usurper'.[28] Some of Elizabeth's advisers favoured a wider-reaching law, to make it treason 'to engender in the heads of the simple ignorant multitude a misliking or murmuring against the quiet government of the realm'.[29] Treason, declared the lawyer Thomas Norton, was 'the crime of violating or abating of majesty', a definition that lacked all statutory precision.[30]

Early Stuart judges in Star Chamber asserted that libelling the king or the state was treason, though they were hard pressed to justify this in law.[31] 'What plot of treason can be more dangerous than that which doth draw the hearts of your people from you', a loyal subject asked Charles I in 1629.[32] Even Pyne's case, which resolved that words by themselves could not be treason, did not completely clarify the matter. Prosecutors and politicians sometimes pushed harder than the law allowed, and threatened capital punishment for words that were merely scandalous or seditious. Their difficulty in determining the weight of such language is suggested by their reference to 'words tending to treason', words 'which we conceive import high treason or are too near it', and 'dangerous and seditious words, bordering upon if not altogether treasonous'.[33] The Restoration treason statute again penalized 'malicious and advised speaking' against the monarch, and took several people to the scaffold.[34] But later in the seventeenth century Justice Holt made the distinction that courts had observed in practice for generations: 'Loose words, spoken without relation to any act or project are not treason; but words of persuasion to kill the king are overt acts of high treason.'[35] Abusive political language remained actionable but would no longer raise the shadow of execution.

Lay opinion tended to imagine the law of treason to have been harsher and more comprehensive than most lawyers would concede. Time and again we hear of ordinary people describing certain expressions as 'a hanging offence', or claiming that 'men have been drawn on a hurdle for less'. Reports to magistrates often began when one person observed of another, 'he speaks treason', prompting the accused to consider that he had but 'a life to lose'.

When a Northamptonshire man declared it 'a pity' that Henry VIII was ever crowned, and 'a pity that he hath lived so long', a neighbour immediately warned him, 'beware what thou sayest, for thou speakest treason'.[36]

'Meanest thou to be hanged, or knowest thou what thou speakest?' asked a Hertfordshire drinker in 1623 when his companion wished King James dead.[37] 'I doubt you speak treason,' a listener rebuked a Northumberland collier in 1636; 'I will make report what you have said in discharge of my duty'.[38] A gentleman in Leicestershire rebuked a kinsman in 1637 for 'dangerous words against that king...saying they were treason'.[39] 'Take heed what you say, I have known men hanged for a less word,' observed an Essex labourer in 1638.[40] In Charles II's reign a drinker said that his companion 'deserved to be hanged for speaking such seditious and treasonable words', that the king had sold out to the French.[41] As late as 1719, long after such punishment for words had lapsed, one Middlesex woman warned another that 'she might be hanged' for damning King George and wishing him dead.[42]

Statements made by witnesses report most of them to have been horrified at hearing abusive and transgressive expressions. Their examinations and depositions reinforced conventional prescriptions encouraging deference and silence. Whether frightened or collusive, they reaffirmed the protocols of the governance of the tongue. Many acknowledged it wrong to meddle in matters that did not concern them, and dangerous to speak against majesty and power.

'I pray, John, turn your heart from any such seditious conversation,' advised a commoner at Norwich in 1554 when talk turned against Queen Mary's Spanish marriage.[43] 'Take heed what you sayest...thou wilt repent these words when thou art sober', warned an Essex artisan in 1560 when his companion declared that Dudley and Queen Elizabeth 'played legerdemain together'.[44] In 1626 one man tried to silence another who spoke ill of the king, saying, 'it is not fit for us to meddle with such matters'.[45] A London diner that year warned his table fellow to 'forbear speaking such things' when the topic verged on sedition.[46] 'Take heed what you speak for you speak unadvisedly,' warned another drinker when conversation turned to 'the king's business'.[47] Hearing talk that 'the king was a dishonest man', a Leicestershire woman in 1637 responded, 'God forbid', and another listener counselled that 'the said words should be buried and never spoken of again'.[48] On another occasion, when a soldier in Worcestershire made speeches verging on sedition, his superior 'bade him hold his peace for shame'.[49] Witnesses evinced a common interest in quieting risky exchanges, or at least in representing themselves as guardians of conventional conversational propriety.

Mitigations

Not surprisingly, the alleged speakers of dangerous words, when brought before authorities, often claimed to have been misheard or misconstrued. Streets and alehouses could be noisy places, where words disappeared in the wind. The most common excuse was that the speaker was so drunk at the time that he had no control of his speech and no recollection of what was said. Others claimed to be victims of malicious prosecution, enmeshed in the law by parties who had enmity or 'spleen' against them. Witnesses needed to be reliable before a prosecution could stand, and their own character and standing could be challenged.

Being drunk did not excuse bad behaviour. Inebriation was no defence at law. Nonetheless a procession of witnesses and defendants drew attention to the consumption of alcohol on occasions when dangerous words were uttered. Their statements show men and women in company together at various times of day and night, downing beer, wine, sack, punch, gin, or brandy. Juries sometimes showed lenience towards victims of excess drink, and magistrates too might be persuaded that words did less damage when the wine did the talking.

Margaret Chaunseler, notorious for calling Henry VIII's Queen Anne 'a goggle-eyed whore', told her examiner that 'she was drunk when she did speak . . . and that the evil spirit did cause her to speak . . . and she was very penitent for her offences'.[50] Edmund Brocke, who thought it no matter if Henry VIII were knocked on the head, likewise claimed 'he was mad or drunk and wist not what he said'.[51] One Elizabethan gentleman sought to excuse his rebellious words by claiming 'that he was overcome by drinking that morning of a great deal of white wine and sack'. Another attributed his seditious outburst to 'drink and heat' and 'excess of drink'.[52]

'Provoked by the devil', a Warwickshire man in 1620 was said to be 'so far in drink' that he knew not what he said when he declared King James 'a villain'. Neighbours testified that Hugh Drayton 'hath a weak brain, by reason of many wounds given him in wars and otherwise on his head, whereby it comes to pass that a little drink doth distemper his brain, and makes him to speak and do at those times such things as he is sorry for afterwards'.[53] Other Jacobean offenders claimed that they 'had with overmuch drinking bereft themselves of the true use of discretion and understanding', though the authorities insisted that should not 'be a privilege to them'.[54]

A workman charged with speaking seditious words in 1635 explained that he 'never held them in his heart', had no remembrance of them, and after downing two pints of sack was 'much afflicted' and 'much weakened in his mind'.[55] Another of Charles I's subjects told authorities in 1640 'that he doth not remember any such words as are informed against him . . . neither is he of any such opinion as the words do import; but if any words of that purport did pass from him in his drink, he is heartily sorry for them'.[56] These were common responses, and some of them may even have been true.

At a time when serious punishment could accrue from a careless tongue it was, perhaps, convenient to offer the alcohol defence by way of exoneration. It helped lessen treason charges to the level of a misdemeanour, and recast sedition as mere disorderly conduct. By the Regency period under George III a magistrate could instruct a jury, 'if you think that this was a drunken conversation, they not knowing what they said, you will acquit the defendant',[57] although that ploy was not always effective. A Yorkshire pros-ecutor declared in 1813 'that the effects of liquor were not to suggest seditious thoughts, but merely to remove those restraints under which evil disposed men were held by the terrors of the law while in a state of sobriety'.[58]

Other weaknesses or disturbances of mind could excuse or mitigate speech offences. An ironmonger gaoled in Cheshire for 'slanderous speeches against the queen's majesty' was released in 1578 on information that he was 'com-monly troubled with a lunacy'.[59] Another man charged in 1596 with 'very undutiful and disloyal speeches' was said to be 'lunatic at the time of uttering'.[60] A Londoner in 1617, 'being distract and mad', was confined to Bedlam for his 'lewd and scandalous words' against King James.[61] Another of James I's ill-spoken subjects was deemed 'distracted . . . mad . . . a kind of brainsick fellow', and was dismissed with a whipping.[62] The cleric Noah Rogers, in trouble in 1634 for seditious words against Charles I, sought exculpation by citing his distemper and melancholy, caused, he said, by 'hard study and deep meditations', and 'upon his knees he beggeth pardon for it'.[63]

Dozens of cases unravelled on report that the informer who brought the accusation did so to discredit an enemy. Even if the allegation were true, the case might founder on suspicion of the prosecution being malicious. The case against Margery Cowpland, who allegedly called Henry VIII 'an extortioner and knave' and his queen 'a strong harlot', stalled in 1535 because her accuser was also in dispute with her about property and money.[64] An alleged speaker of sedition in 1582 explained that his accuser bore a grudge against him, 'upon some falling out at football play more than a month before'.[65] Another complaint of 'scandalous and seditious words' in 1619 lost credibility because the wives of the accuser and the accused had argued over church seating, and the charge appeared to be 'devised and forged in malice'.[66] Reports of a Pembrokeshire man's 'impious, malicious and seditious speeches' against Charles I also appeared less credible on evidence of 'a plot to disgrace' him by local enemies.[67] Any system of justice that allowed witnesses to be challenged was sure to generate charges and counter charges of this sort.

The same system took note of the status and gender of both accusers and accused. In 1596 Edward Francis attempted to discredit witnesses to his treasonable speech against Queen Elizabeth by dismissing them as 'simple creatures' and 'base creatures of no credit', mere women.[68] More success-fully, reports of seditious speech at Ipswich in 1626 were dismissed as the 'mutterings and private whisperings' of 'a man of mean note and unworthy of notice . . . a plain man whose tongue outran his wit'.[69] Hugh Pyne, the lawyer charged with treasonable words, claimed to be 'unredeemably prejudiced . . . by the accusation and confederacy of ill disposed and un-worthy persons'.[70] Other reports of 'fearfully ill-advised words' against Charles I in 1630 were discredited because they came from 'persons of the very lowest and basest rank and conversation', whereas testimony exoner-ating the accused came from 'honest well-known neighbours'.[71] A Restor-ation case collapsed because the witnesses included 'women of ill fame' as well as people with grudges against the defendant.[72] On the other hand, being mean and marginal did not deflect the stern gaze of the authorities from those accused of speaking sedition. James Priest, who in 1629 spread false news 'touching . . . the king's person', was 'a very miserable poor man who . . . can neither read nor write', but his lowly status did not exonerate him.[73] Nor was John Bumstead, described in 1636 as 'a very poor silly fellow', excused his 'evil words and purposes to the king'.[74] Offenders across the seventeenth and eighteenth centuries came from every social level, with witnesses from among their peers with whom they socialized.

The Politics of Everyday Speech

The material collected in the preceding chapters permits only the crudest gender analysis. Perhaps a quarter of all cases involved women. Yet gender involves themes as well as demographics. It was a running refrain in sixteenth-century England that queens were hobbled by their gender. Even women expressed the view that females should not rule. 'We shall never have a merry world so long as we have a woman governor,' declared one of Queen Elizabeth's subjects.[75] 'Let us pray for a father, for we have a mother already,' remarked another.[76] Both male and female monarchs were drawn into the discourse of whoredom, being imagined or blamed for their sexual excesses. There was hardly an early modern ruler who was not called a 'bastard', and several were branded 'cuckolds'. A few kings were challenged for their lack of masculinity, and many were blamed for being overly influenced by their mistresses or wives. The gender constraints of early modern society were also exposed by women prefacing a statement with 'if I were a man'. 'If I were a man, as I am a woman, I would help to pull him to pieces,' declared a London woman of Charles I.[77] 'I will put on the breeches myself to fight for the Duke of Monmouth,' declared another woman a generation later.[78] 'Oh, that I were a man,' sighed the wife of a Middlesex tradesman in 1687, as she contemplated shooting James II.[79]

Observations like these, and hundreds of comparable utterances, expose the politics of everyday speech. They invite the question 'what is political?' and suggest the answer 'almost everything'. There was a politics of the alehouse, a politics of the churchyard, and a politics of the coffee shop, as well as a politics of the nation and the parish. Neighbours at a dinner table, travellers on the road, and loiterers at a shop-board negotiated the valencies of local hierarchy, status, age, wealth, discretion, and access to information. Whether or not they were privileged, literate, or enfranchised, a multitude of commoners passed judgement on their rulers and superiors. Some voiced strong religious opinions, some ventured into commonwealth theory, and some blundered into sedition. Official investigative responses only drew attention to casual remarks, and invested them with greater public significance. The demotic political voice was impossible to suppress, and eventually the state gave up trying.

Notes

PREFACE

1. William Perkins, *A Direction for the Government of the Tongue according to Gods Word* (1593; 1638 edn.), sig. A2.

CHAPTER 1

1. Edward Reynolds, *A Treatise of the Passions and Faculties of the Soule of Man* (1640), 505–7. See also John Abernethy, *A Christian and Heavenly Treatise, Containing Physicke for the Soule* (1622), 464.
2. Edward Reyner, *Rules for the Government of the Tongue* (1656), sig. A3v.
3. Lynn Forest-Hill, 'Sins of the Mouth: Signs of Subversion in Medieval English Cycle Plays,' in Dermot Cavanagh and Tim Kirk (eds.), *Subversion and Scurrility: Popular Discourse in Europe from 1500 to the Present* (Aldershot and Burlington, 2000), 11–25; Carla Mazzio, 'Sins of the Tongue in Early Modern England,' *Modern Language Studies*, 28 (1998), 93–124. See also John Skelton (1460–1529), 'Against Venomous Tongues', in *The Complete Poems of John Skelton*, ed. Philip Henderson (1959), 245–9; Reyner, *Rules for the Government of the Tongue*, 'An Epistle to the Reader,' citing the fourth-century saints Basil and Gregory of Naziazen on these poisonous 'sins of the tongue'.
4. I. D., *A Hedgerow of Busshes, Brambles, and Briers; or, A Fielde full of Tares, Thistles and Tine: Of the Vanities of this Worlde, leading the way to eternall damnation* (1598), title page, sigs. I–Iv.
5. [Edward Nisbet], *Caesars Dialogue or A Familiar Communication containing the first Institution of a Subiect, in allegiance to his Souveraigne* (1601), 33, 37. This was republished in 1623 as *Foode for families: or, An wholsome houshold-discourse: in which all estates and sorts of people whatsoeuer, are taught, their duties towards God, their alegeance to their King, and their brotherly loue and charitie one to another*. See also Jean de Marconville, *A Treatise of the Good and Evell Tounge* (*c.*1592), and William Perkins, *A Direction for the Government of the Tongue according to Gods Word* (1593; 1638 edn.), 103.
6. William Vaughan, *The Spirit of Detraction* (1611), 'to the reader', 104.
7. Perkins, *Direction for the Government of the Tongue*, sig. A2.
8. Abernethy, *Christian and Heavenly Treatise*, ch. 32, 'The Poisonous Tongue'; William Gearing, *A Bridle for the Tongue; or, A Treatise of Ten Sins of the Tongue*

(1663); John Brinsley, *[Glosso-Chalinosis] Or, A Bridle for the Tongue* (1664); T. I., *A Cure for the Tongue-Evill* (1662); Richard Ward, *A Treatise of the Nature, Use, and Abuse of the Tongue and Speech*, in his *Two Very Usefull and Compendious Theological Treatises* (1673); [Matthew Killiray], *The Swearer and the Drunkard* (1673). See also Christopher Blackwood, *Some Pious Treatises Being 1. A Bridle for the Tongue* (1654).

9. Robert Bolton, *Some Generall Directions for a Comfortable Walking with God* (1638), 113.

10. Joseph Bentham, *The Societie of the Saints: or, A Treatise of Good-fellows, and their Good-fellowship* (1630; 1638 edn.), 126. The list included mocking Ishmaels, railing Rabshakehs, reviling Shimeies, scoffing children, backbiting dogs, slandering Tertullus, 'and all the kennels of those doggish barkers against God's children'.

11. George Webbe, *The Araignement of an Unruly Tongue* (1619), sig. A3v; Abernethy, *Christian and Heavenly Treatise*, 463–85; Richard Allestree, *The Government of the Tongue* (Oxford, 1674), sig. A3; Mazzio, 'Sins of the Tongue', 100–1.

12. John Webster, *The Duchess of Malfi* (1613), Act 1, Scene 2.

13. Thomas Adams, *The Taming of the Tongue* (1616), bound with his *The Sacrifice of Thankefulnesse* (1616), 27.

14. Vaughan, *Spirit of Detraction*, 'to the reader', 104.

15. Adams, *Taming of the Tongue*, 36.

16. [John Taylor], *A Iuniper Lecture. With the Description of all sorts of Women* (1639), 27.

17. *The Anatomy of a Woman's Tongue* (1638), in William Oldys and Thomas Park (eds.), *The Harleian Miscellany* (12 vols., 1808–11), ii. 183–93.

18. [Martin Parker], *Keep a Good Tongue in your Head* (1634), broadsheet.

19. Oxford University Archives, Chancellor's Court Papers, 1639/304.

20. Marconville, *Treatise of the Good and Evell Tounge*, sigs. A2, A6v.

21. *Youths Behaviour, or Decency in Conversation Amongst Men* (4th edn., 1646), 33. See also *The Civile Conversation of M. Steeven Guazzo. The First Three Books Translated by George Pettie, anno 1581*, ed. Sir Edward Sullivan (2 vols., 1925).

22. Jacopo Affinati d'Acuto, *The Dumbe Divine Speaker . . . shewing both the dignitie and defectes of the Tongue* (1605), sig. A3. Cf. John Holles, earl of Clare, to his son in 1625, counselling silence: 'more have been hurt by their words than by their deeds' (*Letters of John Holles 1587–1637*, ed. P. R. Seddon (Thoroton Society Record Series, 35, 1983), 314).

23. Affinati, *Dumbe Divine Speaker*, 85. Cf. Helkiah Crooke, *Microcosmographia. A Description of the Body of Man* (1618), 628–9, 'of the tongue and his muscles'.

24. John Ray, *A Compleat Collection of English Proverbs* (3rd edn., 1742), 11. Cf. Perkins, *Direction for the Government of the Tongue*, 18: 'speech is the very image of the heart.'

25. Thomas Wright, *The Passions of the Minde* (1600; 1630 edn.), 32.

26. The National Archives (TNA): Public Record Office (PRO) SP 12/273/35.
27. Sullivan (ed.), *Civile Conversation of M. Steeven Guazzo*, ed. Sullivan, i. 67, 70.
28. *The Reports of Sir George Croke Knight . . . Revised, and Published in English by Sir Harebotle Grimston* (1657), 89, 242.
29. Reynolds, *Treatise of the Passions*, 506; Reyner, *Rules for the Government of the Tongue*, 'To the Reader'.
30. G. L. Apperson (ed.), *English Proverbs and Proverbial Phrases: A Historical Dictionary* (1929; repr. Detroit, 1969), 594; John Ettlinger and Ruby Day (eds.), *Old English Proverbs Collected by Nathan Bailey, 1736* (1992), 104.
31. Wright, *Passions of the Minde*, 107.
32. William Shakespeare, *Much Ado About Nothing*, Act III, Scene 2.
33. Allestree, *Government of the Tongue*, sigs. a2^{v}–a3.
34. Adams, *Taming of the Tongue*, 25, 28.
35. Robert Horn, *The Christian Gouernour, in the Common-wealth, and Priuate Families* (1614), sigs. P8, Q5. See also Perkins, *Direction for the Government of the Tongue*, 16; Stephen Ford, *The Evil Tongue Tryed and found Guilty* (1672); and Allestree, *Government of the Tongue*.
36. Reyner, *Rules for the Government of the Tongue*, 'To the reader', sig. A2^{v}, 5, 94.
37. Killiray, *Swearer and the Drunkard*, 17.
38. Ecclesiastes 28: 17; Psalms 57: 4.
39. Apperson (ed.), *English Proverbs*, 638–9.
40. Skelton, 'Against Venomous Tongues', in *Complete Poems*, ed. Henderson, 247.
41. [John Heywood], *A Ballad against Slander and Detraction* (1562), broadsheet. See also *Civile Conversation of M. Steeven Guazzo*, ed. Sullivan, i. 65, for an 'ill tongue' like stinging bees.
42. William Vaughan, *The Arraignment of Slander* (1630), 123.
43. Killiray, *Swearer and the Drunkard*, 16.
44. Ferdinando Pulton, *De Pace Regis et Regni, viz. A Treatise declaring which be the great and generall Offences of the Realme* (1610), fos. 1–1^{v}.
45. Anthony Anderson, *An Exposition of the Hymne Commonly Called Benedictus* (1574), sig. 30v; id., *The Shield of our Safetie* (1581), sig. T4^{v}.
46. *A Collection of the State Papers of John Thurloe*, ed. Thomas Birch (7 vols., 1742), i. 54.
47. George Webbe, *The Practice of Quietnes: Directing a Christian how to live quietly in this troublesome world* (6th edn., 1633), 249–52.
48. Ford, *Evil Tongue Tryed*, 73, 111, 157.
49. Robert Burton, *The Anatomy of Melancholy*, ed. Thomas C. Faulkner, Nicolas K. Kiessling, and Rhonda L. Blair (6 vols., Oxford, 1989), i. 339.
50. Ford, *Evil Tongue Tryed*, 16.
51. 'Speech act theory' begins with J. L. Austin, *How to Do Things with Words* (Cambridge, MA, 1962; 2nd edn., 1975). It treats language as action, analyses 'performative utterances', and examines the consequences of 'the

perlocutionary act'. Refined by John R. Searle, *Speech Acts: An Essay in the Philosophy of Language* (Cambridge, 1969), and *Mind, Language and Society: Philosophy in the Real World* (New York, 1998), it has transformed the philosophy of language. Pierre Bourdieu, *Language and Symbolic Power* (Cambridge, MA, 1991), understands linguistic exchanges as instruments and relations of power and authority. Legal scholars concerned with 'free speech' analyse 'speech as conduct'—e.g. Franklyn S. Haiman, *'Speech Acts' and the First Amendment* (Carbondale, IL, 1993); Eugene Volokh, 'Speech as Conduct: Generally Applicable Laws, Illegal Courses of Conduct, "Situation-Altering Utterances," and the Uncharted Zones', *Cornell Law Review*, 90 (2005), 1277–348; Anon., 'Rehabilitating the Performative', *Harvard Law Review*, 120 (2007), 2200–21. See also Kent Greenawalt, *Speech, Crime, and the Uses of Language* (Oxford and New York, 1989); Judith Butler, *Excitable Speech: A Politics of the Performative* (New York, 1997).
52. T. F., *Newes from the North* (1579), sig. Biv^v.
53. Perkins, *Direction for the Government of the Tongue*, 2, 41.
54. Paul L. Hughes and James F. Larkin (eds.), *Tudor Royal Proclamations*, ii. *The Later Tudors (1553–1587)* (New Haven and London, 1969), 4.
55. *Civile Conversation of M. Steeven Guazzo*, ed. Sullivan, i. 65–6.
56. William Willymat, *A Loyal Subjects Looking-Glasse, Or A good subjects direction, necessary and requisite for every good Christian* (1604), sig. A2^v–A3^v, 60, 61.
57. [Richard Morison], *A Remedy for Sedition* (1536), sigs. Civ–Civ^v, D^v.
58. TNA: PRO SP 12/44/52.
59. *Homilie agaynst Disobedience and Wylful Rebellion* (1570), part 4.
60. TNA: PRO SP 12/273/35.
61. [Nisbet], *Caesars Dialogue*, 31, 36.
62. Alexander Nowell, *A Catechisme, or Institution of Christian Religion to be learned by all youth* (1570; 1638 edn.), sigs. B^v–B2. It may be no coincidence that Nowell's *Catechism* came out in the same year as the *Homilie agaynst Disobedience and Wylful Rebellion*.
63. William Gouge, *A Short Catechisme, wherein are briefly handled the fundamentall principles of Christian Religion* (7th edn., 1635), sig. A6.
64. John Ball, *A Short Catechisme. Containing the Principles of Religion. Very profitable for all sorts of People* (18th impression, 1637), 34.
65. John Dod, *A Plaine and Familiar Exposition of the Ten Commandements* (18th edn., 1632), 171–2, 177, 216.
66. Robert Blofield in Star Chamber, 1623, TNA: PRO STAC 8/32/20; Attorney General Sir Thomas Coventry in 1624, TNA: PRO STAC 8/29/12.
67. *The Doctrine of the Bible: Or, Rules of Discipline* (1604; 1641 edn.), fos. 2, 19^v–20; Exodus 22: 28.
68. John Hawarde, *Les Reportes del Cases in Camera Stellata, 1593–1609*, ed. William Paley Baildon (1894), 177.
69. TNA: PRO STAC 8/6/10.

70. [Sir John Melton], *A Sixe-folde Politician* (1609), 41.

71. Webbe, *Practice of Quietnes*, 140.

72. Henry Valentine, *God Save the King. A Sermon Preached in St. Pauls Church the 27th of March 1639* (1639), 5, 7, 18, 19; John Swan, *Redde Debitum. Or, A Discourse in defence of three chiefe Fatherhoods* (1640), 7, 11; J. P. Kenyon (ed.), *The Stuart Constitution* (Cambridge, 1966), 18.

73. *Constitutions and Canons Ecclesiasticall . . . 1640* (1640), sigs. B4ᵛ, C.

74. William Laud, sermon before the king at Whitehall, 19 June 1625, in *The Works of . . . William Laud, D.D.*, ed. William Scott and James Bliss (7 vols., Oxford, 1847–60), i. 99, 107, 115.

75. Laud, *Works*, i. 64, 132, 190, 191, 195.

76. Isaac Bargrave, *A Sermon Preached Before King Charles March 27 1627* (1627), 2–3, 19.

77. Thomas Hurste, *The Descent of Authoritie: or, The Magistrates Patent from Heaven* (1637), 16, 23, 24.

78. Henry Peacham, *The Dvty of all Trve Svbiects to their King* (1639), 9–10.

79. Valentine, *God Save the King*, 15, 19, 34.

80. Valentine, *God Save the King*, 19; Robert Mossom, *The King on his Throne: Or, A Discourse maintaining the Dignity of a King, the Duty of a Subject, and the unlawfulnesse of Rebellion* (York, 1642), 39; Richard Towgood, *Disloyalty of Language Questioned and Censured* (Bristol, 1643), title page, 1–8, 16; W. J., *Obedience Active and Passive Due to the Supream Power* (Oxford, 1643), 6, 13, 14.

81. Thomas Starkey, *Exhortation to Unitie and Obedience* (1536), fos. aii, 15ᵛ, 28, 34.

82. Edward Hall quoted in G. W. Bernard, *The King's Reformation: Henry VIII and the Remaking of the English Church* (New Haven and London, 2005), 212–13.

83. [Morison], *Remedy for Sedition*, sigs. Aiiᵛ, Aivᵛ–B, Biv.

84. [John Young], *A Sermon Preached before the Queenes Maiestie* (1576), sigs. B8ᵛ–Ci.

85. Wright, *Passions of the Minde*, 114.

86. TNA: PRO SP 12/273/35.

87. [Melton], *Sixe-folde Politician*, 5–6, 20–2, 58.

88. Bodleian Library, MS Tanner 306, fo. 242. For other versions see *King James VI and I: Selected Writings*, ed. Neil Rhodes, Jennifer Richards, and Joseph Marshall (Aldershot, 2003), 143–8; Alastair Bellany and Andrew McRae (eds.), 'Early Stuart Libels,' www.earlystuartlibels.net/spanish-match-section.

89. Robert Dallington, *Aphorismes Civill and Militarie* (1613), 107, 168, 211, 221.

90. Michael Wigmore, *The Meteors. A Sermon* (1633), sig. C3.

91. Francis Rogers, *A Visitation Sermon Preached* (1633), sig. C4.

92. Bodleian Library, MS Rawlinson C. 421, fo. 27.

93. Thomas Warmstry, *Pax Vobis or A Charme for Tumultuous Spirits* (1641), title page, 10–11, 17, 30; Ephraim Udall, *The Good of Peace and Ill of Warre* (1642), 28, 29. ''Tis no expedient for a vulgar eye/To stare upon superior majesty,' trilled *Fortunes Tennis-ball* (1640), 2.

94. Udall, *The Good of Peace and Ill of Warre*, 28, 29.

95. *The Several Places Where you may Hear News* (1647?).

96. Richard West, *The Court of Conscience* (1607), sig. F.

97. John Taylor, *Wit and Mirth. Chargeably collected out of tauernes, ordinaries, innes, bowling greenes, and allyes, alehouses, tobacco shops, highwayes, and water-passages* (1626). See also John Taylor, *Taylors Travels and Circular Perambulation . . . with an Alphabeticall Description of all the Taverne Signes* (1636).

98. *The Kings Maiesties Declaration to His Subiects, Concering Lawfull Sports* (1633), 8.

99. TNA: PRO STAC 8/27/7.

100. Francis Mawburne, *Eagle 1666: A New Almanac and Prognostication* (York, 1666), in Phil Withington, 'Public Discourse, Corporate Citizenship, and State Formation in Early Modern England,' *American Historical Review*, 112 (2007), 1031. Although this citation is from a Restoration source, it applies equally to earlier eras.

101. T. F., *Newes from the North*, sigs. Bii^v–Biii.

102. Bentham, *Societie of the Saints*, 125.

103. Bodleian Library, MS Rawlinson A. 127, section 2.

104. TNA: PRO STAC 8/27/8.

105. Walter Rye (ed.), *Depositions Taken before the Mayor and Aldermen of Norwich, 1549–1567* (Norwich, 1905), 66–7.

106. I. M. W. Harvey, 'Was there Popular Politics in Fifteenth-Century England?' in R. H. Britnell and A. J. Pollard (eds.), *The McFarlane Legacy: Studies in Late Medieval Politics and Society* (Stroud and New York, 1995), 160.

107. *Mum and the Sothsegger*, ed. Mabel Day and Robert Steele (Early English Text Society, 199, 1936), 31.

108. Skelton, 'Against Venomous Tongues', in *Complete Poems*, ed. Henderson, 248.

109. William Roper, 'The Life of Sir Thomas More,' in Richard S. Sylvester and Davis P. Harding (eds.), *Two Early Tudor Lives* (London and New Haven, 1962), 205.

110. TNA: PRO SP 12/272/35.

111. 'Advertisements touching seditious writings,' *c.*1590, TNA: PRO SP 12/235/81.

112. Charles Gibbon, *Not So New, As True. Being a Verie Necessarie Caveat for All Christians* (1590), sig. B^v.

113. TNA: PRO SP14/18/74.

114. *By the King. A Proclamation against excess of Lavish and Licentious Speech of matters of State* (24 Dec. 1620 and 26 July 1621); James F. Larkin and Paul L. Hughes (eds.), *Stuart Royal Proclamations*, i. *Royal Proclamations of Kings James I 1603–1625* (Oxford, 1973), 495–6, 519–21.

115. [Clarendon], *The History of the Rebellion and Civil Wars in England*, ed. W. Dunn Macray (6 vols., Oxford, 1888), i. 96.

116. Nicholas Darton, vicar of Kilsby, Northamptonshire, in 1639, TNA: PRO SP 16/437/52. Two years earlier Darton had petitioned Archbishop Laud for help against the 'schismatical and seditious molestation' of his parishioners, TNA: PRO SP 16/362/96.

117. *The Diary of Thomas Crosfield*, ed. Frederick S. Boas (Oxford, 1935), 61; TNA: PRO C 115/106, nos. 8413, 8415.

118. Richard Cust, 'News and Politics in Early Seventeenth-Century England,' *Past & Present*, 112 (1986), 60–90; Adam Fox, 'Rumour, News and Popular Political Opinion in Elizabethan and Early Stuart England,' *Historical Journal*, 40 (1997), 597–620; Ian Atherton, ' "The Itch Grown a Disease": Manuscript Transmission of News in the Seventeenth Century', in Joad Raymond (ed.), *News, Newspapers, and Society in Early Modern Britain* (1999), 39–65; Alastair Bellany, *The Politics of Court Scandal in Early Modern England: News Culture and the Overbury Affair, 1603–1660* (Cambridge, 2002).

CHAPTER 2

1. Edward Reyner, *Rules for the Government of the Tongue* (1656), 'To the reader,' sig. A2ᵛ, 5, 94.

2. William Sheppard, *Action upon the Case for Slander. Or a Methodical Collection under Certain Heads, of Thousands of Cases* (1662); Martin Ingram, 'Law, Litigants and the Construction of "Honour": Slander Suits in Early Modern England,' in Peter Coss (ed.), *The Moral World of the Law* (Cambridge, 2000), 134–60.

3. TNA: PRO STAC 8/6/10 and *passim*.

4. Herefordshire Record Office, Quarter Sessions Recognizances and Examinations 1627–35 (1633).

5. Essex Record Office, Quarter Sessions Supplemental Papers, Q/SBa/2/43 (1641).

6. Essex Record Office, Quarter Sessions Supplemental Papers, Q/SBa/2/11 (1628).

7. Herefordshire Record Office, Quarter Sessions Recognizances and Examinations 1627–35 (1634).

8. Sandy Bardsley, *Venomous Tongues: Speech and Gender in Late Medieval England* (Philadelphia, 2006), 141, and chs. 5 and 6 on scolding. See also David Underdown, 'The Taming of the Scold: The Enforcement of Patriarchal Authority in Early Modern England', in Anthony Fletcher and John Stevenson (eds.), *Order and Disorder in Early Modern England* (Cambridge, 1985), 116–36; Martin Ingram, ' "Scolding Women Cucked or Washed": A Crisis in Gender Relations in Early Modern England?' in Jennifer Kermode and Garthine Walker (eds.), *Women, Crime and the Courts in Early Modern England* (1994), 48–80; Laura Gowing, 'Gender and the Language of Insult in Early Modern London', *History Workshop*, 35 (1993), 1–21; Laura Gowing,

Domestic Dangers: Women, Words and Sex in Early Modern London (Oxford, 1996); Garthine Walker, 'Expanding the Boundaries of Female Honour in Early Modern England', *Transactions of the Royal Historical Society*, 6th ser., 6 (1996), 235–45; Bernard Capp, *When Gossips Meet: Women, Family and Neighbourhood in Early Modern England* (Oxford, 2003).

9. William Blackstone, *Commentaries on the Laws of England* (11th edn., 4 vols., 1791), iv. 168.

10. Herefordshire Record Office, Box 17, book 67, fo. 42; Sidney A. Peyton (ed.), *The Churchwardens' Presentments in the Oxfordshire Peculiars of Dorchester, Thame and Banbury* (Oxfordshire Record Society, Oxford, 1928), 292, 298.

11. Cheshire Record Office, Q JF 59/2, fos. 34–5.

12. Norfolk Record Office, Quarter Sessions Rolls, C/S3/26.

13. Norfolk Record Office, Quarter Sessions Rolls, C/S3/27.

14. Leicestershire Archives, I D 41/13/61, fo. 29ᵛ.

15. Lincolnshire Archives, Visitation Book Vj 27, fo. 82.

16. Herefordshire Record Office, BG 11/5/35.

17. East Sussex Record Office, QR/E/82.

18. TNA: PRO CHES 9/6.

19. Cambridge University Library, University Archives, VC Ct. III 17/2.

20. All Souls College, Oxford, Warden's MS 7, *passim*; Oxford University Archives, Hyp/B/6 (Chancellor's Court Depositions, 1628–39), fos. 76–84; Chancellor's Court Papers, 1630/1. The don accused of plagiarism was the Laudian John Arnway, later a royalist polemicist.

21. British Library, Add. MS 72372, fo. 14.

22. Norfolk Record Office, Quarter Sessions Rolls, C/S3/27 (bundle 2).

23. David Cressy, *Travesties and Transgressions in Tudor and Stuart England* (Oxford, 2000), 138–61, quotations on 156, 157.

24. Richard Bernard, *The Faithfull Shepherd* (1621), 32–3. See also John Dod, *A Remedy Against Privat Contentions* (1609), sigs. Bᵛ, E4; Samuel Hieron, 'Penance for Sinne', in *The Workes of Mr Sam. Hieron* (2 vols., 1620; 1635 edn.), ii. 75, 137.

25. TNA: PRO C 115/106, no. 8445; Bodleian Library, MS Carte 77, fo. 397; *The Knyvett Letters (1620–1644)*, ed. Bertram Schofield (Norfolk Record Society, 1949), 85; Historical Manuscripts Commission, *12th Report: The Manuscripts of the Earl Cowper... Preserved at Melbourne Hall, Derbyshire* (1888), app. 2, 46.

26. Blackstone, *Commentaries on the Laws of England*, iii. 123; Ian MacLean, *Interpretation and Meaning in the Renaissance: The Case of Law* (Cambridge, 1992), 186–202. See also citations in notes 2 and 8 above.

27. Richard Burn, *Ecclesiastical Law* (3rd edn., 4 vols., 1775), ii. 115–17, 124.

28. Ralph Houlbrooke, *Church Courts and the People during the English Reformation, 1520–1570* (Oxford, 1979); J. A. Sharpe, *Defamation and Sexual Slander in Early Modern England: The Church Courts at York* (York, 1980); Martin Ingram,

Church Courts, Sex and Marriage in England, 1570–1640 (Cambridge, 1987); Gowing, *Domestic Dangers*. For comparative studies of anger, abuse, and reconciliation, see J. A. Sharpe, ' "Such Disagreement Betwyxt Neighbours": Litigation and Human Relations in Early Modern England', in John Bossy (ed.), *Disputes and Settlements: Law and Human Relations in the West* (Cambridge, 1983), 167–87; David Parkin, 'Exchanging Words', in Bruce Kapferer (ed.), *Transaction and Meaning: Directions in the Anthropology of Exchange and Symbolic Behavior* (Philadelphia, 1976), 163–90; Cheryl English Martin, 'Popular Speech and Social Order in Northern Mexico, 1650–1830', *Comparative Studies in Society and History*, 32 (1990), 305–24; David Garrioch, 'Verbal Insults in Eighteenth-Century Paris', in Peter Burke and Roy Porter (eds.), *The Social History of Language* (Cambridge, 1987), 104–19.

29. William H. Hale (ed.), *A Series of Precedents and Proceedings in Criminal Causes . . . extracted from the Act-Books of the Ecclesiastical Courts of the Diocese of London* (1847), 6, 19.

30. E. D. Stone and B. Cozens-Hardy (eds.), *Norwich Consistory Court Depositions, 1499–1512 and 1518–1530* (Norfolk Record Society, 10, 1938), nos. 145, 394.

31. Burn, *Ecclesiastical Law*, ii. 116, 117.

32. Ingram, *Church Courts, Sex and Marriage*, 300.

33. Borthwick Institute, York, Cause Papers Transmitted on Appeal, 1634/6; Cheshire Record Office, EDC 5 1631/69; EDC 5 1628/7.

34. Walker, 'Expanding the Boundaries of Female Honour'.

35. Houlbrooke, *Church Courts and the People*, 80.

36. Guildhall Library, MS 9064/15, fo. 19; MS 9064/16, fo. 206^v.

37. Burn, *Ecclesiastical Law*, ii. 117.

38. Stone and Cozens-Hardy (eds.), *Norwich Consistory Court Depositions*, nos. 54, 122, 145, 264, 269, 271, 394.

39. Hale, *Precedents*, 14, 27, 68, 99, 208, 245.

40. William Shakespeare, *1 Henry IV*, Act 2, Scene 4; Act 3, Scene 3.

41. William Shakespeare, *The Taming of the Shrew*, Act 4, Scene 1.

42. William Shakespeare, *2 Henry IV*, Act 2, Scene 4.

43. William Shakespeare, *The Comedy of Errors*, Act 4, Scene 4.

44. William Shakespeare, *King Lear*, Act 1, Scene 4; Act 2, Scene 2.

45. William Shakespeare, *Timon of Athens*, Act 4, Scene 3.

46. Sheppard, *Action upon the Case for Slander*; R. H. Helmholz (ed.), *Select Cases on Defamation to 1600* (Selden Society, 101, 1985), *passim*.

47. Burn, *Ecclesiastical Law*, ii. 115; Robert Shoemaker, 'The Decline of Public Insult in London 1660–1800', *Past & Present*, 169 (2000), 97–131.

48. Helmholz (ed.), *Select Cases on Defamation*, c (n. 2), 18, 68, 80, 89.

49. Ferdinando Pulton, *De Pace Regis et Regni, viz. A Treatise declaring which be the great and generall Offences of the Realme* (1610), fo.1^v.

50. Essex Record Office, Q/SR 182/43.

51. John Hawarde, *Les Reportes del Cases in Camera Stellata, 1593–1609*, ed. William Paley Baildon (1894), 104.

52. John Lister (ed.), *West Riding Sessions Records. Vol. II. Orders, 1611–1642. Indictments, 1637–1642* (Yorkshire Archaeological Society Record Series, 53, 1915), 60.

53. Lister (ed.), *West Riding Sessions Records. Vol. II*, 159–60.

54. Hampshire Record Office, Q1/2, 45.

55. Herefordshire Record Office, Quarter Sessions Recognizances and Examinations 1627–35.

56. Common Council Ordinances at Cambridge, 1608, cited in Phil Withington, 'Public Discourse, Corporate Citizenship, and State Formation in Early Modern England', *American Historical Review*, 112 (2007), 1030.

57. Christopher A. Markham and J. Charles Cox (eds.), *The Records of the Borough of Northampton* (2 vols., Northampton, 1898), ii., 20. Suffolk Record Office, General Court Minute Book, 1609–43, C/2/2/3/2, fo. 315.

58. Samuel Crooke, *The Ministeriall Husbandry and Building* (1615), epistle dedicatory; Charles Richardson, *A Workeman That Needeth Not to be Ashamed: Or the Faithfull Steward of Gods House* (1616), 39; William Attersoll, *A Commentarie Vpon the Epistle of Saint Paul to Philemon* (1612), 34; George Downame, *Two Sermons, The One Commending the Ministerie in Generall: The Other Defending the Office of Bishops* (1608), 30, 40, 65–6. Insisting on 'the burden and honour' as well as 'the duty and dignity' of the ministry, Downame set forth his view of the clerical calling: 'to instruct the ignorant, to reduce the erroneous, to heal the diseased, to seek the lost, to admonish the disorderly, to comfort the distressed, to support the weak, to be patient towards all,' as well as to preach and to read. Not surprisingly, he added, 'to abuse the ministers by word or deed, is a sin highly displeasing unto God, and grievously provoking his anger' (ibid., 8, 11, 16–17, 68). See also Bernard, *Faithfull Shepherd*, 1, on 'the high calling of the ministry,' and Stephen Egerton, *The Boring of the Ear* (1623), 20, for the claim that 'the contempt of any true minister is the contempt of God himself'; William Hardwick, *Conformity with Piety, Requisite in Gods Service* (1638), 8, for the view that God saw the clergy as 'his ambassadors, and as shining stars, yea, as angels'.

59. Lincolnshire Archives, Court Papers, Box 61/1, 19, 49; Buckinghamshire Record Office, D/A/V4, fo. 53ᵛ; Norfolk Record Office, DN/VIS/7/1; Borthwick Institute, York, Visitation Court Book 11, 1636, fo. 65.

60. Cressy, *Travesties and Transgressions*, 138–42, 148.

61. Staffordshire Record Office, Bridgeman Correspondence, D1287/18/2/4.

62. Thomas G. Barnes (ed.), *Somerset Assize Orders 1629–1640* (Somerset Record Society, 65, 1959), 49.

63. Robert Horn, *The Christian Gouernour, in the Common-wealth, and Priuate Families* (1614), sig. A2ᵛ.

64. Paul Lathom, *The Power of Kings from God* (1683), 5–6.

65. Thomas Hurste, *The Descent of Authoritie: or, The Magistrates Patent from Heaven* (1637), 1, 3, 15.

66. Statute of Gloucester, 1378, 2 Richard II, c. 5, repeated in 12 Richard II, c. 11 in 1388; Blackstone, *Commentaries on the Laws of England*, iii. 123; John C. Lassiter, 'Defamation of Peers: The Rise and Decline of the Action for *Scandalum Magnatum*, 1497–1773', *American Journal of Legal History*, 22 (1978), 216–36.

67. *Acts of the Privy Council 1575–1577*, 292.

68. *The Reports of Sir Edward Coke* (1658), 227–8.

69. Huntington Library, Ellesmere MSS 2739, 2740.

70. *Acts of the Privy Council 1578–1580*, 357.

71. John Stubbs, *The Discouerie of a Gaping Gulf Whereinto England is like to be Swallowed by Another French Mariage* (1579); David Cressy, 'Book Burning in Tudor and Stuart England', *Sixteenth Century Journal*, 36 (2005), 365.

72. Somerset Record Office, DD/PH 288/26.

73. TNA: PRO C 115/106, no. 8437; Bodleian Library, MS Carte 77, fo. 368ᵛ.

74. House of Lords Record Office, Main Papers, HL/PO/JO/10/1/35, 27 May 1628. See also ibid., 30 May 1628, for another case of 'dangerous speeches' reported to the upper chamber.

75. John Andrews, DD, to Archbishop Laud, 13 June 1636, *CSPD 1635–6*, 556–7; TNA: PRO SP 16/326/18.

76. George Squibb, *The High Court of Chivalry: A Study of the Civil Law in England* (Oxford, 1959); Richard Cust and Andrew Hopper (eds.), *Cases in the High Court of Chivalry 1634–1640* (Harleian Society, NS 18, 2006).

77. University of Birmingham, Calendar of the Court of Chivalry, 1634–1640, www.court-of-chivalry.bham.ac.uk/index.htm, no. 21 Badd v. Rigges, no. 557 Rigges v. Badd, and no. 167 Dorset v. Rigges.

78. Lassiter, 'Defamation of Peers,' 219–29; *The Entering Book of Roger Morrice*, ed. Mark Goldie et al. (6 vols., Woodbridge, 2007), ii. 'The Reign of Charles II,' ed. John Spurr, 298, 318, 334, 474–5.

79. Anchitell Grey (ed.), *Grey's Debates of the House of Commons*, ix (1769), 172–3 (debates on 20 Mar. 1689).

80. Lassiter, 'Defamation of Peers', 233.

81. William Vaughan, *The Arraignment of Slander* (1630), 172–3.

82. John Cowell, *The Interpreter* (1672), sub. 'libel'; Pulton, *De Pace Regis et Regni*, fos. 1ᵛ–2; John March, *The Second Part of Actions for Slanders* (1649), 15–21; Michael Dalton, *The Countrey Justice* (5th edn., 1635), 190; William Hudson, 'A Treatise of the Court of Star-Chamber', in Francis Hargrave (ed.), *Collectanea Juridica* (2 vols., 1791–2), ii. 100. For the Jacobean case '*de libellis famosi, or of scandalous libels*', see [Coke], *The Reports of Sir Edward Coke* (13 parts in 7 vols., 1738), vol. iii, pt. 5, pp. 125–6, and Hawarde, *Reportes del Cases in Camera Stellata*, 222–30.

83. J. S. Cockburn (ed.), *Western Circuit Assize Orders 1629–1648: A Calendar* (Camden Society, 4th ser., 17, 1976), 168.

84. Adam Fox, 'Ballads, Libels and Popular Ridicule in Jacobean England', *Past & Present*, 145 (1994), 47–83; Pauline Croft, 'Libels, Popular Literacy and Public Opinion in Early Modern England', *Historical Research*, 68 (1995), 266–85; Alastair Bellany, 'Libels in Action: Ritual, Subversion and the English Literary Underground, 1603–42', in Tim Harris (ed.), *The Politics of the Excluded, c.1500–1850* (Basingstoke and New York, 2001), 99–124; Andrew McRae, *Literature, Satire, and the Early Stuart State* (Cambridge, 2004).

85. March, *Second Part of Actions for Slanders*, 15–21.

86. Paul L. Hughes and James F. Larkin (eds.), *Tudor Royal Proclamations*, ii. *The Later Tudors (1553–1587)* (New Haven and London, 1969), 400.

87. TNA: PRO SP 12/273/35; *CSPD 1601–1603*, 347–51.

88. TNA: PRO SP 12/273/35.

89. TNA: PRO SP 12/273/35.

90. Hawarde, *Reportes del Cases in Camera Stellata*, 372.

91. 'Advertisements touching seditious writings,' c. 1590, TNA: PRO SP 12/235/81.

92. TNA: PRO C 115/196, no. 8438.

93. Alastair Bellany, ' "Raylinge Rymes and Vaunting Verse": Libellous Politics in Early Stuart England', in Kevin Sharpe and Peter Lake (eds.), *Culture and Politics in Early Stuart England* (Stanford, 1993), 285–310, 367–71; Fox, 'Ballads, Libels and Popular Ridicule', 47–83; Croft, 'Libels, Popular Literacy, and Public Opinion', 266–85; Tom Cogswell, 'Underground Verse and the Transformation of Early Stuart Political Culture', *Huntington Library Quarterly*, 60 (1997), 303–26; Andrew McRae, 'The Literary Culture of Early Stuart Libelling', *Modern Philology*, 97 (2000), 364–92; McRae, *Literature, Satire and the Early Stuart State*.

94. *Acts of the Privy Council 1571–1575*, 387.

95. Essex Record Office, T/A 418/71/69, from Essex Assize files, 18 July 1602.

96. TNA: PRO STAC 8/27/7.

97. Bodleian Library, MS Rawlinson A. 128, fo. 15ᵛ–16ᵛ.

98. British Library, Lansdowne MS 620, fos. 50–1. I am grateful to Alastair Bellany for directing me to this source.

99. Henry Ellis, *Original Letters Illustrative of English History* (2nd edn., 3 vols, 1825), iii. 252; Thomas Birch (ed.), *The Court and Times of Charles the First* (2 vols., 1848), i. 368.

100. TNA: PRO SP 16/142/92.

101. Bodleian Library, MS Carte 77, fo. 404ᵛ.

102. British Library, Add. MS 11045, fo. 5ᵛ.

103. David Cressy, *England on Edge: Crisis and Revolution 1640–1642* (Oxford, 2006), 330–46.

104. Historical Manuscripts Commission, *12th Report*, 305, 310; *CSPD 1641–3*, 273.

105. *Diary of John Rous . . . 1625 to 1642*, ed. Mary Anne Everett Green (Camden Society, 66, 1856), 30, 109.

106. Historical Manuscripts Commission, *Report on the Manuscripts of the Duke of Buccleuch and Queensberry . . . at Montagu House* (1899), 291.

107. Shakespeare, *2 Henry IV*, Prologue.

108. Statute of Westminster, 1275, 3 Edward I, c. 34, *Statutes of the Realm* (10 vols., 1810–28), i. 35.

109. Sir James Dyer, *Reports of Cases in the Reigns of Hen. VIII. Edw. VI. Q. Mary, and Q. Eliz.* (3 vols, 1794), ii. 155a.

110. 26 Hen. VIII, c. 13, *Statutes of the Realm*, iii. 508–9; John Bellamy, *The Tudor Law of Treason: An Introduction* (1979), 31–2; G. R. Elton, *Policy and Police: The Enforcement of the Reformation in the Age of Thomas Cromwell* (Cambridge, 1972), 264–87.

111. *Statutes of the Realm*, 1 and 2 Phil. and Mary, c. 3, 1554–5; *Journals of the House of Commons*, i. *1547–1629* (1802), 37–8.

112. *Statutes of the Realm*, 1 Eliz., c. 6; *Journals of the House of Commons*, i. 54, 57–8; Sir Simonds D'Ewes (ed.), *The Journals of All the Parliaments During the Reign of Queen Elizabeth* (1682), 19, 25, 51.

113. Ethan Shagan, 'Rumours and Popular Politics in the Reign of Henry VIII', in Tim Harris (ed.), *The Politics of the Excluded, c.1500–1850* (Basingstoke and New York, 2001), 30–66; Adam Fox, 'Rumour, News and Popular Political Opinion in Elizabethan and Early Stuart England', *Historical Journal*, 40 (1997), 597–620.

CHAPTER 3

1. William Lambarde, *Eirenarcha: or of the Office of the Iustices of Peace* (1581; 1610 edn.), 226; William Blackstone, *Commentaries on the Laws of England* (11th edn., 4 vols., 1791), iv. 75.

2. Thomas Norton, 'A warning agaynst the dangerous practises of Papistes, and specially the parteners of the late rebellion', in *All such treatises as have been lately published by Thomas Norton* (1570), sigs. Ci, Ci(v). Treason in ancient Rome was '*maiestas minuta populi Romani*', the diminution of the majesty of the Roman people, and this was well known to Tudor statesmen. See R. A. Bauman, *The Crimen Maiestatis in the Roman Republic* (1970).

3. *The Proceedings at the Sessions House . . . Against Anthony Earl of Shaftsbury* (1681), 2.

4. William Perkins, *A Direction for the Government of the Tongue according to Gods Word* (1593; 1638 edn.), 13.

5. *The Description of England by William Harrison*, ed. Georges Edelen (Ithaca, NY, 1968), 187; Sir Francis Bacon, *Cases of Treason* (1641), 4, 6; J. A. Sharpe, *Judicial Punishment in England* (1990), 27. The London merchant Richard Hilles described in 1541 how traitors were 'dealt with in the usual manner, first hung, then cut down from the gallows while yet alive, then drawn, beheaded, and quartered, and their limbs fixed over the gates of the city' (Hastings Robinson (ed.), *Original Letters Relative to the English Reformation . . . Chiefly from the Archives of Zurich* (Parker Society, Cambridge, 1846), 209).

6. Joel Samaha, *Law and Order in Historical Perspective: The Case of Elizabethan Essex* (New York and London, 1974), 63, 118; Sharpe, *Judicial Punishment*, 29.

7. 25 Edward III, statute 5, c. 2, *Statutes of the Realm* (10 vols., 1810–28), i. 319–20; J. G. Bellamy, *The Law of Treason in England in the Later Middle Ages* (Cambridge, 1970).

8. W. S. Holdsworth, *A History of English Law* (rev. edn., 17 vols., Boston, 1922–72), viii. 309.

9. Ferdinando Pulton, *De Pace Regis et Regni, viz. A Treatise declaring which be the great and generall Offences of the Realme* (1610), fos. 106ᵛ, 108; Holdsworth, *History of English Law*, iii. 293; Sir Edward Coke, *The Third Part of the Institutes of the Laws of England* (1644), 1–19. See also Michael Dalton, *The Countrey Justice* (5th edn., 1635), 223–6; Bacon, *Cases of Treason*, 1; Sir Matthew Hale, *Historia Placitorum Coronae: The History of the Pleas of the Crown* (2 vols., 1736), i. 83–9, 107–15; Blackstone, *Commentaries on the Laws of England*, iv. 74–96.

10. Penry Williams, *The Tudor Regime* (Oxford, 1979), 390; Roger B. Manning, 'The Origins of the Doctrine of Sedition', *Albion*, 12 (1980), 99–121.

11. Thomas Blount, *Glossographia: or A Dictionary, Interpreting all such Hard Words* (1656), sub. 'seditious'; Hale, *Historia Placitorum Coronae*, i. 77–8; Holdsworth, *History of English Law*, vi. 266; William Vaughan, *The Arraignment of Slander* (1630), 165; TNA: PRO HO 144/9486.

12. Cambridge University Library, MS Mm. 6. 63/4, fo. 7.

13. Daniel Greenberg and Alexandra Millbrook (eds.), *Stroud's Judicial Dictionary of Words and Phrases* (6th edn., 2000), 2393; Peter Murphy (ed.), *Blackstone's Criminal Practice* (Oxford, 2007), 891. I am grateful to Sir Jeremy Lever, QC, for discussion of this point.

14. Manning, 'Origins of the Doctrine of Sedition', 99–121.

15. *John Bale's King Johan*, ed. Barry B. Adams (San Marino, CA, 1969), 75–6.

16. TNA: PRO SP 12/44/52.

17. John Bullokar, *An English Exposition: Teaching the Interpretation of the Hardest Words Used in Our Language* (1616), sub 'scandall'; John March, *Actions for Slander* (1655), 11, 23, 136; Richard Crompton, *Star-Chamber Cases, Shewing What Causes Properly Belong to the Cognizance of that Court* (1630), 25–36.

18. *The Reports of Sir Edward Coke* (1658), 227–8.

19. 'Advertisements touching seditious writings', c. 1590, TNA: PRO SP 12/235/81.

20. William Lambarde, *Eirenarcha: or of the Office of the Iustices of Peace* (1581), 285–6.
21. TNA: PRO SP 12/118/27.
22. *Acts of the Privy Council 1591*, 323, 346.
23. *CSPD . . . Addenda 1566–1579* (1871), 464. These were almost word for word the same as instructions to the Council in the North in 1549, *CSPD 1601–1603, with Addenda 1547–1565*, 399.
24. TNA: PRO SP 12 /99/53.
25. Pulton, *De Pace Regis et Regni*, fo. 2^{v}.
26. John Pory to Joseph Mead, 3 June 1625, in Thomas Birch (ed.), *The Court and Times of Charles the First* (2 vols., 1848), i. 27. See, however, the case of William Pickering, who in 1638 was recommended to have his tongue bored with an awl; see below, Chapter 7.
27. British Library, Add. MS 11045, fo. 3.
28. Bodleian Library, MS Carte 63, fo. 36^{v}.
29. Henry VI complained to the mayor of Coventry about men who had used 'right unfittyng langage ayenst oure estate and personne' (Mary Dormer Harris (ed.), *The Coventry Leet Book . . . 1420–1555* (Early English Text Society, 134, 1907), 309).
30. I. M. W. Harvey, 'Was There Popular Politics in Fifteenth-Century England?' in R. H. Britnell and A. J. Pollard (eds.), *The McFarlane Legacy: Studies in Late Medieval Politics and Society* (Stroud and New York, 1995), 155–74; Simon Walker, 'Rumour, Sedition and Popular Protest in the Reign of Henry IV', *Past & Present*, 166 (2000), 31–65; Sandy Bardsley, *Venomous Tongues: Speech and Gender in Late Medieval England* (Philadelphia, 2006), 31.
31. Isobel D. Thornley, 'Treason by Words in the Fifteenth Century', *English Historical Review*, 32 (1917), 556–7.
32. R. F. Hunnisett, 'Treason by Words', *Sussex Notes and Queries*, 14 (1954–7), 117–19.
33. *The Brut or The Chronciles of England . . . Part II*, ed. Friedrich W. D. Brie (Early English Text Society, 136, 1908), 480–4; *Chronicle of the Grey Friars of London* (Camden Society, 53, 1852), 15; *The Reports of Sir George Croke Knight . . . Revised, and Published in English by Sir Harebotle Grimston* (1657), 83–9; T. B. Howell (ed.), *A Complete Collection of State Trials* (21 vols., 1816), iii. 359–67.
34. C. A. F. Meekings, 'Thomas Kerver's Case, 1444', *English Historical Review*, 90 (1975), 331–46, quotations at 332, 338; Bertram Wolffe, *Henry VI* (1981), 16–18, 138; Ecclesiastes 10:16.
35. I. M. W. Harvey, *Jack Cade's Rebellion of 1450* (Oxford, 1991), 31–2; Wolffe, *Henry VI*, 16–18.
36. Harvey, 'Was There Popular Politics in Fifteenth-Century England?', 160.
37. Hunnisett, 'Treason by Words', 119–20.
38. Bellamy, *Law of Treason . . . in the Later Middle Ages*, 107, 116–22; E. Kay Harris, 'Censoring Disobedient Subjects: Narratives of Treason and Royal

Authority in Fifteenth-Century England', in Douglas L. Biggs, Sharon D. Michalove, and A. Compton Reeves (eds.), *Reputation and Representation in Fifteenth-Century Europe* (Leiden and Boston, 2004), 211–33; Christopher Randall Duggan, 'The Advent of Political Thought-Control in England: Seditious and Treasonable Speech 1485–1547' (Northwestern University Ph.D. dissertation, 1993).

39. Samuel Rezneck, 'Constructive Treason by Words in the Fifteenth Century', *American Historical Review*, 33 (1928), 544–52, quotations at 548n. and 551.

40. Duggan, 'Advent of Political Thought-Control', 99, 278, 280. This study of the records of King's Bench finds just twenty-seven cases of seditious speech between 1485 and 1509.

41. Ian Arthurson, *The Perkin Warbeck Conspiracy 1491–1499* (Stroud, 1994), 167.

42. Sir Francis Bacon, *The History of the Reign of King Henry the Seventh*, ed. F. J. Levy (Indianapolis and New York, 1972), 166–9.

43. British Library, Lansdowne MS 620, fo. 50ᵛ. In 1539 a monk named Nicholas Balam was charged with denying the royal supremacy but seems to have escaped execution (G. R. Elton, *Policy and Police: The Enforcement of the Reformation in the Age of Thomas Cromwell* (Cambridge, 1972), 341). Richardson may have been using the lawyer's trick of citing a precedent without having done his research.

44. Cited in J. P. D. Cooper, *Propaganda and the Tudor State: Political Culture in the Westcountry* (Oxford, 2003), 95.

45. TNA: PRO SP 1/14, fo. 173; *Letters and Papers, Foreign and Domestic, of the Reign of Henry VIII*, ed. J. S. Brewer et al. (23 vols.; 1862–1932), vol. ii, pt. 1, p. 871; Duggan, 'Advent of Political Thought-Control', 98.

46. *Letters and Papers . . . of Henry VIII*, ed. Brewer et al., vol. iii, pt. 1, p. 522.

47. Duggan, 'Advent of Political Thought-Control', 72, 291, citing TNA: PRO KB 9/487, KB 27/1045.

48. *Letters and Papers . . . of Henry VIII*, ed. Brewer et al., vol. 3, pt. 2, p. 1295.

49. *Statutes of the Realm*, iii. 471, 508; John Bellamy, *The Tudor Law of Treason: An Introduction* (1979), 31–2; Elton, *Policy and Police*, 264–87.

50. Elton, *Policy and Police*, 11; Sharon L. Jansen, *Dangerous Talk and Strange Behavior: Women and Popular Resistance to the Reforms of Henry VIII* (New York, 1996), 77, 181n.; Cooper, *Propaganda and the Tudor State*, 90; Bellamy, *The Tudor Law of Treason*, 14.

51. *Letters and Papers . . . of Henry VIII*, ed. Brewer et al., vol. xii, pt 1, p. 398; vol. xii, pt. 2, 376.

52. Robinson (ed.), *Original Letters . . . from the Archives of Zurich*, 211.

53. Edward Hall, quoted in G. W. Bernard, *The King's Reformation: Henry VIII and the Remaking of the English Church* (New Haven and London, 2005), 212.

54. *Letters and Papers . . . of Henry VIII*, ed. Brewer et al., vol. xiii, pt. 1, p. 36.

55. *Letters and Papers . . . of Henry VIII*, ed. Brewer et al., vol. xiii, pt. 1, p. 266.

56. Elton, *Policy and Police*, 387, 391, counts 63 executions in central government records. Duggan, 'Advent of Political Thought-Control', 156, 186–7, using King's Bench as well as State Papers, finds *c*.550 cases of seditious or treasonable words between 1533 and 1547 and at least 110 executions.

57. Elton, *Policy and Police*, 100, 123–4.

58. Elton, *Policy and Police*, 11; Jansen, *Dangerous Talk*, 89–90.

59. Elton, *Policy and Police*, 137; Jansen, *Dangerous Talk*, 88–9. Cf. Andy Wood, 'The Queen is "a Goggyll Eyed Hoore"': Gender and Seditious Speech in Early Modern England', in Nicholas Tyacke (ed.), *The English Revolution c.1590–1720: Politics, Religion and Communities* (2007), 81–94.

60. Diane Watt, 'Reconstructing the Word: The Political Prophecies of Elizabeth Barton (1506–1534)', *Renaissance Quarterly*, 50 (1997), 136–63; Tim Thornton, *Prophecy, Politics and the People in Early Modern England* (Woodbridge, 2006).

61. Elton, *Policy and Police*, 6, 71–4; Ethan Shagan, 'Rumours and Popular Politics in the Reign of Henry VIII', in Tim Harris (ed.), *The Politics of the Excluded, c.1500–1850* (Basingstoke and New York, 2001), 43–4.

62. Elton, *Policy and Police*, 10, 72.

63. Elton, *Policy and Police*, 9, 368; *Letters and Papers . . . of Henry VIII*, ed. Brewer et al., vol. xiii, pt. 1, pp. 32–3.

64. Elton, *Policy and Police*, 148–50; Jansen, *Dangerous Talk*, 81–2.

65. Elton, *Policy and Police*, 299.

66. *Letters and Papers . . . of Henry VIII*, ed. Brewer et al., vol. xiii, pt. 1, p. 427.

67. TNA: PRO E 111/10; *Letters and Papers . . . of Henry VIII*, ed. Brewer et al., vol. xii, pt. 2, pp. 288, 320–1.

68. *Letters and Papers . . . of Henry VIII*, ed. Brewer et al., vol. xii, pt. 2, p. 376. This may have been a malicious prosecution, for some witnesses claimed never to have heard the incriminating words.

69. *Letters and Papers . . . of Henry VIII*, ed. Brewer et al., vol. xiii, pt. 1, pp. 23, 54.

70. *Letters and Papers . . . of Henry VIII*, ed. Brewer et al., vol. xiii, pt. 1, p. 470; Shagan, 'Rumours and Popular Politics', 51–2.

71. *Letters and Papers . . . of Henry VIII*, ed. Brewer et al., vol. xiii, pt. 1, pp. 341, 423.

72. *Letters and Papers . . . of Henry VIII*, ed. Brewer et al., vol. xiii, pt. 1, p. 221.

73. Duggan, 'Advent of Political Thought-Control', 309, citing TNA: PRO KB 9/542/3.

74. *Letters and Papers . . . of Henry VIII*, ed. Brewer et al., vol. xiii, pt. 1, p. 78; Shagan, 'Rumours and Popular Politics', 43–4.

75. *Letters and Papers . . . of Henry VIII*, ed. Brewer et al., vol. xiii, pt. 1, p. 276.

76. *Letters and Papers . . . of Henry VIII*, ed. Brewer et al., vol. xiii, pt. 1, p. 352.

77. Duggan, 'Advent of Political Thought-Control', 311, citing TNA: PRO KB 9/542/3^v.

78. Duggan, 'Advent of Political Thought-Control', 323, citing TNA: PRO KB 9/550/142.

79. Duggan, 'Advent of Political Thought-Control', 326, citing TNA: PRO KB 9/558/106; also cited in Cooper, *Propaganda and the Tudor State*, 95.

80. *Statutes of the Realm*, vol. iv, pt. 1, p. 18.

81. Sir John Cheke, *The True Subiect to the Rebell. Or the Hurt of Sedition, how Greivous it is to a Common-wealth* (written 1549; 1641 edn.), 15.

82. Walter Rye (ed.), *Depositions Taken before the Mayor and Aldermen of Norwich, 1549–1567* (Norwich, 1905), 18, 20, 22, 25.

83. C. S. Knighton (ed.), *Calendar of State Papers Domestic Series of the Reign of Edward VI 1547–1553* (1992), 134.

84. *Acts of the Privy Council 1552–1554*, 125.

85. British Library, MS Harley 353, fos. 121–3.

86. *Acts of the Privy Council 1550–1552*, 293, 295, 465; *Acts of the Privy Council 1552–1554*, 110, 278.

87. *Acts of the Privy Council 1547–1550*, 385.

88. *Acts of the Privy Council 1550–1552*, 285.

89. *Acts of the Privy Council 1552–1554*, 46.

90. *Acts of the Privy Council 1552–1554*, 274.

91. *Acts of the Privy Council 1550–1552*, 97.

92. *Acts of the Privy Council 1552–1554*, 110.

93. *Acts of the Privy Council 1552–1554*, 211.

94. 1 Mary, St. 1. c. 1, 'An Acte Repealing Certayne Treasons', *Statutes of the Realm*, vol. iv, pt. 1, p. 197.

95. 1 and 2 Phil. and Mary, c. 3, 1554–5, 'An Acte Against Sedityous Woordes and Rumours', *Statutes of the Realm*, vol. iv, pt. 1, p. 240; *Journals of the House of Commons*, i. *1547–1629* (1802), 37–8.

96. 1 and 2 Phil. and Mary, c. 9 and 10, *Statutes of the Realm*, vol. iv, pt. 1, pp. 254–5; *Journals of the House of Commons*, i. 41–2; G. R. Elton, *England under the Tudors* (1956), 219; Bellamy, *The Tudor Law of Treason*, 46.

97. *Acts of the Privy Council 1552–1554*, 363.

98. *Acts of the Privy Council 1554–1556*, 11.

99. *Acts of the Privy Council 1554–1556*, 50, 71, 73.

100. *Acts of the Privy Council 1554–1556*, 27.

101. Sir James Dyer, *Reports of Cases in the Reigns of Hen. VIII. Edw. VI. Q. Mary, and Q. Eliz.* (3 vols, 1794), ii. 155a; Vaughan, *Arraignment of Slander*, 158.

102. *The Diary of Henry Machyn, Citizen and Merchant-Taylor of London, From A.D. 1550 to A.D. 1563*, ed. John Gough Nichols (Camden Society, 1848), 69, 71, 150, 154, 164.

103. John Foxe, *Acts and Monuments* (1583 edn.), 1993.

104. Foxe, *Acts and Monuments*, 2048.

105. Rye (ed.), *Depositions Taken before the Mayor and Aldermen of Norwich*, 56–7.

106. John Cordy Jeaffreson (ed.), *Middlesex County Records. Vol. I...from 3 Edward VI to the end of the Reign of Elizabeth* (Clerkenwell, 1886), 23; *Acts of the Privy Council 1554–1556*, 143.
107. *Acts of the Privy Council 1554–1556*, 290.
108. *Acts of the Privy Council 1554–1556*, 265.
109. C. S. Knighton (ed.), *Calendar of State Papers Domestic Series of the Reign of Mary I, 1553–1558* (1998), 314, 318.

CHAPTER 4

1. TNA: PRO SP 12/273/35.
2. For suggestive glimpses of this current, see Joel Samaha, 'Gleanings from Local Criminal-Court Records: Sedition amongst the "Inarticulate" in Elizabethan Essex', *Journal of Social History*, 8 (1975), 61–79; Carole Levin, '"We shall never have a merry world while the Queene lyveth": Gender, Monarchy, and the Power of Seditious Words', in Julia M. Walker (ed.), *Dissing Elizabeth: Negative Representations of Gloriana* (Durham, NC, 1998), 77–95; Natalie Mears, *Queenship and Political Discourse in the Elizabethan Realms* (Cambridge, 2005), 217–46; Kevin Sharpe, 'Sacralization and De-mystification: The Publicization of Monarchy in Early Modern England', in Jeroen Deploige and Gita Deneckere (eds.), *Mystifying the Monarch: Studies on Discourse, Power and History* (Amsterdam, 2006), 99–115, esp. 104–6.
3. TNA: PRO SP 12/15/39.
4. *Acts of the Privy Council 1558–1570*, 31, 71, 308–9; *Acts of the Privy Council 1571–1575*, 147, 276, 280, 283, 354, 365; *Acts of the Privy Council 1575–1577*, 76–7, 252, 300, 336, etc.
5. 1 Eliz., c. 5 and 6, *Statutes of the Realm* (10 vols. 1810–28), vol. iv, pt .1, pp. 365–7; *Journals of the House of Commons*, i. *1547–1629* (1802), 54, 57–8; Sir Simonds D'Ewes (ed.), *The Journals of All the Parliaments During the Reign of Queen Elizabeth* (1682), 19, 25, 51.
6. TNA: PRO SP 15/18/76.
7. 13 Eliz. I, c. 1, *Statutes of the Realm*, vol. iv, pt .1, 527.
8. Paul L. Hughes and James F. Larkin (eds.), *Tudor Royal Proclamations*, ii. *The Later Tudors (1553–1587)* (New Haven and London, 1969), 329. For the culture of communications in the late 1560s, see K. J. Kesselring, '"A Cold Pye for the Papistes": Constructing and Containing the Northern Rising of 1569', *Journal of British Studies*, 43 (2004), 417–43.
9. Hughes and Larkin (eds.), *Tudor Royal Proclamations*, ii. 400; Paul L. Hughes and James F. Larkin (eds.), *Tudor Royal Proclamations*, iii. *The Later Tudors (1588–1603)* (London and New Haven, 1969), 233.
10. 23 Eliz., c. 2, *Statutes of the Realm*, vol. iv, pt. 1, p. 659. In debate the Commons preferred the phrase 'intending the slander and dishonour of the queen's majesty', to the Lords' 'tending to the slander and dishonour' (T. E.

Hartley (ed.), *Proceedings in the Parliaments of Elizabeth I*, i. *1558–1581* (Leicester, 1981), 530–1, 544–5). See also D'Ewes (ed.), *Journals of All the Parliaments During the Reign of Queen Elizabeth*, 270, 290, 303; *Journals of the House of Commons*, i. 120–1, 133–5.

11. Essex Record Office, T/A 418/28/31, transcript of TNA: PRO ASS 35/19/4/31.

12. J. S. Cockburn (ed.), *Calendar of Assize Records: Home Circuit Indictments. Elizabeth I and James I: Introduction* (1985), 137.

13. J. S. Cockburn (ed.), *Calendar of Assize Records: Hertfordshire Indictments. Elizabeth I* (1975), 48.

14. J. S. Cockburn (ed.), *Calendar of Assize Records: Kent Indictments. Elizabeth I* (1979), 335–6.

15. 1 Eliz., c. 5, section 10; 13 Eliz., c. 1, section 9; 23 Eliz., c. 2, section 13: *Statutes of the Realm*, vol. iv, pt. 1, pp. 366, 528, 661.

16. *Acts of the Privy Council 1591–1592*, 317; *Acts of the Privy Council 1590–1591*, 94, 174–5, 359; *Acts of the Privy Council 1591*, 359.

17. *Acts of the Privy Council 1581–1582*, 417–18.

18. *Acts of the Privy Council 1577–1578*, 404–5; *Acts of the Privy Council 1578–1580*, 6–7; *Acts of the Privy Council 1591*, 360.

19. *Acts of the Privy Council 1575–1577*, 76–7; *Acts of the Privy Council 1577–1578*, 407–8.

20. *Acts of the Privy Council 1591*, 323.

21. Cockburn (ed.), *Calendar of Assize Records: Home Circuit Indictments. Elizabeth I and James I*, 23; *Acts of the Privy Council 1575–1577*, 241, 246, 252.

22. William Lambarde, *Eirenarcha: or of the Office of the Iustices of Peace* (1581), 197, 285–6, 492; J. S. Cockburn (ed.), *Calendar of Assize Records: Essex Indictments. Elizabeth I* (1978), 195; Cockburn (ed.), *Calendar of Assize Records: Kent Indictments. Elizabeth I*, 393.

23. Michael Dalton, *The Countrey Justice* (5th edn., 1635), 191.

24. Richard Burn, *The Justice of the Peace, and Parish Officer* (18th edn., 4 vols., 1797), iv. 400, sub. 'treason'.

25. John Rade to Thomas Hendley, 16 Dec.1594, Staffordshire Record Office, D593/S4/36/15. On Rade's report his neighbour Thomas Delman was detained in prison. Among 'speeches of many matters', Delman 'hoped before Candlemas next coming to see the rich churls plucked out of their houses by the ears'.

26. *Acts of the Privy Council 1586–1587*, 277.

27. *Acts of the Privy Council 1591*, 323–4, 346.

28. TNA: PRO SP 12/44/52.

29. John Hawarde, *Les Reportes del Cases in Camera Stellata, 1593–1609*, ed. William Paley Baildon (1894), 114. They were each fined £200, but being gentlemen were spared the humiliation of pillorying and disfigurement.

30. *Acts of the Privy Council 1571–1575*, 365.

31. *Acts of the Privy Council 1577–1578*, 234, 262.

32. *Acts of the Privy Council 1577–1578*, 404, 421–2.

33. *Acts of the Privy Council 1580–1581*, 328.

34. TNA: PRO SP 12/256/53.

35. Essex Record Office, T/A 418/30/7, transcript of NA ASS 35/30/5A/7; F. G. Emmison, *Elizabethan Life: Disorder* (Chelmsford, 1970), 40–1; Cockburn (ed.), *Calendar of Assize Records: Essex Indictments. Elizabeth I*, 175; *Acts of the Privy Council 1578–1580*, 194, 214–15, 371.

36. Cockburn (ed.), *Calendar of Assize Records: Essex Indictments. Elizabeth I*, 294.

37. *Acts of the Privy Council 1578–1580*, 108; Cockburn (ed.), *Calendar of Assize Records: Essex Indictments. Elizabeth I*, 191.

38. TNA: PRO SP 12/12/51.

39. Richard Newcourt, *Repertorium Ecclesiasticum Parochiale Londinense* (2 vols., 1710), ii. 118; Brett Usher, 'Essex Evangelicals under Edward VI', in David Loades (ed.), *John Foxe at Home and Abroad* (Aldershot and Burlington, 2004), 56.

40. TNA: PRO SP 12/13/21.

41. TNA: PRO SP 12/27/25; *CSPD 1547–1580*, 217; *CSPD 1601–1603 with Addenda 1547–1565*, 534.

42. TNA: PRO SP 12/73/72. Nowell, a Marian exile and a friend to puritans, may have been under attack from more conservative members of the cathedral community.

43. *Acts of the Privy Council 1578–1580*, 405; Cockburn (ed.), *Calendar of Assize Records: Essex Indictments. Elizabeth I*, 195; Samaha, 'Gleanings from Local Criminal-Court Records', 68.

44. TNA: PRO SP 12/148/34.

45. J. S. Cockburn (ed.), *Calendar of Assize Records: Surrey Indictments. Elizabeth I* (1980), 276.

46. TNA: PRO SP 12/190/56.

47. Cockburn (ed.), *Calendar of Assize Records: Surrey Indictments. Elizabeth I*, 290.

48. *CSPD...Addenda 1580–1625*, 256. I am grateful to Geoffrey Parker for discussion of Arthur Dudley's career in Spain.

49. Cockburn (ed.), *Calendar of Assize Records: Essex Indictments. Elizabeth I*, 355. Essex Record Office, T/A 418/53/48, transcript of ASSI 35/32/2/48.

50. Cockburn (ed.), *Calendar of Assize Records: Essex Indictments. Elizabeth I*, 355.

51. TNA: PRO SP 16/118/56.

52. *CSPD 1675–1676*, 547.

53. TNA: PRO SP 12/269/22, SP 12/270/105.

54. TNA: PRO SP 12/269/22, SP 12/270/105.

55. *CSPD 1601–1603*, 23–4; TNA: PRO SP 12/279/48.

56. *CSPD...Addenda 1580–1625*, 278, 280.

57. *CSPD...Addenda 1566–1579*, 363.

58. *CSPD...Addenda 1580–1625*, 54.

59. *CSPD 1601–1603*, 146, 170, 190.

60. *CSPD Ireland, 1588–92*, 142–3, 273, 336, 408, 432, 439, 440; *CSPD 1601–1603*, 146, 190; TNA: PRO SP 12/284/14.

61. Hiram Morgan, ' "Never any realm worse governed" ': Queen Elizabeth and Ireland', *Transactions of the Royal Historical Society*, 14 (2004), 302. Cf. Roger Turvey, 'Sir John Perrot (1528–1592)', *Oxford Dictionary of National Biography*, citing Bodleian Library MS Willis 58 and MS Tanner 299.

62. TNA: PRO SP 12/3/50.

63. *CSPD . . . Addenda 1566–1579*, 521; TNA: PRO SP 15/25/47.

64. TNA: PRO SP 12/118/27.

65. John Cordy Jeaffreson (ed.), *Middlesex County Records. Vol. I . . . from 3 Edward VI to the end of the Reign of Elizabeth* (Clerkenwell, 1886), 147.

66. Cockburn (ed.), *Calendar of Assize Records: Essex Indictments. Elizabeth I*, 203; Samaha, 'Gleanings from Local Criminal-Court Records', 68.

67. Emmison, *Elizabethan Life: Disorder*, 53–4.

68. Cockburn (ed.), *Calendar of Assize Records: Kent Indictments. Elizabeth I*, 246.

69. Jeaffreson (ed.), *Middlesex County Records. Vol. I*, 203. The sailors' names were Balzathar Burrowmaster and Harmon Myne.

70. Jeaffreson (ed.), *Middlesex County Records. Vol. I*, 283.

71. Jeaffreson (ed.), *Middlesex County Records. Vol. I*, 284. See also the case of the London gardener Richard Maidley, who in 1600 referred to the queen as 'a whore' (Cockburn (ed.), *Calendar of Assize Records: Surrey Indictments. Elizabeth I*, 494).

72. Essex Record Office, T/A 418/28/31, transcript of TNA: PRO ASS 35/19/4/31. See later in this chapter for Mary Cleere's treason and execution.

73. Cockburn (ed.), *Calendar of Assize Records: Surrey Indictments. Elizabeth I*, 282.

74. Cockburn (ed.), *Calendar of Assize Records: Essex Indictments. Elizabeth I*, 339; Essex Record Office T/A 418/51/42, transcript of ASSI 35/31/2/42; Samaha, 'Gleanings from Local Criminal-Court Records', 69. See later in this chapter for Wenden's other crimes.

75. Cockburn (ed.), *Calendar of Assize Records: Surrey Indictments. Elizabeth I*, 345.

76. Cockburn (ed.), *Calendar of Assize Records: Essex Indictments. Elizabeth I*, 373; Samaha, 'Gleanings from Local Criminal-Court Records', 69.

77. *CSPD 1601–1603*, 224–5; TNA: PRO SP 12/284/80.

78. *CSPD 1601–1603*, 225; TNA: PRO SP 12/284/80.

79. *CSPD 1601–1603*, 231; TNA: PRO SP 12/284/91.

80. *CSPD 1601–1603 and Addenda 1547–1565*, 525; TNA: PRO SP 15/11/46.

81. Cockburn (ed.), *Calendar of Assize Records: Kent Indictments. Elizabeth I*, 77.

82. Samaha, 'Gleanings from Local Criminal-Court Records', 69.

83. TNA: PRO SP 12/99/53.

84. *Acts of the Privy Council 1578–1580*, 75.

85. Emmison, *Elizabethan Life: Disorder*, 55–6.

86. Cockburn (ed.), *Calendar of Assize Records: Kent Indictments. Elizabeth I*, 336.

87. Jeaffreson (ed.), *Middlesex County Records. Vol. I*, 195.

88. Cockburn (ed.), *Calendar of Assize Records: Kent Indictments. Elizabeth I*, 402.

89. TNA: PRO SP 12/246/49, SP 12/247/73, 74, 75.

90. Cockburn (ed.), *Calendar of Assize Records: Kent Indictments. Elizabeth I*, 7.

91. Essex Record Office, Q/SR 50/10, 12, 18, and 30; Emmison, *Elizabethan Life: Disorder*, 44–5.

92. Essex Record Office T/A 418/30/35 transcript of ASSI 35/20/5B/28; T/A 418/30/20, transcript of ASSI 35/20/5A/20.

93. *Acts of the Privy Council 1578–1580*, 132, 158.

94. East Sussex Record Office, Grantham papers, SAS-WG/873; Emmison, *Elizabethan Life: Disorder*, 52–3.

95. Cockburn (ed.), *Calendar of Assize Records: Kent Indictments. Elizabeth I*, 440.

96. William Averell, *A Mervailous Combat of Contrarieties* (1588), sig. D2ᵛ.

97. Essex Record Office, Q/SR 65/61.

98. Essex Record Office T/A 418/35/36, transcript of ASSI 35/23/H/36. Charles Neville, 6th earl of Westmorland (1542–1601), fled into exile after the failure of the 1569 Northern Rebellion. A Spanish pensioner and inveterate intriguer, he served in the 1580s as colonel of an English Catholic regiment in the Spanish Netherlands. David Brown evidently knew, or believed, that 'the king of Spain hath given him a great dukedom for his good service'.

99. *Acts of the Privy Council 1581–1582*, 180–1.

100. *CSPD . . . Addenda 1580–1625*, 63; TNA: PRO SP 15 /27/93.

101. John Strype, *Brief Annals of the Church and State Under the Reign of Queen Elizabeth* (4 vols., 1725–31), iv. 16. The bishop of Hereford, who reported this to Burghley, noted the possibility that Weir had been charged out of malice.

102. TNA: PRO SP 12/256/54.

103. Cockburn (ed.), *Calendar of Assize Records: Kent Indictments. Elizabeth I*, 404.

104. On the late Elizabethan succession debate see [William Allen, Francis Englefield, and Robert Parsons], *A Conference about the next succession to the crowne of Ingland* (Antwerp, 1595); Peter Wentworth, *A Pithy Exhortation to her Maiestie for establishing her successor* (Edinburgh, 1598); Jean-Christophe Mayer (ed.), *The Struggle for the Succession in Late Elizabethan England: Politics, Polemics and Cultural Representations* (Montpellier, 2004).

105. Essex Record Office, T/A 418/28/31, transcript of TNA: PRO ASSI 35/ 19/4/31; Emmison, *Elizabethan Life: Disorder*, 40, 50–2; Samaha, 'Gleanings from Local Criminal-Court Records', 68.

106. Cockburn (ed.), *Calendar of Assize Records: Surrey Indictments. Elizabeth I*, 262.

107. Cockburn (ed.), *Calendar of Assize Records: Surrey Indictments. Elizabeth I*, 496.

108. *CSPD 1601–1603*, 23.

109. Essex Record Office, T/A 418/56/43, transcript of TNA: PRO ASSI 35/34/2/43. Binks had previously been charged with upholding the mass and rejoicing in the name of papist (Essex Record Office, Q/ SR 64/45 (Michaelmas 1577)).

110. TNA: PRO SP 12/259/21, SP 12/259/16. I am grateful to Paul Hammer and Glyn Parry for insights into this affair. For correspondence in 1600 questioning Beauchamp's fitness to be king, see *CSPD . . . Addenda 1580–1625*, 406.

111. TNA: PRO SP 12/259/16.

112. Essex Record Office, Q/SR 140/171.

113. *CSPD . . . Addenda 1580–1625*, 400.

114. See Chapter 5.

115. For Binks, see above, n. 109.

116. Cockburn (ed.), *Calendar of Assize Records: Essex Indictments. Elizabeth I*, 272. Slater made his remarks while visiting Pleshey, Essex.

117. For Feltwell, see above, n. 76, and Cockburn (ed.), *Calendar of Assize Records: Essex Indictments. Elizabeth I*, 373.

118. Cockburn (ed.), *Calendar of Assize Records: Essex Indictments. Elizabeth I*, 416; Emmison, *Elizabethan Life: Disorder*, 58–9.

119. Cockburn (ed.), *Calendar of Assize Records: Surrey Indictments. Elizabeth I*, 406.

120. Cockburn (ed.), *Calendar of Assize Records: Hertfordshire Indictments. Elizabeth I*, 118.

121. Cockburn (ed.), *Calendar of Assize Records: Kent Indictments. Elizabeth I*, 393.

122. Cockburn (ed.), *Calendar of Assize Records: Home Circuit Indictments. Elizabeth I and James I: Introduction*, 137.

123. Cockburn (ed.), *Calendar of Assize Records: Hertfordshire Indictments. Elizabeth I*, 129.

CHAPTER 5

1. TNA: PRO SP 14/18/69, 73.

2. John Hawarde, *Les Reportes del Cases in Camera Stellata, 1593–1609*, ed. William Paley Baildon (1894), 188.

3. Hawarde, *Reportes del Cases in Camera Stellata*, 372.

4. John Shirley, *The Life of the Valiant & Learned Sir Walter Raleigh, Knight with his Tryal at Winchester* (1677), 85.

5. Edward Coke, *The Third Part of the Institutes of the Laws of England* (1644), 12, 14. For commentary on Coke, see William Hawkins, *A Treatise of the Pleas of the Crown* (2 vols., 1716–21), i. 38–41; Sir Matthew Hale, *Historia Placitorum Coronae: The History of the Pleas of the Crown* (2 vols., 1736), i. 117; W. S. Holdsworth, *A History of English Law* (rev. edn., 17 vols., Boston, 1922–72), viii. 312.

6. Reliable studies of the reign of King James include Maurice Lee, Jr., *Great Britain's Solomon: James VI and I in his Three Kingdoms* (Urbana and Chicago, 1990); Roger Lockyer, *James VI and I* (1998); Pauline Croft, *King James* (Basingstoke and New York, 2003); and Alastair Bellany, *The Politics of Court Scandal in Early Modern England: News Culture and the Overbury Affair, 1603–1660* (Cambridge, 2002). See also Ian Atherton and David Como, 'The Burning of Edward Wightman: Puritanism, Prelacy and the Politics of Heresy in Early Modern England', *English Historical Review*, 120 (2005), 1215–50.

7. J. S. Cockburn (ed.), *Calendar of Assize Records: Sussex Indictments. James I* (1975), 1.

8. J. S. Cockburn (ed.), *Calendar of Assize Records: Hertfordshire Indictments. James I* (1980), 4–5.

9. J. S. Cockburn (ed.), *Calendar of Assize Records: Kent Indictments. James I* (1980), 5.

10. Cockburn (ed.), *Calendar of Assize Records: Kent Indictments. James I*, 7.

11. Cockburn (ed.), *Calendar of Assize Records: Kent Indictments. James I*, 4, 10.

12. Essex Record Office, T/A 418/72/46, transcript of ASSI 35/45/2/46.

13. J. S. Cockburn (ed.), *Calendar of Assize Records: Essex Indictments. James I* (1982), 3. William Bird, vicar of Great Chishall, and John Hoclie, labourer, were called to the Essex Quarter Sessions on 28 Apr. 1603 to give evidence against Bartholomew Ward 'for certain seditious speeches spoken by him against the king's majesty'. Ward and his brother Edward, a labourer of Great Chishall, attempted to turn the charge against Hoclie and Bird 'for such seditious speeches as they should speak of the king's majesty' (Essex Record Office, Q/SR/162/28, 29).

14. Essex Record Office T/A 418/72/41, transcript of ASSI 35/45/2/41; Cockburn (ed.), *Calendar of Assize Records: Essex Indictments. James I*, 2–4.

15. *CSPD 1603–1610* (1857), 31.

16. Cockburn (ed.), *Calendar of Assize Records: Essex Indictments. James I*, 9. He may have had influential friends, for a writ *non molestetis* in favour of Henry Glascocke of High Easter, husbandman, was issued from Westminster on 23 Feb. 1605.

17. TNA: PRO STAC 8/7/3. On resistance to fen drainage, see Clive Holmes, *Seventeenth-Century Lincolnshire* (Lincoln, 1980), 91, 120–30.

18. TNA: PRO STAC 8/6/10.

19. Cockburn (ed.), *Calendar of Assize Records: Kent Indictments. James I*, 16.

20. TNA: PRO SP14/18/69, 73.

21. John Cordy Jeaffreson (ed.), *Middlesex County Records. Vol. II. Indictments, Recognizances . . . and Memoranda, temp. James I* (Clerkenwell, 1887), 76.

22. National Library of Wales, Great Sessions, 4/143/1/68. I am grateful to Lloyd Bowen for supplying this reference.

23. TNA: PRO SP 14/138/21.

24. Jeaffreson (ed.), *Middlesex County Records. Vol. II*, 147.

25. TNA: PRO SP 14/ 122/145, SP 14/123/20.

26. TNA: PRO SP 14/143/18, 19; *Acts of the Privy Council 1621–1623*, 484.

27. TNA: PRO SP 15/40/31.

28. British Library, Add. MS 72421, fos. 110–12.

29. TNA: PRO SP 14/18/69.

30. TNA: PRO STAC 8/11/23.

31. *Acts of the Privy Council 1623–1625*, 19.

32. TNA: PRO STAC 8/32/20.

33. TNA: PRO SP 14 *passim*, quotations from SP 14/127/59, Sir John Mill to Secretary Calvert, Jan. 1622.

34. Cockburn (ed.), *Calendar of Assize Records: Kent Indictments. James I*, 26.

35. Jeaffreson (ed.), *Middlesex County Records. Vol. II*, 20.

36. Cockburn (ed.), *Calendar of Assize Records: Kent Indictments. James I*, 38.

37. National Library of Wales, Great Sessions, 4/143/3/37.

38. *Acts of the Privy Council 1615–1616*, 27–8.

39. *Acts of the Privy Council 1615–1616*, 584.

40. Jeaffreson (ed.), *Middlesex County Records. Vol. II*, 132.

41. *Acts of the Privy Council 1616–1617*, 411.

42. *Acts of the Privy Council 1618–1619*, 147, 246–7.

43. TNA: PRO SP 14/108/43; *Acts of the Privy Council 1618–1619*, 419.

44. *CSPD 1619–1623*, 92–3; TNA: PRO SP 14 /111/14.

45. TNA: PRO SP 14/117/38, 39, 40; *Acts of the Privy Council 1619–1621*, 363.

46. TNA: PRO SP 14/121/99; *Acts of the Privy Council 1619–1621*, 392.

47. TNA: PRO SP 14/123/64; *Acts of the Privy Council 1621–1623*, 81–2.

48. TNA: PRO SP 14/122/111;*Acts of the Privy Council 1621–1623*, 43.

49. *Acts of the Privy Council 1618–1619*, 214; *Acts of the Privy Council 1619–1621*, 14; *CSPD 1619–1623*, 208; TNA: PRO SP 14/118/105.

50. Paul L. Hughes and James F. Larkin (eds.), *Stuart Royal Proclamations*, i. *Royal Proclamations of King James I 1603–1625* (Oxford, 1973), 496n., citing Bibliothèque Nationale, Paris, 15988, fo. 550.

51. *Acts of the Privy Council 1621–1623*, 121–2, 161.

52. TNA: PRO SP 14/128/54; *Acts of the Privy Council 1621–1623*, 156–7, 174.

53. TNA: PRO SP 14/153/26.

54. TNA: PRO SP 14/189/58.

55. TNA: PRO SP 14/18/69, 73.

56. Floyd's case is reconstructed from parliamentary diaries, state papers, and contemporary correspondence: Wallace Notestein, Frances Helen Relf, and Hartley Simpson (eds.), *Commons Debates 1621* (7 vols., New Haven, 1935), ii. 335, 349; iii. 116–27, 135; iv. 281–2, 285–6; v. 126–30, 356–61, 386; vi. 117–23, 397–8; *Acts of the Privy Council 1618–1621*, 8, 10, 24, 37, 41, 42, 97, 262; *Acts of the Privy Council 1621–1623*, 64; TNA: PRO SP 14/121/5, 12, 13, 44, 54, 69. See also *Oxford Dictionary of National Biography*, *sub.* Floyd [Lloyd],

Edward (fl. 1588–1621); Conrad Russell, *Parliaments and English Politics, 1621–1629* (Oxford, 1979), 117–18.

57. *The Letters of John Chamberlain*, ed. Norman Egbert McClure (2 vols., Philadelphia, 1939), ii. 370, 372, 374, 377; Thomas Birch (ed.), *The Court and Times of James the First* (2 vols., 1849), ii. 252–6.

58. TNA: PRO SP 14/128/54, 128/71, 72; *Acts of the Privy Council 1621–1623*, 174.

59. More's case is examined in TNA: PRO STAC 8/32/20.

60. Elisabeth Bourcier (ed.), *Diary of Sir Simonds D'Ewes 1622–1624* (Paris, 1974), 180.

61. *William Whiteway of Dorchester His Diary 1618 to 1635* (Dorset Record Society, 12, Dorchester, 1991), 59.

62. Elizabeth McClure Thomson (ed.), *The Chamberlain Letters* (New York, 1965), 320.

63. Thomas More to Thomas Rant, 28 Feb. 1624, in Michael Questier (ed), *Stuart Dynastic Policy and Religious Politics, 1621–1625* (Camden Society, 5th ser., 2009), newsletter no. 39. I am grateful to Professor Questier for advanced sight of this text.

64. TNA: PRO SP 14/145/65, SP 15/43/12.

65. TNA: PRO SP 14/159/38, 39.

66. Essex Record Office, Clayton MSS. D/DAc66.

67. TNA: PRO SP 14/105/51–3.

68. TNA: PRO SP 14/110/27, 28, 39, 45; *Acts of the Privy Council 1619–1621*, 29.

69. *Acts of the Privy Council 1619–1621*, 257; *Acts of the Privy Council 1621–1623*, 1, 78–9; TNA: PRO STAC 8/225/30; Ronald A. Marchant, *Puritans and the Church Courts in the Diocese of York* (1960), 186–8.

70. TNA: PRO STAC 8/225/30.

71. TNA: PRO STAC 8/180/11.

72. TNA: PRO SP 14/122/71.

73. TNA: PRO STAC 8/29/12.

CHAPTER 6

1. The most important studies include Judith Richards, ' "His Nowe Majestie" and the English Monarchy: The Kingship of Charles I before 1640', *Past & Present*, 113 (1986), 70–96; L. J. Reeve, *Charles I and the Road to Personal Rule* (Cambridge, 1989); Kevin Sharpe, *The Personal Rule of Charles I* (1992); Charles Carlton, *Charles I: The Personal Monarch* (2nd edn., 1995); Michael B. Young, *Charles I* (Basingstoke, 1997); Richard Cust, *Charles I: A Political Life* (Harlow, 2005); Mark Kishlansky, 'Charles I: A Case of Mistaken Identity', *Past & Present*, 189 (2005), 41–80; and Clive Holmes, *Why Was Charles I Executed?* (2006).

2. [George Croke], *The Reports of Sir George Croke . . . Revised, and Published in English by Sir Harebotle Grimston* (1657), 83; T. B. Howell and T. J. Howell (eds.), *A Complete Collection of State Trials* (33 vols., 1809–28), iii. 359. The king had visited Plymouth in September to speed the fleet. The court was travelling in the south-west that autumn, partly to avoid outbreaks of plague at London and Windsor. John Poulett wrote to Secretary Conway on 9 Oct. 1625 with reference to the king's recent visit to his house (TNA: PRO SP 16/7/57).

3. Richard Mulcaster, *Positions . . . for the Training up of Children* (1581), 159; Leonard Wright, *A Display of Dutie* (1589), 16; John Boys, *The Third Part from S. Iohn Baptists Nativitie* (1615), 116; Francis Rous, *Meditations of Instruction* (1616), 447; *Luther and Erasmus: Free Will and Salvation*, ed. E. Gordon Rupp and Philip S. Watson (Philadelphia, 1969), 91. See also [Sir John Melton], *A Sixe-Fold Politician* (1609), 72, on men of 'weak understanding' lured to Jesuit seminaries 'like children . . . with an apple', and [Matthew Killiray], *The Swearer and the Drunkard* (1673), 2, on irreligious men who 'make themselves bondslaves for an apple'.

4. Ecclesiastes 10: 16, 20.

5. Howell and Howell (eds.), *Complete Collection of State Trials*, iii. 359–67; Sir Matthew Hale, *Historia Placitorum Coronae: The History of the Pleas of the Crown* (2 vols., 1736), i. 114–15; William Blackstone, *Commentaries on the Laws of England* (11th edn., 4 vols., 1791), iv. 80; W. S. Holdsworth, *A History of English Law* (rev. edn., 17 vols., 1922–72), viii. 312; Richard L. Greaves and Robert Zaller (eds.), *Biographical Dictionary of British Radicals in the Seventeenth Century* (3 vols., Brighton, 1982), iii. 73.

6. Thomas Garden Barnes, *Somerset 1625–1640: A County's Government during the 'Personal Rule'* (Cambridge, MA, 1961), 34, 70, 262.

7. David Underdown, *Revel, Riot and Rebellion* (Oxford, 1985), 120; *The Diary of Walter Yonge, Esq.*, ed. George Roberts (Camden Society, 1848), 110.

8. Wilfrid R. Prest, *The Rise of the Barristers: A Social History of the English Bar 1590–1640* (Oxford, 1986), 238, 386; *Diary of Walter Yonge*, ed. Roberts, 114.

9. Richard Cust, *The Forced Loan and English Politics 1626–1628* (Oxford, 1987), 192–3.

10. Somerset Record Office, Taunton, DD/CM/72.

11. Frederick Arthur Crisp (ed.), *Abstracts of Somerset Wills* (6 vols., 1887–90), ii. 71–2. TNA: PRO PROB 11/154. Inquisitions post-mortem dated 28 Mar. 1629 list Hugh Pyne's crown leases and holdings as tenant in chief (TNA: PRO C 142/448/96; WARD 7/78/139).

12. Sir William Dugdale, *Origines Juridiciales, or Historical Memorials of the English Laws* (1666), 235; *The Records of the Honorable Society of Lincoln's Inn: The Black Books, Vol. II. From AD 1586 to AD 1660* (1898), 48, 157, 186, 199, 206, 253, 450. I am grateful to Wilfrid Prest for insights into Pyne's legal career.

13. On 11 June 1626, for example, Hugh Pyne presided at the Somerset Quarter Sessions at Somerton (Somerset Record Office, Q/SRD/1/24; E. H. Bates Harbin (ed.), *Quarter Sessions Records for the County of Somerset. Vol. 1. James. I. 1607–1625* (Somerset Record Society, 23, 1907), 216–335; id., *Quarter Sessions Records for the County of Somerset. Vol II. Charles I. 1625–1639* (Somerset Record Society, 24, 1908), 6, 14, 20).

14. TNA: PRO Exchequer King's Remembrancer, Certificates of Residence, E 115/316/65, also E 115/293/25, 296/105, 301/4, 59, 305/57, 307/117, 140; Thomas Birch (ed.), *The Court and Times of Charles the First* (2 vols., 1848), i. 295.

15. TNA: PRO PROB 11/154.

16. Hampshire Record Office, 44M69/L30/58, Hugh Pyne to Henry Sherfield, 8 Apr. 1622.

17. TNA: PRO SP 16/540/24.

18. Robert C. Johnson et al. (eds.), *Commons Debates 1628* (6 vols., New Haven and London, 1977–83), iii. 140, iv. 128.

19. *The Letters, Speeches and Proclamations of King Charles I*, ed. Sir Charles Petrie (1935), 6, 63, 70.

20. *Oxford Dictionary of National Biography*, sub 'Poulett'; Somerset Record Office, DD/BR/ba.

21. TNA: PRO SP 16/36/7; *CSPD 1625–1626*, 121, 238, 357, 431, 436, 445; *CSPD 1627–1628*, 53, 279, 290; Historical Manuscripts Commission, *The Manuscripts of the Earl Cowper, K.G., Preserved at Melbourne Hall, Derbyshire* (3 vols., 1888–9), i. 248, 250.

22. TNA: PRO C 115/108, no. 8632, Roger Palmer to Viscount Scudamore, 19 Oct. 1625.

23. Birch (ed.), *Court and Times*, i. 246, 295.

24. Mary Frear Keeler, *The Long Parliament 1640–1641: A Biographical Study of its Members* (Philadelphia, 1954), 319, mentioning the uncle of John Pyne: 'imprisonment and examination brought him great notoriety in 1627–1628.'

25. Birch (ed.), *Court and Times*, i. 292.

26. *Diary of Walter Yonge*, ed. Roberts, 110, 114.

27. *William Whiteway of Dorchester His Diary 1618 to 1635* (Dorset Record Society, 12, Dorchester, 1991), 93. Another Dorset chronicler, Dennis Bond, made no reference to Pyne's case, although he commented on the forced loan in 1626 and the death of the Duke of Buckingham in 1628 (Dorset History Centre, D/BOC/Box 22).

28. TNA: PRO SP 16/40/58, SP 1 6/438/37; Paul L. Hughes and James F. Larkin (eds.), *Stuart Royal Proclamations*, i. *Royal Proclamations of King James I 1603–1625* (Oxford, 1973), 527–34, for the proclamation of 6 Jan. 1622 'concerning the dissolving of the present convention of parliament'.

29. TNA: PRO C 231/4, 419. Pyne was dismissed on 9 Sept. 1626. I am grateful to Alison Wall for supplying this reference.

30. TNA: PRO SP 16/36/46, SP 16/37/5. Bagg, a naval administrator, was Buckingham's principal political agent in the West Country.

31. TNA: PRO SP 16/40/30.

32. TNA SP 16/526/5, SP 16/40/58, SP 16/438/37; *Acts of the Privy Council 1627–1628*, 298.

33. TNA SP 16/66/78.

34. Bodleian Library, Clarendon MS 4/256; Croke, *Reports*, 83; Howell and Howell (eds.), *Complete Collection of State Trials*, iii. 359.

35. *Acts of the Privy Council 1627–1628*, 297–8.

36. O. Ogle and W. H. Bliss (eds.), *Calendar of the Clarendon State Papers Preserved in the Bodleian Library* (5 vols., Oxford, 1872–1970), i. 31; Bodleian Library, Clarendon MS 4/ 249. The manuscript could be read as 16 June, and has been so calendared, but the 26th is clear on the dorse (SP 16/68/25).

37. Charles to Buckingham, 3 Nov. 1621, Proclamation of 10 Mar. 1629, in *Letters, Speeches and Proclamations*, ed. Petrie, 6, 70, 76.

38. Birch (ed.), *Court and Times*, i. 295. On 27 Aug. 1627 the Cornish loan refuser Sir Bevill Granville wrote to an imprisoned friend of his grief 'at your long suffering, from which there hath not wanted the prayers of many good men to redeem you . . . when now of late also more of the honest knot are fetched away'. There is no direct evidence that this letter was addressed to Hugh Pyne, but its references to the recipient's legal advice, and to his 'worthy nephew' (perhaps John Pyne), as well as the date and the sentiment, suggest the possibility (Roger Granville, *The History of the Granville Family* (Exeter, 1895), 163–4).

39. TNA: PRO SP 16/83/21, SP 16/93/55; *Acts of the Privy Council 1627–1628*, 303; Bodleian Library, Clarendon MS 4/251.

40. Bodleian Library, Clarendon MS 4/251.

41. Bodleian Library, Clarendon MS 4/252, 4/253.

42. TNA SP 16/89/61, undated.

43. Birch (ed.), *Court and Times*, i. 292; Oliver Lawson Dick (ed.), *Aubrey's Brief Lives*, ed. Oliver Lawson Dick (Ann Arbor, 1957), 106, for Noy's excursions with Pyne.

44. Bodleian Library, Clarendon MS 4/254–5.

45. Bodleian Library, Clarendon MS 4/254.

46. Bodleian Library, Clarendon MS 4/257.

47. Bodleian Library, Clarendon MS 4/257. Cf. John Holles to Bishop Williams, 13 Nov. 1626: 'many for refusing the loan are pressed to the ships' (*Letters of John Holles 1587–1637*, ed. P. R. Seddon (Thoroton Society Record Series, 35, 1983), 337).

48. Bodleian Library, Clarendon MS 4/257.

49. Thomas Norton, 'A warning agaynst the dangerous practises of Papistes, and specially the parteners of the late rebellion', in *All such treatises as have been*

lately published by Thomas Norton (1570), sig. Ci(v); British Library, Lansdowne MS 620, fo. 50ᵛ, Chief Justice Richardson in Star Chamber.

50. TNA: PRO SP 16/529/64.

51. *Statutes of the Realm* (10 vols., 1810–28), i., 319–20; John Bellamy, *The Law of Treason in England in the Later Middle Ages* (Cambridge, 1970); John Bellamy, *The Tudor Law of Treason: An Introduction* (Toronto and London, 1979). See also Sir Edward Coke, *The Third Part of the Institutes of the Laws of* England (1644), 14; Rex v. Owen, cited in Holdsworth, *History of English Law*, viii. 312; John Hawarde, *Les Reportes del Cases in Camera Stellata, 1593–1609*, ed. William Paley Baildon (1894), 37; and the discussion in Chapter 3, above.

52. Croke, *Reports*, 83, says 'none other of the judges' were then in town, but *State Trials*, iii. 359, augments the list to include Sir John Dodderidge and Sir James Whitlocke of King's Bench; Sir Richard Hutton, Sir Francis Harvey, and Sir George Croke (who wrote the report) of Common Pleas; and Sir Edward Bromley and Sir John Denham of the Exchequer. I am grateful to Cynthia Herrup for discussion of this point, and her suggestion that there were probably two meetings.

53. See Chapter 3, above, for these and other cases.

54. TNA: PRO SP 16/86/37, 38, 39; SP 16/529/64.

55. *CSPD 1627–8*, 461; TNA: PRO SP 16/76/37–9.

56. Croke, *Reports*, 89; *State Trials*, iii. 367. See also Hale, *Historia Placitorum Coronae*, i. 115.

57. Croke, *Reports*, 89; *State Trials*, iii. 368.

58. Birch (ed.), *Court and Times*, i. 295, 305; *Acts of the Privy Council 1627–1628*, 297. '*Ore tenus*' involved an expedited oral proceeding, not necessarily to the defendant's advantage.

59. Johnson et al. (eds.), *Commons Debates 1628*, i. 39n., 60; ii. 305; iii. 86, 628, 632; iv. 131.

60. TNA: PRO SO 1/1, fo. 344.

61. *Records of the Honorable Society of Lincoln's Inn . . . Vol. II*, 277. Pyne's daughter Christabell Windham enjoyed brief celebrity in 1630 as nurse to Prince Charles (*William Whiteway . . . His Diary*, 111).

CHAPTER 7

1. [George Croke], *The Reports of Sir George Croke . . . Revised, and Published in English by Sir Harebotle Grimston* (1657), 89; T. B. Howell and T. J. Howell (eds.), *A Complete Collection of State Trials* (33 vols., 1809–28), iii. 367; Sir Matthew Hale, *Historia Placitorum Coronae: The History of the Pleas of the Crown* (2 vols., 1736), i. 115.

2. In October 1634 Archbishop Neile of York wrote to Archbishop Laud of Canterbury about a Westmorland man who said that 'greater men had their wives recusants, and yet they had their places; yea, and some privy councillors,

and the king himself had his wife a recusant, yet they continued still in their places'. Neile 'conceived these words to be very seditious, or rather treasonable', but the king 'of his great goodness' was 'pleased to remit these presumptuous speeches' (Bodleian Library, MS Clarendon 6, fos. 40–1). To call someone 'traitor' or to say 'you have spoken treason' exposed the accuser to the risk of an action for slander (William Sheppard, *Action upon the Case for Slander. Or a Methodical Collection under Certain Heads, of Thousands of Cases* (1662), 33).

3. Bodleian Library, MS Rawlinson C. 674, fo. 10: Lord Keeper's speech to parliament, 29 Mar. 1626.
4. *Acts of the Privy Council 1630–1631*, 227–8.
5. Thomas Birch (ed.), *The Court and Times of Charles the First* (2 vols., 1848), i. 27: John Pory to Joseph Mead, 3 June 1625.
6. Statute of Westminster, 1275, 3 Edward I, c. 34, *Statutes of the Realm* (1816), i. 35.
7. Neil Walker and Thomas Craddock, *The History of Wisbech and the Fens* (Wisbech, 1849), 240.
8. The Wisbech stirs are reconstructed from TNA: PRO SP 16/3/53 1–6.
9. *Acts of the Privy Council 1625–1626*, 97.
10. Birch (ed.), *Court and Times*, i. 48–9; Essex Record Office, T/A 418/99/114.
11. TNA: PRO SP 16/6/56; *Acts of the Privy Council 1625–1626*, 206–7.
12. H. Hampton Copnall (ed.), *Nottinghamshire County Records. Notes and Extracts . . . of the 17th Century* (Nottingham, 1915), 107: Hugh Till indicted at Nottingham assizes.
13. Birch (ed.), *Court and Times*, i. 49.
14. TNA: PRO SP 16/10/33.
15. TNA: PRO SP 16/19/46.
16. TNA: PRO SP 16/124/28.
17. TNA: PRO SP 16/110/6.
18. TNA: PRO SP 16/110/41 and postscript.
19. TNA: PRO SP 16/110/21.
20. TNA: PRO SP 16/114/23.
21. *Barrington Family Letters 1628–1632*, ed. Arthur Searle (Camden Society, 4th ser., 28, 1983), 36.
22. TNA: PRO SP 16/100/3.
23. TNA: PRO SP 16/171/37. Buller and Levett would seem to have got wind of John Cosin's remark that 'King Charles is not supreme head of the Church of England next under Christ', discussed later in this chapter.
24. TNA: PRO SP 16/148/66.
25. TNA: PRO SP 16/237/28.
26. TNA: PRO SP 16/237/60.
27. TNA: PRO SP 16/239/61.
28. TNA: PRO SP 16/239/85.

29. TNA: PRO SP 16/26/49.

30. TNA: PRO SP 16/26/49.

31. *Diary of John Rous, Incumbent of Santon Downham, Suffolk, from 1625 to 1642*, ed. Mary Anne Everett Green (Camden Society, 66, 1856), 19–33.

32. TNA: PRO SP 16/29/40: Thomas Brediman in 1626.

33. John Rushworth, *Historical Collections of Private Passages of State* (1659), 639; TNA: PRO SP 16/106/27; Birch (ed.), *Court and Times*, i., 371–3: Mead to Stuteville, 5 July 1628.

34. Birch (ed.), *Court and Times*, i. 368; British Library, Egerton MS 2725, fo. 82^v.

35. TNA: PRO SP 16/106/27.

36. *Letters of John Holles 1587–1637*, ed. P. R. Seddon (Thoroton Society Record Series, 35, 1983), 383.

37. TNA: PRO SP 16/110/13.

38. TNA: PRO SP 16/116/28.

39. TNA: PRO SP 16/116/92; Isaac Bargrave, *A Sermon Preached Before King Charles March 27 1627* (1627). Farrell's words cost him a spell in prison.

40. TNA: PRO SP 16/116/56; *CSPD 1628–29*, 240; Birch (ed.), *Court and Times*, i. 430–1. See *Oxford Dictionary of National Biography* (*ODNB*) for Alexander Gill (1597–1642) and William Chillingworth (1602–44).

41. TNA: PRO C 115/106, no. 8397: John Pory to Viscount Scudamore, 24 Mar. 1632, on news of William Chillingworth turning papist.

42. J. H. Bettey, *Calendar of the Correspondence of the Smyth Family of Ashton Court 1548–1642* (Bristol Record Society, 35, 1982), 93.

43. TNA: PRO SP 16/116/95: Samuel Fisher to William Pickering, 10 Sept. 1628.

44. Henry Ellis, *Original Letters Illustrative of English History* (2nd edn., 3 vols., 1825), iii. 276–7; Birch (ed.), *Court and Times*, i. 430.

45. Most of the Oxford chancellor's court papers for 1628 are missing.

46. TNA: PRO SP 16/116/95; Birch (ed.), *Court and Times*, i. 403.

47. Trumbull papers, British Library, Add. MS 72417, fo. 17; *Aprill 4. The proceeding of the Parliament* (1628). For details of Pyne's case, see above, Chapter 6.

48. Bettey, *Calendar of the Correspondence of the Smyth Family*, 93.

49. *Acts of the Privy Council 1628–1629*, 134; TNA: PRO SP 16/111/5; Bettey, *Calendar of the Correspondence of the Smyth Family*, 93. The lines come from an ambitious libel on 'the five senses', with variants in Alastair Bellany and Andrew McRae (eds.), 'Early Stuart Libels: An Edition of Poetry from Manuscript Sources', *Early Modern Literary Studies* (2005), http://purl.oclc.org/emls/texts/libels/.

50. *Acts of the Privy Council 1628–1629*, 143, 159; TNA: PRO SP 16/116/56, SP 16/117/73, SP 16/118/77; Birch (ed.), *Court and Times*, i. 430–1.

51. Birch (ed.), *Court and Times*, i. 427, 437: Pory to Mead. I am grateful to Simon Healy for sharing his transcription of Harvard Law School Library, MS 1101, fos. 16−16ᵛ, which has John Lightfoot's report of Gill's case.

52. *Diary of John Rous*, ed. Green, 33−4.

53. British Library, Egerton MS 2725, fo. 72.

54. *Milton: Private Correspondence and Academic Exercises*, ed. Phyllis B. Tillyard (Cambridge, 1932), 7, 8, 10. Gill's Latin poems in celebration of Gustavus Adolphus are in Bodleian Library, MS Tanner 306, fos. 76−80ᵛ; MS Wood F. 34, fo. 145 ᵛ; and British Library, Egerton MS 2725, fos. 143−4. More of Gill's poetry can be found in British Library, Add. MS 33998, fos. 64 ᵛ−65, and British Library, Egerton MS 2725, fos. 72, 103−4, 131−2.

55. British Library, Egerton MS 2725, fos. 130−1; Bodleian Library, MS Ashmole 38, Alexander Gill, 'Uppon Ben Jonsons Magnettick Lady', answered by Zouch Townley, 'Against Mr Alexander Gill's Verses'. For the play, see Ben Jonson, *The Magnetick Lady*, ed. Peter Happé (Manchester, 2000).

56. Bodleian Library, MS Rawlinson Poet. 84, fos. 54−6.

57. e.g. TNA: PRO SP 16/163/61, SP 16/171/37.

58. Essex Record Office, Colchester Branch, D/B5/Sb2/7, fo. 121: 'Book of Examinations and Recognizances 1619 to 1645'; John Walter, *Understanding Popular Violence in the English Revolution: The Colchester Plunderers* (Cambridge, 1999), 39, 211.

59. *Acts of the Privy Council 1627 Jan.−Aug.*, 512; TNA: PRO SP 16/83/65; Copnall (ed.), *Nottinghamshire County Records*, 107.

60. Birch (ed.), *Court and Times*, i. 310, 332, 348.

61. TNA: PRO SP 16/148/25; E. H. Bates Harbin (ed.), *Quarter Sessions Records for the County of Somerset. Vol. II. Charles I. 1625−1639* (Somerset Record Society, 24, 1908), 95−6. The court allowed Williams to 'have his reasonable maintenance . . . during his imprisonment'.

62. TNA: PRO SP 16/163/61; Essex Record Office, T/A 418/99/114, T/A 418/107/90.

63. TNA: PRO SP 16/197/35.

64. TNA: PRO SP 16/198/37, SP 16/533/44.

65. John Cordy Jeaffreson (ed.), *Middlesex County Records. Vol. III . . . 1 Charles I to 18 Charles II* (Clerkenwell, 1888), 43.

66. TNA: PRO SP 16/248/60.

67. For Stephens, see later in this chapter.

68. Jeaffreson (ed.), *Middlesex County Records. Vol. III*, 54−5.

69. TNA: PRO SP 16/231/24; Staffordshire Record Office, D1287/18/2/108, Bridgeman correspondence: James Martin reporting words of Dr Robert Floyd.

70. TNA: PRO PC 2/43, 431; SP 16/258/45; Bodleian Library, MS Carte 123, fo. 180.

71. University of Birmingham, Calendar of the Court of Chivalry, 1634–1640, no. 35 Bawde v. Dawson (www.court-of-chivalry.bham.ac.uk/index.htm).
72. Redferne also said 'that the king and peers of the land were not worthy to sit on the seat of judgement because they did not execute true justice'. The justices who examined Redferne's 'reviling and malicious speeches' thought 'his disesteem of the great God of heaven caused him to slight so great a majesty as our gracious sovereign' (TNA: PRO SP 16/258/50, SP 16/260/10; PC 2/43, 443).
73. TNA: PRO SP 16/262/16. For more on Noah Rogers, see below pp. 180–1 and note 222.
74. TNA: PRO SP 16/294/68, 297/11, 12.
75. TNA: PRO SP 16/272/18, 19.
76. TNA: PRO SP 16/293/97, SP 16/296/45.
77. TNA: PRO PC 2/44, 136, PC 2/45, 121, PC 2/45, 401.
78. Bodleian Library, MS Bankes 43/35, fo. 76; CSPD 1635–6, 253, 260; CSPD 1637–8, 124.
79. TNA: PRO SP 16/317/6.
80. TNA: PRO SP 16/326/75, SP 16/536/79.
81. Bodleian Library, MS Bankes 41/53, fo. 99; TNA: PRO SP 16/426/41.
82. TNA: PRO SP 16/248/60.
83. Bodleian Library, MS Bankes 41/54, fo. 100.
84. TNA: PRO SP 16/318/76.
85. Essex Record Office, T/A 418/117/70, T/A 418/117/79, 80, transcript of ASSI 35/81/1/10, ASSI 35/81/1/79, 80.
86. Bodleian Library, MS Bankes 18/7, fo. 12; MS Bankes 18/25; MS Bankes 43/36.
87. Bodleian Library, MS Bankes 18/28.
88. TNA: PRO PC 2/48, fo. 88^v.
89. TNA: PRO SP 16/369/25, SP 16/362/96.
90. TNA: PRO C 115/108, no. 8615; CSPD 1636–7, 560; CSPD 1637, 44–5, 106, 109–10, 176.
91. Bodleian Library, MS Bankes 42/57, 58; TNA: PRO PC 2/48, fos. 251, 259^v–60.
92. TNA: PRO SP 16/385/37, 64, 76.
93. TNA: PRO SP 16/389/64; PC 2/49, fo. 84; Lambeth Palace Library, Bramston Papers, MS 3391, fo. 37.
94. Bodleian Library, MS Bankes 42/65, fo. 137; TNA: PRO SP 16/395/40.
95. Bodleian Library, MS Bankes 18/3, 18/38, 58/1–2; British Library, Add. MS 11045, fos. 3v–4; TNA: PRO SP 16/397/26–8, SP 16/427/115, SP 16/439/18.
96. Bodleian Library, MS Bankes 13/13, fo. 20; MS Bankes 37/57, fo. 118.
97. TNA: PRO PC 2/49, fo. 119.
98. British Library, Add. MS 11045, fo. 3.
99. Copnall (ed.), Nottinghamshire County Records, 108.

100. Bodleian Library, MS Bankes 37/54, fo. 112; *CSPD 1638–1639*, 596. Not surprisingly, Glascocke claimed 'he was distempered and intoxicated with drink at that time', and sought pardon.

101. British Library, Add. MS 11045, fo. 7; *CSPD 1638–1639*, 523; TNA: PRO PC 2/50, fo. 67.

102. Bodleian Library, MS Bankes 18/1, 18/2.

103. *CSPD 1640*, 228.

104. Staffordshire RO, Q/SO/5. fo. 16; Q/SR/243, fos. 6–7, 11.

105. Bodleian Library, MS Bankes 18/8, fos. 13–14; MS Bankes, 18/10, fo. 17. The minister John Denison claimed not to have heard Warner's offending words, but noted that 'there was a falling out' between him and his accusers, Thomas and Margery Laward. Denison, however, was a lodger in Robert Warner's house, and perhaps had his own agenda (MS Bankes 18/9, fo. 15).

106. East Sussex Record Office, QR/E/56/18.

107. Essex Record Office, Quarter Sessions Rolls, Q/SR/314/130; Quarter Sessions Depositions, Q/SBa/2/44.

108. TNA: PRO Chester 24/126/1.

109. John Lister (ed.), *West Riding Records. Vol. II, Orders, 1611–1642. Indictments, 1637–1642* (Yorkshire Archaeological Society Record Series, 53, 1915), 367.

110. Jeaffreson (ed.), *Middlesex County Records. Vol. III*, 174.

111. Essex Record Office, D/Deb/16/1–4, Bramston Papers, certified copies from Glamorganshire Quarter Sessions.

112. TNA: PRO ASSI 45/1/4, Northern Circuit Depositions, nos. 55–8; James Raine (ed.), *Depositions from the Castle of York, Relating to Offences Committed in the Northern Counties in the Seventeenth Century* (Surtees Society, Durham, 40, 1861), 4–5.

113. TNA: PRO SP 16/318/55.

114. TNA: PRO PC 2/50, fos. 251^v, 253.

115. Thomas G. Barnes (ed.), *Somerset Assize Orders 1629–1640* (Somerset Record Society, 65, 1959), 47.

116. TNA: PRO SP 16/248/93, 250/58, 327/140, 372/109, etc., examples from Apr.–June 1639; *CSPD 1639*, 43–4, 260, 300; *CSPD 1640*, 474, 487.

117. Bodleian Library, MS Bankes 18/24, reporting remarks by Archie Armstrong in the White Lion at Westminster in March 1638.

118. TNA: PRO SP 16/361/117. This Mr Shepherd was 'a silenced minister' at Sion College, London.

119. *CSPD 1639*, 43, 260, 300; Bodleian Library, MS Bankes 18/1, 18/2.

120. British Library, Add. MS 11045, fo. 7: Sir Edward Powell in March 1639.

121. TNA: PRO SP 16/417/97.

122. Bodleian Library, MS Bankes 18/1, 18/2.

123. *The Works of . . . William Laud, D.D.*, ed. William Scott and James Bliss (7 vols., Oxford, 1847–60), iii. 210; Lambeth Palace Library, MS 943, 719. Another libel against Laud in 1629 described him as 'the fountain of

wickedness' (John Rushworth, *Historical Collections of Private Passages of State* (8 vols., 1680–1701), i. 662).

124. Lambeth Palace Library, MS 943, 717, 721.

125. [Lucy Hutchinson], *Memoirs of the Life of Colonel Hutchinson*, ed. Julius Hutchinson, rev. C. H. Firth (1906), 72.

126. British Library, Add. MS 11045, fo. 3.

127. TNA: PRO SP 16/140/44.

128. TNA: PRO SP 16/140/44.

129. TNA: PRO SP 16/152/82.

130. *Diary of John Rous*, ed. Green, 54.

131. See Chapters 8 and 9.

132. TNA: PRO SP 16/382/17.

133. Bodleian Library, MS Top. Oxon. C. 378, fo. 298. See also Margaret Grigg's criticism in 1640 of expenditures for the queen mother, Essex Record Office, D/Deb 94/20, papers of Sir John Bramston; Lambeth Palace Library, Bramston Papers, MS 3391, fos. 50, 52; PC 2/51, fo. 260v.

134. TNA: PRO PC 2/51, fos. 347^v, 356, 360^v, 361; Bodleian Library, MS Bankes 18/19.

135. TNA: PRO SP 16/392/61, SP 16/393/2. On the Petres, see William Hunt, *The Puritan Moment: The Coming of Revolution in an English County* (Cambridge, MA, 1983), 15, 27; Walter, *Understanding Popular Violence*, 48, 207, 222. I am grateful to James Kelly for discussion of the Petre family.

136. TNA: PRO SP 16/393/24.

137. British Library, MS Harley 1026, 'Memorandum Book of Justinian Pagit', fo. 45, Birch (ed.), *Court and Times*, ii. 225: Pagit to Dr Charles Twysden, 2 Feb. 1633; *CSPD 1633–34*, 480.

138. Lambeth Palace Library, Bramston Papers, MS 3391, fos. 39–41.

139. *CSPD 1640*, 193.

140. TNA: PRO SP 16 474/4.

141. Jeaffreson (ed.), *Middlesex County Records. Vol. III*, 74. Joan Worrall was included in the Middlesex gaol delivery in June 1641 'for scandalous words against his majesty' (Bodleian Library, MS John Johnson C. 1, fo. 5).

142. TNA: PRO PC 2/51, fos. 347^v, 356, 360^v, 361; Bodleian Library, MS Bankes 18/19.

143. TNA: PRO ASSI 45/1/3, Northern Circuit Depositions, no. 47; Raine (ed.), *Depositions from the Castle of York*, 3–4.

144. J. S. Cockburn (ed.), *Calendar of Assize Records: Kent Indictments. Charles I* (1995), 424.

145. Jeaffreson (ed.), *Middlesex County Records. Vol. III*, 81.

146. Lambeth Palace Library, Bramston Papers, MS 3391, fo. 72.

147. Lambeth Palace Library, Bramston Papers, MS 3391, fos. 74, 80. The offending words were spoken by Enoch Grey at St Ethelburgh's 'about a

fortnight before Easter' 1641. Manasseh was a Jewish king who reinstituted paganism.

148. Lambeth Palace Library, Bramston Papers, MS 3391, fo. 78. The speaker was Henry Pryme on 4 Jan. 1642, the day of the king's failed coup at Westminster.

149. Devon Record Office, Exeter Quarter Sessions Order Book, no. 64, fo. 6ᵛ.

150. Birch (ed.), *Court and Times*, i. 58; TNA: PRO SP 16/11/42.

151. Richard Johnson, *The Baronetage of England* (3 vols., 1771), i. 34; G. E. Cockayne (ed.), *Complete Baronetage* (6 vols., Exeter, 1800–1909), i. 22; William Farrer and J. Brownbill (eds.), *The Victoria History of the County of Lancaster*, iv (1911), 144–5. Gerard was born *c*.1584, succeeded to the baronetcy in 1621, served as MP for Liverpool 1624–5, and died *c*.1630. His daughter Frances became a nun at Gravelines.

152. Bridgeman correspondence, Staffordshire Record Office, D1287/18/2/18, 20. Lord Keeper Williams had twice warned Bridgeman not to proceed against Gerard without his express approval.

153. TNA: PRO SP 16/7/69, SP 16/9/31; *CSPD 1625–1626*, 115.

154. TNA: PRO SP 16/7/69, SP 16/10/42.

155. *Acts of the Privy Council 1625–1626*, 202–3, 205, 206; Bridgeman correspondence, Staffordshire Record Office, D1287/18/2/28.

156. Birch (ed.), *Court and Times*, i. 58.

157. Birch (ed.), *Court and Times*, i. 58.

158. *Acts of the Privy Council 1625–1626*, 247; TNA: PRO SP 16/10/42.

159. *Acts of the Privy Council 1625–1626*, 247, 263.

160. TNA: PRO SP 16/11/42.

161. *Acts of the Privy Council 1625–1626*, 349–50; TNA: PRO SP 16/12/8.

162. TNA: PRO SP 16/31/54, SP 16/32/37; Bridgeman correspondence, Staffordshire Record Office, D1287/18/2/28.

163. TNA: PRO SO 3/9, not foliated; *CSPD 1627–1628*, 590; Huntington Library, Hastings MS, HA 3434, 3437.

164. TNA: PRO SP 16/39/35. As an agent for Elizabeth of Bohemia, Nethersole would have particular interest in such predictions.

165. *Acts of the Privy Council 1626, June–Dec.* (1938), 348, 350.

166. TNA: PRO SP 16/29/40.

167. TNA: PRO SP 16/29/41.

168. TNA: PRO SP 16/52/57.

169. Birch (ed.), *Court and Times*, i. 167–8.

170. Historical Manuscripts Commission, *12th Report: The Manuscripts of the Earl Cowper, K.G., Preserved at Melbourne Hall, Derbyshire* (3 vols., 1888–9), i. 296; TNA: PRO SP 16/55/67.

171. Historical Manuscripts Commission, *Manuscripts of the Earl Cowper*, i. 282, 319.

172. *Diary of John Rous*, ed. Green, 12.

173. *Diary of John Rous*, ed. Green, 19.

174. TNA: PRO SP 16/105/67.

175. TNA: PRO PC 2/41, 346–7, 349.

176. *The Godly End, and wofull lamentation of one Iohn Stevens, a youth, that was hang'd, drawne, and quartered for High-Treason, at Salisbury in Wilshire, upon Thursday being the seventh day of March last 1632, with the setting up of his quarters on the City gates. To the tune of Fortune my foe* (1633).

177. TNA: PRO SP 16/231/65, SP 16/534/4.

178. Details of Crohagan's case are found in *Reports of Sir George Croke*, 242; British Library, Harley MS 1026, fos. 47ᵛ–48; *William Whiteway of Dorchester His Diary 1618 to 1635* (Dorset Record Society, 12, Dorchester, 1991), 135; *Diary of John Rous*, ed. Green, 5–6; TNA: PRO C 115/105, no. 8212; Bodleian Library, MS Rawlinson D. 392, 362.

179. Thomas S. Flynn, *The Irish Dominicans 1536–1641* (Dublin, 1993), 119–20; Martin J. Havran, *The Catholics in Caroline England* (Stanford, 1962), 114. I am grateful to James Lenaghan, OP, for discussion of this case.

180. Gerald Aylmer, *Rebellion or Revolution? England 1640–1660* (Oxford, 1986), 7; Kevin Sharpe, *The Personal Rule of Charles I* (1992), 930; Ian Gentles, *The English Revolution and the Wars in the Three Kingdoms, 1638–1652* (Harlow, 2007), 71.

181. Bodleian Library, MS Bankes 19/4, fos. 6–7.

182. Birch (ed.), *Court and Times*, ii. 250; *Winthrop Papers*, iii. *1631–1637* (Massachusetts Historical Society, Boston, 1943), 355–6.

183. Essex Record Office, T/A 418/117/9, 79, 80, transcript of ASSI 35/81/1/9, 80.

184. TNA: PRO SP 16/387/64.

185. Moore's case can be reconstructed from *CSPD 1638–39*, 167, 321, 360–1; TNA: PRO SP 16/404/64, 409/102, 410/6, 7; University of Birmingham, Calendar of the Court of Chivalry, 1634–1640, no. 405, Mansergh v. Moore.

186. TNA: PRO SP 16/441/36, SP 16/441/55.

187. TNA: PRO ASSI 45/1/3, Northern Circuit Depositions, no. 47; Raine (ed.), *Depositions from the Castle of York*, 3–4. The Scot Alexander Leslie, of course, had no claim to any British throne.

188. London Metropolitan Archives, MJ/SBB/15, fo. 34.

189. Peter Heylyn, *Examen Historicum* (1659), 131.

190. TNA: PRO SP 16/263/65.

191. Birch (ed.), *Court and Times*, ii. 250: Edward Rossingham to Sir Thomas Puckering.

192. Bodleian Library, MS Bankes 18/34.

193. TNA: PRO PC 2/48, fo. 88ᵛ.

194. TNA: PRO SP 16/440/78, 79.

195. Thomas Hurste, *The Descent of Authoritie: or, The Magistrates Patent from Heaven* (1637), 19.
196. TNA: PRO PC 2/43, 247.
197. TNA: PRO SP 16/284/24; PC 2/44, 465.
198. TNA: PRO SP 16/367/73.
199. *CSPD 1637–1638*, 140.
200. TNA: PRO SP 15/42/76, 77, SP 14/120/13, SP 14/130/127, SP 16/278/65.
201. David Cressy, *Coming Over: Migration and Communication between England and New England in the Seventeenth Century* (Cambridge, 1987), 65, 134, 140, 152, 154; John Camden Hotten (ed.), *Original Lists of Persons of Quality . . . Who Went from Great Britain to the American Plantations, 1600–1700* (1874; repr. Baltimore, 1974), 289–92.
202. TNA: PRO SP 16/289/46.
203. *CSPD 1637–1638*, 140; TNA: PRO PC 2/48, fo. 251.
204. TNA: PRO SP 16/119/42; Birch (ed.), *Court and Times*, i. 439: John Pory to Joseph Mead, 28 Nov. 1628; *Barrington Family Letters*, ed. Searle, 51; Bodleian Library, MS Rawlinson D. 821, fo. 4ᵛ, papers of Peter Smart.
205. TNA: PRO SP 16 /121/33.
206. British Library, Add. MS 38,490, 12; Bodleian Library, Oxford, Tanner MS 65, fo. 223.
207. Birch (ed.), *Court and Times*, i. 335: Mead to Stuteville, 29 Mar. 1628; TNA: PRO SP 16/147/15, 35, 42; SP 16/150/92, 93; John Cosin, *A Collection of Private Devotions* (3 editions in 1627); Peter Smart, *The Vanitie and Downe-fall of Superstitious Popish Ceremonies* (Edinburgh, 1628).
208. Letters and reports concerning Williams are collected and copied in Bodleian Library, MS Cherry 2.
209. TNA: PRO SP 16/221/41.
210. TNA: PRO C 115/108, no. 8616.
211. Samuel Rawson Gardiner (ed.), *Reports of Cases in the Courts of Star Chamber and High Commission* (Camden Society, 1886), 89, 91–2.
212. Andy Wood, *The Politics of Social Conflict: The Peak Country, 1520–1770* (Cambridge, 1999), 184, 186, 219–226, quotation at 225. See also Jill R. Dias, 'Lead, Society and Politics in Derbyshire before the Civil War', *Midland History*, 6 (1981), 39–57; Gardiner (ed.), *Reports of Cases*, 89–91, 94, 106.
213. Gardiner (ed.), *Reports of Cases*, 99, 101, 102, 103, 107.
214. Gardiner (ed.), *Reports of Cases*, 100.
215. Gardiner (ed.), *Reports of Cases*, 108; *Theeves, Theeves: or, a relation of Sir John Gell's proceedings in Darbyshire* (Oxford, 1643), 7. 'Some things well charged against him in the bill were but weakly proved, and other things well proved were weakly charged,' observed John Pory of Carrier's case in Star Chamber (TNA: PRO C 115/106, no. 8391).

216. TNA: PRO SP 16/190/45. For more on the Forest of Dean riots, see TNA: PRO SP 16/188/20, SP 16/195/5, SP 16/215/5; Buchanan Sharp, *In Contempt of All Authority: Rural Artisans and Riot in the West of England, 1586–1660* (Berkeley, 1980).

217. TNA: PRO SP 16/197/33, 34; SP 16/198/17.

218. TNA: PRO C 115/106, nos. 8414, 8415.

219. British Library, Harley MS 1026, 'Memorandum Book of Justinian Pagitt', fo. 45; Birch (ed.), *Court and Times*, ii. 225.

220. *CSPD 1633–34*, 480. Vicar since 1618, Preston was in trouble again in 1640 for naming his hogs after leading members of parliament.

221. TNA: PRO SP 16/324, fo. 13.

222. TNA: PRO SP 16/262/16, SP 16/262/67. Noah Rogers was scholar in 1609 and sophister in 1611 at Trinity College (George Dames Burtchaell and Thomas Ulick Sadleir (eds.), *Alumni Dublinenses . . . 1593–1860* (2nd edn., Dublin, 1935), 714). There is no trace of him in standard New England sources.

223. A. Percival Moore (ed.), 'The Metropolitical Visitation of Archdeacon [*sic*] Laud', in *Associated Architectural Societies Reports and Papers*, 29 (1907), 524–34; *CSPD 1637–1638*, 240; TNA: PRO SP 16/267/6.

224. Bodleian Library, MS Rawlinson C. 573, 28.

225. TNA: PRO SP 16/397/91.

226. TNA: PRO SP 16/267/6.

227. Lambeth Palace Library, Bramston Papers, MS 3391, fos. 39–41; British Library, Add. MS 11045, fo. 33.

228. Lambeth Palace Library, Bramston Papers, MS 3391, fos. 42–42ᵛ; *ODNB* sub Burroughs, Jeremiah. On Covenanter resistance theory, see John Morrill (ed.), *The Scottish National Covenant in its British Context, 1638–1651* (Edinburgh, 1990).

229. TNA: PRO PC 2/49, fo. 267ᵛ; Bodleian Library, MS Bankes 44, fo. 13.

230. Staffordshire Record Office, Bridgeman Correspondence, D1287/18/2/183.

231. *CSPD 1638–1639*, fos. 554–5; TNA: PRO SP 16/414/82; PC 2/50, fos. 73ᵛ, 74ᵛ.

232. British Library, Add. MS 11045, fo. 3.

233. Cheshire Record Office, Q JF 68/2, fos. 28–33. In a previous rant Girtam declared England 'full of treason', saying 'he alone stood for the king'. He was assigned to appear at the next assizes, but no further trace of him can be found.

234. Cockburn (ed.), *Calendar of Assize Records: Kent Indictments. Charles I*, 438.

235. Lambeth Palace Library, Bramston Papers, MS 3391, fos. 74, 80. See also Enoch Grey's narrative in his printed petition, *To the Supreame Authority of this Nation, the Commons of England in Parliament Assembled* (1649).

236. *CSPD 1628–1629*, 347; TNA: PRO SP 16/118/35, SP 16/118/56.

237. TNA: PRO SP 16/174/18.

238. TNA: PRO SP 16/174/41.

239. TNA: PRO SP 16/252/26, SP 16/260/60, SP 16/262/57.

240. TNA: PRO PC 2/44, 621; SP 16/290/18.

241. TNA: PRO SP 16/294/87, SP 16/293/117.

242. Bodleian Library, MS Bankes 37/37, fo. 80; TNA: PRO SP 16/391/85, SP 16/406/82.

243. Bodleian Library, MS Rawlinson B. 243, fo. 19, the Lord Keeper's speech, 14 June 1638.

244. Historical Manuscripts Commission, *Report on the Manuscripts of the Family of Gawdy* (1885), 168: William Davy to Framlingham Gawdy, 7 June 1638.

245. TNA: PRO SP 16/392/61.

246. Charles I, *Basilika. The Workes of King Charles the Martyr* (2 vols., 1662), i. 363.

247. *The Letters, Speeches and Proclamations of King Charles I*, ed. Charles Petrie (1935), 47.

248. William Laud, sermon before the king at Whitehall, 19 June 1625, in *Works*, i. 99, 107, 115.

249. Bodleian Library, MS Carte 1, fo. 89, 4 Apr. 1628.

250. *The Knyvett Letters (1620–1644)*, ed. Bertram Schofield (Norfolk Record Society, 1949), 103.

CHAPTER 8

1. Examples in Bodleian Library, MS Nalson 13.

2. Marchamont Nedham, *Certain Considerations Tendered in all Humility, to an Honorable Member of the Councell of State* (1649), 1, 12.

3. *Constitutions and Canons Ecclesiasticall . . . 1640* (1640), canon 1, sigs. B4, C, C^v.

4. John Swan, *Redde Debitum. Or, A Discourse in defence of three chiefe Fatherhoods* (1640), 7, 9, 21.

5. Henry King, *A Sermon Preached at St Pauls March 27.1640*, in *The Sermons of Henry King*, ed. Mary Hobbs (Cranbury, NJ, and Aldershot, 1992), 222.

6. Richard Gardyner, *A Sermon Appointed . . . on the Day of His Maiesties Happy Inauguration* (1642), 9.

7. Robert Mossom, *The King on his Throne: Or, A Discourse maintaining the Dignity of a King, the Duty of a Subject, and the unlawfulnesse of Rebellion* (York, 1642), 5, 39, 40.

8. *Gods Good Servant, and the Kings Good Subject* (1642), 6–8.

9. Bodleian Library, MS Nalson 13, fo. 208.

10. For example, William Sclater, *Papisto-Mastix, or Deborah's Prayer against God's Enemies* (1642), 39; Edward Reynolds, *Evgenia's Teares for great Brittaynes Distractions* (1642), 44; John Taylor, *A Plea for Prerogative: Or, Give Caesar his due* (1642), title page; *The Soveraignty of Kings* (1642).

11. Bodleian Library, MS Tanner 69, fo. 108: Elizabeth Felton to Sir John Hobart.

12. Richard Towgood, *Disloyalty of Language Questioned and Censured* (Bristol, 1643), 36–7, 43–4.

13. Towgood, *Disloyalty of Language*, 1–2, 5–9, 36, 43, 51.

14. David Jenkins in 1647, quoted in Janelle Greenberg, *The Radical Face of the Ancient Constitution* (Cambridge, 2001), 192.

15. Bodleian Library, MS Nalson 13, fo. 163.

16. 'You are not firm in your designs,' she charged him in Mar. 1642; in Oct. she urged him 'to continue in your constant resolution to die rather than to submit basely' (*Letters of Queen Henrietta Maria*, ed. Mary Anne Everett Green (1857), 56, 129).

17. *The Knyvett Letters (1620–1644)*, ed. Bertram Schofield (Norfolk Record Society, 1949), 103.

18. British Library, Add. MS 70,003, fos. 236–7. For the curses of Shimei, see 2 Samuel, 16: 5–13.

19. Bodleian Library, MS Tanner 63, fos. 66–7; Historical Manuscripts Commission, *Fifth Report*, pt. 1 (1876), 24; John Cordy Jeaffreson (ed.), *Middlesex County Records. Vol. III . . . 1 Charles I to 18 Charles II* (Clerkenwell, 1888), 179.

20. Vernon F. Snow and Anne Steele Young (eds.), *The Private Journals of the Long Parliament 2 June to 17 September 1642* (New Haven and London, 1992), 136–7.

21. Leicestershire Archives, BR II/18/22/176.

22. TNA: PRO Chester 24/126.4.

23. Bodleian Library, MS Nalson 13, fo. 303.

24. Jeaffreson (ed.), *Middlesex County Records. Vol. III*, 88.

25. *Journals of the House of Lords*, vol. 5, *1642–1643* (1802), 656; House of Lords Record Office, Main Papers, HL/PO/JO/10/1/145.

26. Jeaffreson (ed.), *Middlesex County Records. Vol. III*, 89.

27. Norfolk Record Office, C/S3/34.

28. *Journals of the House of Lords*, vol. 7, *1644* (1802), 175.

29. Jeaffreson (ed.), *Middlesex County Records. Vol. III*, 97.

30. TNA: PRO ASSI 45/1/5, nos. 15–18.

31. Jeaffreson (ed.), *Middlesex County Records. Vol. III*, 101.

32. Jeaffreson (ed.), *Middlesex County Records. Vol. III*, 103.

33. Jeaffreson (ed.), *Middlesex County Records. Vol. III*, 118.

34. Jeaffreson (ed.), *Middlesex County Records. Vol. III*, 93.

35. Jeaffreson (ed.), *Middlesex County Records. Vol. III*, 94.

36. Bodleian Library, MS Tanner 69, fo. 108.

37. Bodleian Library, MS Nalson 12, fo. 23; MS Nalson 13, fo. 194; Huntington Library, MSS El. 7802, El. 8879, El. 8880 for verse libels against John Pym. See also Lloyd Bowen, 'Seditious Speech and Popular Royalism, 1649–60', in

Jason McElligott and David Smith (eds.), *Royalists and Royalism during the Interregnum* (Manchester, 2009).

38. Bodleian Library, MS Nalson 2, fo. 161.

39. Jeaffreson (ed.), *Middlesex County Records. Vol. III*, 82, 84. In August 1642 a Middlesex jury found guilty Elizabeth Humphries, wife of a Whitechapel yeoman, for scandalous words against the parliament, and fined her forty nobles (£13 13s. 4d.).

40. *Englands Ioyalty, in Ioyful expressions, for the City of Londons safety* (1641/2), 2–5. Rabshakeh was the Assyrian who taunted the Hebrews of Hezekiah, 2 Kings 18: 19–37, Isaiah 36: 1–22.

41. Bodleian Library, MS Nalson 13, fos. 163–163ᵛ. Elliot claimed to have been a tutor to Prince Charles.

42. Bodleian Library, Tanner MS 63, fo. 83.

43. Bodleian Library, MS Tanner 63, fo. 67.

44. Bodleian Library, MS Nalson 13, fos. 197, 198.

45. Bodleian Library, MS Nalson 13, fo. 208.

46. Bodleian Library, MS Nalson 2, fos. 56, 87–90.

47. Bodleian Library, MS Nalson 13, fo. 215.

48. TNA: PRO Chester 24/126/3.

49. Bodleian Library, MS Tanner 63, fos. 142–142ᵛ, words of William Lord, reported 1 Sept. 1642.

50. Bodleian Library, MS Nalson 2, fos. 206–7.

51. Jeaffreson (ed.), *Middlesex County Records. Vol. III*, 90.

52. Jeaffreson (ed.), *Middlesex County Records. Vol. III*, 90, 178.

53. Norfolk Record Office, C/S3/34.

54. Jeaffreson (ed.), *Middlesex County Records. Vol. III*, 96. For more in this vein, see ibid., 92, 117, 123, 135.

55. Essex Record Office, Q/SBa 2/57–61.

56. Jeaffreson (ed.), *Middlesex County Records. Vol. III*, 98.

57. Ian Gentles, *The English Revolution and the Wars in the Three Kingdoms, 1638–1652* (Harlow, 2007), 131; TNA: PRO SP 24, *passim*.

58. C. H. Firth and R. S. Rait (eds.), *Acts and Ordinances of the Interregnum, 1642–1660* (3 vols., 1911), ii. 120–1, 193–4; Adele Hast, 'State Treason Trials during the Puritan Revolution, 1640–1660', *Historical Journal*, 15 (1972), 37–53.

59. Firth and Rait (eds.), *Acts and Ordinances of the Interregnum*, ii. 831–5, 844, 1038–42.

60. *A Collection of State Papers of John Thurloe*, ed. Thomas Birch (7 vols., 1742), iii. 398.

61. Firth and Rait (eds.), *Acts and Ordinances of the Interregnum*, ii. 397–402.

62. B. C. Redwood (ed.), *Quarter Sessions Order Book, 1642–1649* (Sussex Record Society, 54, 1954), 175: the case of Mr William Hippesley of Hurstpeirpoint, Sussex, in Apr. 1649.

63. James Raine (ed.), *Depositions from the Castle of York, Relating to Offences Committed in the Northern Counties in the Seventeenth Century* (Surtees Society, Durham, 40, 1861), 24.

64. TNA: PRO ASSI 45/3/2, no. 102; Raine (ed.), *Depositions from the Castle of York*, 25.

65. TNA: PRO ASSI 45/3/2, no. 165; Raine (ed.), *Depositions from the Castle of York*, 25–6.

66. TNA: PRO ASSI 45/4/1, no. 190; Raine (ed.), *Depositions from the Castle of York*, 46.

67. Raine (ed.), *Depositions from the Castle of York*, 50.

68. TNA: PRO ASSI 45/5/5, fos. 73–6; Raine (ed.), *Depositions from the Castle of York*, 55, 53n.

69. TNA: PRO SP 24/59.

70. TNA: PRO ASSI 45/4/3, nos. 98, 99.

71. Jeaffreson (ed.), *Middlesex County Records. Vol. III*, 194, 195, 207–8, 212, 250; TNA: PRO ASSI 45, *passim*.

72. TNA: PRO ASSI 45/5.5, fo. 27.

73. Jeaffreson (ed.), *Middlesex County Records. Vol. III*, 192, 284.

74. Jeaffreson (ed.), *Middlesex County Records. Vol. III*, 195.

75. TNA: PRO ASSI 45/3/2, no. 98.

76. Raine (ed.), *Depositions from the Castle of York*, 39.

77. Jeaffreson (ed.), *Middlesex County Records. Vol. III*, 203.

78. TNA: PRO ASSI 45/4/1, no. 189; Raine (ed.), *Depositions from the Castle of York*, 48.

79. Raine (ed.), *Depositions from the Castle of York*, 53.

80. *State Papers of John Thurloe*, ed. Birch, i. 591.

81. *State Papers of John Thurloe*, ed. Birch, iii. 169.

82. *State Papers of John Thurloe*, ed. Birch, ii. 128–9.

83. *State Papers of John Thurloe*, ed. Birch, ii. 129.

84. TNA: PRO ASSI 45/5/1, fos. 72, 79.

85. *State Papers of John Thurloe*, ed. Birch, ii. 382–4.

86. TNA: PRO ASSI 45/5/1, fo. 120; Raine (ed.), *Depositions from the Castle of York*, 67. Meaning punishment in store, the phrase refers to the soaking of birch rods in urine to strengthen them for beating children or malefactors.

87. Raine (ed.), *Depositions from the Castle of York*, 72–3, 80n.

88. TNA: PRO ASSI 45/5/2, no. 57.

89. Jeaffreson (ed.), *Middlesex County Records. Vol. III*, 259, 264, 268, 271, 272, 274.

90. *State Papers of John Thurloe*, ed. Birch, iv. 55.

91. Bodleian Library, MS Rawlinson A. 26, fo. 431.

92. TNA: PRO ASSI 45/5/4, no. 7, ASSI 45/5/, fo. 6; Raine (ed.), *Depositions from the Castle of York*, 73–4. Browne is variously described as a labourer and a yeoman.

93. J. S. Cockburn (ed.), *Calendar of Assize Records. Kent Indictments 1649–1659* (1989), 281.
94. Cockburn (ed.), *Calendar of Assize Records. Kent Indictments 1649–1659*, 242.
95. Jeaffreson (ed.), *Middlesex County Records. Vol. III*, 252.
96. Jeaffreson (ed.), *Middlesex County Records. Vol. III*, 259.
97. Jeaffreson (ed.), *Middlesex County Records. Vol. III*, 272,
98. Raine (ed.), *Depositions from the Castle of York*, 80.
99. Jeaffreson (ed.), *Middlesex County Records. Vol. III*, 274, 276.
100. Historical Manuscripts Commission, *Fifth Report*, app., 146.

CHAPTER 9

1. James Raine (ed.), *Depositions from the Castle of York, Relating to Offences Committed in the Northern Counties in the Seventeenth Century* (Surtees Society, Durham, 40, 1861), 94, 95.
2. John Cordy Jeaffreson (ed.), *Middlesex County Records. Vol. III . . . 1 Charles I to 18 Charles II* (Clerkenwell, 1888), 304, 305, 306, 314, and *passim*. The essential studies are Buchanan Sharp, 'Popular Political Opinion in England, 1660–1685', *History of European Ideas*, 10 (1989), 13–29, and Tim Harris, ' "There is None that Loves him but Drunk Whores and Whoremongers": Popular Criticisms of the Restoration Court', in Julia Marciari Alexander and Catherine Macleod (eds.), *Politics, Transgression, and Representation at the Court of Charles II* (New Haven, 2008), 33–56. Recent scholarship on Restoration political culture includes Tim Harris, *Restoration: Charles II and his Kingdoms, 1660–1685* (2005), and Grant Tapsell, *The Personal Rule of Charles II 1681–85* (Woodbridge, 2007).
3. My calculation from the admittedly incomplete Jeaffreson (ed.), *Middlesex County Records. Vol. III*, and John Cordy Jeaffreson (ed.), *Middlesex County Records. Vol. IV. Indictments, Recognizances . . . 19 Charles II to 4 James II* (Clerkenwell, 1892).
4. Sharp, 'Popular Political Opinion in England 1660–1685', 14. Indictments offer less precise identification of status than recognizances, for which see T. J. G. Harris, 'Politics of the London Crowd in the Reign of Charles II', Cambridge University Ph.D. thesis, 1984, app. one, where 152 'Whig' speakers of seditious words include 23 gentlemen, 14 professionals, 45 retailers, 49 artisans, and 21 labourers.
5. Historical Manuscripts Commission, *Fifth Report* (1876), 150.
6. *Journal of the House of Commons*, viii. *1660–1667* (1802), 36, 40.
7. *Journal of the House of Lords*, xi. *1660–1667* (1832), 26, 29, 30, 45–6.
8. Raine (ed.), *Depositions from the Castle of York*, 84.
9. Jeaffreson (ed.), *Middlesex County Records. Vol. III*, 316.
10. Jeaffreson (ed.), *Middlesex County Records. Vol. III*, 304.
11. Sharp, 'Popular Political Opinion in England 1660–1685', 16.

12. J. S. Cockburn (ed.), *Calendar of Assize Records. Kent Indictments. Charles II 1676–1688* (1997), 153; Jeaffreson (ed.), *Middlesex County Records. Vol. IV*, 2; *CSPD 1677–1678*, 634; *CSPD 1678*, 27; *CSPD Jan.–June 1683*, 279, 280, 303; *CSPD July–Sept. 1683*, 364; *CSPD 1684–1685*, 228.

13. Jeaffreson (ed.), *Middlesex County Records. Vol. III*, 304.

14. Raine (ed.), *Depositions from the Castle of York*, 86–7. Hodgson had been involved in the alleged Sowerby plot of 1660 to kill the newly returned king (Richard L. Greaves, *Deliver Us from Evil: The Radical Underground in Britain, 1660–1663* (Oxford and New York, 1986), 30–1).

15. Jeaffreson (ed.), *Middlesex County Records. Vol. III*, 308.

16. Raine (ed.), *Depositions from the Castle of York*, 83; TNA: PRO SP 29/7/145.

17. TNA PRO: ASSI 45/5/7, fos. 17, 24.

18. Raine (ed.), *Depositions from the Castle of York*, 83.

19. TNA PRO: ASSI 45/5/7, fo. 81.

20. Jeaffreson (ed.), *Middlesex County Records. Vol. III*, 303.

21. Jeaffreson (ed.), *Middlesex County Records. Vol. III*, 304.

22. Jeaffreson (ed.), *Middlesex County Records. Vol. III*, 306.

23. Jeaffreson (ed.), *Middlesex County Records. Vol. III*, 305–6.

24. Jeaffreson (ed.), *Middlesex County Records. Vol. III*, 305.

25. Raine (ed.), *Depositions from the Castle of York*, 85.

26. Jeaffreson (ed.), *Middlesex County Records. Vol. III*, 311.

27. Essex Record Office, Q/SR 392/52.

28. Jeaffreson (ed.), *Middlesex County Records. Vol. III*, 327.

29. Historical Manuscripts Commission, *Fifth Report* (1876), 150, 154.

30. J. S. Cockburn (ed.), *Calendar of Assize Records. Kent Indictments. Charles II 1660–1675* (1995), 23–4.

31. Raine (ed.), *Depositions from the Castle of York*, 84, 94.

32. Jeaffreson (ed.), *Middlesex County Records. Vol. III*, 309–10.

33. Raine (ed.), *Depositions from the Castle of York*, 93n.

34. Jeaffreson (ed.), *Middlesex County Records. Vol. III*, 304.

35. *CSPD 1675–1676*, 547.

36. *CSPD 1678*, 256, 605.

37. Raine (ed.), *Depositions from the Castle of York*, 176; *CSPD 1670*, 214–15.

38. Raine (ed.), *Depositions from the Castle of York*, 99, 144.

39. Historical Manuscripts Commission, *Fifth Report*, 174.

40. *CSPD 1670, with Addenda, 1660 to 1670*, 683.

41. 'An act for safety and preservation of his majesties person and government against treasonable and seditious practices and attempts' (13 Charles II. c. 1, 1661).

42. *The Proceedings at the Sessions House...Against Anthony Earl of Shaftsbury* (1681), 3–5, 33; *A Complete Collection of State-Trials* (6 vols., 1730), iii. 415.

43. *The Speech and Declaration of John James* (1661); *The True and Perfect Speech of John James, a Baptist, and Firth-Monarchy-Man* (1661); *A Narrative of the*

Apprehending, Committment, Arraignment, Condemnation, and Execution of John James (1662); 'The Trial of John James, at the King's Bench, for High-Treason', in 'A Barrister at Law', *Legal Recreations, or Popular Amusements in the Laws of England* (2 vols., 1792), i. 245–60, which misdates it to 1662; T. B. Howell and T. J. Howell (eds.), *A Complete Collection of State Trials* (33 vols., 1809–28), vi. 67–104.

44. Rex v. Alicock, *The English Reports*: (1793), 1 Lev 57/ 83 ER 295. The statute of 13 Car. II c. 1 was also invoked in Rex v. Field, Field having preached that the Church of England was popish and superstitious, and that God would demand of all who obeyed it, 'who required this at your hands?' (*English Reports*: (1685), 1 Keb 209/ 98 ER 914).

45. *CSPD 1678*, 377, 380, 410, 570; *Journal of the House of Commons*, viii. 1667–1687, 517.

46. Jeaffreson (ed.), *Middlesex County Records. Vol. III*, 304, 305, 306, 314; *CSPD Jan.–June 1683*, 3, 181; *The Proceedings of the Old Bailey, 1674–1913* (www.oldbaileyonline.org), trial of Phillip Wallis, 10 Dec. 1684.

47. *CSPD 1682*, 292, 506, 575–7, the case of Ferdinando Gorges.

48. Jeaffreson (ed.), *Middlesex County Records. Vol. IV*, 227.

49. Clarendon to Charles II, quoted in Brian Cowan, *The Social Life of Coffee: The Emergence of the British Coffeehouse* (New Haven and London, 2005), 194.

50. Cowan, *Social Life of Coffee*, 195–8, 200–3, 208; *CSPD 1675–1676*, 465; *CSPD 1678*, 295. On the Parisian 'mouches', see Arlette Farge, *Subversive Words: Public Opinion in Eighteenth-Century France* (University Park, PA, 1995), 137, 167; G. A. Kelly, 'From Lèse-Majesté to Lèse-Nation: Treason in Eighteenth-Century France', *Journal of the History of Ideas*, 42 (1981), 269–86.

51. Steven Pincus, ' "Coffee politicians does create" : Coffeehouses and Restoration Political Culture', *Journal of Modern History*, 67 (1995), 807–34; Cowan, *Social Life of Coffee*.

52. Jeaffreson (ed.), *Middlesex County Records. Vol. III*, 306, 310, 316, 335, 339.

53. Raine (ed.), *Depositions from the Castle of York*, 88n.

54. Jeaffreson (ed.), *Middlesex County Records. Vol. III*, 327.

55. Jeaffreson (ed.), *Middlesex County Records. Vol. III*, 335, *Vol. IV*, 268–9.

56. Raine (ed.), *Depositions from the Castle of York*, 101. For similar indictments in 1663, see S. C. Ratcliff and H. C. Johnson (eds.), *Warwick County Records Volume VI. Quarter Sessions Indictment Book Easter, 1631, to Epiphany, 1674* (Warwick, 1941), 149.

57. Raine (ed.), *Depositions from the Castle of York*, 116.

58. Jeaffreson (ed.), *Middlesex County Records. Vol. III*, 338.

59. Jeaffreson (ed.), *Middlesex County Records. Vol. III*, 339.

60. Raine (ed.), *Depositions from the Castle of York*, 158n. Mayling was acquitted.

61. Jeaffreson (ed.), *Middlesex County Records. Vol. IV*, 2. Northit's case came to the Middlesex sessions in June 1667, when a jury found him 'not guilty'.

62. Raine (ed.), *Depositions from the Castle of York*, 176; *CSPD 1670*, 214–15. John Browne, the alleged speaker of these sedititious words, was acquitted at the York assizes and bound over to keep the peace.

63. *CSPD 1671*, 190.

64. Jeaffreson (ed.), *Middlesex County Records. Vol. IV*, 26.

65. TNA PRO: ADM 106/283, fos. 209–10.

66. Jeaffreson (ed.), *Middlesex County Records. Vol. IV*, 48.

67. *CSPD 1676–1677*, 308; *CSPD Jan.–June 1683*, 13, 22; *CSPD July–Sept. 1683*, 42.

68. Cockburn (ed.), *Calendar of Assize Records. Kent Indictments. Charles II 1676–1688*, 36; *CSPD 1682*, 15.

69. Cockburn (ed.), *Calendar of Assize Records. Kent Indictments. Charles II 1676–1688*, 23.

70. Jeaffreson (ed.), *Middlesex County Records. Vol. IV*, 75. Said to be 'diabolically affected' to his majesty, Morris was found 'not guilty' in January 1677.

71. Jeaffreson (ed.), *Middlesex County Records. Vol. IV*, 77.

72. Cockburn (ed.), *Calendar of Assize Records. Kent Indictments. Charles II 1676–1688*, 81.

73. *CSPD July–Sept. 1683*, 430–1.

74. Cockburn (ed.), *Calendar of Assize Records. Kent Indictments. Charles II 1676–1688*, 157; Jeaffreson (ed.), *Middlesex County Records. Vol. IV*, 162.

75. Jeaffreson (ed.), *Middlesex County Records. Vol. IV*, 54.

76. Jeaffreson (ed.), *Middlesex County Records. Vol. IV*, 47.

77. *CSPD 1675–1676*, 142.

78. *CSPD 1675–1676*, 432, 437.

79. *CSPD 1678*, 295.

80. Sharp, 'Popular Political Opinion in England 1660–1685', 17, 19.

81. *CSPD July–Sept. 1683*, 430–1.

82. *CSPD 1682*, 549; *CSPD Jan.–June 1683*, 77, 252, 262, 273.

83. Cockburn (ed.), *Calendar of Assize Records. Kent Indictments. Charles II 1660–1675*, 56.

84. Raine (ed.), *Depositions from the Castle of York*, 98, 101.

85. Raine (ed.), *Depositions from the Castle of York*, 118.

86. Cockburn (ed.), *Calendar of Assize Records. Kent Indictments. Charles II 1660–1675*, 119. Bromley was acquitted in 1664.

87. Richard L. Greaves, *Enemies under his Feet: Radicals and Nonconformists in Britain, 1664–1677* (Stanford, 1990); Gary De Krey, *London and the Restoration, 1659–1683* (Cambridge, 2005).

88. Raine (ed.), *Depositions from the Castle of York*, 116n.

89. Raine (ed.), *Depositions from the Castle of York*, 130.

90. Raine (ed.), *Depositions from the Castle of York*, 83n.

91. Jeaffreson (ed.), *Middlesex County Records. Vol. III*, 339.

92. Raine (ed.), *Depositions from the Castle of York*, 134n.

93. Cockburn (ed.), *Calendar of Assize Records. Kent Indictments. Charles II 1660–1675*, 176.

94. Jeaffreson (ed.), *Middlesex County Records. Vol. IV*, 4.

95. Ratcliff and Johnson (eds.), *Warwick County Records Volume VI*, 177.

96. Cockburn (ed.), *Calendar of Assize Records. Kent Indictments. Charles II 1660–1675*, 290.

97. *CSPD 1672*, 72.

98. *CSPD 1672–1673*, 453.

99. Raine (ed.), *Depositions from the Castle of York*, 238.

100. Jeaffreson (ed.), *Middlesex County Records. Vol. IV*, 78; *CSPD 1680–1681*, 151; *CSPD 1682*, 43; *CSPD July–Sept. 1683*, 81.

101. *CSPD 1682*, 292, 506, 575–7.

102. Jeaffreson (ed.), *Middlesex County Records. Vol. IV*, 263.

103. Cockburn (ed.), *Calendar of Assize Records. Kent Indictments. Charles II 1660–1675*, 11.

104. Raine (ed.), *Depositions from the Castle of York*, 126, 134, 147, 267.

105. Sharp, 'Popular Political Opinion in England 1660–1685', 17.

106. *CSPD 1671*, 190.

107. *CSPD 1675–1676*, 142.

108. *CSPD 1677–1678*, 369, 407.

109. Jeaffreson (ed.), *Middlesex County Records. Vol. IV*, 78.

110. For healths to the Duke of York, *CSPD1673–1675*, 95–6, 100; *CSPD Jan.–June 1683*, 3, 181; *Proceedings of the Old Bailey*, trial of Phillip Wallis, Dec. 1684. For healths to Monmouth, *CSPD Jan.–June 1683*, 3, 181; *CSPD July–Sept. 1683*, 218. When Bartholomew Taylor raised his cup of ale in Dec. 1678 to offer a health to King Charles II, his drinking companion, William Shaw, labourer, responded: 'God damn him! I will not pledge him.' Shaw, a Catholic, was arraigned at the Middlesex sessions for 'this extremely shocking speech', and was fined £16 13*s*. and sent to Newgate until the fine was paid (Jeaffreson (ed.), *Middlesex County Records. Vol. IV*, 100).

111. *CSPD 1675–1676*, 464, 466.

112. *CSPD 1678*, 449.

113. *The Tryal of William Stayley, Goldsmith; For Speaking Treasonable Words Against his Most Sacred Majesty* (1678), 4–8, 10–11; *Treason Justly Punished: Or, A Full Relation of the Condemnation, and Execution of Mr William Staley* (1678), broadsheet; *Complete Collection of State-Trials*, ii. 652–6. The diarist Roger Morrice recorded on 15 Nov. 1678 that Stayley, 'a young man that had travelled much beyond sea, and lives in Covent Garden, is apprehended and committed for speaking very desperate and horrid words against the king' (*The Entering Book of Roger Morrice*, ed. Mark Goldie et al. (6 vols., Woodbridge, 2007), ii. 80).

114. *Proceedings at the Sessions House . . . Against Anthony Earl of Shaftsbury*, 9, 11, 25, 27, 29, 43; *Complete Collection of State-Trials*, iii. 414–37. See also *An*

Account at Large, of the Proceedings at the Sessions-House in the Old-Bayly, on the 24 of November 1681 (1681), 1–8.

115. *Proceedings at the Sessions House . . . Against Anthony Earl of Shaftsbury,* and various shorter printed summaries. For an example of the pressure on witnesses to provide incriminating testimony, see *The Information of Capt. Hen. Wilkinson, of What hath passed betwixt him and some other Persons, who have attempted to prevail with him to Swear High Treason against the Earl of Shaftesbury* (1681). For the diarist, see *Entering Book of Roger Morrice,* ed. Goldie et al., ii. 292. On Shaftesbury's acquittal, Morrice reports: 'the shout was very great and of long continuance, and very many bonfires made that night, it is said eighty between Aldersgate and Stocks market' (ibid. 294).

116. *CSPD 1682,* 528–30.

117. Jeaffreson (ed.), *Middlesex County Records. Vol. IV,* 152.

118. Jeaffreson (ed.), *Middlesex County Records. Vol. IV,* 153.

119. *CSPD Jan.–June 1683,* 338. The truth of this report was undermined when it emerged that £600 was in dispute between Hugh Speke and his principal accuser, Robert Gargrave.

120. Cockburn (ed.), *Calendar of Assize Records. Kent Indictments. Charles II 1676–1688,* 190.

121. Jeaffreson (ed.), *Middlesex County Records. Vol. IV,* 201. He was fined £6 3s. 4d. in Feb. 1683.

122. *CSPD 1682,* 15.

123. Jeaffreson (ed.), *Middlesex County Records. Vol. IV,* 162; *CSPD 1682,* 326.

124. *CSPD 1680–1681,* 151.

125. *CSPD July–Sept. 1683,* 81.

126. *CSPD 1682,* 201, 203, 359.

127. *CSPD 1682,* 327.

128. *CSPD 1682,* 358.

129. *CSPD 1682,* 549; *CSPD Jan.–June 1683,* 77, 252, 262, 273.

130. *CSPD Jan.–June 1683,* 276–7.

131. *CSPD July–Sept. 1683,* 42.

132. *CSPD July–Sept. 1683,* 94, 91. This may be connected to Rex v. Baker in 1687, in which Baker was found guilty at a second trial for speaking seditious words, *English Reports:* (1741) Carth 6/90 ER 609.

133. William Clifford, *The Power of Kings, Particularly the British Monarchy Asserted and Vindicated* (1682), 1, 18.

134. John Burrell, *The Divine Right of Kings, Proved from the Principles of the Church of England* (Cambridge, 1683), 11.

135. Paul Lathom, *The Power of Kings from God* (1683), 2, 14, 36, 38.

136. Cockburn (ed.), *Calendar of Assize Records. Kent Indictments. Charles II 1676–1688,* 221. Cf. the statement of the London vintner Francis White in 1674, 'that he cared not for a justice of the peace more than he valued a bog or a fart' (Jeaffreson (ed.), *Middlesex County Records. Vol. IV,* 54).

CHAPTER 10

1. David Cressy, *Literacy and the Social Order: Reading and Writing in Tudor and Stuart England* (Cambridge, 1980), 177, based on ability to sign signatures.

2. James Raine (ed.), *Depositions from the Castle of York, Relating to Offences Committed in the Northern Counties in the Seventeenth Century* (Surtees Society, Durham, 40, 1861), 265.

3. Buchanan Sharp, 'Popular Political Opinion in England, 1660–1685', *History of European Ideas*, 10 (1989), 22–4; John Cordy Jeaffreson (ed.), *Middlesex County Records. Vol. IV. Indictments, Recognizances . . . 19 Charles II to 4 James II* (Clerkenwell, 1892), 289–94; *The Proceedings of the Old Bailey, 1674–1913* (www.oldbaileyonline.org), trials of Phillip Wallis and John Ward, 10 Dec. 1684.

4. Thomas Crookhall was set in the stocks at Lytham, Lancashire, for speaking seditious words in 1687 (Lancashire Record Office, QSP/628/4).

5. *CSPD 1685*, 137–8. Mary of Modena had a series of stillborn and short-lived children, but no English queen died in 1685.

6. Worcestershire Record Office, Quarter Sessions, 1/1/185/6a-c. The claim that Charles II had been poisoned appeared in the Duke of Monmouth's rebellion manifesto.

7. Jeaffreson (ed.), *Middlesex County Records. Vol. IV*, 285–6.

8. *CSPD 1685*, 61.

9. Jeaffreson (ed.), *Middlesex County Records. Vol. IV*, 284.

10. *CSPD 1685*, 11, 30, 37.

11. J. S. Cockburn (ed.), *Calendar of Assize Records. Kent Indictments. Charles II 1676–1688* (1997), 237.

12. Raine (ed.), *Depositions from the Castle of York*, 283.

13. *Proceedings of the Old Bailey*, trial of James Audley, 14 Jan. 1687. He was acquitted, 'it being looked upon as a malicious prosecution'.

14. Lancashire Record Office, Kenyon papers, DDKE/acc.7840 HMC/599. See also the report from May 1686 that Monmouth had been seen alive in female disguise in Bristol and Somerset, British Library, Add. MS 41804, fo. 168, cited in Tim Harris, 'Scott [Crofts], James, Duke of Monmouth and First Duke of Buccleuch (1649–1685)', *Oxford Dictionary of National Biography* (Oxford) 2004.

15. Raine (ed.), *Depositions from the Castle of York*, 284.

16. Jeaffreson (ed.), *Middlesex County Records. Vol. IV*, 315.

17. Raine (ed.), *Depositions from the Castle of York*, 283.

18. *The Entering Book of Roger Morrice*, ed. Mark Goldie et al. (6 vols., Woodbridge, 2007), iii. 49, 309.

19. Jeaffreson (ed.), *Middlesex County Records. Vol. IV*, 292.

20. Jeaffreson (ed.), *Middlesex County Records. Vol. IV*, 313.

21. Jeaffreson (ed.), *Middlesex County Records. Vol. IV*, 319.
22. *Proceedings of the Old Bailey*, trial of John Seyton, 24 Feb. 1686.
23. Jeaffreson (ed.), *Middlesex County Records. Vol. IV*, 319.
24. *The Sentence of Samuel Johnson, at the Kings-Bench-Barr at Westminster* (1686), broadsheet.
25. *The Diary of John Evelyn*, ed. E. S. De Beer (6 vols., Oxford, 1955), iv. 609. R. B. Walker, 'The Newspaper Press in the Reign of William III', *Historical Journal*, 17 (1974), 691–709; E. S. De Beer, 'The English Newspapers from 1695 to 1702', in Mark Almeras Thomson, Ragnhild Marie Hatton, and J. S. Bromley (eds.), *William III and Louis XIV* (Liverpool and Toronto, 1968), 117–29.
26. *CSPD 1689–1690*, 112, 123, 308, 325, 341.
27. *CSPD 1689–1690*, 175.
28. Raine (ed.), *Depositions from the Castle of York*, 290, 298, 299.
29. W. J. Hardy (ed.), *Middlesex County Records. Calendar of Sessions Books 1689 to 1709* (1905), 5, 8, 11, 20, 21.
30. *CSPD 1689–1690*, 341, 343.
31. *CSPD 1689–1690*, 402, 420, 421, 459, 462, 492, 545; *CSPD 1690–1691*, 308; East Kent Archives, Dover Borough Quarter Sessions, Do/JS/d/03.
32. *CSPD 1689–1690*, 373.
33. *CSPD 1689–1690*, 2, 3, 196, 239, 270; *CSPD 1690–1691*, 74.
34. *CSPD 1690–1691*, 263.
35. *The Post Boy and Historical Account*, 23 July 1695; *The Flying Post and Postmaster*, 11 Apr. 1696; *The Postman and the Historical Account*, 17 Sept. 1696.
36. *Proceedings of the Old Bailey*, trial of James Weames, 3 Sept. 1690.
37. Hardy (ed.), *Middlesex County Records. Calendar of Sessions Books 1689 to 1709*, 54.
38. *Proceedings of the Old Bailey*, trial of Ann Knot, 31 Aug. 1692.
39. *CSPD 1695* and addenda, 51. See also *CSPD 1696*, 415; Hardy (ed.), *Middlesex County Records. Calendar of Sessions Books 1689 to 1709*, 139.
40. TNA: PRO ADM 106/482/242.
41. Worcestershire Record Office, Quarter Sessions Rolls, 1/1/176.
42. W. S. Holdsworth, *A History of English Law* (rev. edn., 17 vols., Boston, 1922–72), viii. 313–16.
43. *CSPD 1700–1702*, 454, 461.
44. *CSPD 1700–1702*, 455.
45. *CSPD 1700–1702*, 454–5.
46. *The Full Tryal, Examination, and Conviction of Mr James Taylor* (1703); *The English Reports*: 2 Ld Raym 879 SC / (1795) 3 Salk 198 / 91 ER 775; TNA: PRO KB 33/5/5.
47. *CSPD 1702–1703*, 59, 66.
48. *CSPD 1702–1703*, 395.
49. *CSPD 1702–1703*, 638.

50. Richard Burn, *Ecclesiastical Law* (3rd edn., 4 vols., 1775), ii. 117.
51. TNA: PRO SP 34/3/43; *CSPD 1703–1704*, 144, 147–8.
52. *London Gazette, no.* 4252 (8–12 Aug. 1705).
53. *Statutes of the Realm*, 4 Anne. c. 8; 6 Anne, c. 7.
54. TNA: PRO SP 34/8/62.
55. Hardy (ed.), *Middlesex County Records. Calendar of Sessions Books 1689 to 1709*, 327, 346, 351.
56. TNA: PRO SP 34/12/80.
57. TNA: PRO SP 34/14/78.
58. TNA: PRO SP 34/15/160.
59. *Proceedings of the Old Bailey*, trial of Charles Collins, 11 Jan. 1712.
60. TNA: PRO SP 34/20/84.
61. *The Evening Post*, 23 July 1713.

CHAPTER 11

1. The social, cultural and political history of Hanoverian England is best approached through Paul Langford, *A Polite and Commercial People. England 1727–1783* (Oxford, 1989); H. T. Dickinson, *The Politics of the People in Eighteenth-Century Britain* (1995); Julian Hoppit, *A Land of Liberty? England 1689–1727* (Oxford, 2000); Boyd Hilton, *A Mad, Bad, and Dangerous People. England 1783–1846* (Oxford, 2006); and Hannah Smith, *Georgian Monarchy: Politics and Culture, 1714–1760* (Cambridge, 2006).
2. *The London Journal*, 4 Feb. 1721/2; *The Public Advertiser*, 12 Mar. 1766.
3. William Hawkins, *A Treatise of the Pleas of the Crown* (2 vols., 1716–21), i. 38, 39, 41.
4. Hawkins, *Treatise of the Pleas of the Crown*, i. 38, 39, 60.
5. Michael Foster, A Report of Some Proceedings ... to which are added Discourses upon a few Branches of the Crown Law (Oxford, 1762), 200–7.
6. William Blackstone, *Commentaries on the Laws of England* (4 vols., Oxford, 1765–9), iv. 75, 79–80. See also 'A Barrister at Law', *Legal Recreations, or Popular Amusements in the Laws of England* (2 vols., 1792), i. 194–9 for a summary or plagiarism of Blackstone.
7. Nicholas Rogers, 'Popular Protest in Early Hanoverian London', *Past & Present*, 79 (1978), repr. in Paul Slack (ed.), *Rebellion, Popular Protest and the Social Order in Early Modern England* (Cambridge, 1984), 263–93; Nicholas Rogers, 'Riot and Popular Jacobitism in Early Hanoverian England', in Eveline Cruickshanks (ed.), *Ideology and Conspiracy: Aspects of Jacobitism, 1689–1759* (Edinburgh, 1982), 70–88; Jonathan D. Oates, 'Jacobitism and Popular Disturbances in Northern England, 1714–1719', *Northern History*, 41 (2004), 111–28. Contrast especially Paul Kléber Monod, *Jacobitism and the English People, 1688–1788* (Cambridge, 1989), esp. 233–66, and Nicholas Rogers, *Crowds, Culture, and Politics in Georgian Britain* (Oxford, 1998), esp. 50–4.

8. *The Proceedings of the Old Bailey, 1674–1913* (www.oldbaileyonline.org), trials of William Wide, 23 Feb. 1715, and John Bournois, 2 June 1715; *The Evening Post*, 12 Jan. 1717. See also *The Weekly Journal with Fresh Advices*, 30 Apr. 1715, for the case of George Goodwin, and *The Flying Post or the Post Master*, 28 June 1715, for Jacobites at Leeds.

9. Monod, *Jacobitism and the English People*, 247, 257; Rogers, *Crowds, Culture, and Politics*, 54.

10. *St James's Post*, 11 July 1718; *Proceedings of the Old Bailey*, trial of Robert Harrison, 9 July 1718; TNA: PRO SP 35/12, fo. 225, cited in Robert B. Shoemaker, *The London Mob: Violence and Disorder in Eighteenth-Century England* (2004), 98. See also *Proceedings of the Old Bailey*, trial of Henry Whitehead, 10 Jan. 1718, for speaking 'very flightingly of the king's title and government', calling King George a usurper.

11. *The Evening Post*, 25 Nov. 1718; *The Annals of King George, Year the Sixth* (1721), 391.

12. *Proceedings of the Old Bailey*, trial of Margaret Hicks, Apr. 1719, also cited in Rogers, *Crowds, Culture, and Politics*, 215.

13. *The Evening Post*, 3 Sept. 1719.

14. *The Weekly Journal or Saturday's Post*, 22 Apr. 1721. See also *The London Journal*, 28 July 1722, and *The Evening Post*, 4 Sept. 1722, for the case of Philip and Elizabeth Jones; and *The London Journal*, 20 Aug. 1726, for Clement Hubbard at Norwich.

15. *The Daily Post*, 27 Feb. 1727/8. See also the case of George Farnham, *The Daily Post*, 25 Oct. 1728.

16. TNA: PRO SP 36/13, fo. 50.

17. TNA: PRO SP 36/20, fo. 36.

18. TNA: PRO SP 36/20, fos. 37, 39; SP 36/22. fos. 141–2.

19. TNA: PRO KB 33/5/6.

20. TNA: PRO SP 36/64, fos. 131–3.

21. TNA: PRO SP 36/64, fo. 156; *The London Evening Post*, 17 July 1744.

22. TNA: PRO TS 11/179, no. 785.

23. TNA: PRO TS 11/179, no. 792; TS 11/944, no. 3424.

24. East Riding of Yorkshire Archives and Records Service, QSF/159/B/19.

25. Surrey History Centre, Sessions Bundles, QS2/6/1747/Xms/30.

26. *English Reports*, 1 Black W 37/ 96 ER 20.

27. *Proceedings of the Old Bailey*, trial of Charles Farrel, 3 June 1756.

28. W. Stubbs and G. Talmash, *The Crown Circuit Companion* (4th edn., 1768), 479–81; 'Barrister at Law', *Legal Recreations*, i. 204–5; [Spencer Perceval, attrib.], *The Duties and Powers of Public Officers* (1792?), 7–8.

29. G. A. Kelly, 'From Lèse-Majesté to Lèse-Nation: Treason in Eighteenth-Century France', *Journal of the History of Ideas*, 42 (1981), 269–86; Arlette Farge, *Subversive Words: Public Opinion in Eighteenth-Century France*

(University Park, PA, 1995), 137, 167; Lisa Jane Graham, *If the King Only Knew: Seditious Speech in the Reign of Louis XV* (Charlottesville, VA, 2000), 1–2.

30. Home Office 'Information', 26 Nov. 1792; Lord Grenville to Buckingham, 1 Dec. 1792, quoted in Clive Emsley, 'The London "Insurrection" of December 1792: Fact, Fiction, or Fantasy?' *Journal of British Studies*, 17 (1978), 73, 81.

31. John Barrell, *Imagining the King's Death: Figurative Treason, Fantasies of Regicide 1793–1796* (Oxford, 2000); Michael Lobban, 'Treason, Sedition and the Radical Movement in the Age of the French Revolution', *Liverpool Law Review*, 22 (2000), 210–17; Clive Emsley, 'The Home Office and its Sources of Information and Investigation 1791–1801', *English Historical Review*, 94 (1979), 532–61.

32. *By the King. A Proclamation* (21 May 1792).

33. *The Trial of John Frost for Seditious Words* (1794), 9; Lobban, 'Treason, Sedition and the Radical Movement', 206, 208.

34. *The World*, 6 Nov. 1793, the trial of William Powis.

35. Philip Harling, 'The Law of Libel and the Limits of Repression, 1790–1832', *Historical Journal*, 44 (2001), 107–34. See also the coverage of these trials in such newspapers as *The Morning Post* and *The Evening Mail*.

36. *The Evening Mail*, 27 May 1793; *The Morning Post*, 14 June 1793; *The Trial of John Frost for Seditious Words*, 2, 9; T. B. Howell and T. J. Howell (eds.), *A Complete Collection of State Trials* (33 vols., 1809–28), xxii. 471–522.

37. *The Trial of Wm. Winterbotham . . . For Seditious Words* (1794).

38. *The Morning Post*, 7 Dec. 1793; *The Trial of Thomas Briellat, For Seditious Words* (1794). The victualler William Francis of Prittlewell, Essex, was likewise tried for saying 'Damn the king and country too: if the French come I wonder who the hell will not join them' (TNA: PRO TS 11/924, no. 3238). Three years later Briellat was in America, settled on a farm in Kentucky (*The Telegraph*, 8 Sept. 1796).

39. *The Law of Treason. A Concise and Comprehensive View of the Power and Duty of Grand Juries* (1794).

40. Harling, 'Law of Libel', 108–10. See also Clive Emsley, *Crime and Society in England 1750–1900* (1987), 21, 204; Steve Poole, *The Politics of Regicide in England, 1760–1850: Troublesome Subjects* (Manchester, 2000), 96. Among many reports that did not lead to indictment was that of Ebenezer Hollick of Whittlesford, Cambridgeshire, who allegedly said in Feb. 1793 that it would have been better to burn George III than Paine's *Rights of Man* (Emsley, 'The Home Office and its Source of Information', 542).

41. TNA: PRO ASSI 23/8 (pt. 2), fo. 411.

42. *The World*, 13 and 20 Aug. 1793.

43. TNA: PRO TS 11/506, no. 1662.

44. *The Sun*, 1 Aug. 1793.

45. *The Morning Post*, 4 Nov. 1793; *The News*, 4 Nov. 1793; *The World*, 10 Dec. 1793. *Proceedings of the Old Bailey*, trial of William Hudson, 4 Dec. 1793.

46. *The World*, 12 Apr. 1794.

47. *The Oracle and Public Advertiser*, 10 Sept. 1794.

48. TNA: PRO ASSI 23/8 (pt. 2), fo. 426.

49. *The Times*, 17 Jan. 1794, cited in Lobban, 'Treason, Sedition and the Radical Movement', 207.

50. TNA: PRO ASSI 23/8 (pt. 2), fo. 424.

51. TNA: PRO HO 42/32/263, HO 42/33/41.

52. *The Oracle and Public Advertiser*, 3 Apr. 1794, 2 May 1794.

53. *The Morning Chronicle*, 16 Sept. 1794.

54. TNA: PRO TS 11/944, no. 3433; HO/47/20. Evidence that Swift was 'very much intoxicated', and had given a lifetime to the king's naval service, did not protect him from eighteen months in gaol.

55. TNA PRO KB 33/6/5; TS 11/45, no. 167; *The Times*, 28 July 1795, 3; *The Trial of Henry Yorke for Conspiracy* (1795).

56. William Cobbett and T. C. Hansard (eds.), *Parliamentary History* (36 vols., 1806–20). xxxii. 1818.

57. *The Star*, 30 July 1796; *The Telegraph*, 1 Aug. 1796; *The True Briton*, 1 Aug. 1796.

58. TNA: PRO TS 11/505, no. 1661.

59. Treasonable and Seditious Practices Act of 1795 (36 Geo. III, c. 7), in E. Neville Williams (ed.), *The Eighteenth-Century Constitution 1688–1815* (Cambridge, 1960), 425–6; Barrell, *Imagining the King's Death*, 30–6, 583.

60. 36 Geo. III. c. 8.

61. Clive Emsley, 'Repression, "Terror" and the Rule of Law in England during the Decade of the French Revolution', *English Historical Review*, 100 (1985), 801–25.

62. Iain McCalman, 'Ultra-Radicalism and Convivial Debating-Clubs in London, 1795–1838', *English Historical Review*, 102 (1987), 309, 312; E. P. Thompson, *The Making of the English Working Class* (1963), 676.

63. Howell and Howell (eds.), *Complete Collection of State Trials*, xxii. 477–8.

64. Justin Champion, ' "May the last king be strangled in the bowels of the last priest": Irreligion and the English Enlightenment, 1649–1789', in Timothy Morton and Nigel Smith (eds.), *Radicalism in British Literary Culture, 1650–1830: From Revolution to Revolution* (Cambridge, 2002), 29.

65. Surrey History Centre, Borough of Guildford Quarter Sessions, BR/QS/2/8.

66. TNA: PRO ASSI 23/8 (pt. 2), fo. 498.

67. *The True Briton*, 15 Apr. 1800.

68. *The London Packet or New Lloyd's Evening Post*, 16 June 1800. See also the case of Francis Brooks, labourer, in 1803, who said: 'Damn and bugger the bloody king, if I had him here and a pistol I would shoot him.' He was sentenced to a public whipping and three months in prison (TNA TS 11/506, no. 1659).

Richard Mountain, a former militia man, disappointed of a seat on the mail coach from Deptford to London, launched into an invective against the king, saying 'he wished he had the shaking of his bloody head, and that he did not mind putting him to death', and damned all kings and aristocrats. A jury at Maidstone in 1801 found him guilty of speaking seditious words (*The Times*, 31 July 1801 (repr. in *The Times*, 31 July 1901, 13)).

69. *Proceedings of the Old Bailey*, trial of Jesse Hilliar, 3 Dec. 1800.

70. *The Times*, 10 Jan. 1807.

71. *The Times*, 7 May 1810, 3.

72. Linda Colley, 'The Apotheosis of George III: Loyalty, Royalty and the British Nation 1760–1820', *Past & Present*, 102 (1984), 113. On hostile cartoons, see M. D. George, *English Political Caricature: A Study of Opinion and Propaganda* (2 vols., Oxford, 1959–60); Kenneth Baker, *The Kings and Queens: An Irreverent Cartoon History of the British Monarchy* (1996); Tamara Hunt, *Defining John Bull: Political Caricature and National Identity in Late Georgian England* (2003).

73. [House of Commons], *Political Libel and Seditious Conduct* (1821); TNA: PRO KB 33/24/2.

74. TNA: PRO TS 11/1047, no. 4560; *The Times*, 13 Aug. 1813, 4.

75. A Yorkshire prosecutor declared in 1813 'that the effects of liquor were not to suggest seditious thoughts, but merely to remove those restraints under which evil disposed men were held by the terrors of the law while in a state of sobriety' (*The Times*, 13 Aug. 1813, 4).

76. 57 Geo. III, c. 6.

77. Michael Lobban, 'From Seditious Libel to Unlawful Assembly: Peterloo and the Changing Face of Political Crime', *Oxford Journal of Legal Studies*, 10 (1990), 310.

78. 60 Geo. III. c. 4.

79. Lobban, 'From Seditious Libel to Unlawful Assembly', 307–52; Michael Bush, *The Casualties of Peterloo* (Lancaster, 2005); Robert Poole, ' "By the Law or the Sword": Peterloo Revisited', *History*, 91 (2006), 254–76; Robert Poole, 'The March to Peterloo: Politics and Festivity in Late Georgian England', *Past & Present*, 192 (2006), 109–53.

80. *The Leeds Mercury*, 28 Aug. 1819; *The Morning Chronicle*, 31 Aug. 1819 and 18 Mar. 1820.

81. TNA: PRO TS 11/45, no. 167; Malcolm Chase, 'Wedderburn, Robert (1762–1835/6?)', *Oxford Dictionary of National Biography* (2004–7).

82. TNA: PRO TS 11/48, no. 186.

83. TNA: PRO TS 11/91, no. 295.

84. TNA: PRO TS 11/48, no. 190.

85. *The Times*, 13 Nov. 1837, 5; *The Times*, 20 Nov. 1837, 6; *English Reports*, (1837) 7 Ad & E 536// 112 ER 572.

86. 11 and 12 Victoria, c. 12; Poole, *Politics of Regicide*, 198–9. For 'certain scandalous and seditious words of and concerning our lady the queen and government' allegedly spoken by Chartists, see *The Times*, 8 June 1848, 8; 26 June 1848, 3; 11 July 1848, 6; 4 Aug. 1848, 8; 24 Aug. 1848, 7.

87. *The New Gagging Bill* (1848), Bodleian Library, Firth ballads, c. 16 (45).

88. *The Times*, 24 June 1846.

89. *The Graphic*, 22 Nov. 1879.

90. Trial of John Burns, Henry Hyde and others, *The Manchester Times*, 20 Feb. 1886; *The Daily News*, 12 Apr. 1886; *The Times*, 6 Apr. 1886, 10; 7 Apr. 1886, 6; 12 Apr. 1886, 9.

91. 2 and 3 Victoria, c. 47, section 54, item 13; The Public Order Act, 1986, section 40, schedule 3.

92. *The Times*, 17 Feb. 1919, 7; 10 Mar. 1919, 7.

93. TNA: PRO HO 144/1514/376831, minutes, 23 Apr. 1919.

94. TNA: PRO HO 144/1514/376831, minutes and reports, 18 June–8 July 1919.

95. TNA: PRO HO 144/1514/376831, Home Office circular, 18 Feb. 1919; 'secret' memorandum, 22 Apr. 1919.

96. TNA: PRO HO 144/1514/376831, memoranda, Nov. 1919.

97. TNA: PRO HO 144/9486. This archived document was closed until 2029, but later received 'accelerated opening'. The reference to tares and wheat invoked the Christian parable of the sower.

98. Law Commission of England and Wales, *Working Paper No 72 . . . Codification of the Criminal Law—Treason, Sedition and Allied Offences* (1977).

99. *European Convention on Human Rights* (1950–1966); Human Rights Act, 1998 (C. 42).

100. Public Order Act, 1986 (C. 64), section 18.

101. Crime and Disorder Act, 1998 (C. 37), amended 2001; Racial or Religious Hatred Act, 2006 (C. 1).

102. Terrorism Act 2006 (C. 11), section 1; Ralf Dahrendorf, 'Free Speech on Trial', www.project-syndicate.org/commentary/dahrendorf45, at 24 Nov. 2006.

103. See the website www.throneout.com, 'dedicated to removing the royal pimple from the arse of Britain'; 'Diana murdered, Al Fayed claims', http://news.bbc.co.uk (18 Feb. 2008).

CHAPTER 12

1. Quotes and references are from Chs. 3 and 4.

2. See Ch. 5 for sources.

3. See Chs. 6 and 7.

4. See Ch. 8.

5. See Ch. 9.

6. See Chs. 10 and 11.

7. *CSPD... Addenda 1566–1579*, 521; TNA: PRO SP 15/25/47.

8. TNA: PRO SP 12/259/16.

9. *The Letters of John Chamberlain*, ed. Norman Egbert McClure (2 vols., Philadelphia, 1939), ii. 370.

10. *Acts of the Privy Council 1628–1629*, 143, 159; TNA: PRO SP 16/116/56, SP 16/117/73, SP 16/118/77.

11. TNA: PRO SP 16/221/41.

12. TNA: PRO SP 12/44/52, SP 12/235/81, SP 12/99/53.

13. TNA: PRO SP 16/116/92.

14. *The Works of... William Laud, D.D.*, ed. William Scott and James Bliss (7 vols., Oxford, 1847–60), i. 191, 195.

15. *A Collection of State Papers of John Thurloe*, ed. Thomas Birch (7 vols., 1742), ii. 2, 382–4.

16. *CSPD 1675–1676*, 465; *CSPD 1678*, 295.

17. *CSPD 1682*, 576.

18. William Hawkins, *A Treatise of the Pleas of the Crown* (2 vols., 1716–21), i. 38, 39, 60.

19. *Letters and Papers, Foreign and Domestic, of the Reign of Henry VIII*, ed. J. S. Brewer et al. (23 vols., 1862–1932), vol. xiii, pt. 1, p. 36.

20. J. S. Cockburn (ed.), *Calendar of Assize Records: Home Circuit Indictments. Elizabeth I and James I: Introduction* (1985), 23.

21. TNA: PRO SP14/128/54; *Acts of the Privy Council 1621–1623*, 156–7, 174.

22. TNA: PRO SP14/18/69, 73.

23. *Acts of the Privy Council 1627–1628*, 297–8; *Acts of the Privy Council 1630–1631*, 227–8.

24. TNA: PRO SP 16/106/27, SP 16/25/65.

25. TNA: PRO PC 2/48, fo. 88^v.

26. Samuel Rezneck, 'Constructive Treason by Words in the Fifteenth Century', *American Historical Review*, 33 (1928), 544–52, quotations at 548n. and 551.

27. John Bellamy, *The Tudor Law of Treason: An Introduction* (1979), 31–2; G. R. Elton, *Policy and Police: The Enforcement of the Reformation in the Age of Thomas Cromwell* (Cambridge, 1972), 264–87.

28. *Statutes of the Realm*, 13 Eliz. I, c. 1.

29. Paul L. Hughes and James F. Larkin (eds.), *Tudor Royal Proclamations*, ii. *The Later Tudors (1553–1587)* (London and New Haven, 1969), 341.

30. Thomas Norton, 'A warning agaynst the dangerous practises of Papistes, and specially the parteners of the late rebellion', in *All such treatises as have been lately published by Thomas Norton* (1570), sigs. Ci, Ci(v).

31. John Hawarde, *Les Reportes del Cases in Camera Stellata, 1593–1609*, ed. William Paley Baildon (1894), 372.

32. TNA: PRO SP 16/135/35.

33. John Cordy Jeaffreson (ed.), *Middlesex County Records. Vol. III* (Clerkenwell, 1888), 304, 305, 306, 314; *CSPD Jan.–June 1683*, 3, 181; *The Proceedings of the Old Bailey, 1674–1913* (www.oldbaileyonline.org), trial of Phillip Wallis, 10 Dec. 1684.

34. 'An act for safety and preservation of his majesties person and government against treasonable and seditious practices and attempts' (13 Charles II. c. 1, 1661).

35. W. S. Holdsworth, *A History of English Law* (rev. edn., 17 vols., Boston, 1922–72), viii. 313–16.

36. *Letters and Papers of Henry VIII*, vol. xii, pt. 2, p. 376.

37. TNA: PRO SP 14/143/18, 19; *Acts of the Privy Council 1621–1623*, 484.

38. TNA: PRO SP 16/318/76.

39. TNA: PRO SP 16/369/25.

40. TNA: PRO SP 16/393/24.

41. *CSPD 1675–1676*, 432, 437.

42. *Proceedings of the Old Bailey*, trial of Margaret Hicks, Apr. 1719.

43. Walter Rye (ed.), *Depositions Taken before the Mayor and Aldermen of Norwich, 1549–1567* (Norwich, 1905), 56–7.

44. TNA: PRO SP12/13/21.

45. TNA: PRO SP16/26/49.

46. TNA: PRO SP16/29/40.

47. TNA: PRO SP 16/25/65.

48. TNA: PRO SP 16/369/25.

49. House of Lords Record Office, Main Papers, HL/PO/JO/10/1/35.

50. Elton, *Policy and Police*, 137.

51. Elton, *Policy and Police*, 100, 123–4.

52. TNA: PRO SP 12/259/16, 21; Hawarde, *Les Reportes del Cases in Camera Stellata*, 114.

53. TNA: PRO SP14/117/38, 39, 40; *Acts of the Privy Council 1619–1621*, 363.

54. TNA: PRO SP14/ 122/145, SP 14/123/20.

55. TNA: PRO SP 16/293/97, SP 16/296/45.

56. TNA: PRO 16/447/104.

57. *Proceedings of the Old Bailey*, trial of Jesse Hilliar, 3 Dec. 1800.

58. *The Times*, 13 Aug. 1813, 4.

59. *Acts of the Privy Council 1577–1578*, 404, 421–2.

60. TNA: PRO SP 12/256/53.

61. *Acts of the Privy Council 1616–1617*, 411.

62. TNA: PRO SP 14/143/18, 19; *Acts of the Privy Council 1621–1623*, 484.

63. TNA: PRO SP 16/262/16, SP 16/262/67.

64. Elton, *Policy and Police*, 11.

65. *Acts of the Privy Council 1581–1582*, 417–18.

66. *CSPD 1619–1623*, 92–3; TNA: PRO SP 14/111/14.

67. Bodleian Library, MS Bankes 51/54, fo. 100.

68. TNA: PRO SP 12/269/22, SP 12/270/105.

69. TNA: PRO SP 16/33/60, SP 16/38/20.

70. TNA: PRO SP 16/89/61.

71. TNA: PRO SP 16/163/61.

72. Rex v. Alicock, *The English Reports:* (1793) 1 Lev 57/ 83 ER 295.

73. TNA: PRO SP 16/148/66.

74. Bodleian Library, MS Bankes 19/4, fos. 6–7.

75. J. S. Cockburn (ed.), *Calendar of Assize Records: Kent Indictments. Elizabeth I* (1979), 77.

76. J. S. Cockburn (ed.), *Calendar of Assize Records: Essex Indictments. Elizabeth I* (1978), 373.

77. Jeaffreson (ed.), *Middlesex County Records. Vol. III*, 93.

78. John Cordy Jeaffreson (ed.), *Middlesex County Records. Vol. IV* (Clerkenwell, 1892), 285–6.

79. Jeaffreson (ed.), *Middlesex County Records. Vol. IV*, 319.

Bibliography

PRIMARY SOURCES

Manuscript Sources
All Souls College, Oxford
Warden's MS 7.

Bodleian Library, Oxford
MS Ashmole 38.
MS Bankes 13, 18, 19, 37, 41, 42, 43, 44, 51, 65.
MS Carte 1, 63, 77, 123.
MS Cherry 2.
MS Clarendon 4, 6.
MS John Johnson C.
MS Nalson 2, 12, 13.
MS Rawlinson A. 26, 127, 128.
MS Rawlinson B. 243.
MS Rawlinson C. 421, 573, 674.
MS Rawlinson D. 392, 821.
MS Rawlinson Poet. 84.
MS Tanner 63, 65, 69, 306.
MS Top. Oxon. C. 378.
MS Wood F. 34.
Firth Ballads, c.16.
Oxford University Archives, Chancellor's Court Papers and Depositions.

Borthwick Institute, York
Cause Papers Transmitted on Appeal.
Visitation Court Book 11, 1636.

British Library, London
Add. MS 11045: Rossingham Newsletters.
Add. MS 33998: English Poetry.
Add. MS 38490: Henry Townsend Diary.
Add. MS 41804: Middleton Papers.
Add. MS 70003: Harley Papers.

Add. MS 72372: Trumbull Papers.
Add. MS 72417: Trumbull Papers.
Add. MS 72421: Trumbull Papers.
MS Egerton 2725: Poetical Miscellany.
MS Harley 353: Starkey Papers.
MS Harley 1026: Justinian Pagitt Memoranda.
MS Lansdowne 620: Star Chamber Reports.

Buckinghamshire Record Office, Aylesbury
D/A/V: Archdeaconry Act Books.

Cambridge University Library
MS Mm. 6. 63: Littleton Papers.
University Archives, Vice Chancellor's Court Papers.

Cheshire Record Office, Chester
EDC 5: Diocesan Cause Papers.
QJF: Quarter Sessions Files.

Devon Record Office, Exeter
Quarter Sessions Order Book.

Dorset History Centre, Dorchester
D/BOC/Box 22: Chronicle of Dennis Bond.

East Kent Archives, Dover
Dover Borough Quarter Sessions: Do/JS/d/03.

East Sussex Record Office, Lewes
QR/E: Quarter Sessions Rolls.
SAS-WG: Grantham Papers.

Essex Record Office, Chelmsford
D/DAc66: Clayton MSS.
D/Deb/: Bramston Papers.
Q/SR: Quarter Sessions Rolls.
Q/SBa: Quarter Sessions Depositions and Supplemental Papers.
T/A 418: Assizes Transcripts.

Essex Record Office, Colchester Branch
D/B5/Sb2/7: Examinations and Recognizances.

Guildhall Library, London
MS 9064: Commissary Act Books.

Hampshire Record Office, Winchester
Q1/2: Quarter Sessions Orders.
44M69/L30: Jervoise Papers.

Herefordshire Record Office, Hereford
Quarter Sessions Recognizances and Examinations.

House of Lords Record Office, London
HL/PO/JO/10: Main Papers.

Huntington Library, San Marino
Ellesmere MSS 2739, 2740.
Hastings MSS HA 3434, 3437.

Lambeth Palace Library
MS 943: Laudian Papers.
MS 3391: Bramston Papers.

Lancashire Record Office, Preston
DDKE/: Kenyon Papers.
QSP/: Quarter Sessions Papers.

Leicestershire Archives, Leicester
I D 41/: Archdeaconry Act Books.
BR II/: Borough Hall Book.

Lincolnshire Archives, Lincoln
Visitation Books.
Consistory Court Papers.

London Metropolitan Archives
MJ/SBB/: Session Books.

The National Archives (TNA)
ADM 106: Admiralty (Navy Board).
ASSI 1, 23, 35, 45: Assizes.
C 115, 142, 231: Chancery.
CHES 9: Palatinate of Chester Papers.
CHESTER 24: Chester Court of Sessions.
E 111, 115: Exchequer.
HO 42, 45, 47, 144: Home Office.
KB 9, 33: King's Bench.
PC 2: Privy Council.
PROB 11: Probate.
SO 1: Signet Office.
SP 1, 12, 14, 15, 16, 24, 25, 29, 34, 35, 36: State Papers.
STAC 8: Star Chamber.
TS 11: Treasury Solicitor.
WARD 7: Wards.

National Library of Wales, Aberystwyth
Great Sessions, 4/143.

Norfolk Record Office, Norwich
C/S3: Quarter Sessions Rolls.
DN/VIS/7: Visitation Returns.

Somerset Record Office, Taunton
DD/BR/ba: Poulett Papers.
DD/CM/72: Combe Papers.
DD/PH 288: Phelips Papers.
Q/SRD/: Quarter Sessions.

Staffordshire Record Office, Stafford
D593: Leveson Papers.
D1287: Bridgeman Correspondence.
Q/SO: Quarter Sessions Orders.
Q/SR: Quarter Sessions Rolls.

Suffolk Record Office, Ipswich
C/2/: General Court Minutes.

Surrey History Centre, Woking
QS2/: Sessions Bundles.
BR/QS/2/8: Guildford Quarter Sessions.

Worcestershire Record Office, Worcester
1/1/: Quarter Sessions Rolls.

Printed Sources

Abernethy, John, *A Christian and Heavenly Treatise, Containing Physicke for the Soule* (1622).
An Account at Large, of the Proceedings at the Sessions-House in the Old-Bayly, on the 24 of November 1681 (1681).
Acts of the Privy Council 1542–1631, ed. J. R. Dasent et al. (46 vols., 1890–1964).
Adams, Thomas, *The Taming of the Tongue* (1616).
Affinati d'Acuto, Jacopo, *The Dumbe Divine Speaker . . . shewing both the dignitie and defectes of the Tongue* (1605).
[Allen, William, Francis Englefield, and Robert Parsons], *A Conference about the next succession to the crowne of Ingland* (Antwerp, 1595).
Allestree, Richard, *The Government of the Tongue* (Oxford, 1674).
The Anatomy of a Woman's Tongue (1638), in William Oldys and Thomas Park (eds.), *The Harleian Miscellany* (12 vols., 1808–11), ii. 183–93.
Anderson, Anthony, *An Exposition of the Hymne Commonly Called Benedictus* (1574).
——, *The Shield of our Safetie* (1581).
The Annals of King George, Year the Sixth (1721).
Aprill 4. The proceeding of the Parliament (1628).
Attersoll, William, *A Commentarie Vpon the Epistle of Saint Paul to Philemon* (1612).
[Aubrey], *Aubrey's Brief Lives*, ed. Oliver Lawson Dick (Ann Arbor, 1957).

Averell, William, *A Mervailous Combat of Contrarieties* (1588).

Bacon, Sir Francis, *Cases of Treason* (1641).

——, *The History of the Reign of King Henry the Seventh*, ed. F. J. Levy (Indianapolis and New York, 1972).

[Bale], *John Bale's King Johan*, ed. Barry B. Adams (San Marino, CA, 1969).

Ball, John, *A Short Catechisme. Containing the Principles of Religion. Very profitable for all sorts of People* (18th impression, 1637).

Bargrave, Isaac, *A Sermon Preached Before King Charles March 27 1627* (1627).

Barnes, Thomas G. (ed.), *Somerset Assize Orders 1629–1640* (Somerset Record Society, 65, 1959).

[Barrington], *Barrington Family Letters 1628–1632*, ed. Arthur Searle (Camden Society, 4th ser., 28, 1983).

'A Barrister at Law', *Legal Recreations, or Popular Amusements in the Laws of England* (2 vols., 1792).

Bentham, Joseph, *The Societie of the Saints: or, A Treatise of Good-fellows, and their Good-fellowship* (1630; 1638 edn.).

Bernard, Richard, *The Faithfull Shepherd* (1621).

Bettey, J. H., *Calendar of the Correspondence of the Smyth Family of Ashton Court 1548–1642* (Bristol Record Society, 35, 1982).

Birch, Thomas (ed.), *The Court and Times of Charles the First* (2 vols., 1848).

—— (ed.), *The Court and Times of James the First* (2 vols., 1849).

Blackstone, William, *Commentaries on the Laws of England* (4 vols., Oxford, 1765–9).

——, *Commentaries on the Laws of England* (11th edn., 4 vols., 1791).

Blackwood, Christopher, *Some Pious Treatises Being 1. A Bridle for the Tongue* (1654).

Blount, Thomas, *Glossographia: or A Dictionary, Interpreting all such Hard Words* (1656).

Bolton, Robert, *Some Generall Directions for a Comfortable Walking with God* (1638).

Boys, John, *The Third Part from S. Iohn Baptists Nativitie* (1615).

Brinsley, John, *[Glosso-Chalinosis] Or, A Bridle for the Tongue* (1664).

[Brut], *The Brut or The Chronicles of England . . . Part II*, ed. Friedrich W. D. Brie (Early English Text Society, 136, 1908), 480–4.

Bullokar, John, *An English Exposition: Teaching the Interpretation of the Hardest Words Used in Our Language* (1616).

Burn, Richard, *Ecclesiastical Law* (3rd edn., 4 vols., 1775).

——, *The Justice of the Peace, and Parish Officer* (18th edn., 4 vols., 1797).

Burrell, John, *The Divine Right of Kings, Proved from the Principles of the Church of England* (Cambridge, 1683).

Burton, Robert, *The Anatomy of Melancholy*, ed. Thomas C. Faulkner, Nicolas K. Kiessling, and Rhonda L. Blair (6 vols., Oxford, 1989).

Calendar of State Papers, Domestic [*CSPD*, Edward VI to Queen Anne], ed. Mary Anne Everett Green et al. (84 vols., 1856–2006).

[Chamberlain] *The Letters of John Chamberlain*, ed. Norman Egbert McClure (2 vols., Philadelphia, 1939).

[Charles I], *The King Maiesties Declaration to His Subiects, Concering Lawfull Sports* (1633).

——, *Basilika. The Workes of King Charles the Martyr* (2 vols., 1662).

——, *The Letters, Speeches and Proclamations of King Charles I*, ed. Sir Charles Petrie (1935).

Cheke, Sir John, *The True Subiect to the Rebell. Or the Hurt of Sedition, how Greivous it is to a Common-wealth* (1549; 1641 edn.).

Chronicle of the Grey Friars of London (Camden Society, 53, 1852).

[Clarendon], *The History of the Rebellion and Civil Wars in England*, ed. W. Dunn Macray (6 vols., Oxford, 1888).

Clifford, William, *The Power of Kings, Particularly the British Monarchy Asserted and Vindicated* (1682).

Cobbett, William, and T. C. Hansard (eds.), *Parliamentary History.* (36 vols., 1806–20).

Cockburn, J. S. (ed.), *Calendar of Assize Records: Hertfordshire Indictments. Elizabeth I* (1975).

—— (ed.), *Calendar of Assize Records: Sussex Indictments. James I* (1975).

—— (ed.), *Western Circuit Assize Orders 1629–1648: A Calendar* (Camden Society, 4th ser., 17, 1976).

—— (ed.), *Calendar of Assize Records: Essex Indictments. Elizabeth I* (1978).

—— (ed.), *Calendar of Assize Records: Kent Indictments. Elizabeth I* (1979).

—— (ed.), *Calendar of Assize Records: Hertfordshire Indictments. James I* (1980).

—— (ed.), *Calendar of Assize Records: Kent Indictments. James I* (1980).

—— (ed.), *Calendar of Assize Records: Surrey Indictments. Elizabeth I* (1980).

—— (ed.), *Calendar of Assize Records: Essex Indictments. James I* (1982).

—— (ed.), *Calendar of Assize Records: Home Circuit Indictments. Elizabeth I and James I: Introduction* (1985).

—— (ed.), *Calendar of Assize Records. Kent Indictments 1649–1659* (1989).

—— (ed.), *Calendar of Assize Records: Kent Indictments. Charles I* (1995).

—— (ed.), *Calendar of Assize Records: Kent Indictments. Charles II 1660–1675* (1995).

—— (ed.), *Calendar of Assize Records: Kent Indictments. Charles II 1676–1688* (1997).

Coke, Sir Edward, *The Third Part of the Institutes of the Laws of England* (1644).

[Coke], *The Reports of Sir Edward Coke* (1658).

——, *The Reports of Sir Edward Coke* (13 parts in 7 vols., 1738).

A Complete Collection of State-Trials (6 vols., 1730).

Constitutions and Canons Ecclesiasticall . . . 1640 (1640).

Copnall, H. Hampton (ed.), *Nottinghamshire County Records. Notes and Extracts . . . of the 17th Century* (Nottingham, 1915).

Cosin, John, *A Collection of Private Devotions* (1627).

Cowell, John, *The Interpreter* (1672).

Crisp, Frederick Arthur (ed.), *Abstracts of Somerset Wills* (6 vols., 1887–90).

[Croke], *The Reports of Sir George Croke Knight . . . Revised, and Published in English by Sir Harebotle Grimston* (1657).

Crooke, Helkiah, *Microcosmographia. A Description of the Body of Man* (1618).

Crooke, Samuel, *The Ministeriall Husbandry and Building* (1615).

Crompton, Richard, *Star-Chamber Cases, Shewing What Causes Properly Belong to the Cognizance of that Court* (1630).

[Crosfield], *The Diary of Thomas Crosfield*, ed. Frederick S. Boas (Oxford, 1935).

Cust, Richard, and Andrew Hopper (eds.), *Cases in the High Court of Chivalry 1634–1640* (Harleian Society, NS 18, 2006).

D., I., *A Hedgerow of Busshes, Brambles, and Briers; or, A Fielde full of Tares, Thistles and Tine: Of the Vanities of this Worlde, leading the way to eternall damnation* (1598).

Dallington, Robert, *Aphorismes Civill and Militarie* (1613).

Dalton, Michael, *The Countrey Justice* (5th edn., 1635).

[Erasmus], *Luther and Erasmus: Free Will and Salvation*, ed. E. Gordon Rupp and Philip S. Watson (Philadelphia, 1969).

D'Ewes, Sir Simonds (ed.), *The Journals of All the Parliaments During the Reign of Queen Elizabeth* (1682).

[D'Ewes], *The Diary of Sir Simonds D'Ewes 1622–1624*, ed. Elisabeth Bourcier (Paris, 1974).

The Doctrine of the Bible: Or, Rules of Discipline (1604; 1641 edn.).

Dod, John, *A Remedy Against Privat Contentions* (1609).

——, *A Plaine and Familiar Exposition of the Ten Commandements* (18th edn., 1632).

Downame, George, *Two Sermons, The One Commending the Ministerie in Generall: The Other Defending the Office of Bishops* (1608).

Dugdale, Sir William, *Origines Juridiciales, or Historical Memorials of the English Laws* (1666).

Dyer, Sir James, *Reports of Cases in the Reigns of Hen. VIII. Edw. VI. Q. Mary, and Q. Eliz.* (3 vols, 1794).

Egerton, Stephen, *The Boring of the Ear* (1623).

Ellis, Henry, *Original Letters Illustrative of English History* (2nd edn., 3 vols, 1825).

Englands Ioyalty, in Ioyful expressions, for the City of Londons safety (1641/2).

The English Reports (176 vols., 1865).

European Convention on Human Rights (1950–66).

[Evelyn], *The Diary of John Evelyn*, ed. E. S. De Beer (6 vols., Oxford, 1955).

F., T., *Newes from the North* (1579).

Farrer, William, and J. Brownbill (eds.), *The Victoria History of the County of Lancaster* (8 vols., 1906–11).

Firth, C. H., and R. S. Rait (eds.), *Acts and Ordinances of the Interregnum, 1642–1660* (3 vols., 1911).

Foode for families: or, An wholsome houshold-discourse: in which all estates and sorts of people whatsoeuer, are taught, their duties towards God, their alegeance to their King, and their brotherly loue and charitie one to another (1623).

Fortunes Tennis-ball (1640).

Ford, Stephen, *The Evil Tongue Tryed and found Guilty* (1672).

Foster, Michael, *A Report of Some Proceedings . . . to which are added Discourses upon a few Branches of the Crown Law* (Oxford, 1762).

Foxe, John, *Acts and Monuments* (1583 edn.).

The Full Tryal, Examination, and Conviction of Mr James Taylor (1703).

Gardiner, Samuel Rawson (ed.), *Reports of Cases in the Courts of Star Chamber and High Commission* (Camden Society, 1886).

Gardyner, Richard, *A Sermon Appointed ... on the Day of His Maiesties Happy Inauguration* (1642).

Gearing, William, *A Bridle for the Tongue; or, A Treatise of Ten Sins of the Tongue* (1663).

[George III], *By the King. A Proclamation* (21 May 1792).

Gibbon, Charles, *Not So New, As True. Being a Verie Necessarie Caveat for All Christians* (1590).

The Godly End, and wofull lamentation of one Iohn Stevens, a youth, that was hang'd, drawne, and quartered for High-Treason, at Salisbury in Wilshire, upon Thursday being the seventh day of March last 1632, with the setting up of his quarters on the City gates. To the tune of Fortune my foe (1633).

Gods Good Servant, and the Kings Good Subject (1642).

Gouge, William, *A Short Catechisme, wherein are briefly handled the fundamentall principles of Christian Religion* (7th edn., 1635).

Grey, Anchitell (ed.), *Grey's Debates of the House of Commons*, 10 vols. (1769).

[Grey, Enoch], *To the Supreame Authority of this Nation, the Commons of England in Parliament Assembled, The Humble Petition of Enoch Grey, minister* (1649).

[Guazzo], *The Civile Conversation of M. Steeven Guazzo. The First Three Books Translated by George Pettie, anno 1581*, ed. Sir Edward Sullivan (2 vols., 1925).

Hale, Sir Matthew, *Historia Placitorum Coronae: The History of the Pleas of the Crown* (2 vols., 1736).

Hale, William H. (ed.), *A Series of Precedents and Proceedings in Criminal Causes ... extracted from the Act-Books of the Ecclesiastical Courts of the Diocese of London* (1847).

Harbin, E. H. Bates (ed.), *Quarter Sessions Records for the County of Somerset. Vol. 1. James. I. 1607–1625* (Somerset Record Society, 23, 1907).

—— (ed.), *Quarter Sessions Records for the County of Somerset. Vol II. Charles I. 1625–1639* (Somerset Record Society, 24, 1908).

Hartley, T. E. (ed.), *Proceedings in the Parliaments of Elizabeth I*, i. *1558–1581* (Leicester, 1981).

Hardwick, William, *Conformity with Piety, Requisite in God's Service* (1638).

Hardy, W. J. (ed.), *Middlesex County Records. Calendar of Sessions Books 1689 to 1709* (1905).

Harris, Mary Dormer (ed.), *The Coventry Leet Book ... 1420–1555* (Early English Text Society, 134, 1907).

[Harrison], *The Description of England by William Harrison*, ed. Georges Edelen (Ithaca, NY, 1968).

Hawarde, John, *Les Reportes del Cases in Camera Stellata, 1593–1609*, ed. William Paley Baildon (1894).

Hawkins, William, *A Treatise of the Pleas of the Crown* (2 vols., 1716–21).

Helmholz, R. H. (ed.), *Select Cases on Defamation to 1600* (Selden Society, vol. 101, 1985).

[Henrietta Maria], *Letters of Queen Henrietta Maria*, ed. Mary Anne Everett Green (1857).

Heylyn, Peter, *Examen Historicum* (1659).

[Heywood, John], *A Ballad against Slander and Detraction* (1562).

Hieron, Samuel, *The Workes of M. Sam. Hieron* (2 vols., 1620; 1635 edn.).

Historical Manuscripts Commission, *Fifth Report* (1876).

Historical Manuscripts Commission, *12th Report: The Manuscripts of the Earl Cowper, K.G., Preserved at Melbourne Hall, Derbyshire* (3 vols., 1888–9).

Historical Manuscripts Commission, *Report on the Manuscripts of the Duke of Buccleuch and Queensberry . . . at Montague House* (1899).

Historical Manuscripts Commission, *Report on the Manuscripts of the Family of Gawdy* (1885).

[Holles], *Letters of John Holles 1587–1637*, ed. P. R. Seddon (Thoroton Society Record Series, 35, 1983).

Holy Bible (1611).

Homilie agaynst Disobedience and Wylful Rebellion (1570).

Horn, Robert, *The Christian Gouernour, in the Common-wealth, and Priuate Families* (1614).

[House of Commons], *Political Libel and Seditious Conduct* (1821).

Howell, T. B., and T. J. Howell (eds.), *A Complete Collection of State Trials* (33 vols., 1809–28).

Hudson, William, 'A Treatise of the Court of Star-Chamber', in Francis Hargrave (ed.) *Collectanea Juridica* (2 vols., 1791–2), vol. ii.

Hughes, Paul L., and James F. Larkin (eds.), *Tudor Royal Proclamations*, ii. *The Later Tudors (1553–1587)* (New Haven and London, 1969).

——— (ed.), *Tudor Royal Proclamations*, iii. *The Later Tudors (1588–1603)* (London and New Haven, 1969).

Hurste, Thomas, *The Descent of Authoritie: or, The Magistrates Patent from Heaven* (1637).

[Hutchinson, Lucy], *Memoirs of the Life of Colonel Hutchinson*, ed. Julius Hutchinson, rev. C. H. Firth (1906).

I., T., *A Cure for the Tongue-Evill* (1662).

J., W., *Obedience Active and Passive Due to the Supream Power* (Oxford, 1643).

[James], *The Speech and Declaration of John James* (1661).

———, *The True and Perfect Speech of John James, a Baptist, and Firth-Monarchy-Man* (1661).

———, *A Narrative of the Apprehending, Commitment, Arraignment, Condemnation, and Execution of John James* (1662).

[James I], *By the King. A Proclamation against excesse of Lavish and Licentious Speech of matters of State* (24 Dec. 1620 and 26 July 1621).

———, *King James VI and I: Selected Writings*, ed. Neil Rhodes, Jennifer Richards, and Joseph Marshall (Aldershot, 2003).

Jeaffreson, John Cordy (ed.), *Middlesex County Records. Vol. I . . . from 3 Edward VI to the end of the Reign of Elizabeth* (Clerkenwell, 1886).

Jeaffreson, John Cordy (ed.), *Middlesex County Records. Vol. II. Indictments, Recognizances . . . and Memoranda, temp. James I* (Clerkenwell, 1887).

—— (ed.), *Middlesex County Records. Vol. III . . . 1 Charles I to 18 Charles II* (Clerkenwell, 1888).

—— (ed.), *Middlesex County Records. Vol. IV. Indictments, Recognizances . . . 19 Charles II to 4 James II* (Clerkenwell, 1892).

Johnson, Robert C., Mary Frear Keeler, Maija Jansson Cole, and William B. Bidwell (eds.), *Commons Debates 1628* (6 vols., New Haven and London, 1977–83).

Jonson, Ben, *The Magnetick Lady*, ed. Peter Happé (Manchester, 2000).

Journals of the House of Commons (12 vols., 1802).

Journals of the House of Lords (15 vols., 1832–4).

[Killiray, Matthew], *The Swearer and the Drunkard* (1673).

[King], *The Sermons of Henry King*, ed. Mary Hobbs (Cranbury, NJ, and Aldershot, 1992).

Knighton, C. S. (ed.), *Calendar of State Papers Domestic Series of the Reign of Edward VI 1547–1553* (1992).

—— (ed.), *Calendar of State Papers Domestic Series of the Reign of Mary I, 1553–1558* (1998).

[Knyvett], *The Knyvett Letters (1620–1644)*, ed. Bertram Schofield (Norfolk Record Society, 1949).

Lambarde, William, *Eirenarcha: or of the Office of the Iustices of Peace* (1581; 1610 edn.).

Larkin, James F. (ed.), *Stuart Royal Proclamations*, ii. *Royal Proclamations of King Charles I 1625–1646* (Oxford, 1983).

——, and Paul L Hughes (eds.), *Stuart Royal Proclamations*, i. *Royal Proclamations of Kings James I 1603–1625* (Oxford, 1973).

Lathom, Paul, *The Power of Kings from God* (1683).

[Laud], *The Works of . . . William Laud, D.D.*, ed. William Scott and James Bliss (7 vols., Oxford, 1847–60).

The Law of Treason. A Concise and Comprehensive View of the Power and Duty of Grand Juries (1794).

Law Commission of England and Wales, *Working Paper No 72 . . . Codification of the Criminal Law—Treason, Sedition and Allied Offences* (1977).

Letters and Papers, Foreign and Domestic, of the Reign of Henry VIII, ed. J. S. Brewer et al. (23 vols., 1862–1932).

Lister, John (ed.), *West Riding Sessions Records. Vol. II. Orders, 1611–1642. Indictments, 1637–1642* (Yorkshire Archaeological Society Record Series,53, 1915).

[Machyn], *The Diary of Henry Machyn, Citizen and Merchant-Taylor of London, From A.D. 1550 to A.D. 1563*, ed. John Gough Nichols (Camden Society, 1848).

March, John, *Actions for Slander* (1655).

——, *The Second Part of Actions for Slanders* (1649).

Marconville, Jean de, *A Treatise of the Good and Evell Tounge* (*c.*1592).

Markham, Christopher A., and J. Charles Cox (eds.), *The Records of the Borough of Northampton* (2 vols., Northampton, 1898).

Mawburne, Francis, *Eagle 1666: A New Almanac and Prognostication* (York, 1666).

[Melton, Sir John], *A Sixe-Folde Politician* (1609).

[Milton], *Milton: Private Correspondence and Academic Exercises*, ed. Phyllis B. Tillyard (Cambridge, 1932).

Moore, A. Percival (ed.), 'The Metropolitical Visitation of Archdeacon [*sic*] Laud', in *Associated Architectural Societies Reports and Papers*, 29 (1907), 524–34.

[Morison, Richard], *A Remedy for Sedition* (1536).

[Morrice], *The Entering Book of Roger Morrice*, ed. Mark Goldie et al. (6 vols., Woodbridge, 2007).

Mossom, Robert, *The King on his Throne: Or, A Discourse maintaining the Dignity of a King, the Duty of a Subject, and the unlawfulnesse of Rebellion* (York, 1642).

Mulcaster, Richard, *Positions . . . for the Training up of Children* (1581).

Mum and the Sothsegger, ed. Mabel Day and Robert Steele (Early English Text Society, 199, 1936).

Nedham, Marchamont, *Certain Considerations Tendered in all Humility, to an Honorable Member of the Councell of State* (1649).

The New Gagging Bill (1848).

Newcourt, Richard, *Reportorium Ecclesiasticum Parochiale Londinense* (2 vols., 1710).

[Nisbet, Edward], *Caesars Dialogue or A Familiar Communication containing the first Institution of a Subiect, in allegiance to his Souveraigne* (1601).

[Norton, Thomas], *All such treatises as have been lately published by Thomas Norton* (1570).

Notestein, Wallace, Frances Helen Relf, and Hartley Simpson (eds.), *Commons Debates 1621* (7 vols., New Haven, 1935).

Nowell, Alexander, *A Catechisme, or Institution of Christian Religion to be learned by all youth* (1570; 1638 edn.).

Ogle, O., and W. H. Bliss (eds.), *Calendar of the Clarendon State Papers Preserved in the Bodleian Library* (5 vols., Oxford, 1872–1970).

[Parker, Martin], *Keep a Good Tongue in your Head* (1634).

Peacham, Henry, *The Dvty of all Trve Svbiects to their King* (1639).

[Perceval,Spencer, attrib.], *The Duties and Powers of Public Officers* (1792?), 7–8.

Perkins, William, *A Direction for the Government of the Tongue according to Gods Word* (1593; 1638 edn.).

Peyton, Sidney A. (ed.), *The Churchwardens' Presentments in the Oxfordshire Peculiars of Dorchester, Thame and Banbury* (Oxfordshire Record Society, Oxford, 1928).

The Proceedings at the Sessions House . . . Against Anthony Earl of Shaftsbury (1681).

Pulton, Ferdinando, *De Pace Regis et Regni, viz. A Treatise declaring which be the great and generall Offences of the Realme* (1610).

Raine, James (ed.), *Depositions from the Castle of York, Relating to Offences Committed in the Northern Counties in the Seventeenth Century* (Surtees Society, Durham, 40, 1861).

Ratcliff, S. C., and H. C. Johnson (eds.), *Warwick County Records Volume VI. Quarter Sessions Indictment Book Easter, 1631, to Epiphany, 1674* (Warwick, 1941).

Ray, John, *A Compleat Collection of English Proverbs* (3rd edn., 1742).

The Records of the Honorable Society of Lincoln's Inn: The Black Books, Vol. II. From AD 1586 to AD 1660 (1898).

Redwood, B. C. (ed.), *Quarter Sessions Order Book, 1642–1649* (Sussex Record Society, 54, 1954).

Reyner, Edward, *Rules for the Government of the Tongue* (1656).

Reynolds, Edward, *A Treatise of the Passions and Faculties of the Soule of Man* (1640).

——, *Evgenia's Teares for great Brittaynes Distractions* (1642).

Richardson, Charles, *A Workeman That Needeth Not to be Ashamed: Or the Faithfull Steward of Gods House* (1616).

Robinson, Hastings (ed.), *Original Letters Relative to the English Reformation . . . Chiefly from the Archives of Zurich* (Parker Society, Cambridge, 1846).

Rogers, Francis, *A Visitation Sermon Preached* (1633).

Roper, William, 'The Life of Sir Thomas More', in Richard S. Sylvester and Davis P. Harding (eds.), *Two Early Tudor Lives* (London and New Haven, 1962).

Rous, Francis, *Meditations of Instruction* (1616).

[Rous], *Diary of John Rous, Incumbent of Santon Downham, Suffolk, from 1625 to 1642*, ed. Mary Anne Everett Green (Camden Society, 66, 1856).

Rushworth, John, *Historical Collections of Private Passages of State* (1659).

——, *Historical Collections of Private Passages of State* (8 vols., 1680–1701).

Rye, Walter (ed.), *Depositions Taken before the Mayor and Aldermen of Norwich, 1549–1567* (Norwich, 1905).

Sclater, William, *Papisto-Mastix, or Deborah's Prayer against God's Enemies* (1642).

The Sentence of Samuel Johnson, at the Kings-Bench-Barr at Westminster (1686).

The Several Places Where you may Hear News (1647?).

Shakespeare, William, *Comedy of Errors; 1 and 2 Henry IV; King Lear; Much Ado About Nothing; The Taming of the Shrew; Timon of Athens.*

Sheppard, William, *Action upon the Case for Slander. Or a Methodical Collection under Certain Heads, of Thousands of Cases* (1662).

Shirley, John, *The Life of the Valiant & Learned Sir Walter Raleigh, Knight with his Tryal at Winchester* (1677).

Skelton, John, *The Complete Poems of John Skelton*, ed. Philip Henderson (1959).

Smart, Peter, *The Vanitie and Downe-fall of Superstitious Popish Ceremonies* (Edinburgh, 1628).

The Soveraignty of Kings (1642).

Snow, Vernon F., and Anne Steele Young (eds.), *The Private Journals of the Long Parliament 2 June to 17 September 1642* (New Haven and London, 1992).

Statutes of the Realm (10 vols., 1810–28).

Starkey, Thomas, *Exhortation to Unitie and Obedience* (1536).

Stone, E. D., and B. Cozens-Hardy (eds.), *Norwich Consistory Court Depositions, 1499–1512 and 1518–1530* (Norfolk Record Society, vol. 10, 1938).

Strype, John, *Brief Annals of the Church and State Under the Reign of Queen Elizabeth* (4 vols., 1725–31).

Stubbs, John, *The Discouerie of a Gaping Gulf Whereinto England is like to be Swallowed by Another French Mariage* (1579).

Stubbs, W., and G. Talmash, *The Crown Circuit Companion* (4th edn., 1768).

Swan, John, *Redde Debitum. Or, A Discourse in defence of three chiefe Fatherhoods* (1640).

Taylor, John, *Wit and Mirth. Chargeably collected out of tauernes, ordinaries, innes, bowling greenes, and allyes, alehouses, tobacco shops, highwayes, and water-passages* (1626).

——, *Taylors Travels and Circular Perambulation . . . with an Alphabeticall Description of all the Taverne Signes* (1636).

[Taylor, John], *A Iuniper Lecture. With the Description of all sorts of Women* (1639).

——, *A Plea for Prerogative: Or, Give Caesar his due* (1642).

Theeves, Theeves: or, a relation of Sir John Gell's proceedings in Darbyshire (Oxford, 1643).

[Thurloe], *A Collection of the State Papers of John Thurloe*, ed. Thomas Birch (7 vols., 1742).

Towgood, Richard, *Disloyalty of Language Questioned and Censured* (Bristol, 1643).

Treason Justly Punished: Or, A Full Relation of the Condemnation, and Execution of Mr William Staley (1678).

The Trial of Henry Yorke for Conspiracy (1795).

The Trial of John Frost for Seditious Words (1794).

The Trial of Thomas Briellat, For Seditious Words (1794).

The Trial of Wm. Winterbotham . . . For Seditious Words (1794).

The Tryal of William Stayley, Goldsmith; For Speaking Treasonable Words Against his Most Sacred Majesty (1678).

Udall, Ephraim, *The Good of Peace and Ill of Warre* (1642).

Vaughan, William, *The Spirit of Detraction* (1611).

——, *The Arraignment of Slander* (1630).

Valentine, Henry, *God Save the King. A Sermon Preached in St Pauls Church the 27th of March 1639* (1639).

Walker, Neil, and Thomas Craddock, *The History of Wisbech and the Fens* (Wisbech, 1849).

Ward, Richard, *Two Very Usefull and Compendious Theological Treatises* (1673).

Warmstry, Thomas, *Pax Vobis or A Charme for Tumultuous Spirits* (1641).

Webbe, George, *The Araignement of an Unruly Tongue* (1619).

——, *The Practice of Quietnes: Directing a Christian how to live quietly in this troublesome world* (6th edn. 1633).

Webster, John, *The Duchess of Malfi* (1613).

Wentworth, Peter, *A Pithy Exhortation to her Maiestie for establishing her successor* (Edinburgh, 1598).

West, Richard, *The Court of Conscience* (1607).

[Whiteway], *William Whiteway of Dorchester His Diary 1618 to 1635* (Dorset Record Society, 12, Dorchester, 1991).

Wigmore, Michael, *The Meteors. A Sermon* (1633).

[Wilkinson], *The Information of Capt. Hen. Wilkinson, of What hath passed betwixt him and some other Persons, who have attempted to prevail with him to Swear High Treason against the Earl of Shaftesbury* (1681).

Willymat, William, *A Loyal Subjects Looking-Glasse, Or A good subjects direction, necessary and requisite for every good Christian* (1604).

Wright, Leonard, *A Display of Dutie* (1589).

Wright, Thomas, *The Passions of the Minde* (1600; 1630 edn.).

[Yonge], *The Diary of Walter Yonge, Esq.*, ed, George Roberts (Camden Society, 1848).

[Young, John], *A Sermon Preached before the Queenes Maiestie* (1576).

Youths Behaviour, or Decency in Conversation Amongst Men (4th edn., 1646).

Winthrop Papers, iii. *1631–1637* (Massachusetts Historical Society, Boston, 1943).

Newspapers

The Daily News, 1886.

The Daily Post, 1728.

The Evening Mail, 1793.

The Evening Post, 1713, 1718, 1719, 1722.

The Flying Post and Postmaster, 1696.

The Flying Post or the Post Master, 1715.

The Graphic, 1879.

The Leeds Mercury, 1819.

The London Evening Post, 1744.

London Gazette, 1705.

The London Journal, 1722, 1726.

The London Packet or New Lloyd's Evening Post, 1800.

The Manchester Times, 1886.

The Morning Chronicle, 1794, 1819, 1820.

The Morning Post, 1793.

The News, 1793.

The Oracle and Public Advertiser, 1794.

The Post Boy and Historical Account, 1695.

The Postman and the Historical Account, 1696.

The Public Advertiser, 1766.

St James's Post, 1718.

The Star, 1796.

The Sun, 1793.

The Telegraph, 1796.

The Times, 1794, 1795, 1801, 1807, 1810, 1813, 1837, 1846, 1848, 1886, 1901, 1919.

The True Briton, 1796, 1800.

The Weekly Journal or Saturday's Post, 1721.

The Weekly Journal with Fresh Advices, 1715.

The World, 1793, 1794.

Parliamentary Statutes

3 Edward I, c. 34.

25 Edward III, statute 5, c. 2.

2 Richard II, c. 5.

12 Richard II, c. 11.

26 Hen. VIII, c. 13.

1 Edw. VI, c. 12.

1 Mary, St. 1. c. 1.

1 and 2 Phil. and Mary, c. 3.

1 and 2 Phil. and Mary, c. 9.

1 and 2 Phil. and Mary, c. 10.

1 Eliz. I, c. 5.

1 Eliz. I, c. 6.

13 Eliz. I, c. 1.

23 Eliz. I, c. 2.

13 Charles II. c. 1.

4 Anne. c. 8.

6 Anne, c. 7.

36 Geo. III. c. 7.

36 Geo. III. c. 8.

57 Geo. III. c. 6.

60 Geo. III. c. 4.

2 and 3 Victoria, c. 47.

11 and 12 Victoria, c. 12.

The Public Order Act, 1986.

Human Rights Act, 1998.

Racial or Religious Hatred Act, 2006.

Terrorism Act, 2006.

SECONDARY SOURCES

Anon., 'Rehabilitating the Performative', *Harvard Law Review*, 120 (2007), 2200–21.

Apperson, G. L. (ed.), *English Proverbs and Proverbial Phrases: A Historical Dictionary* (1929; repr. Detroit, 1969).

Arthurson, Ian, *The Perkin Warbeck Conspiracy 1491–1499* (Stroud, 1994).

——, '"The Itch Grown a Disease": Manuscript Transmission of News in the Seventeenth Century', in Joad Raymond (ed.), *News, Newspapers, and Society in Early Modern Britain* (1999), 39–65.

Atherton, Ian, and David Como, 'The Burning of Edward Wightman: Puritanism, Prelacy and the Politics of Heresy in Early Modern England', *English Historical Review*, 120 (2005), 1215–50.

Austin, J. L., *How to Do Things with Words* (Cambridge, Mass., 1962; 2nd edn., 1975).

Aylmer, Gerald, *Rebellion or Revolution? England 1640–1660* (Oxford, 1986).

Baker, Kenneth, *The Kings and Queens: An Irreverent Cartoon History of the British Monarchy* (1996).

Bardsley, Sandy, *Venomous Tongues: Speech and Gender in Late Medieval England* (Philadelphia, 2006).

Barnes, Thomas Garden, *Somerset 1625–1640: A County's Government during the 'Personal Rule'* (Cambridge, MA, 1961).

Barrell, John, *Imagining the King's Death: Figurative Treason, Fantasies of Regicide 1793–1796* (Oxford, 2000).

Bauman, R. A., *The Crimen Maiestatis in the Roman Republic* (1970).

Bellamy, J. G., *The Law of Treason in England in the Later Middle Ages* (Cambridge, 1970).

Bellamy, John, *The Tudor Law of Treason: An Introduction* (Toronto and London, 1979).

Bellany, Alastair, ' "Raylinge Rymes and Vaunting Verse": Libellous Politics in Early Stuart England', in Kevin Sharpe and Peter Lake (eds.), *Culture and Politics in Early Stuart* England (Stanford, 1993), 285–310, 367–71.

——, 'Libels in Action: Ritual, Subversion and the English Literary Underground, 1603–42', in Tim Harris (ed.), *The Politics of the Excluded, c.1500–1850* (Basingstoke and New York, 2001), 99–124.

Bellany, Alastair, *The Politics of Court Scandal in Early Modern England: News Culture and the Overbury Affair, 1603–1660* (Cambridge, 2002).

Bernard, G. W., *The King's Reformation: Henry VIII and the Remaking of the English Church* (New Haven and London, 2005).

Bourdieu, Pierre, *Language and Symbolic Power* (Cambridge, MA, 1991).

Bowen, Lloyd, 'Seditious Speech and Popular Royalism, 1649–1660', in Jason McElligott and David Smith (eds.), *Royalists and Royalism during the Interregnum* (Manchester, 2009).

Burtchaell, George Dames, and Thomas Ulick Sadleir (eds.), *Alumni Dublinenses . . . 1593–1860* (2nd edn., Dublin, 1935).

Butler, Judith, *Excitable Speech: A Politics of the Performative* (New York, 1997).

Bush, Michael, *The Casualties of Peterloo* (Lancaster, 2005).

Capp, Bernard, *When Gossips Meet: Women, Family and Neighbourhood in Early Modern England* (Oxford, 2003).

Carlton, Charles, *Charles I: The Personal Monarch* (2nd edn., 1995).

Champion, Justin, ' "May the last king be strangled in the bowels of the last priest": Irreligion and the English Enlightenment, 1649–1789', in Timothy Morton and Nigel Smith (eds.), *Radicalism in British Literary Culture, 1650–1830: From Revolution to Revolution* (Cambridge, 2002), 29–44, 220–6.

Cockayne, G. E. (ed.), *Complete Baronetage* (6 vols, Exeter, 1800–1909).

Cogswell, Thomas, 'Underground Verse and the Transformation of Early Stuart Political Culture', *Huntington Library Quarterly*, 60 (1997), 303–26.

Colclough, David, *Freedom of Speech in Early Stuart England* (Cambridge, 2005).

Colley, Linda, 'The Apotheosis of George III: Loyalty, Royalty and the British Nation 1760–1820', *Past & Present*, 102 (1984), 94–129.

Cooper, J. P. D., *Propaganda and the Tudor State: Political Culture in the Westcountry* (Oxford, 2003).

Cowan, Brian, *The Social Life of Coffee: The Emergence of the British Coffeehouse* (New Haven and London, 2005).

Cressy, David, *Literacy and the Social Order: Reading and Writing in Tudor and Stuart England* (Cambridge, 1980).

——, *Coming Over: Migration and Communication between England and New England in the Seventeenth Century* (Cambridge, 1987).

——, *Travesties and Transgressions in Tudor and Stuart England* (Oxford, 2000).

——, 'Book Burning in Tudor and Stuart England', *Sixteenth Century Journal*, 36 (2005), 359–74.

——, *England on Edge: Crisis and Revolution 1640–1642* (Oxford, 2006).

Croft, Pauline, 'Libels, Popular Literacy and Public Opinion in Early Modern England', *Historical Research*, 68 (1995), 266–85.

——, *King James* (Basingstoke and New York, 2003).

Cust, Richard, 'News and Politics in Early Seventeenth–Century England', *Past & Present*, 112 (1986), 60–90.

——, *The Forced Loan and English Politics 1626–1628* (Oxford, 1987).

——, *Charles I: A Political Life* (Harlow, 2005).

De Beer, E. S., 'The English Newspapers from 1695 to 1702', in Mark Almeras Thomson, Ragnhild Marie Hatton, and J. S. Bromley (eds.), *William III and Louis XIV* (Liverpool and Toronto, 1968), 117–29.

De Krey, Gary, *London and the Restoration, 1659–1683* (Cambridge, 2005).

Dias, Jill R., 'Lead, Society and Politics in Derbyshire before the Civil War', *Midland History*, 6 (1981), 39–57.

Dickinson, H. T., *The Politics of the People in Eighteenth-Century Britain* (1995).

Duggan, Christopher Randall, 'The Advent of Political Thought-Control in England: Seditious and Treasonable Speech 1485–1547' (Northwestern University Ph.D. dissertation, 1993).

Elton, G. R., *England under the Tudors* (1956).

——, *Policy and Police: The Enforcement of the Reformation in the Age of Thomas Cromwell* (Cambridge, 1972).

Emsley, Clive, 'The London "Insurrection" of December 1792: Fact, Fiction, or Fantasy?' *Journal of British Studies*, 17 (1978), 66–86.

——, 'The Home Office and its Sources of Information and Investigation 1791–1801', *English Historical Review*, 94 (1979), 532–61.

——, 'Repression, "Terror" and the Rule of Law in England during the Decade of the French Revolution', *English Historical Review*, 100 (1985), 801–25.

——, *Crime and Society in England 1750–1900* (1987).

Emmison, F. G., *Elizabethan Life: Disorder* (Chelmsford, 1970).

Ettlinger, John, and Ruby Day (eds.), *Old English Proverbs Collected by Nathan Bailey, 1736* (1992).

Farge, Arlette, *Subversive Words: Public Opinion in Eighteenth-Century France* (University Park, PA, 1995).

Flynn, Thomas S., *The Irish Dominicans 1536–1641* (Dublin, 1993).

Forest-Hill, Lynn, 'Sins of the Mouth: Signs of Subversion in Medieval English Cycle Plays', in Dermot Cavanagh and Tim Kirk (eds.), *Subversion and Scurrility: Popular Discourse in Europe from 1500 to the Present* (Aldershot and Burlington, 2000), 11–25.

Fox, Adam, 'Ballads, Libels and Popular Ridicule in Jacobean England', *Past & Present*, 145 (1994), 47–83.

——, 'Rumour, News and Popular Political Opinion in Elizabethan and Early Stuart England', *Historical Journal*, 40 (1997), 597–620.

——, *Oral and Literate Culture in England, 1500–1700* (Oxford, 2000).

Freist, Dagmar, *Governed by Opinion: Politics, Religion and the Dynamics of Communication in Stuart London 1637–1645* (1997).

Garrioch, David, 'Verbal Insults in Eighteenth-Century Paris', in Peter Burke and Roy Porter (eds.), *The Social History of Language* (Cambridge, 1987), 104–19.

Gentles, Ian, *The English Revolution and the Wars in the Three Kingdoms, 1638–1652* (Harlow, 2007).

George, M. D., *English Political Caricature: A Study of Opinion and Propaganda* (2 vols., Oxford, 1959–60).

Gowing, Laura, 'Gender and the Language of Insult in Early Modern London', *History Workshop*, 35 (1993), 1–21.

—— *Domestic Dangers: Women, Words and Sex in Early Modern London* (Oxford, 1996).

Graham, Lisa Jane, *If the King Only Knew: Seditious Speech in the Reign of Louis XV* (Charlottesville, VA, 2000).

Granville, Roger, *The History of the Granville Family* (Exeter, 1895).

Greaves, Richard L., *Deliver Us from Evil: The Radical Underground in Britain, 1660–1663* (Oxford and New York, 1986).

——, *Enemies under his Feet: Radicals and Nonconformists in Britain, 1664–1677* (Stanford, 1990).

——, and Robert Zaller (eds.), *Biographical Dictionary of British Radicals in the Seventeenth Century* (3 vols., Brighton, 1982).

Greenberg, Daniel, and Alexandra Millbrook (eds.), *Stroud's Judicial Dictionary of Words and Phrases* (6th edn., 2000).

Greenberg, Janelle, *The Radical Face of the Ancient Constitution* (Cambridge, 2001).

Greenawalt, Kent, *Speech, Crime, and the Uses of Language* (Oxford and New York, 1989).

Haiman, Franklyn S., *'Speech Acts' and the First Amendment* (Carbondale, Ill., 1993).

Harling, Philip, 'The Law of Libel and the Limits of Repression, 1790–1832', *Historical Journal*, 44 (2001), 107–34.

Harris, E. Kay, 'Censoring Disobedient Subjects: Narratives of Treason and Royal Authority in Fifteenth-Century England', in Douglas L. Biggs, Sharon

D. Michalove, and A. Compton Reeves (eds.), *Reputation and Representation in Fifteenth-Century Europe* (Leiden and Boston, 2004), 211–33.

Harris, T.J. G., 'Politics of the London Crowd in the Reign of Charles II' (Cambridge University Ph.D. thesis, 1984).

Harris, Tim (ed.), *The Politics of the Excluded, c.1500–1850* (Basingstoke and New York, 2001).

——, *Restoration: Charles II and his Kingdoms, 1660–1685* (2005).

——, ' "There is None that Loves him but Drunk Whores and Whoremongers": Popular Criticisms of the Restoration Court', in Julia Marciari Alexander and Catherine Macleod (eds.), *Politics, Transgression, and Representation at the Court of Charles II* (New Haven, 2008), 33–56.

Harvey, I. M. W., *Jack Cade's Rebellion of 1450* (Oxford, 1991).

——, 'Was there Popular Politics in Fifteenth-Century England?' in R. H. Britnell and A. J. Pollard (eds.), *The McFarlane Legacy: Studies in Late Medieval Politics and Society* (Stroud and New York, 1995), 155–74.

Hast, Adele, 'State Treason Trials during the Puritan Revolution, 1640–1660', *Historical Journal*, 15 (1972), 37–53.

Havran, Martin J., *The Catholics in Caroline England* (Stanford, 1961).

Hilton, Boyd, *A Mad, Bad, and Dangerous People: England 1783–1846* (Oxford, 2006).

Holdsworth, W. S., *A History of English Law* (rev. edn., 17 vols., Boston, 1922–72).

Holmes, Clive, *Seventeenth-Century Lincolnshire* (Lincoln, 1980).

——, *Why Was Charles I Executed?* (2006).

Hoppit, Julian, *A Land of Liberty? England 1689–1727* (Oxford, 2000).

Hotten, John Camden (ed.), *Original Lists of Persons of Quality . . . Who Went from Great Britain to the American Plantations, 1600–1700* (1874; repr. Baltimore, 1974).

Houlbrooke, Ralph, *Church Courts and the People during the English Reformation, 1520–1570* (Oxford, 1979).

Hunnisett, R. F., 'Treason by Words', *Sussex Notes and Queries*, 14 (1954–7), 117–19.

Hunt, Tamara, *Defining John Bull: Political Caricature and National Identity in Late Georgian England* (2003).

Hunt, William, *The Puritan Moment: The Coming of Revolution in an English County* (Cambridge, MA, 1983).

Ingram, Martin, *Church Courts, Sex and Marriage in England, 1570–1640* (Cambridge, 1987).

——, ' "Scolding Women Cucked or Washed": A Crisis in Gender Relations in Early Modern England?' in Jennifer Kermode and Garthine Walker (eds.), *Women, Crime and the Courts in Early Modern England* (1994), 48–80.

——, 'Law, Litigants and the Construction of "Honour": Slander Suits in Early Modern England', in Peter Coss (ed.), *The Moral World of the Law* (Cambridge, 2000), 134–60.

Jansen, Sharon L., *Dangerous Talk and Strange Behavior: Women and Popular Resistance to the Reforms of Henry VIII* (New York, 1996).

Johnson, Richard, *The Baronetage of England* (3 vols., 1771).

Keeler, Mary Frear, *The Long Parliament 1640–1641. A Biographical Study of its Members* (Philadelphia, 1954).

Kelly, G. A., 'From Lèse-Majesté to Lèse-Nation: Treason in Eighteenth-Century France', *Journal of the History of Ideas*, 42 (1981), 269–86.

Kenyon, J. P. (ed.), *The Stuart Constitution* (Cambridge, 1966).

Kermode, Jennifer, and Garthine Walker (eds.), *Women, Crime and the Courts in Early Modern England* (1994).

Kesselring, K. J., ' "A Cold Pye for the Papistes": Constructing and Containing the Northern Rising of 1569', *Journal of British Studies*, 43 (2004), 417–43.

Kishlansky, Mark, 'Charles I: A Case of Mistaken Identity', *Past & Present*, 189 (2005), 41–80.

Langford, Paul, *A Polite and Commercial People: England 1727–1783* (Oxford, 1989).

Lassiter, John C., 'Defamation of Peers: The Rise and Decline of the Action for *Scandalum Magnatum*, 1497–1773', *American Journal of Legal History*, 22 (1978), 216–36.

Lee, Maurice, Jr., *Great Britain's Solomon: James VI and I in his Three Kingdoms* (Urbana and Chicago, 1990).

Levin, Carole, ' "We shall never have a merry world while the Queene lyveth": Gender, Monarchy, and the Power of Seditious Words', in Julia M. Walker (ed.), *Dissing Elizabeth: Negative Representations of Gloriana* (Durham, NC, 1998), 77–95.

Lobban, Michael, 'From Seditious Libel to Unlawful Assembly: Peterloo and the Changing Face of Political Crime', *Oxford Journal of Legal Studies*, 10 (1990).

——, 'Treason, Sedition and the Radical Movement in the Age of the French Revolution', *Liverpool Law Review*, 22 (2000), 210–17.

Lockyer, Roger, *James VI and I* (1998).

McCalman, Iain, 'Ultra-Radicalism and Convivial Debating-Clubs in London, 1795–1838', *English Historical Review*, 102 (1987), 309–33.

MacLean, Ian, *Interpretation and Meaning in the Renaissance: The Case of Law* (Cambridge, 1992).

McRae, Andrew, 'The Literary Culture of Early Stuart Libelling', *Modern Philology*, 97 (2000), 364–92.

——, *Literature, Satire, and the Early Stuart State* (Cambridge, 2004).

Manning, Roger B., 'The Origins of the Doctrine of Sedition', *Albion*, 12 (1980), 99–121.

Marchant, Ronald A., *Puritans and the Church Courts in the Diocese of York* (1960).

Martin, Cheryl English, 'Popular Speech and Social Order in Northern Mexico, 1650–1830', *Comparative Studies in Society and History*, 32 (1990), 305–24.

Mayer, Jean-Christophe (ed.), *The Struggle for the Succession in Late Elizabethan England: Politics, Polemics and Cultural Representations* (Montpellier, 2004).

Mazzio, Carla, 'Sins of the Tongue in Early Modern England', *Modern Language Studies*, 28 (1998), 93–124.

Mears, Natalie, *Queenship and Political Discourse in the Elizabethan Realms* (Cambridge, 2005).

Meekings, C.A.F., 'Thomas Kerver's Case, 1444', *English Historical Review*, 90 (1975), 331–46.

Monod, Paul Kléber, *Jacobitism and the English People, 1688–1788* (Cambridge, 1989).

Morgan, Hiram, ' "Never any realm worse governed": Queen Elizabeth and Ireland', *Transactions of the Royal Historical Society*, 14 (2004), 295–308.

Morrill, John (ed.), *The Scottish National Covenant in its British Context, 1638–1651* (Edinburgh, 1990).

Murphy, Peter (ed,), *Blackstone's Criminal Practice* (Oxford, 2007).

Oates, Jonathan D., 'Jacobitism and Popular Disturbances in Northern England, 1714–1719', *Northern History*, 41 (2004), 111–28.

Parkin, David, 'Exchanging Words', in Bruce Kapferer (ed.), *Transaction and Meaning: Directions in the Anthropology of Exchange and Symbolic Behavior* (Philadelphia, 1976), 163–90.

Pincus, Steven, ' "Coffee politicians does create" : Coffeehouses and Restoration Political Culture', *Journal of Modern History*, 67 (1995), 807–34.

Poole, Robert, ' "By the Law or the Sword: Peterloo Revisited', *History*, 91 (2006), 254–76.

——, 'The March to Peterloo: Politics and Festivity in Late Georgian England', *Past & Present*, 192 (2006), 109–53.

Poole, Steve, *The Politics of Regicide in England, 1760–1850: Troublesome Subjects* (Manchester, 2000).

Prest, Wilfrid R., *The Rise of the Barristers: A Social History of the English Bar 1590–1640* (Oxford, 1986).

Questier, Michael (ed), *Stuart Dynastic Policy and Religious Politics, 1621–1625* (Camden Society, 5th ser., 2009), Raymond, Joad (ed.), *News, Newspapers, and Society in Early Modern Britain* (1999).

Reeve, L. J., *Charles I and the Road to Personal Rule* (Cambridge, 1989).

Rezneck, Samuel, 'Constructive Treason by Words in the Fifteenth Century', *American Historical Review*, 33 (1928), 544–52.

Richards, Judith, ' "His Nowe Majestie" and the English Monarchy: The Kingship of Charles I before 1640', *Past & Present*, 113 (1986), 70–96.

Rogers, Nicholas, 'Popular Protest in Early Hanoverian London', *Past & Present*, 79 (1978), repr. in Paul Slack (ed.), *Rebellion, Popular Protest and the Social Order in Early Modern England* (Cambridge, 1984), 263–93.

——, 'Riot and Popular Jacobitism in Early Hanoverian England', in Eveline Cruickshanks (ed.), *Ideology and Conspiracy: Aspects of Jacobitism, 1689–1759* (Edinburgh, 1982), 70–88.

——, *Crowds, Culture, and Politics in Georgian Britain* (Oxford, 1998).

Russell, Conrad, *Parliaments and English Politics, 1621–1629* (Oxford, 1979).

Samaha, Joel, *Law and Order in Historical Perspective: The Case of Elizabethan Essex* (New York and London, 1974).

Samaha, Joel, 'Gleanings from Local Criminal-Court Records: Sedition amongst the "Inarticulate" in Elizabethan Essex', *Journal of Social History*, 8 (1975), 61–79.

Searle, John R., *Speech Acts: An Essay in the Philosophy of Language* (Cambridge, 1969).

——, *Mind, Language and Society: Philosophy in the Real World* (New York, 1998).

Shagan, Ethan, 'Rumours and Popular Politics in the Reign of Henry VIII', in Tim Harris (ed.), *The Politics of the Excluded, c.1500–1850* (Basingstoke and New York, 2001), 30–66.

Sharp, Buchanan, *In Contempt of All Authority: Rural Artisans and Riot in the West of England, 1586–1660* (Berkeley, 1980).

Sharp, Buchanan, 'Popular Political Opinion in England, 1660–1685', *History of European Ideas*, 10 (1989), 13–29.

Sharpe, J. A., *Defamation and Sexual Slander in Early Modern England: The Church Courts at York* (York, 1980).

——, ' "Such Disagreement Betwyxt Neighbours": Litigation and Human Relations in Early Modern England', in John Bossy (ed.), *Disputes and Settlements: Law and Human Relations in the West* (Cambridge, 1983), 167–87.

——, *Judicial Punishment in England* (1990).

Sharpe, Kevin, *The Personal Rule of Charles I* (1992).

——, 'Sacralization and Demystification. The Publicization of Monarchy in Early Modern England', in Jeroen Deploige and Gita Deneckere (eds.), *Mystifying the Monarch: Studies on Discourse, Power and History* (Amsterdam, 2006), 99–115.

Shoemaker, Robert, 'The Decline of Public Insult in London 1660–1800', *Past & Present*, 169 (2000), 97–131.

Shoemaker, Robert R., *The London Mob: Violence and Disorder in Eighteenth-Century England* (2004).

Smith, Hannah, *Georgian Monarchy: Politics and Culture, 1714–1760* (Cambridge, 2006).

Squibb, George, *The High Court of Chivalry: A Study of the Civil Law in England* (Oxford, 1959).

Tapsell, Grant, *The Personal Rule of Charles II 1681–85* (Woodbridge, 2007).

Thompson, E. P., *The Making of the English Working Class* (1963).

Thomson, Elizabeth McClure (ed.), *The Chamberlain Letters* (New York, 1965).

Thornley, Isobel D., 'Treason by Words in the Fifteenth Century', *English Historical Review*, 32 (1917), 556–7.

Thornton, Tim, *Prophecy, Politics and the People in Early Modern England* (Woodbridge, 2006).

Underdown, David, *Revel, Riot and Rebellion* (Oxford, 1985).

——, 'The Taming of the Scold: The Enforcement of Patriarchal Authority in Early Modern England', in Anthony Fletcher and John Stevenson (eds.), *Order and Disorder in Early Modern England* (Cambridge, 1985), 116–36.

Usher, Brett, 'Essex Evangelicals under Edward VI', in David Loades (ed.), *John Foxe at Home and Abroad* (Aldershot and Burlington, 2004), 51–61.

Volokh, Eugene. 'Speech as Conduct: Generally Applicable Laws, Illegal Courses of Conduct, "Situation-Altering Utterances," and the Uncharted Zones', *Cornell Law Review*, 90 (2005), 1277–348.

Walker, Garthine, 'Expanding the Boundaries of Female Honour in Early Modern England', *Transactions of the Royal Historical Society*, 6th ser., 6 (1996), 235–45.

Walker, R. B., 'The Newspaper Press in the Reign of William III', *Historical Journal*, 17 (1974), 691–709.

Walker, Simon, 'Rumour, Sedition and Popular Protest in the Reign of Henry IV', *Past & Present*, 166 (2000), 31–65.

Wall, Alison D., *Power and Protest in England, 1525–1640* (2000).

Walter, John, *Understanding Popular Violence in the English Revolution: The Colchester Plunderers* (Cambridge, 1999).

Watt, Diane, 'Reconstructing the Word: The Political Prophecies of Elizabeth Barton (1506–1534)', *Renaissance Quarterly*, 50 (1997), 136–63.

Williams, E. Neville (ed.), *The Eighteenth-Century Constitution 1688–1815* (Cambridge, 1960).

Williams, Penry, *The Tudor Regime* (Oxford, 1979).

Withington, Phil, 'Public Discourse, Corporate Citizenship, and State Formation in Early Modern England', *American Historical Review*, 112 (2007), 1016–38.

Wolffe, Bertram, *Henry VI* (1981).

Wood, Andy, *The Politics of Social Conflict: The Peak Country, 1520–1770* (Cambridge, 1999).

——, 'Fear, Hatred and the Hidden Injuries of Class in Early Modern England', *Journal of Social History*, 39 (2006), 803–26.

——, 'The Queen is "a Goggyll Eyed Hoore": Gender and Seditious Speech in Early Modern England', in Nicholas Tyacke (ed.), *The English Revolution c.1590–1720: Politics, Religion and Communities* (2007), 81–94.

Young, Michael B., *Charles I* (Basingstoke, 1997).

INTERNET SOURCES

Bellany, Alastair, and Andrew McRae (eds.), 'Early Stuart Libels', www.earlystuartlibels.net.

Dahrendorf, Ralf, 'Free Speech on Trial', www.project-syndicate.org/commentary/dahrendorf45, at 24 Nov. 2006.

Oxford Dictionary of National Biography (ODNB), www.oxforddnb.com.

The Proceedings of the Old Bailey, 1674–1913, www.oldbaileyonline.org.

University of Birmingham, Calendar of the Court of Chivalry, 1634–1640, www.court-of-chivalry.bham.ac.uk/index.htm.

www.throneout.com.

Index